Justinian

DEBATES AND DOCUMENTS IN ANCIENT HISTORY

GENERAL EDITORS

Emma Stafford, *University of Leeds*, and
Shaun Tougher, *Cardiff University*

Focusing on important themes, events or periods throughout ancient history, each volume in this series is divided into roughly equal parts. The first introduces the reader to the main issues of interpretation. The second contains a selection of relevant evidence supporting different views.

PUBLISHED

Diocletian and the Tetrarchy
Roger Rees

Julian the Apostate
Shaun Tougher

Rome and its Empire, AD 193–284
Olivier Hekster with Nicholas Zair

Roman Imperialism
Andrew Erskine

King and Court in Ancient Persia 559 to 331 BCE
Lloyd Llewellyn-Jones

Sex and Sexuality in Classical Athens
James Robson

Justinian: Empire and Society in the Sixth Century
F. K. Haarer

FORTHCOMING

The Family in the Roman World
Mary Harlow and Nikki Rollason

Justinian

Empire and Society in the Sixth Century

F. K. Haarer

EDINBURGH
University Press

Edinburgh University Press is one of the leading university presses in the UK. We publish academic books and journals in our selected subject areas across the humanities and social sciences, combining cutting-edge scholarship with high editorial and production values to produce academic works of lasting importance. For more information visit our website: edinburghuniversitypress.com

© F. K. Haarer, 2022

Edinburgh University Press Ltd
The Tun – Holyrood Road, 12(2f) Jackson's Entry, Edinburgh EH8 8PJ

Typeset in 11/13 pt Minion Pro
by IDSUK (DataConnection) Ltd

A CIP record for this book is available from the British Library

ISBN 978 0 7486 3677 8 (hardback)
ISBN 978 0 7486 3678 5 (paperback)
ISBN 978 0 7486 3979 2 (webready PDF)
ISBN 978 1 4744 1429 6 (epub)

The right of F. K. Haarer to be identified as the author of this work has been asserted in accordance with the Copyright, Designs and Patents Act 1988, and the Copyright and Related Rights Regulations 2003 (SI No. 2498).

Contents

Series Editors' Preface — ix
Preface — xi
Acknowledgements — xiii
Abbreviations — xiv
Maps — xv

Part I Debates

Introduction: Discovering Justinian – Sources and Scholarship — 3
Chapter 1   Rise to Power — 12
Chapter 2   Conflict and Diplomacy on the Eastern Frontier — 33
Chapter 3   The Wars of Reconquest — 49
Chapter 4   Church and State — 75
Chapter 5   Governing the Empire — 95
Chapter 6   Culture and Society — 120
Conclusion: Longevity and Legacy — 140

Part II Documents

1. *Collectio Avellana* 147 — 145
2. Anonymus Valesianus 85–7 — 146
3. Marcellinus *Comes* 521 — 146
4. Diptych announcing the consulship of Justinian, 521 — 146
5. *Greek Anthology* I.10, On the Church of the Holy Martyr Polyeuktos, lines 14–33, 42–50 — 147
6. Church of SS Sergius and Bacchus inscription — 149
7. Procopius, *Secret History* 9.20-2 — 150
8. John of Ephesus, *Lives of the Eastern Saints* 13 — 150
9. Cassiodorus, *Variae* X.20 — 151
10. Procopius, *Buildings* I.9.5–10 — 152
11. C.J. I.5.12.4–10 — 153
12. Gold coin of Justin and Justinian, 527 — 154

13.	Procopius, *Wars* I.24.33–7	154
14.	Menander the Guardsman, fragment 6.1	155
15.	*C.J.* I.29.5	156
16.	The *Chronicle* of Pseudo-Zachariah Rhetor, IX.8a	157
17.	Procopius, *Wars* I.14.45–54	157
18.	Malalas, *Chronicle* 477–8	158
19.	Procopius, *Secret History* 24.12–14	159
20.	Evagrius, *Ecclesiastical History* IV.27	159
21.	Agathias, *The Histories* IV.30.7–10	160
22.	John of Ephesus, *Church History* 3.4.6–9	161
23.	Procopius, *Wars* VIII.17.1–8	162
24.	Procopius, *Wars* IV.6.30–4	162
25.	John the Lydian, *de Magistratibus* III.55	163
26.	Corippus, *In laudem Iustini minoris* 1.276–87	163
27.	Victor of Tonnena, *Chronicon* 534	164
28.	Procopius, *Buildings* I.10.16–18	164
29.	*C.J.* I.27.1, 12–14	164
30.	Procopius, *Secret History* 18.5–10	165
31.	Inscription from Aïn Djelloula (*Cululis*)	166
32.	Cyril of Scythopolis, *Life of St Sabas* 74	166
33.	*Novel* 37, preface, 1, 5	166
34.	Facundus of Hermiane, *In Defence of the Three Chapters*, preface	167
35.	Procopius, *Wars* VII.37.1–7	168
36.	*Epistulae Austrasicae* XX	169
37.	Procopius, *Wars* III.2.1–6	169
38.	Cassiodorus, *Variae* XI.1	170
39.	Pope Pelagius, *Letters* 4 and 85	171
40.	*Novels*, Appendix 7: Pragmatic Sanction, 554	171
41.	Procopius, *Secret History* 11.5–8	172
42.	Procopius, *Wars* II.4.4–11	173
43.	*Novel* 11, preface, 4	173
44.	Agathias, *The Histories* V.13.5–6	174
45.	Agathias, *The Histories* V.15.7–8	175
46.	Theophanes AM 6050	175
47.	Isidore, *History of the Goths* 47	175
48.	The *Chronicle* of Pseudo-Zachariah Rhetor, IX.15j	175
49.	*C.J.* I.1.6 and *Chronicon Paschale* 533	176
50.	'Only-begotten Son' troparion	178
51.	Victor of Tonnena, *Chronicon* 540	178
52.	*Novel* 42, preface	178

53.	Victor of Tonnena, *Chronicon* 543	179
54.	Evagrius, *Ecclesiastical History* IV.38	180
55.	Cyril of Scythopolis, *Life of St Sabas* 85	181
56.	Justinian, *On the Orthodox Faith*	181
57.	Evagrius, *Ecclesiastical History* IV.39	182
58.	Agapetus, *Advice to the Emperor Justinian*	183
59.	*Novel* 131, preface, 1–4	183
60.	Pseudo-Dionysius of Tel-Mahre, *Chronicle* 844	184
61.	Pseudo-Dionysius of Tel-Mahre, *Chronicle* 845	184
62.	Cyril of Scythopolis, *Life of St Sabas* 72	185
63.	Evagrius, *Ecclesiastical History* IV.10	185
64.	*Institutes*, preface	186
65.	*Novel* 25, preface	187
66.	*Novel* 47, preface	188
67.	Justinian, the first dated copper coin, AD 538	189
68.	*Novel* 38, preface	189
69.	Evagrius, *Ecclesiastical History* IV.29	190
70.	Procopius, *Secret History* 17.5	192
71.	Romanos, *Kontakion* 54, 14–25	192
72.	Paul the Silentiary, *Ekphrasis of Hagia Sophia*, lines 1–80	194
73.	Procopius, *Buildings* I.2.1–12	196
74.	Procopius, *Buildings* V.8.4–9	197
75.	Procopius, *Buildings* I.11.10–15	198
76.	*Greek Anthology* IX.641	198
77.	*C.J.* I.5.18.4	198
78.	*C.J.* I.11.10	199
79.	Agathias, *The Histories* II.30.3–4	199
80.	Pseudo-Dionysius of Tel-Mahre, *Chronicle* 852	200
81.	Choricius, *Oratio* XIII, preface, 10–16	200
82.	*Greek Anthology* I.8	202

Chronology	203
Popes and Patriarchs	205
Glossary	207
Further Reading	215
Essay Questions and Exercise Topics	218
Primary Sources	221
Bibliography	228
Index	260

For Peter

Series Editors' Preface

With the addition of this volume on the Roman emperor Justinian I (527–565) the chronological scope of the series *Debates and Documents in Ancient History* extends even further into late antiquity, bringing us to the critical century of the sixth century AD. Apparently by quirk of fate this century is dominated by a number of major and highly significant rulers in Europe and the Near East: Justinian finds himself in the company of the kings Clovis the Frank and Theoderic the Ostrogoth, as well as the Persian King of Kings Chosroes I. As ruler of the Roman Empire for thirty-eight years, and whose significance pre-dated his reign as the nephew and then heir of his uncle the emperor Justin I (518–527), Justinian demands attention.

Justinian is certainly not an unfamiliar figure, for many reasons. His legal projects (including the major achievement of his *Code*) and the reconquest of parts of the Western Roman Empire (primarily North Africa and Italy) make him especially well known, as do his building projects, in particular the breath-taking Hagia Sophia. The depiction of him in mosaic in the sanctuary of the Church of San Vitale in Ravenna is a truly iconic image of a later Roman emperor. The partner mosaic reveals another element of his reign that makes him celebrated, for it depicts his wife the empress Theodora, whose background as an entertainer and possible power within the regime of her husband are intriguing subjects. Justinian has the reputation of being a great talent spotter and a harnesser of the skills of others to attain the achievements of his reign, and Theodora ranks among figures such as Belisarius the general, Tribonian the quaestor, and the chamberlain-turned-general Narses the eunuch. Other aspects of the reign add to the interest of the period, such as the *Nika* riot of 532, the relationship with Persia, the ongoing theological disputes, and the pandemic which Justinian himself was afflicted by. Broader questions concern the nature and identity of the Roman Empire in the period: was Justinian the last

Roman emperor, or in fact presiding over and contributing to the transformation of antiquity into the middle ages? As Fiona Haarer says in this volume all these subjects are familiar, and she skilfully avoids presenting just another tired narrative of the reign by highlighting the key issues and outlining new areas of debate, such as the greater interest in and understanding of the provinces and peoples affected by Justinian's diplomatic and military policies, reflecting current concerns with the impact of war and imperialism on local peoples.

A particular problem with studying the age of Justinian is the risk of simply reproducing the image of it created by the dominating voice for the period, that of the contemporary writer Procopius. From Caesarea in Palestine and an eye witness to events of the reign as legal adviser to the general Belisarius, Procopius wrote three apparently contrasting texts: his major work the *Wars* (a classicising history focused on the campaigns conducted under Justinian), the *Buildings* (a panegyrical work on the construction activity of the emperor), and the notorious *Secret History* (a companion piece to the *Wars* but an explicit blistering attack on the regime of Justinian, focused on the married couples of Belisarius and Antonina and Justinian and Theodora). However, there is a wealth of other sources available for studying Justinian and his age – and there are in fact far more sources than there are for the reign of Constantine the Great (306–337) – as this volume makes clear in the Documents section. In her account of the reign of Justinian Fiona Haarer draws on the full range of available evidence, including legislation, poetry, hagiography, chronicles, church history, inscriptions, documents, treatises, panegyrics and material evidence. Thus, this volume enables readers to see well beyond Procopius' vision of Justinian and his age.

Emma Stafford
Shaun Tougher

Preface

Justinian used the prefaces to his *Novels* (new laws) not only to introduce the subject matter of the law which followed but also to explain the rationale behind the law. This format makes a fitting model for this preface which follows below.

Justinian himself needs very little introduction. Most people will know that European law today is still heavily influenced by Justinian's *Corpus of Civil Law*, the result of his massive effort to codify Roman law. Many people will have visited Hagia Sophia in Istanbul, constructed by Justinian in the 530s. Many will know of the Goths and Vandals who threatened and eventually conquered parts of the Roman Empire: after Justinian's wars of reconquest in North Africa and Italy, the Vandals and Ostrogoths were defeated, dispersed and disappeared from history. Those who have visited the churches of Ravenna decorated with splendid mosaics will have seen the panels of Justinian and Theodora facing each other across the apse in the Church of San Vitale. And those who are familiar with the general history of the late antique and Byzantine world will know that Justinian ruled an empire still familiar from the classical world. However, in the seventh century the world looked very different: the territory in the west so carefully restored by Justinian was lost again (Italy would not be unified again until 1861) and significant parts of the eastern empire, including Jerusalem and the Holy Land, fell to the Arab armies of Muhammed in the rise of Islam.

But if Justinian needs little introduction then why do we need another book? There have been numerous monographs, edited volumes, articles and conferences exploring every aspect of Justinian's reign and the large body of source material. This is not a narrative of his reign but a snapshot and analysis of the current questions we are asking about Justinian today. Alongside the enduring fascination with Theodora, and continued interest in the theological controversies, new areas of interest are opening up, especially concerning the peoples and lands affected by Justinian's foreign policies (the Persians, the Arabs, the Ostrogoths and the Vandals). An increase in translated editions and commentaries of the primary sources has helped to make the study of Justinian more accessible, and new editions and translations of the laws have done much to aid our understanding of Justinian's governance of his empire.

The first part of the book (Debates) considers the key aspects of Justinian's reign and the current debates. References to sources which appear in Part II, Documents, are highlighted in bold (e.g. **II 1**). References to other primary sources not in bold may be found in the list of Primary Sources and the key to references to secondary literature (by author and year of publication) is provided by the Bibliography. I have provided my own translation of the Greek and Latin texts; the translated editions of the Syriac texts used are listed in the Acknowledgements and are referenced with the individual extracts.

Many people have helped with the production of this book. I would like to thank everyone at Edinburgh University Press, especially Carol Macdonald for her patience over the years; John Watson for producing the maps; and the series editors, Emma Stafford and Shaun Tougher, for their encouragement and helpful comments. Amongst many late antique colleagues, I would especially like to thank Geoffrey Greatrex and Brian Croke. Finally, family and friends have provided encouragement and invaluable help in reading drafts: thank you to you all.

Acknowledgements

Part I
3.1 Theudebert gold solidus © The Trustees of the British Museum
3.3 Theodahad bronze coin © The Trustees of the British Museum
5.1 Justinian gold solidus and lightweight solidus © Classical Numismatic Group LLC MBS 60, lot 1976 and EA 383, lot 574

Part II
II.8 John of Ephesus – *Patrologia Orientalis Translated from the Syriac by E. W. Brooks, PO 17 (1923), 187–9* permission granted by Brepols and the Pontificio Istituto Orientale.
II.12 Justin and Justinian gold coin © Classical Numismatic Group LLC Auction 108, lot 717
II.16 *Chronicle* of Pseudo-Zachariah Rhetor, IX.8a – © Liverpool University Press.
II.48 *Chronicle* of Pseudo-Zachariah Rhetor, IX.15j – © Liverpool University Press.
II.60 Pseudo-Dionysius of Tel-Mahre, *Chronicle* 844 – © Liverpool University Press.
II.61 Pseudo-Dionysius of Tel-Mahre, *Chronicle* 845 – © Liverpool University Press.
II.67 Justinian, first dated copper coin, AD 538 © The Trustees of the British Museum
II.80 Pseudo-Dionysius of Tel-Mahre, *Chronicle* 852 – © Liverpool University Press.

Abbreviations

BAR	British Archaeological Reports, Oxford
BMGS	Byzantine and Modern Greek Studies
CQ	Classical Quarterly
DOP	Dumbarton Oaks Papers
GRBS	Greek, Roman and Byzantine Studies
IGLS	Inscriptions grecques et latines de la Syrie
JHS	Journal of Hellenic Studies
JRS	Journal of Roman Studies
MGH	Monumenta Germaniae Historica
ZAC	Zeitschrift für Antikes Christentum. Journal of Ancient Christianity
ZPE	Zeitschrift für Papyrologie und Epigraphik

Maps

1 Constantinople
2 Eastern Frontier
3 Egypt and the Arabian Peninsula
4 The Balkans
5 North Africa
6 Italy

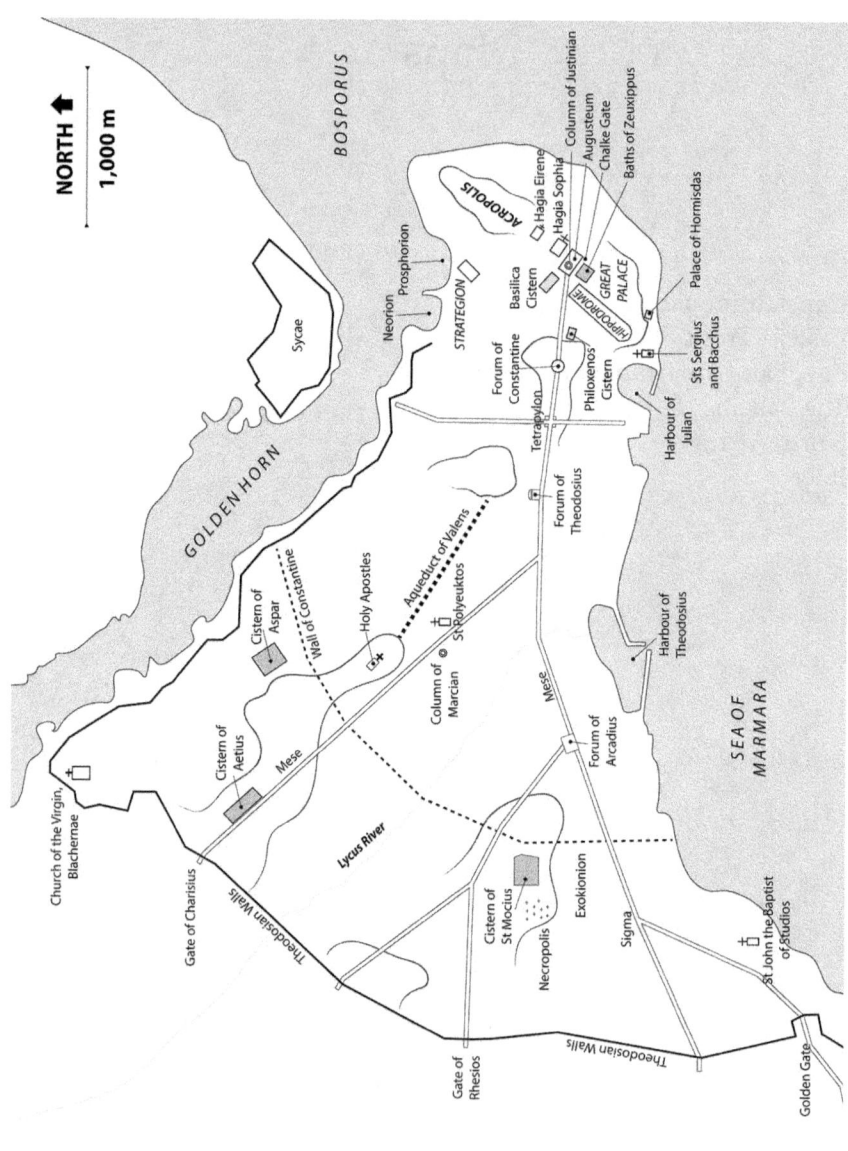

Map 1 Constantinople

Map 2 Eastern Frontier

Map 3 Egypt and the Arabian Peninsula

Map 4 The Balkans

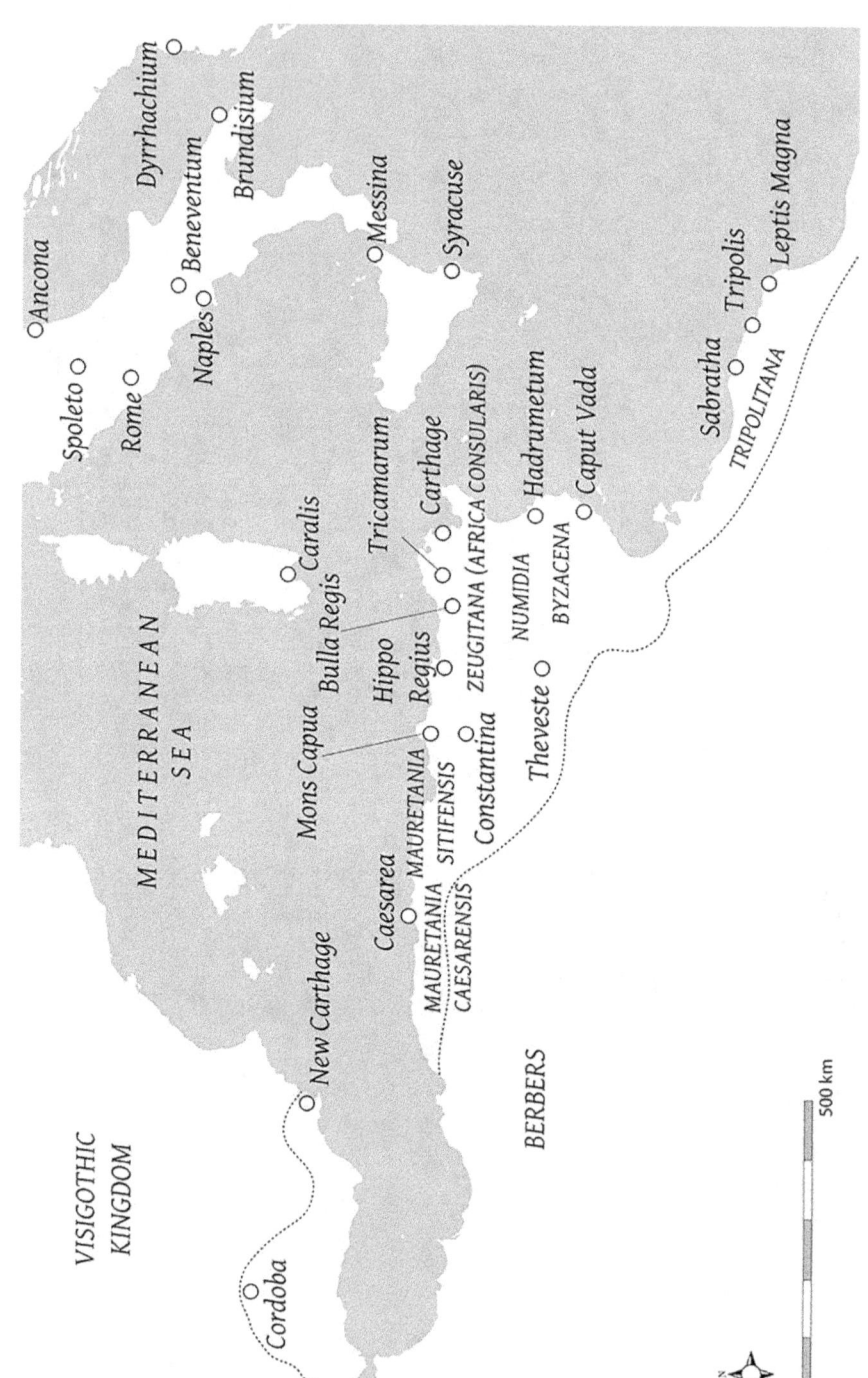

Map 5 North Africa

Map 6 Italy

Part I
Debates

Introduction: Discovering Justinian – Sources and Scholarship

> From the time when God set us up to reign over the Romans, we have been making every effort to do everything to help the subjects of the state entrusted to us by God. (*Novel* 86)

Justinian's overhaul and updating of Roman law has been a major influence on European law; the programme of provincial reform; the construction of Hagia Sophia in Constantinople; the recovery of the western provinces of North Africa and Italy; and his determination to eliminate heresy and bring unity to the Church: each one of these achievements or 'efforts' suggests that Justinian was doing everything he could for the welfare of his subjects. There was, indeed, a lot to do, as he remarked in the preface to another law: 'it so happens that we pass every day and night in full study and thought as to how something useful and pleasing to God might be granted to our subjects' (*Novel* 8). And it seems that God had planned it this way, for example, deliberately keeping the 'disorder' in Egypt 'for our time', thus giving Justinian the opportunity to restore order (*Edict* 13).

The themes of order and unity are key to Justinian's reign. He travelled very little during his long reign (527–565), but from his palace in Constantinople, he conducted himself as a traditional Roman emperor. He despatched generals to defend his frontiers and to conquer (or at least *re*conquer) Roman lands; he entertained embassies and sought to create client kings; he orchestrated an extensive building programme in his capital and throughout the empire; and he strove to stamp out corruption and improve efficiency in provincial administration. But as the Emperor Constantine had discovered in the early fourth century, the expansion of the Christian Church and its relationship with the Roman state added another dimension to the rule of an emperor. As it was important for there to be unity within the empire, so it would be important for there to be unity within the Church. As Constantine had found from his efforts to reconcile the disagreements over the nature of Christ at the first oecumenical council held in Nicaea in 325, this was far from easy. By the time Justinian reached the throne, further disagreements about the nature of Christ arising from the councils of 431 at Ephesus and 451 at Chalcedon had caused fractures within the eastern provinces and with the pope in Rome. A great deal of Justinian's time would also be spent trying to effect a reconciliation between the Chalcedonians and non-Chalcedonians (miaphysites) at the fifth oecumenical council, held in Constantinople in 553. That Justinian saw himself with a divine right to rule has been seen from some of the *Novels* quoted above.

Justinian's struggle to impose order on schismatic clergy and unity on the Church was only one of the difficulties which would beset his reign. There were plenty of setbacks in his wars against Persia and his recovery of North Africa and Italy, including notable misfortunes such as the destruction of Milan by the Ostrogoths in 539 and the sack of Antioch by the Persians in 540. His grip on the throne was challenged at the outset of his reign during the *Nika* riot which saw the centre of his capital destroyed by fire. He endured the personal grief of the death of his wife, Theodora, in 548. And the prosperity of his reign was dented by a pandemic: the plague struck in the 540s and the vivid description written by the historian Procopius includes images of a population confined to their houses, caring for the sick and unable to work. The sequence and the influence of these disappointments on Justinian's policies and strategies must be considered in the study of his rule.

So much for a short introduction to Justinian himself. His long and influential reign from AD 527 to 565 has been the subject of a growing number of studies and conferences over recent years which have sought to understand the emperor himself and the sixth-century world he dominated. Some have emphasised the role of Justinian in the transition between antiquity and the middle ages (Maas 2005), or have been concerned with evaluating the extent to which Justinian weakened the empire, thus allowing the rise of Islam in the seventh century (Heather 2018). Others have looked to portray Justinian's reign as a game of two halves: the successful early years up to the end of the 530s, but, following military setbacks and the plague, a disappointing second part given over to theological controversies (Evans 1996b, Meier 2003a, 2004a). Scholars have endeavoured to describe and analyse every aspect of his reign and this book does not aim to add to the narrative of events. Instead, it seeks to highlight the key issues and to outline the new areas of debate which are emerging. Examples include our enhanced understanding of the provinces and peoples affected by Justinian's diplomatic and military policies, such as the Persians (Canepa 2009, Sauer et al. 2013), the Arab tribes (Fisher 2011, Dijkstra and Fisher 2014, Fisher 2015), the Ostrogoths (Arnold, Bjornlie and Sessa 2016), North Africa (Stevens and Conant 2016) and the Balkans (Sarantis 2016). These areas of new study are perhaps a reflection of our interest today in local peoples caught up in issues of war and imperialism.

The reign of Justinian also introduces us to the wider issues of the culture and society of the sixth century. In the period AD 200–700, which we habitually refer to as 'late antiquity', the sixth century is often seen as a period of transition from a world recognisable for its classical traditions to the new world of Byzantium which, by the end of the seventh century, had not only lost the western provinces which Justinian had sought to recover, but had also lost a significant part of territory in the east (including Jerusalem and the Holy Land) to the armies of Muhammed. This is a subject too large for this book, but it is right to consider Justinian's own contribution to the period of transition. The fusion between church and state and the notion of 'caesaropapism' was hastened by Justinian, who involved himself fully in the affairs of the Church, legislating on ecclesiastical matters, actively seeking to reconcile the schisms, and composing his own theological works. Changes to festivals and public ceremony which now highlighted the role of the Church affected the everyday lives of ordinary people. Prolific church building in Constantinople and throughout the empire continued the transformation in the appearance and fabric of cities, as temples decayed, and even baths, theatres and public spaces became less important. Lastly, his own use of Greek instead of Latin, the traditional language of the Roman Empire and until recent times the language of the army and the law, led him to compose the majority of his *Novels* in Greek. Although they may have continued to refer to themselves as *Romaioi*, as a result of Justinian's actions, the Greek-speaking inhabitants of the Eastern Roman Empire lived in a world where churches increasingly dominated the landscape of towns and cities, and ceremonies and the imperial cult were increasingly sacralised.

Back in the second century, the Christian scholar Tertullian had asked, 'what has Athens to do with Jerusalem?' This question queried the relevance of the (pagan) literature of the classical world in the new Christian world. In 529, so it is often claimed, Justinian was responsible for the closing of the Academy of Athens which, albeit with some gaps and changes to the curriculum, could trace its roots back to the fifth century BC. As part of his efforts to impose order and unity on his empire, Justinian was determined to stamp out heresy and paganism. Yet the deep influence of the classical world continued and can be seen, for example, in the Graeco-Roman myths which still decorated silverware and the mosaic hunting scenes on the floors of the Great Palace in Constantinople. At the same time, the sixth century saw the introduction of the first icons which would come to be so evocative of Byzantium.

A wide range of genres is also reflected in the contemporary written sources both in Constantinople and in the provinces. Histories, chronicles, church histories, collections of letters, edicts, laws, religious works, the records of church councils, hymns, epigrams: we have numerous primary sources which are increasingly made accessible to us in translated editions with commentaries. We also have epigraphic and numismatic evidence, as well as the visual images of the imperial couple. The introduction will end with a review of these sources which give us an incredibly detailed, if often diverse and contradictory, insight into Justinian and Theodora. In these cases, acclaim or disapprobation are portioned often according to the doctrinal sympathies of the author (Chalcedonian or non-Chalcedonian).

One of the most debated issues of Justinian's reign surrounds our most well-known and complex source. Procopius of Caesarea, a lawyer by training who subsequently became an *assessor* to Belisarius, Justinian's famous general, and accompanied him on his early campaigns, has left us three very different works. The *Wars* recount the conflict with Persia (Books I and II), the Vandal wars and subsequent battles with the Moors in North Africa (Books III and IV), and the campaign against the Ostrogoths in Italy (Books V to VII). Book VIII continues the account of the war on the eastern frontier in Lazica and completes the operation in Italy and in the Balkans. The *Wars* are composed very much in the classicising style familiar from Herodotus and Thucydides. Scholars have detected a modicum of criticism, especially in the last book, but the *Wars* are predominantly a narrative. Procopius also composed the *Buildings*, a work in which he describes and praises the emperor's building projects in Constantinople, the east, the Balkans, Anatolia and Palestine, Egypt and Africa. Some constructions are described at length, especially, for example, Hagia Sophia, whilst at other times he merely provides lists of fortifications. Procopius' third work is the highly controversial *Secret History*, a critical invective of Justinian and Theodora, Belisarius and his wife, Antonina. His salacious account of Theodora's early life in the theatre and depiction of Justinian as a demon initially caused outrage and puzzlement, when the text was discovered in modern times, that the author of the sober *Wars* and panegyrical *Buildings* could also have penned the *Secret History*: it was not published at the time and was only found centuries later in the Vatican Library in Rome and published for the first time in 1623. On the other hand, although the criticism of imperial policy is exaggerated, it is not inaccurate and can be shown to be referring to particular reforms and policies of which Procopius did not approve.

Procopius' works (translated by Dewing) are easily accessible in the Loeb series, and there is now an updated version of Dewing's translation of the *Wars* by Kaldellis. He has also produced an English translation of the *Secret History*, and there is a revised Penguin edition (by Sarris) of the Williamson translation. Procopius is also the subject of a huge amount of scholarship. In 2014, an article by Greatrex considered the recent works, including three important monographs (Cameron 1985, Brodka 2004 and Kaldellis 2004b). Against the conventional view that Procopius was a Christian and broadly in favour of Justinian's western campaigns, Kaldellis argues most strongly that Procopius was a crypto-pagan and firmly anti-imperialist. Studies on Procopius continue, with the publication of edited volumes (Lillington-Martin and Turquois 2017 and Greatrex and Janniard 2018) and the *Brill Companion to Procopius* (forthcoming 2021).

Procopius' *Wars* was continued by Agathias, lawyer, historian and poet. Agathias covered the years 552–559, focusing on the Persian wars and campaigns of Narses against the Franks. He wrote 'to record the momentous events' of his own time which would be valuable for posterity. He also composed a number of epigrams in a classicising style which he included, along with a number of poems by his friends, in a collection called the *Cycle*. Again, the conventional view suggests that for all his enthusiasm for classical themes and style, he was undoubtedly a Christian, a view challenged again by Kaldellis (Kaldellis 1997, 1999 *contra* Cameron 1970, Lung 2017). Agathias' history was, in turn, continued by Menander the Guardsman (*Protector*) whose work survives in fragments, although some of these are extensive (Blockley 1985). Menander concentrates on foreign policy, especially diplomatic relations between Rome and Persia, and he preserves for us a copy of the important fifty years' peace treaty of 561/562 which ended the war which had run, on and off, for the duration of Justinian's reign.

Like Procopius' *Wars*, the works of Agathias and Menander were written in the style of traditional classicising histories, following

Herodotus, Thucydides and Polybius. However, a new and popular form of writing was emerging in this period. World chronicles, giving data per year starting from the Creation and often reaching as far as the author's own day, were usually composed in everyday (vernacular) Greek, rather than the literary classicising Greek used by Procopius, and were frequently dismissed as unreliable historical sources. However, although some of the entries could be very brief, the chronicles might also include longer narratives or copies of contemporary documents. One of the most important sources for the reign of Justinian and someone who, like Procopius, has been the subject of increased attention lately is John Malalas. Believed to have worked as a bureaucrat in the office of the *comes Orientis* in Antioch, and later in Constantinople, he produced a chronicle from the time of Adam up to 565 in eighteen books. Amidst some short annalistic entries, his longer narratives provide a very useful alternative contemporary source to Procopius. The chronicle was first made accessible by the English translation and accompanying study by the Australian team (Jeffreys et al. 1986 and 1990). Since then, Malalas studies have proliferated and a major research project, 'Historical and Philological Commentary on John Malalas' Chronicle', is now under way in Tübingen to produce a commentary and edited volumes from regular conferences. One of the major problems in reading Malalas is the complicated manuscript tradition. The single surviving manuscript (Oxford, Bodleian Barroccianus 182) lacks a beginning and end and has many gaps, and the text has to be reconstructed from later chronicles which draw on it. One of these, known as the *Chronicon Paschale*, was composed in Constantinople c. 630, and supplements the text of Malalas' chronicle for the sixth century. It includes a very detailed account of the *Nika* riot and incorporates Justinian's Theopaschite Edict of 533. There is a helpful translation and commentary in the Translated Texts for Historians (TTH) series published by Liverpool University Press (Whitby and Whitby 1989) which provides an invaluable service in making available a large number of texts with detailed commentaries.

Not all Greek chronicles survived in their original language and another important source for Justinian published in the TTH series is the surviving Syriac version of the *Chronicle* of Pseudo-Zachariah Rhetor (Greatrex 2011). Although part of the work is based on the *Ecclesiastical History* of the bishop of Mytilene, Zachariah the Rhetor, the compiler again did not confine himself to church matters, but included an account of the Persian war, the *Nika* riot and events in the west, and incorporated a number of documents, especially the correspondence of churchmen. Not all chronicles were written in Greek in the first place, however, and an example is the Latin chronicle by the Illyrian Marcellinus *Comes*, a *cancellarius* to Justinian in Constantinople, which provides us with helpful details of Justinian's reign up to the year 534 (with an anonymous continuation to 548). An English translation and commentary are available in the Byzantina Australiensia series (Croke 1995).

Apart from classicising histories on secular subjects such as war and politics, ecclesiastical histories which focused primarily on church matters were also popular. One such example is Evagrius Scholasticus who composed a church history in Greek covering the years 428 to 592 (Whitby 2000). Book IV is dedicated to the reign of Justinian and includes not only church matters, but also a summary of some parts of Procopius' *Wars* and a moving personal account of the plague. Another useful source for us is the *Life of St Sabas* in the *Lives of the Monks of Palestine*, a collection compiled by Cyril of Scythopolis, a monk in Palestine closely familiar with the monasteries (*lavrae*) in the desert around Jerusalem. Although he spent most of his life there, Sabas did travel to Constantinople and the *Life* gives us a fascinating insight into these visits, which concerned not only doctrinal issues, but also practical issues such as tax relief. The *Lives of the Eastern Saints* composed by John of Ephesus also reveals useful details, as does his *Ecclesiastical History*. Part I of the *History* does not survive but sections of Part II can be recovered from Part III of the *Chronicle* of Pseudo-Dionysius of Tel-Mahre, also known as the *Chronicle of Zuqnin*, for which there is a translation and commentary in the TTH series (Witakowski 1996). Part III of John's *Ecclesiastical History* also survives and has been translated into English (Payne Smith 1860) and into Latin (Brooks 1923–6). The strongly pro-Chalcedonian view of Cyril and the strongly anti-Chalcedonian view of John, who was responsible for the conversion of thousands to miaphysitism during Justinian's reign, are clearly evident in their works.

The church politics of the sixth century were hugely complicated and we are indebted to the work of Price in providing a translation with a thorough introduction and commentary of the Acts of the Council of Constantinople of 553 and associated letters and edicts on the Three Chapters Controversy (Price 2009). Further insights into the correspondence between emperors and popes are provided by the documents included in the *Collectio Avellana*, a collection of 244 documents dating from 367 to 553. Much work has been carried out on the *Collectio Avellana* recently (Lizzi Testa and Marconi 2019), but no complete English translation yet exists.

There are also secular collections and one important example is Cassiodorus' *Variae*, for which a partial translation exists in the TTH series (Barnish 1992) and there is now also a full translation (Bjornlie 2019). The *Variae* are a series of documents comprising the correspondence and edicts of the Ostrogothic royal family collected by the statesman and writer Cassiodorus. They offer an invaluable window on to the workings of Ostrogothic Italy and its relationship with the Eastern Roman Empire (see Chapter 3). Cassiodorus came to Constantinople, probably after the fall of Ostrogothic Ravenna to Belisarius in 540, where it is likely he met other writers, such as Malalas and John the Lydian (John Lydus). A civil servant, John also held an advanced teaching position in Latin at the imperial institute, or university. An encomium to Justinian and possible history of the Persian war are lost, unfortunately, but his antiquarian works on the calendar and portents remain, as does his *de Magistratibus* (*On the Magistracies*) which preserves his critical view on Justinian's reforms (though not the emperor himself) and on the finance minister, John the Cappadocian. John the Lydian's love of antiquarian learning, the classical pagan past and divination, and his praise of the praetorian prefect Phocas, who committed suicide during one of the purges of pagans, has led some (such as Kaldellis 2003a) to believe that John (like Procopius and Agathias) was pagan (*contra* Maas 1992, Cameron 1996).

Praise of Justinian can be found in a variety of contemporary literary sources from across the empire and in a variety of genres, and three important examples will be highlighted here. The first is a highly classicising work from the imperial court, an *Ekphrasis (Description) of Hagia Sophia*, by one of Agathias' friends, Paul the Silentiary. This was a poem written for the re-dedication of Hagia Sophia in early 563 after repairs to the dome, and it is particularly interesting not only for the detailed description of the church but also for the panegyrical passages at the beginning and end in praise of Justinian and the Patriarch Eutychius. A partial English translation exists in Mango (1986) and also in Bell (2009). Bell's volume is entitled *Three Political Voices from the Age of Justinian*; the other two works are Agapetus' *Advice to the Emperor* and the anonymous *Dialogue on Political Science*, both of which give an insight into imperial government and the political problems of sixth-century Constantinople.

The second example of a panegyrical work is a composition by Choricius who was the head of a prolific literary circle (the so-called 'School of Gaza') in the flourishing provincial town of Gaza in Palestine. The writings of the poets and orators of this Christian town were infused with classical and mythological influences. Amongst Choricius' copious works was an oration (*Oratio* XIII) celebrating the *Brumalia*, one of the pagan festivals which Justinian had sought to reformulate to suit a more Christian audience. For the third example, we return to the capital, and to the hymns of Romanos. Romanos composed a large number of hymns, mostly on sacred subjects (those on repentance are translated by Mellas, 2020), but a few contained allusions to contemporary politics. His *Kontakion* 54, *On Earthquakes and Fires*, alludes to the *Nika* riot and the rebuilding of Hagia Sophia.

We started with a quotation from the *Novels* and the last key primary source to introduce are the laws of Justinian. The many laws of Justinian from 527 to 534 are included in the *Code*. Those issued after 534 are to be found in the *Novels*. We are fortunate in having a new translation (with a parallel Greek and Latin text) of the *Codex of Justinian* (Frier 2016) and an English translation of the *Novels* (Miller and Sarris 2018) with a helpful introduction and commentary. As with Justinian's theological works, this is our opportunity to hear the voice of the emperor.

From this vast collection of sources, I have aimed in Part II to choose a balanced selection to reflect the aims and achievements of Justinian and the responses and actions of his officials, churchmen, subjects, enemies and allies, and to give a flavour of the culture and society of the sixth century. In Part I, I have divided up his reign between foreign policy (Chapters 2 and 3), religious policy (Chapter 4), governance (Chapter 5) and culture and society (Chapter 6). We start, however, in Chapter 1, with Justinian's rise to the throne and the early years of his reign.

1

Rise to Power

The reign of Justin (518–527)

The remarkable story of his rise 'from swineherd to emperor', thus characterised by the imaginatively named second chapter of the only monograph on Justin I (Vasiliev 1950: chapter 2), is well known. In about 470, three peasants, Justin, Zimarchus and Dityvistus, set out to walk from their village of Bederiana in Thrace to Constantinople, carrying some toasted bread wrapped in their rough cloaks. They were fortunate to be enrolled into the new body of palace guards (*excubitors*) formed by Leo I, and Justin rose up the ranks. He became a *dux*, and during the reign of Anastasius he played an important role in the wars against the Isaurians, the Persians and the rebel Vitalian. By the time Anastasius died in 518, he held the top position, *comes excubitorum*.

However, it is not Justin's undoubted distinguished military career but subsequent events which are of most interest. His nine-year reign as emperor is significant for several key religious and military policies which had far-reaching consequences for Justinian's reign and beyond. However, the most controversial question about the years 518 to 527 concerns Justinian's influence over his uncle and to what extent he wielded imperial power himself. It is known that Justin sent for his nephews, ensured they benefited from a good education in the capital, and promoted their careers. One of them, Germanus, became a successful general. The other (who was to become known as Justinian), born Petrus Sabbatius, joined the palace guards and is attested as a *comes* in 519 and the following year as the *magister militum praesentalis* (*PLRE* II.646). From this point, traditional accounts of this period of late Roman history have tended to compound the two reigns, following the lead of Procopius of Caesarea who depicts Justin as old and decrepit ('an old man tottering to his grave') and attributes the governance of the empire to Justinian (*Secret History* 6.11, 6.19). The standard narratives of Bury (1923), Jones (1964) and the *Cambridge Ancient History* (volume 14) all contain chapters entitled 'Justin and Justinian', and Stein (1949), Rubin (1960), Browning (1987), Evans (1996a) and Meier (2003a, 2004a) all tend to portray Justinian as the dominant force behind the throne. Even Vasiliev (1950: 6) draws attention to his subtitle: *An Introduction to the Epoch of Justinian the Great*, remarking that 'the reign of Justin is to be regarded as the unofficial reign of Justinian'. This view has now been questioned by Croke (2007) who suggests, on the contrary, that Justin was a highly competent and vigorous ruler throughout his reign. And the natural corollary to this argument must be a reduction in the role of Justinian, which Croke proceeds to argue.

The means by which Justin ascended to the throne after the death of the elderly Anastasius are unclear. The story goes that since Anastasius was childless and had not nominated any of his perfectly eligible three nephews, there was a brief period of uncertainty and unrest, before the senate agreed on the accession of Justin. Soon, however, a rumour circulated that Justin had used for his own campaign the money provided by one of the chief ministers, Amantius, for the promotion of another minister, the *comes domesticorum*, Theocritus. There are varying opinions on the association of Justin and this conspiracy of Amantius. Greatrex (2007: 99–105), after a thorough examination of the sources, suggests that the conspiracy of Amantius was fabricated by the new regime to account for the execution of Amantius who had spoken out against Justin. Croke (2007: 16–26), however, argues that it was 'no surprise' that as one of the 'empire's most senior military dignitaries' Justin might become emperor, and that therefore the assumption that he was somehow implicated in the plot of Amantius is unnecessary. Croke also dismisses the suggestion that Justin's accession was orchestrated by Justinian. Croke emphasises that although Justinian was one of the imperial *candidati* (an elite unit of the *scholae palatinae*) serving the emperor and would have had an excellent knowledge of the workings of the imperial court, there were plenty of other similarly well-connected courtiers, ministers and generals who were favoured and promoted by Justin, while his nephew remained a *candidatus*.

One of these men who benefited from Justin's policy of replacing the favourites of the previous regime with its enemies was Vitalian. A pro-Chalcedonian rebel who had waged a civil war (ostensibly on religious grounds) against the miaphysite Anastasius (Haarer 2006: 164–79), Vitalian was now recalled to Constantinople and appointed *magister militum praesentalis*. Justin overlooked his own role in defeating

Vitalian in a sea battle at the Golden Horn, although he did insist on an oath of allegiance first. Vitalian played a crucial role in the negotiations with the pope to end the Acacian schism (Croke 2007: 26–33, Ruscu 2008: 779ff), and as the most important man at court after the emperor, he succeeded Justin as consul for 520. However, in July 520 he was murdered during some disturbances in the hippodrome races. Greatrex (2007: 105–6) again examines the sources to throw light on the relationship of Vitalian not just with Justinian, who is usually held to account for his murder, but with the whole regime. Croke (2007: 34–5) develops this argument, suggesting that it was the emperor himself who caught the unreliable Vitalian plotting his overthrow and had him murdered. Less convincing is the argument that Justinian was behind the assassination, motivated by fear of Vitalian's popularity among the Scythian monks in Constantinople and their recognition of him as the true defender of the eastern orthodox tradition against Rome (Ruscu 2008: 783–5).

The healing of the schism with Rome was a major achievement for Justin (see Chapter 4). The breach had occurred back in 484 when Acacius (Patriarch of Constantinople) and Peter Mongus (Patriarch of Alexandria) were excommunicated by Pope Felix III and Acacius promptly removed the pope's name from the diptychs. These retaliatory actions followed the publication of Zeno's compromise document, the *Henoticon*, which sought to patch up the divisions following the 451 Council of Chalcedon. While the eastern sees had largely been prepared to accept the decree, Rome refused to sanction a document which overruled Chalcedon and which had been imposed by imperial edict (Frend 1972: 81–183). During the reign of the anti-Chalcedonian Anastasius, the battle-lines between Rome and the east had hardened, despite a strong desire for reconciliation in the imperial capital itself (Charanis 1974, Haarer 2006: 125ff). Within a couple of months of Justin's accession, the legate Gratus set out from Constantinople carrying a letter from Justin asking Pope Hormisdas to send envoys who would be in favour of peace (*Collectio Avellana* 143), and an invitation from Justinian to Hormisdas himself to visit Constantinople (*Collectio Avellana* 147 – **II 1**). Throughout the subsequent negotiations carried out by the papal legates leading up to the signing of the pope's *libellus* (*Collectio Avellena* 159) by the patriarch of Constantinople, John, on Maundy Thursday 519, Croke emphasises Justin's personal involvement and seeks to portray Justinian as only one of a number of papal correspondents who included Celer, Anicia Juliana and Euphemia (*contra* Vasiliev 1950: 199–200 who argued that the missives of the future emperor carried far greater weight). Croke highlights Justin's attention to detail in passing legislation requiring all soldiers to be orthodox (Jacob of Edessa, *Chronicon* 3.4.240, *C.J.* I.4.20), and his instruction to Hypatius (Anastasius' nephew and *magister militum per Orientem*) to investigate the report of the bishop of Cyrrhus, Sergius, who had organised a procession in honour of the now questionable former bishop, Theodoret. Finally, he sees in Hormisdas' replies, which arrived in the early summer of 521, a personal appreciation of the effort Justin himself had expended to achieve unity. Hormisdas' *libellus* required the condemnation of key miaphysite patriarchs, the Constantinopolitan patriarchs from Acacius to Macedonius, and two emperors, Zeno and Anastasius, a major triumph for the pope.

The healing of the Acacian schism, however, was not perhaps so advantageous to Theoderic, the Arian Ostrogothic ruler of Italy, who felt that his position was stronger when there was dissension between the Chalcedonians and anti-Chalcedonians. The fullest discussions of the subsequent tension between Ravenna and Constantinople are to be found in many studies of the senator and philosopher Boethius, who, along with his father-in-law, Symmachus, became the most famous casualties of the atmosphere of suspicion (Chadwick 1981: 43–67, Matthews 1981: 15–43, Moorhead 2009: 13–22; see Chapter 3).

In a move to protect the line of succession, Theoderic invited Justin to adopt his son-in-law, Eutharic, according to Germanic custom and recognise him as his heir. Eutharic also became the consul for 519, along with the emperor. The year 519 was also a significant one for Boethius who was appointed *magister officiorum* and his sons were designated consuls for 522. However, Eutharic died in 522, leaving his widow, Amalasuntha, and two children, Athalaric and Matasuntha. Previously close relations between the Ostrogoths and Burgundians degenerated, there was rebellion in Spain, and in Africa, Hilderic succeeded Thrasamund as the Vandal king and imprisoned Amalafrida, Thrasamund's wife and Theoderic's sister. Hilderic favoured the Nicene African Church over the Arians, and sought an alliance with Justin; it has even been suggested that their new relationship was celebrated with a series of coins, but the eastern emperor depicted on the coins is now thought to be Justin II (Wroth 1908: I, 21 *contra* Grierson 1982: 79, Grierson and Blackburn 2007: 20). The success of Justin's religious policy meant that Catholics in Italy were no longer in schism with the eastern empire, and might again feel stronger allegiance to Constantinople than to the Arian Ostrogoths. At the same time, Theoderic heard that Arians in the east were being persecuted by

Justin, and he sent Pope John (Hormisdas' successor) to investigate. The emperor was persuaded to return the Arian churches he had confiscated, and the pope was persuaded to perform a coronation ceremony. Theoderic expressed his displeasure by imprisoning, on his return, the already sick John, who died shortly thereafter. It was in the context of this period of anxiety and suspicion that correspondence from the senator, Albinus, to Justin was intercepted, and when accusations of treachery were brought, Boethius suggested that if Albinus was guilty, then so was the whole senate, including himself. Boethius was imprisoned by Theoderic in Pavia, where he composed his famous *Consolation of Philosophy*, before he was put to death (Anonymus Valesianus 85-7 - **II 2**).

There are many uncertainties in the narrative and the motivation of the major players. The extent of Boethius' own desire to see an alliance between the emperor in the east and the Roman Senate is debatable (O'Daly 1991: 4-8), and Theoderic's uncharacteristic tyrannical behaviour has been much discussed. His letter to the praetorian prefect Abundantius, in which he refers to the building of a fleet as a precaution against the Greeks (i.e. the Romans) and Africans (Cassiodorus, *Variae* V.17), and his decree ordering the Arians to take over the Catholic churches (Anonymus Valesianus 94-5), if true, suggest a high degree of hostility towards the eastern empire. Most interesting is the question of Justinian's role. The achievement of church unity, the alliance with the Vandals, and the persecution of the Arians in the east might be isolated policies of Justin, or a clever plan by Justinian to weaken Ostrogothic rule in Italy as a prelude to reconquest (Chadwick 1981: 66-8, *contra* Moorhead 1994: 73-4, Croke 2007: 48). After the death of Theoderic in 526, under the regency of the pro-Roman Amalasuntha, Athalaric wrote a conciliatory letter to Justin. However, the reconciliation was short-lived, and whatever the extent of premeditation on Justinian's part, the tragedy of Boethius and the decline in Theoderic's government clearly marked an important stage in events leading to the restoration of Italy (Matthews 1981: 29; see Chapter 3).

It was not only in the west that politics and theology came together. Justin turned his attention to Ethiopia (Abyssinia), whose ruler, Ella Asheba (variously spelt, and also known as Caleb), was a miaphysite, and Yemen (Himyar), whose ruler, Dhu Nuwas (variously spelt and also known as Masruq), was Jewish. A massacre of Christians in the Ḥimyarite town of Najran by Dhu Nuwas in 518 or 523 provided Justin with the opportunity to invade the strategically important Yemen and install a Christian (albeit miaphysite) on the throne. The troops were provided by the Ethiopians and their alliance with Justin was facilitated by the patriarch of Alexandria, Timothy, an indication of the Chalcedonian emperor's willingness to support miaphysites outside the empire. The massacre had come to light at an international conference in Ramla (519 or 524) at which Persian and Roman envoys convened with the Lakhmid chief, Mundhir. Justin's envoy, Abraham, was successful in ransoming two Roman commanders captured by the Lakhmids who had raided Osrhoene in 519/520, perhaps with the encouragement of their Persian allies.

Narratives of this episode are offered aimed at elucidating events, the relationships between these world powers, and establishing the chronology (the consensus is now for the later years of 523/524) (Vasiliev 1950: 283–302, Shahîd 1964, Rubin 1989, Greatrex 1998: 226–31, Beaucamp, Briquel-Chatonnet and Robin 1999–2000). However, much detailed analysis may also be found in the editions of the key sources: the *Book of the Himyarites* (Moberg 1924), the *Martyrdom of Arethas* (Detoraki 2007), the letters of Simeon of Bet Arsham (Jeffery 1945, Shahîd 1971), and the *Chronicles* of Pseudo-Dionysius of Tel-Mahre 57–67/53–62 (Witakowski 1996) and Pseudo-Zachariah Rhetor VIII.3 (Greatrex 2011).

Justin's dealings with Persia are naturally significant, given that the ongoing conflict would command so much of Justinian's attention. The standard account for what follows may be found in Greatrex (1998: 130–8). Trouble started initially with Tzath, the king of Lazica, who feared that Kavadh, the Persian king, would impose Zoroastrianism on the people of Lazica, and sought an alliance with Justin. Kavadh considered this a hostile action, and both Rome and Persia solicited aid from Zilgibis, the king of the Sabir Huns. After accepting a bribe from the Romans, Zilgibis proceeded to make an alliance with the Persians, but was executed by Kavadh when he heard of his treachery from Justin (Malalas 414–16). Otherwise, Kavadh was preoccupied by problems within Persia, including the succession of his son, Chosroes. Following the example of Arcadius whose son, Theodosius, had been formally adopted by the Persian king, Yezdgerd, Kavadh asked Justin to adopt Chosroes. Concern that Chosroes might one day claim that he was heir to the Roman Empire prompted Justin to agree only to adoption by arms, according to a custom used for barbarian kings (Procopius, *Wars* I.11.7–30). Insulted by this response, Kavadh successfully annexed Iberia and the Romans were hard pressed to retain Lazica; the latter kingdom would play an important role in the subsequent conflict (Greatrex 1998: 139–47). Meanwhile, Justin sent Belisarius and Sittas (on whom more below) to invade Persian Armenia (Greatrex 1998: 147–8). Libelarius, the *dux* of Mesopotamia, made an unsuccessful foray into Persian territory, as a result of which he was replaced by Belisarius, and Hypatius (Anastasius' nephew) was re-appointed as *magister militum per Orientem* to protect the empire from the incursions of the Lakhmid Al-Mundhir (Shahîd 1995: I.1.42–8, Greatrex 1998: 148–50). The absence of the pro-Roman (and miaphysite) Ghassānids who had provided a counter-balance to the Lakhmids during the reign of Anastasius may be explained by Justin's harsh attitude towards anti-Chalcedonianism (Shahîd 1995: I.1.32–9; for further discussion on the significance of doctrinal loyalties, Shahîd 1995 I.2.716–33).

The above discussion highlights the fact that the focus of Justin's reign was on theological and foreign policy. There has been little discussion on his attention to domestic and administrative affairs, although Vasiliev presents the evidence for the economic conditions of the empire (including natural disasters, trade and commerce, expenses and coinage) in his chapter 7 (1950: 344–88) and his legislation in chapter 8 (1950: 389–413). Croke (2007: 49) picks up on Malalas and Theophanes who chronicle the aid dispensed by Justin to cities affected by floods and earthquakes, as well as the renaming of two cities (Edessa and Anazarbus) as Iustinopolis, to underline his argument that Justin (not Justinian) was fully in charge (Malalas 417–19, Theophanes AM 6014–17). Even in 526, when the news of the terrible earthquake in Antioch reached Constantinople, Justin himself was very active in organising relief and planning the rebuilding programme (Croke 2007: 50–1). Vasiliev's third chapter, devoted to 'domestic rule', largely concerns the Amantius conspiracy, Vitalian, and the other advisors and courtiers with whom Justin surrounded himself (1950: 102–31, now mostly superseded by Croke 2007 and Greatrex 2007). One aspect which Vasiliev raises and which is of great importance is that of the factions, and this brings us neatly back to the question of the significance of Justinian's role during the reign of his uncle.

The rise of Justinian and Theodora

Factional violence, sometimes but not always connected to doctrinal differences, and more often than not instigated by the Greens, had been an increasing problem throughout the reign of Anastasius (Cameron 1973, Cameron 1976, Liebeschuetz 1996a, Haarer 2006: 223–9). With the accession of Justin, however, it was the constant rioting of the Blues which threatened the social security of the empire. From the early days, Justinian's fortunes seemed to have been linked to the factions and a thirst for popularity in the hippodrome. Vitalian's downfall had come after he had enjoyed the favour of the factions following his consular games in 520. Just a year later in 521, Justinian's own consular games, featuring large numbers of exotic animals, were considered to be the finest and most costly ever to be staged, and were surely a deliberate attempt to gain favour (Marcellinus *Comes* 521 – **II 3**). He also sent to senators the customary ivory diptychs, carrying his full names and titles and the inscription: 'I, the consul, offer these gifts, small indeed in value but rich in honours, to my senators' (Weitzman 1979: 51; **II 4**). It has been suggested that the abolition of the Olympic games in Antioch in 520 resulted not from the risk of rioting (or their cost, or their association with paganism) but from Justinian's desire to centralise and control spectacles in Constantinople (Lim 1997; see Chapter 6). However, although this argument fits with the view that elevates the position of Justinian, it is unlikely that in the early 520s the future emperor had formed such a coherent policy. Indeed, in 523 his outright support for the Blues almost made him a victim of his uncle's policy to control the factions. Justin ordered his city prefect, Theodotus, to deal with the persistent unrest caused by the Blues. He arrested and executed Theodosius, an imperial minister, and began to make arrangements for the arrest of Justinian himself. Fortunately for Justinian, he became ill, and by the time he recovered, Justin had decided to spare him. As soon as he was safe, Justinian took action against Theodotus who fled from Constantinople and later died in Jerusalem (Greatrex 1997: 66, Croke 2007: 39–40). We will return to Justinian's most notorious involvement with the factions on the occasion of the *Nika* riot at the end of this chapter.

The rise of Justinian after this time may be traced with reference to the bestowal of titles by Justin: patrician, just after his recovery from illness; the rank of *nobilissimus*, probably in 524 and at the urging of the senate; *Caesar*, in 525, prompted by the debate over the adoption of Kavadh's son, Chosroes (Croke 2006: 27–9, 2007: 40–9). The main point of Croke's argument is to question the process of succession planning and to suggest the slow emergence of Justinian as the natural successor to Justin. Another issue which merits consideration is the role which Anicia Juliana played in the formation of Justinian's imperial ambitions. With impeccable royal lineage (she was the daughter of the western emperor, Olybrius, and on her mother's side she could trace connections back to Valentinian III and Theodosius II), she

Figure 1.1 Church of St Polyeuktos. Photo: author.

was the only other holder of the rank of *nobilissima*. She had maintained her Chalcedonian faith throughout the reign of the miaphysite Anastasius, and was one of the papal correspondents in 519. She was immensely wealthy and was well known for her acts of patronage: the donor portrait on the frontispiece of the lavish illuminated manuscript, the Vienna Dioscorides, attests to her generous patronage of art. She was also responsible for commissioning at least three churches in Constantinople, and it is the most famous of these, St Polyeuktos, which aroused Justinian's greatest envy (Harrison 1989). The dedicatory inscription in hexameter verse is preserved in the *Greek Anthology* I.10, and fragments remain in the Istanbul Archaeological Museum (**II 5**). Justinian's triumphant words on the completion of Hagia Sophia in 537, 'O Solomon, I have surpassed thee' (*Narratio de Aedificatione Templi S. Sophiae* 27), also alluded to by Romanos in his *Kontakion* 54, are a reference to this dedicatory inscription in St Polyeuktos which compares Juliana to King Solomon (see Chapter 5). However, even before Hagia Sophia, there are signs that Justinian sought to challenge the pretensions of Juliana's church building. It has been argued that the Church of SS Sergius and Bacchus, often ascribed to Theodora in the early 530s as a church for the miaphysites sheltering under the empress's protection in the Palace of Hormisdas, in fact

Figure 1.2 SS Sergius and Bacchus, today known as the Little Hagia Sophia Mosque. Photo: author.

belongs to the mid-520s and was designed by Justinian as a response to the Church of St Polyeuktos now re-dated to the early 520s. The inscribed epigram inside SS Sergius and Bacchus includes claims of the superiority of Justinian over other rulers, and the efficacy of St Sergius over other saints 'whose labour was unprofitable', perhaps a reference to St Polyeuktos (Croke 2006: 47–8; **II 6**). If this view is correct, then not only may we add SS Sergius and Bacchus to the list of Justinian's churches built prior to his accession, but we may see it as a deliberate attempt by Justinian to stamp his own mark on the courtly politics of Constantinople: Juliana was no doubt hoping for the advancement of her own son, Olybrius, a patrician who had held the consulship in 491 at an early age, and who was advantageously married to the niece of the Emperor Anastasius.

Theodora

One event which certainly had important consequences was the death, probably in 524, of Justin's wife, Euphemia. Originally a barbarian and a slave, she had been Justin's concubine and known as Lupicina, a name associated with prostitution. Justin freed her and subsequently married her, and on his accession, she had been persuaded by the factions to change her name to the more respectable Euphemia. This had the further significance of identifying her with the local saint, Euphemia of Chalcedon, and thus associating her with the pro-Chalcedonian policy of the new regime. There is little evidence for Euphemia's involvement in affairs of state, apart from encouraging the reconciliation with Rome. However, she strongly objected to the marriage of Justinian to Theodora, and if the rhetoric of Procopius persuades, we should believe that once Euphemia was out of the way, Justinian pressurised Justin to alter the legislation to allow a senator to marry a former actress (*C.J.* V.4.23, *Secret History* 9.51). It is commonly believed that an additional clause referring to women of patrician rank was a specific allusion to the position of Theodora (Daube 1966–7, Angold 1996: 26, Garland 1999: 14–15 *contra* Vasiliev 1950: 395, who argued that if Theodora was already a patrician, then a change in the legislation would not have been necessary). Justin's marriage law was addressed to the prefect, Demosthenes, but cannot be dated any more precisely than between 520 and 524, and the marriage of Justinian and Theodora has been dated variously to 524 and 525 (Browning 1987: 40–1, Honoré 1978: 9–12, Evans 2002: 20).

The scandalous rise of Theodora from the stage to the imperial court is a story which never fails to fascinate and one that has formed the subject of a huge number of books, both scholarly and fictional, and even plays, such as the 1884 *Théodora*, written by Victorien Sardou and starring Sarah Bernhardt. A cluster of studies over the last decade have sought to elucidate the character of this most notorious and enigmatic

Figure 1.3 Theodora panel, San Vitale, Ravenna. Photo: author.

empress, posing questions such as 'Was she a saint or a troublemaker?' (Evans 2011: xiv). 'To some she was the "beloved queen". To others she was the demon incarnate' (Potter 2015: 2). We struggle to understand the complexity of her relationship with Justinian: the wife whom he described in one of his laws as 'our most pious consort given us by God' (*Novel* 8.1), yet who did not hesitate to thwart his pro-Chalcedonian policy to protect her miaphysite allies. Even the two most distinctive sources left to us offer contradictory portrayals. Her characterisation by Procopius in the *Secret History* as 'licentious and depraved, spiteful, greedy, an intriguer, a demon in human form' (James 2001: 16) may be set against the visual impression offered by the mosaic in San Vitale in Ravenna which reveals her imperial power and her close relationship to God (James 2001: 39–41; see Chapter 6). Other key written sources are provided by John of Ephesus: his *Lives of the Eastern Saints* and the remaining part of his *Ecclesiastical History*. John was a fellow miaphysite who records the deeds of his 'believing queen', thereby offering a counter-balance to the scurrilous tales of Procopius. Theodora's suggested modern counterpart, Eva Perón of Argentina, evokes the notion of the rise of an actress to the highest pinnacle of government (Foss 2002, Evans 2011: xiii–xiv).

The story of Theodora's early hardships has been retold many times. Her father, Acacius, the bear-keeper for the Greens, died when she was about five, leaving his widow and Theodora's two sisters, Comito and Anastasia. Her mother quickly remarried and hoped that her new husband would take over Acacius' position. However, even the appearance of Theodora and her sisters dressed as suppliants in the hippodrome failed to persuade Asterius, the lead dancer of the Greens, not to accept a bribe from another candidate. Fortunately, the Blues were also in need of a new bear-keeper and they offered the post to Theodora's step-father; her subsequent support for the Blue faction is hardly surprising. Her career in the theatre is well known from the oft-quoted account in Procopius' *Secret History*, especially her stage-act of having geese peck barley grains from her almost naked body as a loose representation of Leda and the swan (II 7). A brief reference from John of Ephesus confirms her origins in a brothel (II 8). She managed to escape from the theatre as the concubine of one Hecebolus of Tyre who had purchased the governorship of Cyrenaica, and she travelled with him to Alexandria. It is assumed that it was here, where its most ardent exponents (including the extreme Severus of Antioch, and Patriarch Timothy) were based, that she became familiar with miaphysitism (John of Nikiu 514). However, after a quarrel with Hecebolus, she was left to make her way back to Constantinople, and it is likely that she met Justinian through their connections to the Blues shortly after her return. About the same time as her marriage, her elder sister, Comito, married Justinian's friend and *magister militum*, Sittas. Theodora's early days in power are well documented (most recently, Evans 2011: 48–62).

Apart from her astonishing rise, important questions remain to be answered about this seemingly dominant empress: how extensive was her imperial power and to what extent could she influence her husband? These issues have been widely debated (Fisher 1978, Moorhead 1994: 38–40, Evans 2005: 33–47, Angold 1996: 26–32, Garland 1999: 29–39, Foss 2002: 148–54, 170–5, Evans 2002 and Evans 2011 *passim*). There are plenty of signs of their co-rule, alluded to by John the Lydian (*de Magistratibus* III.69) and in the laws (*Novel* 8.1 and *Novel* 8 *ad fin.* stating that the oath that they would carry out their duties should be sworn by officials to both the emperor and his wife). There are examples of inscriptions citing both their names (*IGLS* I.146, Dagron et al. 1987: 97, no. 52), and Theodora appears to deal independently with foreign rulers. Procopius refers to her letter to the Persian ambassador, Zaberganes, in which she claimed that Justinian did nothing without her, a claim which Chosroes was pleased to use to ridicule the Roman Empire where a woman was reputedly in charge (*Secret History* 2.32–5). Correspondence between Theodora and the Ostrogoths, including letters from Theodahad and his wife, Gudeliva, which refer to a secret mission, possibly confirms the accusation that Theodora was implicated in the murder of Amalasuntha (see Chapter 3). It is also clear that Theodora had requested Theodahad to consult her first before Justinian (Cassiodorus, *Variae* X.10 (from Amalasuntha), X.20 (**II 9**) and X.23 from Theodahad, and X.21 and X.42 from Gudeliva).

Theodora was successful in eventually bringing about the exile of John the Cappadocian (on whom see below), and in promoting the cause of the miaphysites and in negotiations with the pope (see Chapter 4). Even if she was not directly responsible for Justinian's legislation which sought to improve the status of women (see Chapter 5), she was certainly involved with his measures to stamp out prostitution. Procopius presents two sides to this reform: in the *Buildings* (**II 10**), he describes how Justinian and Theodora converted a palace into a convent for prostitutes; in the *Secret History* (17.5–6), he represents the girls as fiercely resisting the move and even committing suicide in their attempt to escape. Malalas (440–1) records Theodora's arrangement that brothel-keepers should be paid five *nomismata* as a recompense for the girls they had employed; the girls were to be released with a new set of clothes and one *nomisma*.

In general, she enjoyed the acts of patronage she was able to perform. Malalas (423) gives evidence for her church building in Antioch, still recovering from the earthquake, and records her gift of a precious cross, decorated with pearls, to Jerusalem. On her visit to the springs at Pythion (Bythinia) in 529, she was accompanied by a retinue of over 4,000, including the *comes sacrarum largitionum*, whose presence was no doubt useful for the distribution of donations to churches and monasteries along the way, and the establishment of a palace and aqueduct in Pythion itself (*Buildings* V.3.16–20). Otherwise, her name is often linked with Justinian's in a wide variety of projects: religious, humanitarian and practical.

Finally, Theodora was also well able to look after the interests of her own family. Her illegitimate daughter married into the family of Anastasius. Her three grandsons prospered: Athanasius was an eminent miaphysite churchman, Anastasius married Belisarius' daughter, Joannina (albeit against Antonina's wishes), and John (an ambassador and consul) married into a good miaphysite family. Her niece, Sophia, was married to Justin, the son of Justinian's sister, Vigilantia, and future emperor.

When evaluating the extent of Theodora's imperial authority, it is often noted that she does not feature in the coinage (Moorhead 1994: 39). However, it has been convincingly argued that this omission has more to do with the changes in iconography associated with the coinage reform of Anastasius, rather than a deliberate indication that Theodora was any less influential than, for example, any of the Theodosian empresses. Apart from the initial coins of 491, the Empress Ariadne had not appeared on any subsequent issues, and the design of the new bronze coins which showed the emperor on the obverse and the value on the reverse did not allow for the inclusion of the empress (Brubaker and Tobler 2000: 582–3). As to the issue of the extent of Justinian's discomfort at his wife's actions which appeared contrary to his own wishes (such as her support for miaphysitism or her opposition to Amalasuntha, John the Cappadocian and others), there are various views. Foss (2002: 170ff) argues that Theodora exercised no independent power herself and all her actions were in fact carefully planned to help Justinian's purpose: her support for the miaphysites obviated the need for them to rebel against Justinian, allowing him to favour the pro-Chalcedonians and maintain peace with Rome; the murder of Amalasuntha provided him with an opportunity to invade Italy. The twelfth-century chronicler Zonaras (XIV.6.1–10, 8.4–7) would characterise their reign as one in which Theodora exercised equal power (or perhaps a little more) and actively collaborated with Justinian in raising and appropriating revenue and perpetrating injustice.

The final key debate to be had about Theodora is one of gender: as a powerful woman in antiquity who suffered the negative bias of a male historian, she naturally forms an important subject in gender studies (Fisher 1978, James 2001: 16–18, 39–41, *passim*, Brubaker 2004). Brubaker presents a careful study of the *Secret History*, showing that it 'neatly inverts all of the imperial virtues meant to be incorporated into a *basilikos logos*', that Justinian and Theodora 'stand ... gender roles on their heads' and that 'the imperial couple invert the ideals of Roman social order' (2004: 86–7). She highlights the fact that Procopius focused on 'sex, family, marriage, emotions and decorum' (91–4) and concludes that Procopius used Theodora to point out Justinian's bad judgement (in selecting her as his wife) and weak character (in being unable to control her). Fisher notes how Procopius presents 'excessive and shocking' behaviour of Theodora and Antonina which is offset by the portrayal of several virtuous women of royal status including Domitian's wife, Justin's wife (Euphemia) and Amalasuntha. From another angle, it is possible to use the portrayal of Theodora to analyse the composition of the *Secret History* and the extent of its factual accuracy. Angold (1996) sees the work as an investigation into the abuse of power. Foss (2002) takes a different approach, considering what we know about Theodora other than that learned from the *Secret History*. This leads to a section on 'Checking the Secret History' in which he concludes that 'as far as Theodora is concerned, it has a greater foundation in fact than is usually accepted' (159–64).

The joint reign of Justin and Justinian

By March 527, Justin was becoming frail and the senate persuaded him to elevate Justinian to sit alongside him as co-emperor. This accession duly took place: Justinian was crowned *Augustus* on 1 April 527 in the triclinium of the palace, and ratified on 4 April in the delphax by the army and officials. Theodora was crowned *Augusta* at the same time (*de Caeremoniis* I.95). There is some debate about the significance of the setting: Meier (2003a: 122–3 and 2004a: 10–12) suggests that Justinian was keen to demonstrate that his imperial authority was divinely inspired rather than being conferred by the populace in the hippodrome. However, Zonaras (XIV.40) provides evidence that

Justinian's accession was approved by the people in addition to the ceremonies in the triclinium and delphax which had been dictated by Justin's ill health (Croke 2007: 51). At any rate, the two emperors now embarked on a brief period of great activity.

They passed a number of laws (*C.J.* I.5.12, I.15.2, I.31.5, XII.19.15) and several others may be attributed to 527. One important early piece of legislation was directed against heretics (*C.J.* I.5.12 – **II 11**; see Chapter 6). Malalas (422) also records decrees against factional rioters, and there is evidence of a rescript to the clergy of the Church of St John in Pamphylia in response to their request for imperial support against the purloining of local resources by Roman soldiers (Diehl 1893). They also granted assistance to Antioch, still suffering the effects of the 526 earthquake, at the request of a delegation led by Zacharias, the new *comes Orientis*.

To further cement the idea of joint rule, Justin and Justinian also issued a series of gold coins at Constantinople and Thessalonica, depicting them both as *Augusti*. The obverses display various images including the globe, cross, throne and different spellings of Justinian. It is suggested by numismatists that these variations are the result of a sudden proclamation and the hasty production of these coins (Bellinger 1966: 92, Metcalf 1988: 26; **II 12**).

The period of joint rule was to last only four months. Justin died on 1 August 527 from an ulcer on his foot caused by an old war wound (Malalas 424). Croke (2007: 53) emphasises that there is no evidence of the senility so often ascribed to him (for example, Browning 1987: 23).

The *Nika* riot

The first years of Justinian's rule saw the start of a number of major projects which will be discussed in later chapters. These include the war on the eastern front and the negotiation of the so-called Eternal Peace with Persia in 532; the persecution of the non-orthodox (the Manichaeans, Samaritans, Montanists and Jews); his action against pagans; the reform of the law code; financial subventions for the provinces and the start of an ambitious building programme. These achievements were undoubtedly made possible by his team of outstanding generals and ministers, and much has been made of Justinian's skill in selecting these talented individuals (Browning 1987: 42–53; see Chapter 5). John the Cappadocian, uncultured but efficient, was quickly promoted to the praetorian prefecture where he effectively controlled taxation, the army and provincial governance, instituting a huge reform programme. Tribonian, learned but corrupt, was *magister officiorum* in 528 and quaestor of the sacred palace in 529, and oversaw the reform of the law codes. Belisarius was surely the most famous of Justinian's generals, his military exploits known to us from the pages of the *Wars* written by his military secretary, Procopius. Despite an indifferent performance against the Persians, Belisarius was promoted to the position of *magister militum per Orientem* in 529 and would go on to lead Justinian's campaigns in Africa and Italy. He married Theodora's actress friend, Antonina, about whom we know so much, of a less glorious nature, from the pages of the *Secret History* (Evans 2011). Belisarius' charismatic personality and military successes as described by Procopius have made him the subject of several popular books (Graves 1938). Belisarius' greatest rival general was Narses, a eunuch from Persarmenia. He was initially in charge of Justinian's bodyguard and was later sent twice to Italy to intervene in the war effort there (Fauber 1990).

In 532, a major event occurred which affected these men in different ways. A factional disturbance, usually easily controlled by swift imperial action, spiralled out of control. Justinian yielded to popular pressure and removed the unpopular John the Cappadocian and Tribonian from office (though they were later reinstated). Belisarius and Narses worked together to control the crowd resulting in the slaughter of 30,000 citizens in the hippodrome, for which service Justinian and Theodora would have cause to be grateful. Apart from the exciting unfolding of the drama, the violence of the street fighting and destruction of the city centre, the striking intervention of Theodora, and the brutal conclusion in the hippodrome, a number of serious issues arise. Why did the violence escalate to such a pitch? What was the role of Hypatius? And how had such discontent arisen in the first place? In 528, Justinian had held the consulship for a second time, and the sources (Malalas 426 followed by the *Chronicon Paschale* 528 and Theophanes AM 6020) comment on the generous largesse expended. Four busy years followed with activity in all the areas of governance listed above, but wars, reforms and aid are all costly and the financial and social consequences are usually seen as the root causes leading to the *Nika* riot. Following Bury's study of the *Nika* riot published in the *Journal of Hellenic Studies* in 1897, a full century elapsed before Greatrex's reappraisal of the *Nika* riot appeared (*Journal of Hellenic Studies*, 1997). This is the most thorough treatment in English available today. Greatrex's study not only throws light upon the 532 riot itself, but also considers the broader context of factional rioting. There has been much speculation on the exact nature of the factions, which included not just the Blues and Greens but also the Reds and Whites, and their relationship with other divisions in society. The work of Cameron (1973 and especially 1976) has been critical in establishing that the factions were not tied to any particular religious or political view or social stratum and that although they led acclamations in favour of the emperor, or to express grievances, no faction was consistently associated with a particular political stance (Liebeschuetz 1996a: 170ff). It is Procopius who draws our attention to the fact that, although the factions had existed for a long time, it was only recently that they had started to cause trouble (*Wars* I.24.2). Three different types of riots are identified by Greatrex: those related to doctrinal differences; mêlées arising from sporting rivalries; and disturbances caused by dissatisfaction with the authorities, especially the city prefect and the emperor.

In this case, it appears that the *Nika* riot took place against a backdrop of muted but growing discontent with the financial position of the empire, perhaps exacerbated by the stringent tax collection masterminded by John the Cappadocian. And once under way, Greatrex suggests that although the *Nika* riot shared a number of common features with other faction riots, the violence escalated to an unprecedented

Figure 1.4 Gambling machine with scenes of chariot racing, Constantinople (Bode Museum, Berlin). Photo: author.

level due to a number of accidental incidents and especially due to the conduct of the emperor. Greatrex therefore approaches the problem by dividing the riot into ten phases and then comparing and contrasting each phase with other riots in order to chart the stages at which the *Nika* riot got out of hand. The trouble started in early January 532, when seven members of the Blues and Greens were found guilty of murder during the course of street scuffles and were condemned to death. However, the scaffold broke and two (one Green and one Blue) were saved, but although the crowds clamoured for the men to be pardoned, Justinian did not yield. On 13 January, during the races, the factions, shouting *Nika* (win!), very unusually united, and widespread rioting ensued. They first attacked the praetorium of the city prefect, Eudaemon, freeing the prisoners and setting fire to the building. The next day, Justinian attempted to continue with the games, perhaps hoping to defuse the situation, but the mob continued with further incendiary attacks, including setting fire to the hippodrome. It was at this point that they also called for the dismissal of Eudaemon and, as noted above, John the Cappadocian and Tribonian. The crowd's disapproval for Eudaemon can be easily explained, and it is likely that both John and Tribonian were seen as close advisors to the emperor and directly responsible for his most unpopular measures (Greatrex 1997: 71–2). Justinian agreed to these demands via, it seems, three intermediaries, Basilides (Tribonian's replacement) and two generals, Constantiniolus and Mundus, whom he sent to negotiate with the rioters on his behalf. The crowd, however, was not calmed by Justinian's acquiescence, and on 14 or 15 January, Belisarius and his troops were despatched against the mob which was engaged both in burning down much of the city centre and in trying to acclaim Probus (one of Anastasius' nephews) emperor. Probus had prudently left the city, however, and so the crowd set fire to his house. This reminds us of the 512 riot when the mob had acclaimed the general, Areobindus, emperor, but finding him not at home had proceeded to burn down his house. And, as Greatrex points out, there are parallels in previous instances of rioting for all the events up to this point.

As the incendiary attacks in the city centre around Hagia Sophia continued, Justinian ordered troops stationed in Thrace to come to Constantinople. They arrived on Saturday 17 January but the ensuing street fighting led to even more destruction of the capital when many buildings along the Mese were burnt down. The chronology of events on the Saturday evening and Sunday 18 January, following the accounts of Procopius, Malalas and the *Chronicon Paschale*, is difficult to establish, but the main events are as follows. On the Saturday evening, Justinian dismissed from the palace Anastasius' remaining nephews, Hypatius and Pompey, either because he feared an assassination attempt or because Hypatius was to act as an agent on Justinian's behalf. The next day, Justinian attempted to imitate Anastasius' successful performance in 512 when he won over the rioters by appearing in the hippodrome without his diadem. Justinian, carrying the Gospels, accepted his opposition to the factions had been misguided and offered a pardon to the rioters. However, although some were sympathetic, many abused him and he hastily withdrew. Greatrex (1997: 77) suggests that Justinian did not have his troops standing by for this eventuality as he still wished to avoid indiscriminate slaughter, or because their presence would have hardly lent credence to his apology, or because he was optimistic of his success. As for the people, they now sought out Hypatius, conveyed him to the Forum of Constantine where there was an impromptu crowning ceremony, and from there they processed to the hippodrome where he was installed in the *kathisma*. This outcome was not due to either the people's will or Hypatius' ambition, Greatrex argues, but was part of a careful plan laid between Justinian and Hypatius to lure the people back to the hippodrome where they could be more easily dealt with (76–7). While Hypatius was receiving the acclamations of the crowd, Procopius, the *Chronicon Paschale* and Theophanes all present versions of Justinian's suggestion that he leave Constantinople, followed by Theodora's famous spirited speech in which she advocated death over flight (Procopius, *Wars* I.24.33–7 – **II 13**). Greatrex focuses not on Justinian's cowardice in contrast to his wife's bravery (Evans 2002: 45–6) but rather on Justinian's expediency: if he left the capital while his generals did the dirty work in quelling the riot, he might be able to maintain the appearance of his personal leniency and benevolence on his return. Following Greatrex's argument, the sequel now involves the breakdown of communication between Justinian and Hypatius, who was mistakenly informed that Justinian had indeed fled and began to accept the acclamations on his own behalf. The emperor was now forced to allow his generals, Narses, Belisarius, Mundus and Maurice, to end the hopes of the usurper by attacking the crowd in the hippodrome. The next day, Hypatius and Pompey were executed, and their property and that of other disloyal senators confiscated.

In summing up this inglorious episode, it appears that a general atmosphere of discontent meant that the factions were more ready to react adversely to Justinian's stubborn refusal to pardon the two rioters saved when the scaffold broke. Many aspects of this riot were not new, such as the demands to sack unpopular officials, the street scuffles and the conflagrations in the city centre. Even the attempt to crown a usurper emperor was not unknown. But, as Greatrex argues, Justinian's desire to retain his popularity led him to act inconsistently, sometimes acceding to the demands of the people, sometimes remaining firm, and this unpredictability meant that the final solution had to be uncompromisingly harsh. Ironically, as is well known, the ruin of the city centre paved the way for Justinian's imposing building programme which would include Hagia Sophia (see Chapter 5).

The *Nika* riot was one reason that Justinian sought to call a halt to the hostilities with Persia which had marked the first years of his reign, and which would continue to demand his attention almost until his final years. It is to imperial foreign policy on the eastern frontier we turn next.

2

Conflict and Diplomacy on the Eastern Frontier

Introduction: The scope of the conflict

In late 561, two high-ranking ambassadors, Peter the Patrician and Yazdgushnasp, met in the border region of Dara to agree the terms of a peace treaty. After extensive discussions, terms were agreed in 562 and the treaty composed in both Greek and Persian with twelve interpreters on hand to ensure that there were no discrepancies between the two versions.

The treaty, preserved by Menander the Guardsman (**II 14**), was comprehensive. Its major terms provide an excellent guide to the issues which had proved sticking points over the previous sixty years of conflict, and the geographical references are a fair reflection of the sheer length and complexity of the border stretching as it did from Lazica and Armenia in the north, through Mesopotamia in the central section, and down towards Arabia and Egypt in the south. While it was one frontier, each section had its own history, features and disputes. The long middle section along the Euphrates naturally saw some of the key action, especially in the early 530s and 540s. The significance of the destruction of Antioch in 540 was particularly mentioned at the talks, and clauses eight and ten dealt with the fortification of Dara which the Persians had repeatedly argued contravened an earlier agreement that neither side should erect new defences on the frontier (in this case, Dara was allowed to remain but no further border fortifications were to be undertaken). Relations between the two great states were often influenced by their neighbours and allies, and clause two required that the Arab allies of each should also abide by the treaty. Finally, Lazica, which had seen the longest span of fighting, was to be returned to the Romans. Clause nine stipulated that neither side should make war against any other territory or peoples, thus ruling out the possibility that Persia or Rome should continue their hostility towards Lazica.

Only the ownership of Suania (a small but strategically significant region with valuable access to Lazica (Braund 1994: 311–14)) was left unresolved. General conduct at the border, such as trade and customs duties, was also included. In return for keeping the peace, the Persians would receive an annual sum of 30,000 gold coins from the Romans, a reference to the long-held belief of the Persians that they should receive some financial compensation for the defence of the Caspian Gates (also known as the Dariel Pass). Defence of this pass in the Caucasus Mountains was essential to block the raids of the Sabir Huns which threatened both Persian and Roman territory. Back in 363, the Persians and Romans had reportedly agreed to share the defence, but since then the Persians had complained that the Romans were not making their financial contribution. The peace was to last for fifty years, which was obviously felt to be a rather more realistic timespan than the failed 'Eternal' Peace of 532. In fact, this treaty was to be broken by 572 (Dignas and Winter 2007: 138–48, Lee 2008).

The major players

The debates which surround events and imperial policy along the eastern frontier are wide-ranging and fast-moving as research into all possible relevant areas develops apace. A greater appreciation of internal affairs at the Persian court helps to explain the motivation of Kavadh and Chosroes in pursuing military action (Howard-Johnston 2006, Farrokh 2007, Dignas and Winter 2007, Daryaee 2009, Canepa 2009, McDonough 2013, Shayegan 2011 and Sauer et al. 2013). Comparison between the two empires has been explored by Howard-Johnston (1995) who concluded that the two empires commanded similar military forces, an argument supported by Sauer et al. (2013: 613–16), while Rubin (1995), exploring in detail the reforms of Chosroes, argued that there was rather less mutual influence and continuity than allowed for by Howard-Johnston. The extent of influence and rivalry continues to be debated (Canepa 2009). While the rulers may have referred to themselves as brothers during treaty negotiations, Canepa argues that their competitive relationship was responsible for creating a whole new culture of court ceremonial ritual and exchange of artistic motifs; he gave the example of Sasanian elements in the churches of St Polyeuktos and Hagia Sophia, and the appearance of the magi on the hem of Theodora's chlamys in San Vitale at Ravenna.

Even greater strides have been made in studies on the Arabs before the rise of Islam, and a clearer knowledge of the history, policies and aspirations of the Arab allies in turn informs our understanding of their relationship with neighbouring tribes as well as with Constantinople and Ctesiphon. Studies of the Arabs were developed by Shahîd, following Nöldeke (1897), Rothstein (1899) and later Sartre (1982). Many shorter studies culminated in a series of exhaustive tomes covering Byzantium and the Arabs in the fourth (1984), fifth (1989) and sixth centuries (1995, 2002, 2010). Shahîd's thesis was that the Ghassānids were miaphysite allies of Byzantium and crucial to the defensive policy of Anastasius and Justinian against Persia and their Arab allies. An initial challenge to this view came from Whittow (1999) and, since then, others have taken up the challenge to review and develop Shahîd's studies, looking to understand the Arabs before Islam (Hainthaler 2007), to investigate how the political and social development of the Arabs was influenced by Rome and Persia (Hoyland 2001), and to develop a more nuanced understanding of the relationship between Rome, Persia and their allies (Millar 2010, Fisher 2011 and 2015). Even determining the most appropriate terminology has been the subject of much debate. Gone is the casual referencing to the Ghassānids (Rome's allies) and Lakhmids (Persia's allies) and the easy equivalence with the Jafnids and Naṣrids, and even the assumption that an imperial treaty was made with these groups. Instead, it is believed that treaties were made with the individual leaders (for example, with al-Ḥārith or al-Mundhir) (Robin 2008, Millar 2010, Fisher 2011: 1–14, Hoyland 2014: 268–73). At any rate, the prevailing view certainly prefers a terminology that refers to the Jafnids, Naṣrids and Ḥujrids (the Kindites). Building on Fisher's 2011 monograph, a volume edited by Dijkstra and Fisher (2014) seeks to further understand the Arabs, as well as the peoples on the Egyptian frontier, thus opening up the same avenues of enquiry as those explored in the Transformation of the Roman World project, which focused on the Germanic peoples of Western Europe. Put simply, this is the rehabilitation of the Arabs, often characterised as 'barbarians', using the technique of inverting our usual perception of the source material, referring to Graeco-Roman sources as the 'outsider' sources, in contrast to the 'insider' Arab sources. The volume of sources edited by Fisher (2015) helps to make this Arab world more accessible to us. The task is helped by taking advantage of the recent archaeology in Syria and Jordan (for example, Resafa and Nitl), epigraphic finds in Saudi Arabia (for example, Hegra/Al-Hijr (Madâin Sâlih)), plus new frontier studies which stress interaction rather than confrontation. Dijkstra and Fisher also seek to compare the situation on the Arabian frontier with that on the Egyptian frontier for a wider picture of Roman imperial activity in the very southern reaches of their influence, on which more below.

At the other end of the frontier, strategically placed Lazica has also found itself at the centre of discussion. The staple work on Armenia (although now a little outdated) remains Adontz's *Armenia in the Period of Justinian* (translated by Garsoïan in 1970). For us the most relevant chapters of this major study are 6, 7 and 8, in which Adontz sets Justinian's military reforms in the context of the increasing centralisation of the empire, using the Persian war as a pretext for his actions. More recent is Braund's important 1994 study, *Georgia in Antiquity* (especially chapter 9), where he notes the significance of Lazica, whose broad-based empire encompassed a number of peoples (including the Suani, Scymni, Abasgi, Apsilii and Misimiani) and which controlled crucial access to the Black Sea and thence by sea to Constantinople (in the west), to the Caucasus passes (north), towards Iberia (east), Pontus Polemoniacus (south-west), and Armenia and Persarmenia (south-east).

The key issue remains Justinian's policy: as he tried to swing the focus of his reign to the reconquest and restoration of the west, it is sometimes argued that the problems of the east were merely a distraction. Others think that Justinian went out of his way to provoke the Persians (Heather 2018: 98). Without agreeing that he deliberately incited hostility, we can find plenty of occasions where Justinian took the opportunity to develop policy on the eastern frontier using administrative reform, religion and culture.

Timeline and key events

The 562 treaty was the latest in a series of attempts to make peace since war had broken out in the 520s. Conflict on the eastern frontier can therefore be divided into a number of distinct phases, although clashes in Lazica were fairly continuous from 541 to 561. As we saw in Chapter 1, hostile manoeuvring along the length of the frontier was already in progress when Justinian came to the throne in 527. His accession took place shortly after the Romans had lost Iberia to Kavadh and were barely holding on to Lazica; Belisarius had just been appointed the *dux* of Mesopotamia where it was hoped he would make successful incursions, while Hypatius was re-appointed *magister militum per Orientem* to stop the raids of the pro-Persian al-Mundhir. The narrative for this initial phase up to the Eternal Peace of 532 may be found in Greatrex (1998), Greatrex and Lieu (2002) and Meier (2003a: 191–8). The spotlight falls upon the activities of al-Mundhir whose audacious raids as far as the territory of Antioch, including the sacrifice of 400 virgins to the goddess al-'Uzza, were obviously significant (Pseudo-Zachariah Rhetor VIII.5a, with Greatrex 2011: 298). At the other end of the frontier, Justinian, prompted by the escalation of hostilities in Lazica, turned his attention to a wide-ranging reorganisation of the defences of Armenia (*C.J.* I.29.5 – **II 15**). He completed or strengthened fortifications at key sites such as Citharizon, Theodosiopolis and Martyropolis, and he sought to create a more unified command for this part of the frontier by appointing Sittas as the *magister militum per Armeniam et Pontum Polemoniacum et gentes* with overall authority. The first task for the new commander was the subjugation of one of Lazica's neighbouring tribes, the mountainous Tzani. Sittas constructed roads to ease accessibility, established garrisons and a key fortress on the frontier with Persarmenia, and supported Christianity in the region. Justinian was also able to encourage the loyalty of the Iberians through shared beliefs, for, following Kavadh's decision to impose Persian religious customs, the king, Gourgenes, and a number of Iberians fled to Constantinople. They remained there until the Eternal Peace of 532 when some returned, leaving Gourgenes to incite unrest in Iberia and to advise Justinian on his Lazican policy.

After a rather unsuccessful campaign in 528 by the newly appointed Belisarius in Mesopotamia and Osrhoene (Greatrex 1998: 156–9), the year 529 saw a number of key developments. Following a raid by al-Mundhir, Justinian granted the Jafnid chief al-Ḥārith (son of Jabala) 'the dignity of king' (supreme phylarch), making him the equal of the Naṣrid al-Mundhir (Shahîd 1995: 95–124). Of particular importance for the role of the Arabs, this appointment was also part of Justinian's replacement of the men of Justin's generation with his own, including Sittas and Belisarius. However, at this time, Kavadh was in a strong position. He knew first-hand of the devastation caused by an earthquake in Antioch and was heartened by the news of the rioting in Scythopolis. This was the first of two violent clashes between the Samaritans against the Jews and Christians, possibly caused by Justinian's intolerant legislation against non-Christians. The second revolt took place in 556, mainly in Caesarea in Palestine, when the Jews and Samaritans acted together. In this earlier rebellion (529–531), the Samaritan leader, Julian, seized control of Neapolis and enjoyed watching the chariot races before being defeated and beheaded by the *dux* of Palestine, Theodore Simus. There are a number of accounts (Winkler 1965, Crown 1986, Rabello 1987: 409–22, Shahîd 1995: 82–95, Meier

2003a: 194, 209–15, Noethlichs 2007), while Pummer (2002) helpfully examines the sources (Pseudo-Zachariah Rhetor IX.8a (**II 16**), Malalas 445–7, Cyril of Scythopolis, *Life of St Sabas* 71–3). Coincidentally, Kavadh himself was secure in Persia since the powerful Mazdakite sect had been suppressed, and he therefore made one of his demands for financial aid. His letter to Justinian is helpfully preserved for us by Malalas (449–50): 'Koades (Kavadh), king of kings, of the rising sun, to Flavius Justinian Caesar, of the setting moon. We have found it written in our ancient records that we are brothers of one another and that if one of us should stand in need of men or money, the other should provide them.'

Justinian was not prepared for war and duly sent off his ambassadors, Hermogenes and Rufinus, but Kavadh was certainly prepared, and if the years 527–530 had witnessed nothing more than skirmishing and manoeuvring along the frontier, the years 530–531 are distinctive for their decisive set-piece battles (Greatrex 1998: 168–212, Greatrex and Lieu 2002: 88–93). Our key source for these events is Procopius, who gives an eye-witness account (accepted by Lee 1993b: 115–16, challenged by Kaldellis 2004b). The first of these was the battle of Dara, the most remarkable Roman triumph since the campaigns of 421–422 and responsible for establishing Belisarius' reputation as a brilliant young general. Sadly, such a victory was not repeated in Justinian's reign. A detailed account of the battle is provided by Procopius, *Wars* I.13.9–14.55 (**II 17**) with an impressionistic account in Pseudo-Zachariah IX.3. Haldon (2001: 30–5) offers an account, as does Greatrex (1998: 168–85) with plans. But the most important recent research is that carried out by Lillington-Martin (2007 and 2013) who uses satellite technology to resite the location of the battle to approximately three kilometres from Dara (rather than just outside the walls) and suggests that an archaeological survey is needed to confirm this new position.

Just as the battle of Dara gave the Romans a sound footing in Mesopotamia, they also scored a notable success in this year along the northern sector of the frontier, with victory at the battle of Satala. Here the 30,000-strong force of the Persian general Mihr-Mihroe (Mermeroes) was halted by Sittas and Dorotheus (the *magister militum per Armeniam*). The Romans gained significant and long-reaching advantage from this victory: three Armenian chiefs defected from the Persians (Narses, Aratius and Isaac) and they handed over the border forts of Bolum and Pharangium, depriving the Persians of the revenues from the goldmining areas around the latter (Greatrex 1998: 185–90).

On the other hand, the Roman victory at Satala contributed to

Kavadh's decision not to pursue the peace talks he had begun with Rufinus in 530 and instead he sent an army to make a direct invasion along the Euphrates, crossing into Roman territory by Circesium from where the 20,000-strong force (15,000 Persians, 5,000 Arabs) proceeded north-west to Callinicum. Here a battle was fought as disastrous for the Romans and Belisarius personally as Dara had been successful. Belisarius, who had unsuccessfully tried to dissuade his troops from engaging with the enemy in unfavourable circumstances, was criticised by the formal enquiry set up to investigate the loss of the battle; he was dismissed from his command and ordered back to Constantinople (Shahîd 1995: 134–42, Greatrex 1998: 193–212). The most detailed accounts of the battle are given by Procopius, *Wars* I.18.24–56 (pro-Belisarius) and Malalas 462–6 (anti-Belisarius); they have divided the opinion of scholars ever since.

After these three major battles, there was another short period of manoeuvring and minor campaigns, leading up to the accession of Chosroes following the death of Kavadh in September 531. With both rulers facing internal problems (for Chosroes, the plotting of his younger brother, Zames; for Justinian, the *Nika* riot), conditions were ripe for agreement, and terms were fairly easily settled. In return for an indefinite peace, the Romans were to pay a subsidy of 110 *centenaria* (11,000 pounds of gold) for the defence of the Caspian Gates and the headquarters of the *dux* of Mesopotamia were to be moved from Dara back to Constantia, thus addressing the two issues raised previously by Kavadh. The only point of contention was the ownership of the Lazican and Armenian forts, but after some negotiation the Romans recovered the Lazican forts at Sarapanis and Scanda and returned the Armenian forts of Pharangium and Bolum to the Persians. Greatrex (1998: 216–17) points out the significance of the financial clause: by agreeing to a one-off payment, Justinian avoided paying an annual tribute and the size of the payment did not overstretch the treasury; on the other hand, it was the largest sum ever paid to the Persians, and no doubt beneficial for Chosroes' reputation. The first 'Eternal' Peace, coming at the end of a thirty-year war (counting from the outbreak of hostilities under Anastasius in 502), was a cause for celebration. Malalas (**II 18**) noted 'a great shower of stars from dawn to dusk', and a fragmentary inscription on a column in Hierapolis acclaims the peace (Roussel 1939: 367, Greatrex and Lieu 2002: 97).

There was little to disrupt the peace at first. An isolated incident of an Arab incursion into Euphratesia in 536 was resolved by the *dux* Batzas, while an uprising at Dara was quickly put down. However,

Justinian was active in continuing his systematic reorganisation of Armenia, establishing four provinces of Armenia (*Novel* 31, 18 March 536). He also sent troops to Lazica, making Petra a city and calling it Justiniana (*Novel* 28 preface). Adontz (1970: chapter 7) argues that Justinian set out to destroy the old socio-political structure of Armenia in the hope that Romanisation and centralisation of its customs would draw it out of the orbit of Persia, although many of the reforms (such as updating marriage and inheritance legislation for women) also fitted into his broader programme of provincial legislation.

But while Justinian may have been attending to the northern sector of his eastern frontier, perhaps enjoying the peaceful conditions, he neglected to keep the fortifications along the rest of the border in good repair or to maintain an adequate military force. Many troops were sent off to Africa and Italy where the focus of war now was; the remaining troops were paid poorly and sporadically, and the *limitanei* not at all (Procopius, *Secret History* 24.12–14 – **II 19**). There was, therefore, little opposition in 540 when a large army led by Chosroes invaded Roman Mesopotamia and Syria and brought to an end the optimistically termed Eternal Peace, agreed only eight years earlier. Various reasons for the termination have been suggested; a detailed analysis can be found in Börm (2006). It is likely that Chosroes was once more motivated by the hope of financial gain and was encouraged to believe that an invasion might be successful, knowing of Justinian's inattention to both troops and fortifications on the eastern frontier whilst he was preoccupied with his campaigns in North Africa and Italy. From Procopius (*Wars* II.2–3) we learn that he was encouraged by deputations from both the Ostrogothic king, Vitigis, and the Armenians who were discontented by Roman rule. Chosroes also tried to stir up trouble via the Jafnids and Naṣrids before making his incursion in May. The cities of Sura and Beroea were early casualties but the spotlight of disaster rightly falls upon the sack of Antioch in June. Justinian had despatched his cousin, the general Germanus, to strengthen the defences of Antioch but granted him only 300 troops. Having such a small military force, Germanus decided to offer a bribe of 1,000 pounds of gold to persuade Chosroes to leave Antioch in peace, but after this decision was overturned by a messenger from Justinian, Germanus prudently withdrew. Six thousand Roman troops were later despatched but they soon also abandoned the city when the Persians gained control, despite fierce resistance from the citizens led by the circus factions. Antioch was plundered and razed to the ground, except one church, according to the possibly exaggerated account of

Procopius (*Wars* II.9.14–18). The Antiochenes who were taken to Persia were given their own city, Veh-Antioch-Chosroes (the better Antioch of Chosroes), near Ctesiphon. After the destruction of the city, Chosroes returned to his demands for financial compensation for the Caspian Gates and Dara (Procopius, *Wars* II.10.19–24), asking for a one-off payment of fifty *centenaria* followed by an annual payment of five *centenaria*. Whilst he waited for a response from Justinian, he continued his tour of Roman territory, enjoying bathing in the Mediterranean at Seleucia and watching the chariot races at Apamea (Meier 2003a: 365–73). From there he journeyed via Chalcis, Edessa, Carrhae and Constantia (with mixed fortunes), eventually reaching Dara, which he attacked. Although Justinian had by this time agreed to Chosroes' demands, the agreement was nullified by this aggression towards Dara.

Campaigning continued during the years 541–545 along the central sector of the frontier. Belisarius took advantage of Chosroes' absence in Lazica (see below) to invade Persian territory, whilst al-Ḥārith was sent to plunder Assyria. However, al-Ḥārith returned the Roman troops who had been sent to accompany him, while Belisarius withdrew, lacking information. This is another occasion where there are contradictory opinions as to Belisarius' competence, but this time from the same author. In the *Wars* (II.19), Procopius blames al-Ḥārith, the other Roman commanders and the poor condition of the troops, while in the *Secret History* (3.31), he argues that Belisarius could have reached as far as Ctesiphon itself had he not turned back to meet his wife, Antonina (Shahîd 1995: 220–30). Belisarius did win great acclaim in the following year when he deflected Chosroes' attempt to invade Palestine, enticed by the riches of Jerusalem, but this was to be his last triumph on the eastern frontier: he was recalled to Constantinople, accused of treason, and subsequently sent to Italy. As for Chosroes, he had to be content with destroying Callinicum which had been in the process of repairing its walls (*Wars* II.21.30–2) before hastily withdrawing to his own territory, no doubt partly as a result of the plague (Kislinger and Stathakopoulos 1999: 84). He did return the following year when he again unsuccessfully occupied Edessa and eventually, after receiving five *centenaria*, he departed. Procopius (*Wars* II.27.18–46) tells us this much, though he does not mention the role of the miraculous image of Edessa described by Evagrius (**II 20**; Whitby 2000: 225–7). This was the last hostile incident of this part of the war in this area before a five-year peace agreement was made. Again, Chosroes had a financial settlement in mind, for he first requested a payment of twenty *centenaria* to ensure the armistice. Curiously, he also requested (and was granted) that the doctor, Tribunus, who had previously cured him of a disease, spend a year with him. After the year was up, he allowed Tribunus to return to Constantinople and freed 3,000 prisoners.

Meanwhile, the Transcaucasus now became the major theatre of war, dominating the news until almost the end of Justinian's reign (Braund 1994: 292–311). Encouraged by the complaints of the Armenians and the Lazi of abusive treatment by the Romans (not all appreciated the interventions of the Romans or the expensive improvements to Petra, the costs of which were charged to the Lazi), and possibly by their argument that possession of Lazica offered a route to attack Constantinople via the Black Sea, Chosroes, pretending that he was assembling forces against the Huns, easily entered Lazica. He received control of the country from the Lazican king, Gubazes, including possession of Petra, but when he heard about the Roman incursions into his territory in 541, he immediately withdrew.

However, like the Iberians, it was not long before the Armenians and the Lazi began to resent their new rulers: as Christians they felt no affinity with the Zoroastrian Persians, and they felt aggrieved at being cut off from trading in the Black Sea. They therefore returned their support to the Romans, and in 548, Justinian sent 8,000 troops under the *magister militum per Armeniam*, Dagisthaeus. Despite the spirited resistance of the Persian general, Mihr-Mihroe, especially in holding on to Petra, the Roman forces in conjunction with Gubazes, and the Sabir Huns and Alans (at a cost of three *centenaria*), eventually forced the Persians to withdraw, although they did manage to retain Petra. The Romans made inroads into Iberia and established a strong garrison to guard the pass between Iberia and Lazica. The Persian campaign in 549 accomplished little and, in 551, Bessas (replacing the unpopular Dagisthaeus) managed to capture Petra, burning the acropolis in which the remaining Persians had taken refuge, and destroying the walls. The Romans also succeeded in subduing a rebellion of the Abasgi, who had also expressed dissatisfaction at their treatment, and reconciling the Apsilii, who had made a temporary alliance with the Persians.

Notwithstanding these victories, under the experienced leadership of Mihr-Mihroe, the Persians continued to enjoy success. They recaptured the forts of Sarapanis and Scanda, and the strategic fort of Uthimereos which allowed them to control eastern Lazica, Scymnia and Suania. They made overtures to King Gubazes and, with the help of the Sabir Huns, proceeded west towards Phasis and the Black Sea. Winning over the Lazi with civil constructions and supplies, this was to be the peak of their achievement, for in the summer of 555, Mihr-Mihroe returned to Iberia where he died. He was replaced by a general named as Nakhoragon by Agathias (which may in fact be the Persian title *nakhveragan*; see Greatrex and Lieu 2002: 121).

Meanwhile, King Gubazes complained about the incompetence of the Roman generals. Bessas was recalled, but two other generals, Martin and Rusticus, remained and carried out a plot to assassinate Gubazes in September/October 555. Martin continued to operate with indifferent success against the Persians, but the Lazi refused to co-operate further and sent to Justinian to complain about the assassination of their king. Justinian despatched the senator, Athanasius, to conduct an enquiry. Agathias presents the deliberations of the Lazi as a set-piece debate, in the best traditions of Greek historiography (III.8.4–13.11). Rusticus and his brother John were subsequently executed. In spring 556, Gubazes' younger brother, Tzath, newly invested by Justinian, arrived, along with the *magister militum* Soterichus. Although he was bringing gold for the neighbouring peoples (and here we can note Justinian's willingness to provide financial incentives for loyalty), Soterichus was killed by the Misimiani, who then went over to Persia. Meanwhile, the *nakhveragan* attempted to march on Phasis but was outwitted by Martin and consequently withdrew to Iberia. In the summer, the Romans enjoyed various successes, including the recovery of Misimia (and the money brought by Soterichus), and the *nakhveragan* was executed by Chosroes for his failures. Realising that waging war in Lazica was almost impossible because of the difficulty of supplying his troops, Chosroes despatched Yazdgushnasp to negotiate a truce. Both sides agreed to keep whatever they had gained so far in the war and desist from further hostile engagement (Agathias IV.30.7–10 – **II 21**) although the Tzani had to be subdued again in 558, and the treaty did not include the region of Suania. This treaty was the precursor of the version signed at Dara in 562.

Whilst these events had been taking place in this northern sector of the frontier, the five-year truce agreed in 545 had held good for the rest of the border, marred only by two incidents. Procopius (*Wars* II.28.12–14) reports on the continuing warfare between al-Ḥārith and al-Mundhir: the latter captured one of al-Ḥārith's sons and sacrificed him to al-'Uzza before al-Ḥārith won a significant victory over al-Mundhir, finally proving his loyalty to the Romans (Shahîd 1995: 237–379). Procopius (*Wars* II.28.31–44) also reports on the attempted capture by ruse of Dara by Chosroes' ambassador, Yazdgushnasp, who later continued to Constantinople where he was treated with great honour. In 551, he enjoyed another distinguished reception in Constantinople when he was sent there to settle the terms proposed by Peter the Patrician at the Persian court earlier that year. Yazdgushnasp referred to the recent hostilities between the Saracens as a breach of the truce but eventually a five-year armistice was agreed (excluding Lazica) at a cost of twenty *centenaria* to the Romans, plus an extra six for the previous eighteen months of negotiations (Procopius, *Wars* VIII.15.1–7). An account by Peter the Patrician survives within the *de Caeremoniis* (89–90) compiled by Constantine Porphyrogenitus. It is not certain whether the description relates to this episode but it surely reflects the elaborate diplomatic protocol which was generally followed by this period (Greatrex and Lieu 2002: 124–8).

Although the truce continued in Mesopotamia and Armenia, al-Mundhir continued his raids into Roman territory, south of the Euphrates, but he was killed by al-Ḥārith in June 554, as foretold by Symeon the Younger (*Life of St Symeon Stylites the Younger* 186–7, Shahîd 1995: 240–4). After the 562 treaty, there was only one infraction in the remaining years of Justinian's reign (again involving the Arabs) when the Naṣrid king ʿAmr attacked al-Ḥārith's territory in 562 or 563. Al-Ḥārith complained to Justinian, who offered him a subsidy (Shahîd 1995: 282–8).

Strategies and themes: Acculturation and Christianisation

The traditional Roman strategy of conquest by civilisation and acculturation, including religious conversion, was clearly part of Justinian's arsenal in managing and securing the loyalty of those on the periphery of his empire (Maas 2003). As we have seen, Justin and then Justinian were able to encourage and win back, if necessary, the loyalty of the Lazi through their shared culture and beliefs. In 521/522 Justin provided a lavish reception for King Tzath in Constantinople when he was baptised and endowed with the regalia of office, and Justinian repeated the same exercise when he bestowed the traditional regalia on Tzath in 555 following the murder of his brother, Gubazes. And while Gubazes and the Lazi might have been tempted to defect to the Persians on occasion (as in 541), their dislike of Zoroastrianism proved to be more powerful than the incompetence or interference of the Romans. Shared beliefs also helped to encourage the allegiance of the Iberian king Gourgenes, and Justinian used conversion in controlling some of the neighbouring Caucasus peoples, such as the Tzani and Abasgi. These tactics, alongside the legislation for the administrative reorganisation of Armenia, appear to form a cohesive imperial policy to reinforce Roman rule within their own territory and to strengthen Roman influence over their allies in the all-important buffer zones in this northern sector of the frontier.

At the southern end of the frontier, Justinian's use of the Jafnids, who emerged in the sixth century as one of the most influential Arab groups, reflects the traditional client management long practised by the Romans, and helped to balance Persia's connection with the Naṣrids. However, although these Arab tribes did fulfil the expectations of their respective allied states (for example, al-Mundhir's raiding of Roman territory in the late 520s or al-Ḥārith's victory over the Naṣrids in 554), there were other occasions when they operated separately, quarrelling amongst themselves (for example, their dispute over ownership of the *Strata* (the region of the *Strata Diocletiana*), important grazing land) or negotiating on their own initiative (al-Ḥārith sent envoys to the Ḥimyarite king Abraham in 548). Much has been written about the implication of the Jafnids' Christianity and specifically their adherence to miaphysitism. Several issues may be highlighted here. One is that great importance has been attached to some key sites which have been particularly linked to the Jafnids, such as Nitl in Jordan (Piccirillo 2001) and Resafa (Sergiopolis) in Syria. In particular, Key Fowden (1999 and 2000) has explored the role of Resafa in trade and transhumance patterns, its importance as a pilgrimage centre, and the attempts of the Romans, Persians and Arabs to tap into the widespread popularity of St Sergius throughout Syria and Mesopotamia (including those parts lying within Persian territory). However, just as perceptions of the Ghassānids and Lakhmids as coherent tribes led by one dynastic family have been broken down, so the neat solution which sees the Ghassānids as loyal Christians and patrons of miaphysitism in the region has also been challenged. Fisher (2011: 49–64) argues that the Jafnids preferred to maintain some distance in order to preserve their connections with Arabs less closely tied to Roman imperial and Christian ideology.

The debate crystallises around an episode in 542 when Theodora, at the request of the Jafnid leader al-Ḥārith, sent two bishops to provide suitable spiritual care for the miaphysites of Syria and Arabia. One of the bishops was Jacob Baradaeus who went on to become one of the foremost miaphysite leaders, being responsible for the conversion of huge numbers of Arabs. Since the persecutions of Justin there had been a shortage of bishops, and al-Ḥārith was viewed as a benefactor to all the miaphysites in the region. He therefore gained prestige from this action, and he and his son, al-Mundhir, held the honorific title *patricius*. However, Wood (2014) in a neat exploration of the complexities of Arabs and Christianisation warns against making superficial assumptions. He challenges the significance of the role of al-Ḥārith, playing down the connections between al-Ḥārith and Jacob Baradaeus, and suggests that within the Jafnid dynasty and certainly wider Ghassānid confederation there was some strongly rooted Chalcedonianism. As for Justinian, he sought to keep the Jafnids within the Roman political orbit by any possible means and it was only much later that their adherence to miaphysitism became a problem.

A similar set of issues applies to the Egyptian frontier about which we are well-informed by Procopius and John of Ephesus. We know that by the sixth century the Blemmyes, an ensemble of tribes who originated in the Eastern Desert and whose raids into the Egyptian Nile valley during the Roman and late Roman period caused the Romans much disquiet, became marginalised, paving the way for the emergence of the Kingdom of Nobadia, one of the three medieval kingdoms of Nubia, in the sixth century (Welsby 2002, Dijkstra 2008, Dijkstra and Fisher 2014). In his *Church History*, John of Ephesus (**II 22**) describes the missions sent to Nubia, including the supposedly rival Chalcedonian/miaphysite delegations sent by Justinian and Theodora in either 549 or 554. This passage is often drawn on to show the Christianisation of Lower Nubia related to the closure of the temples at Philae in 536, or used to comment on the relationship between the imperial couple as regards their doctrinal policy (see Chapters 4 and 6 for further discussion on these issues). However, this was first and foremost a diplomatic operation, rather than merely a matter of religious conversion: a continuation of the Roman policies towards the southern Egyptian frontier in the fifth century where several treaties were made with the Nobadae to persuade them to stop raiding Egypt. Justinian wanted to continue or renew his ties with the new emerging Nobadian kingdom, and for his part, this allowed the client king an opportunity to associate himself with Rome and win a powerful ally (Grillmeier and Hainthaler 1996: II.4, 267–71, Dijkstra 2008: 271–304).

In addition to these efforts, Justinian also turned his attention further south towards the Red Sea. Following the incident in the 520s narrated in Chapter 1 when Justin avenged the Najran massacre and installed the Christian Sumyafʿa Ashwʿa (Hellestheaeus/Ella Asbeha) on the throne in Ethiopia (later replaced in a coup by Abramus who was to rule until 569/570; Robin 2014: 65–79), Justinian sent a number of embassies, including the ambassador Nonnosus, who left an account (*FHG* IV, 178–81), to both the Ḥimyarites (Axumites) and the Ethiopians (Homeritae). He asked them to support him against the Persians directly, by attacking them, and indirectly, by taking over the silk trade to India. Although both kings agreed, neither carried out their promises, most likely because of serious internal problems in the region amongst the various Arab groups, rather than because Abramus was merely exemplifying the standard 'barbarian' quality of 'untrustworthiness' as argued by Procopius (Procopius, *Wars* I.20.13, Greatrex 1998: 225–39, Shahîd 1995: 144–66). Incidentally, it was not until the 550s when the monks commissioned by the emperor finally returned from Serinda (Sogdiana) with the eggs of the silk worm that the Persian monopoly on the silk trade finally ended, although the Romans continued to rely on imported silk to some extent (Procopius, *Wars* VIII.17.1–8 – **II 23**; Browning 1987: 154–6, Tate 1999, Zuckerman 2013). As for the complex politics and inter-tribal rivalries of the Arabs, Fisher (2011: 84–91, 2014) and Robin (2008, 2012) have done much to elucidate the relationship between the Jafnids, Naṣrids, Ḥujrids, Ma'add, Mudar and the Ḥimyarites, and to emphasise the promising opportunities for enrichment and political advancement offered by northern and central Arabia which meant it was certainly worth the efforts of the Roman and Persian courts to continue to press for alliances.

Conclusions

Justinian did not seek war with Persia, and his strategy was therefore defensive and usually reactive. Along the major central section of the frontier, it seems that cities were often left to fend for themselves, offering a small number of *centenaria* to deflect the Persian army and with the local bishop in charge of the negotiations. Although some effort was made to defend Antioch in 540, in the end it was the circus factions who put up the strongest fight to save their city. Tales of squabbling between commanders and especially the question marks raised over the competence of Belisarius, along with the suggested neglect of fortifications and troops, indicate that Justinian's efforts to manage the eastern frontier of his empire were not entirely successful.

On the other hand, we have witnessed plenty of occasions when Justinian did pursue a pragmatic policy of consolidation and expansion when possible. Although Procopius may have criticised Justinian's efforts in the *Secret History*, from the *Buildings* we learn that the emperor did seek to strengthen fortifications and repair war damage (for example, II.10 on Antioch). And if he did not always commit sufficient military resources, he compensated by the use of diplomacy (Lee 1993b, 2008, 2013), payments, assimilation, acculturation and Christianisation. Relying upon his Jafnid allies to counteract the help afforded to the Persians by the Naṣrid al-Mundhir, he was content to encourage close ties through shared miaphysite beliefs (even if miaphysitism was not the official doctrine of the empire), and the same was true for the Nobadae. At the other end of the frontier, it was crucial to retain possession of the strategically important Lazica and again, Justinian's reorganisation of Armenia as part of his administrative reforms helped to consolidate Roman rule in this area, and his care in fostering close cultural and religious bonds with the peoples of the Caucasus region helped to strengthen their loyalty. These strategies, which we will also be able to see at work in the chapters on governance of the empire and religious policy, allowed Justinian to focus his military efforts on the reconquest of the western provinces, to which we now turn.

3

The Wars of Reconquest

Recovering North Africa

The story of Justinian's recovery of North Africa from the Vandals in 533–534 is well known. Belisarius' rapid military victory culminating in his entry to Carthage where he enjoyed the banquet prepared the previous day for the defeated Vandal king, Gelimer (Procopius, *Wars* III.21.1–6), and the contrasting vignettes of Gelimer's surrender when he called for a loaf of bread (to assuage his hunger), a sponge (to bathe an infected eye) and a harp (to accompany his lament) are images which nicely convey the mood of imperial triumph characteristic of the early part of Justinian's reign (Procopius, *Wars* IV.6.30–4 – **II 24**; John the Lydian, *de Magistratibus* III.55 – **II 25**). The easy victory was still proudly recalled long after on his funeral pall commissioned by the new empress, Sophia (Corippus, *In laudem Iustini minoris* 1.276–87 – **II 26**). However, the emperor's assumption of titles *Vandalicus* and *Africanus* (*CIC* I, *Inst.* 21) and his triumph in Constantinople had been over hasty, for although the Vandals were defeated, the native Moors (later referred to as the Berbers) remained a hostile force until their subjugation in 548. Since the early work of Averil Cameron (1982, 1984, 1989) noting the dearth of work on North Africa, much has been published, including individual studies (Modéran 2003b, Merrills 2010, Conant 2012, Miles 2015, Wilhite 2017) and collaborative volumes (the 2001 and 2002 *Antiquité Tardive* volumes and the 2016 Dumbarton Oaks papers). New excavations and epigraphic studies have thrown light on the building programmes of the Vandals and Romans, their civic life, the local economy and governance, religious policy and military practice. Innovative studies in identity and ethnicity have helped us to understand the key groups; our perception of the native Moors, the Vandals and the Romano-Africans, and how they interacted, has a major impact on how we assess the 'recovery' of North Africa. Finally, literary studies have led to a more varied and critical assessment of our two major sources, Procopius and Corippus. The recent work of both Wood (2011) and Kaldellis (2016) highlights the ways in which Procopius subverts his initial favourable view of the war, and there has been a spate of recent editions, commentaries and studies on Corippus (Vinchesi 1983, Shea 1998, Tommasi Moreschini 2001, Zarini 2003, Gärtner 2008, Schindler 2009, Riedlberger 2010, Hays 2016).

From Vandal kingdom to Roman province

In the years 429–442 the Vandals, under their king, Geiseric, had succeeded in wresting a number of regions (Proconsular Africa, Byzacena (Byzacium), Tripolitania and part of Numidia) from Roman rule. Many Romans fled from the new political regime and also from religious persecution as the Vandals imposed their Arian beliefs on the Roman Nicene Church. However, the new Vandal kingdom occupied about one ninth of the total area of the Maghrib, the area of northwestern Africa from the Gulf of Syrtes to the Atlantic coast of Morocco, less than one half of the Roman diocese of Africa. The remainder was occupied by the native Moorish communities.

Justinian's excuse to reconquer North Africa was the usurpation of Gelimer in 530. He had imprisoned the ruling king, Hilderic, a guest friend of Justinian who had passed an Edict of Toleration towards the Nicene Church. Gelimer disregarded the emperor's embassies, but Justinian had a strong motivation for invasion. A victorious military campaign in a wealthy former Roman province would divert criticism following the disastrous *Nika* riot of the previous year, enhance the optimistic rhetoric of the early years, and – should the projected recovery of Italy succeed – restore Africa to its customary role as breadbasket for the western empire. However, the expedition was opposed by his advisers in Constantinople, especially by John the Cappadocian, on grounds of expense, previous failures, and the reluctance of the troops to embark on another campaign so soon after the Persian conflict. But Justinian's purpose was strengthened by hearing the dream of a priest in which God promised his support (Procopius, *Wars* III.9–10).

In June 533, the expedition led by Belisarius, accompanied by his *assessor*, Procopius, left Constantinople, and sailing via Sicily, they reached Caput Vada on the African coast in August, and Carthage by mid-September. After a number of defeats, and spending three months of hardship in Numidia, Gelimer surrendered, and by the summer of 534 Belisarius had returned to Constantinople with Gelimer and 2,000 Vandals (Victor of Tonnena, *Chronicon* 534 – **II 27**). Justinian celebrated with a traditional Roman triumph, and a mural on the ceiling of the vestibule of the imperial palace depicted the imperial couple approached in supplication by the defeated Vandal king (Procopius, *Buildings* I.10.16–18 – **II 28**). However, the following years were marred by incursions of the Moors, and a mutiny within the Roman army. The praetorian prefect, Solomon, escaped an assassination plot, but it took successive campaigns of Belisarius and Justinian's cousin, Germanus, to put down this insurrection. Solomon returned as praetorian prefect in charge of the army in 539, and the campaigns against the Moors recommenced. He was killed in 544, and poor appointments of commanders, like his unpopular nephew, Sergius, antagonised even the Moorish allies of the Romans, and led to further rebellions, such as that by Guntarith, the *dux Numidiae*, who gained possession of Carthage. The Roman cause was saved on this occasion by the Armenian commander, Artabanes, who feigned support for Guntarith but killed him and his supporters at a banquet in early 546. John Troglita, well known as the hero of Corippus' epic (*Iohannis* or *de Bellis Libycis*), succeeded Artabanes, arriving in Carthage at the end of 546. He enjoyed initial success and sent the standards of Solomon, recaptured from the Moors, to Justinian. A couple of years of reverses followed, the Romans struggling with the harsh conditions of combat in the desert, but eventually, with the help of the allied Moorish leaders, the rebel Moors were defeated. As the accounts of both Procopius and Corippus come to an end in 548 we know little of the later period, except that John remained in command of the army until c. 552 and North Africa at last enjoyed a spell of peace and reconstruction.

Much work has been done recently to understand the native Moors and their relationship with the Vandals, Romans and Arabs. As studies of the Moorish groups have become more sophisticated, distinctions are now drawn between the 'interior' Moors (such as the tribes of Antalas, Cusina and Iaudas, who all ruled territory within the network of fortifications erected by Justinian in the frontier zone) and 'exterior' Moors. While the latter were portrayed as typically 'barbarian' by Procopius and Corippus, who were no doubt influenced by traditional Roman histories (such as Sallust's *Jugurthine War*), many of the 'interior' Moors were allies. Interestingly, the latest thinking appears to show that despite the hostilities, and some unreliability (especially that of Antalas), the Romans and these Moors enjoyed a reciprocal dependence upon each other: the Moors policed the *limes* in return for imperial recognition of their leaders and annual cash payments (Modéran 2003b: chapters 13–15, Merrills 2004: 3–24, Conant 2012: chapter 5, Fentress and Wilson 2016).

Governance and the economy

In April 534, Justinian outlined his plan for the civil and military administration of his new province (*C.J.* I.27.1–2 – **II 29**). Although there is debate about how much territory was actually reclaimed by the imperial forces (Trousset 2003, Laporte 2003), the organisation into seven provinces (Proconsularis (renamed Zeugitana), Byzacena (Byzacium), Tripolitania, Numidia, Mauritania Sitifensis, Mauritania Caesariensis and Sardinia) shows that Justinian was aiming to restore the original boundaries before the Vandal and Moorish invasions. The praetorian prefect responsible for civil administration was to be based in Carthage while Belisarius retained overall military authority supported by *duces*. Following Belisarius' departure, Solomon was appointed with joint responsibility for civil and military matters (Zuckerman 2003, Merrills 2010, Conant 2012: chapter 4). A detailed analysis of the men appointed to the positions of highest command in the major cities reveals that Justinian carefully selected his most trusted advisors, regardless of their geographical origins, indicating the importance the emperor placed on ensuring the security of the province. It was only in the 540s that local Africans filled more of the principal positions. Exact calculations were made for the minor appointments and allocation of rations, including provision for two grammarians and two orators.

Apart from ensuring the smooth running of local government, the success of Justinian's rule of Africa may be measured in terms of economic stability and prosperity. It is clear that the burden of taxation imposed was harsher than it had been during the Vandal era, since the costs of civil administration, the army and the building programme were high. The great landowners were able to use their influence to escape as far as possible, and Procopius is suitably critical (**II 30**). However, after the initial complaints about taxation, there was no further unrest. Furthermore, although the abandonment of agricultural land resulting from the Moorish raids had been a problem since the mid-fifth century, it is likely that Roman rule aided farmers by facilitating access to markets and by eventually curtailing the raiding. There was a revival of trade in corn, oil, dates, camels and pottery.

Advances in the studies of African red slip ware, the UNESCO excavations in Carthage, and various surveys (the UNESCO Libyan Valleys and Kasserine Archaeological Surveys) have allowed us to build up a much more nuanced picture of life in North Africa. The partial rehabilitation of the Vandals and more positive view of their legacy (Merrills 2004, 2016, Reynolds 2016) points to a general trend which allows for much more continuity during the fifth and sixth centuries and beyond than previously thought (von Rummel 2016). On the other hand, the detailed analysis of the movement of people, documents, administrative ties, both secular and ecclesiastical, and economic exchange amply demonstrates the successful reintegration of Africa into the Roman Empire and it is clear that networks between North Africa, Rome, Constantinople and further afield flourished (Conant 2012: 330–53). Evidence from the circulation of coinage (Morrisson 2004, 2016) and ceramics (Reynolds 2016) reveals a wide distribution, although detailed studies distinguish between the exportation of ceramics from different regions of North Africa along specific trade routes to targeted ports and regions.

Building programme

A key criterion for the economic success of Justinian's project should be the evidence from the building programme, but here the picture is complicated by a number of factors. First, our main source, Procopius' *Buildings* VI, remains a draft and cannot be accepted at face value. However, while Procopius' narrative may reflect Justinian's aspiration to provide security, and it is true that he does ask Belisarius for a list of places to be fortified (*C.J.* I.27.2.14), the extent of the emperor's direct involvement in the building programme is unclear. The general consensus is that although imperial permission may have been sought for some of the work, and the government retained overall co-ordination (in *Novel* 67 Justinian instructs donors to repair churches rather than endowing new ones), much was commissioned at a local level by military officials, bishops and other secular and religious functionaries, as the epigraphic record demonstrates (Durliat 1981, Feissel 2000). Of Durliat's collection of thirty-eight inscriptions, twenty-four are securely dated to Justinian's reign and specifically to the second praetorian prefecture of Solomon (539–544). The inscriptions allude to an imperial plan but rely on Solomon to carry it out with the help of the locals. A famous example, in ten lines of dactylic hexameters, from Aïn Djelloula (*Cululis*) refers to the pious emperor, the empress, great-hearted Solomon and the tribune, Nonnus (**II 31**; Durliat 1981: 37–42, Modéran 1996, Feissel 2000: 102, Pringle 2002: 269–82, Hays 2016: 278–81). Another argument for proactive imperial participation has been the marble pieces imported in prefabricated form in designs familiar from Constantinople and Ravenna. As the marble quarries were imperially owned, it has been assumed that these were gifts from Justinian. However, it is probable that there was a private trade in marble by the sixth century and, as the dating is insecure, it is possible that these pieces were made earlier and stockpiled until needed, making the involvement of bishops and laymen rather more likely than direct imperial involvement (Reynolds 2000).

The second issue concerns our view of the Vandal legacy already discussed above. The traditional assumption that repairs were necessary because of destruction and neglect has been reconsidered since, during the Vandal era, Carthage flourished not just as a mere provincial capital, but as the royal capital. There is evidence for continued prosperity in the commercial sphere, in domestic building (fine houses) and in church building (Merrills 2004, Miles 2015).

Thirdly, on the other hand, the unmistakable signs of urban decline in the fabric of the classical city, including the abandonment of public spaces, the deterioration of city walls, and the decay of public buildings such as baths, temples and theatres, were not particular to North African cities but part of an empire-wide trend (Modéran 1996, Lassère 2015: 695–733, von Rummel 2016). The work carried out in Carthage – for example, the repair of the Theodosian walls, the restoration of the Antonine baths, and the proconsular palace on the Byrsa Hill, the ancient administrative centre – demonstrates the concern to use building work as an expression of empire (Leone 2007: 168–78, Miles 2015). Modifications, such as the siting of olive presses and lime kilns within prestige buildings, are now thought to be examples of new economic impulses rather than simple civic decline (Leone 1999, 2003). The *Codex Justinianus* still included laws preserving public spaces, so Leone (2007: 284f) argues that these changes were part of a careful reorganisation planned by the state in which urban and rural activities were merged for greater efficiency. It was more convenient for production centres to be situated within towns which were securely defended and close to the harbour where goods were ready for immediate export. The trend whereby olive presses have been found in churches reflects the new structure familiar from the rest of the empire where the clergy were now in charge of commercial activity (Leone 2007: 236f). As excavations in Carthage have shown, the commercial ports were redeveloped as part of Justinian's plan to exploit agricultural produce and restore the *annona* supply (noted cynically by Procopius, *Secret History* 25.7–10). The monumental gate and colonnade in the north sector of the circular harbour were reconstructed and may in fact be the location of Justinian's maritime agora mentioned by Procopius (*Buildings* VI.5.10, Hurst 1994).

Building work elsewhere, such as at Lepcis Magna, also shows evidence of thriving commercial activity (Leone 2007: 185–7), while numerous studies on fortifications (Pringle 1981, Mattingly and Hitchner 1995, Sarantis 2013) reveal a range of defensive works to protect the local populations, including city walls, and forts constructed in disused public buildings, such as baths, temples or theatres.

Lastly, we come to ecclesiastical complexes. While the Vandals had not neglected church building, and there was no discernible difference in the architecture of Arian and Nicene churches, it is suggested that the ambitious programme of rebuilding and redesign helped the Nicene authorities to reassert their authority, and it was a subtle way for the Romano-African elite who had previously collaborated with the Vandals to now distance themselves from this episode. In Carthage, at least eight Christian basilicas, two monasteries and other cult structures were built or remodelled (Merrills 2010: 241ff). Basilicas were now reorientated east-west, and there was an emphasis on baptism and the veneration of relics with the addition of crypts and reliquaries, and ambulatories to aid the circulation of pilgrims. The new popularity of liturgical processions in Constantinople, along with the adoption of these eastern architectural practices, provides evidence for a strong Eastern Mediterranean influence (Conant 2016b).

The African Church

A final complication for Justinian was his dealings with the Nicene African Church. For all the rhetoric about rescuing the Nicene Church from the hands of Arian Vandals (Cyril of Scythopolis, *Life of St Sabas* 74 – **II 32**; Mîrşanu 2008), it appears that Justinian's support was limited by his pragmatism in two respects. First, he was inclined towards compromise with the Arians who were ordered to hand over their sacraments to the Nicenes immediately, but other property was to be surrendered only after a delay, and the Arian clergy were allowed to keep their former status once rebaptised and admitted to the Nicene Church. Naturally, this conciliatory approach did not suit the Nicene Church and a council of 220 bishops met January–August 335. A petition was sent to Justinian requesting full restitution of church properties confiscated by the Arians, and a letter to Pope John II regarding the matter of Arian clerics retaining their status (*Collectio Avellana* 85). In *Novel* 37 (1 August 535) (**II 33**) Justinian acceded to both demands (Kaegi 1965, Sotinel 2005: 277). However, it was unfortunate that shortly afterwards, the Church world-wide was soon embroiled in the Three Chapters Controversy (see Chapter 4, Sotinel 2000, Modéran 2007, Conant 2012: chapter 6, Patout Burns and Jensen 2014: 67–80, Lassère 2015: 722ff, Conant 2016a, Dossey 2016). This Controversy concerned the writings of Theodore of Mopsuestia, Ibas of Edessa and Theodoret of Cyrrhus, declared orthodox by the 451 Council of Chalcedon, but later denounced by the miaphysites as tainted with Nestorianism. In order to reconcile these miaphysites, in the mid-540s, Justinian issued an edict demanding the condemnation of the three, but it was rejected in Italy and Africa on the grounds that if one decision could be overturned, all resolutions could be questioned, putting the whole council at risk. Bishop Pontianus of Thaenae complained to Justinian but suggested that copies of the writings should be sent to Africa where they were not very well known. It was not until the 550s that the Carthaginian Liberatus obliged with an explanatory document but in the meantime a number of Africans wrote extensively in protest. Ferrandus, the deacon of Carthage, sent letters to his contacts in Rome, southern Italy and Constantinople, and Bishop Facundus of Hermiane composed a treatise, *In Defence of the Three Chapters*, in which he invited Justinian to admit his error (**II 34**). In 550, the African bishops held a synod at which they excommunicated the pope and wrote to Justinian to explain why they disagreed with his policy. Justinian responded by summoning the African opponents to Constantinople, where he deposed Reparatus, the bishop of Carthage. However, even at the very end of his reign, recalcitrant African churchmen were still being threatened, bribed, imprisoned or brought to Constantinople, including the historian Victor of Tonnena. Eventually those who did not die were persuaded to return to communion.

The initial easy and celebrated recovery of Carthage in 533–534 was only the beginning. The subsequent necessary military action, and the governance of this province which had not been part of the empire for a century, proved, as we saw above, far more difficult, in terms of the relationship between Romans, Vandals and native Moors, the economy and the Church. These issues were also to be features of Justinian's Italian campaign, and it is to this which we now turn.

Recovering Italy: The military highlights

The campaign began promisingly with the successful capture of Sicily by Belisarius and an equally successful offensive in Dalmatia led by Mundo. However, Justinian's recovery of Italy from the Ostrogoths rapidly degenerated into a tortuous conflict lasting twenty-seven years (535–562). The narrative of the war may be followed in Procopius (*Wars* V–VIII), whose account is followed by Bury (1923), Wolfram (1988: 332–62 and 1997: chapter 10), Heather (1996: 259–76) and Wiemer (2013). The war may be divided into three phases: 536/7–540: early success for the imperial army under Belisarius; 540–551: the Gothic comeback under Totila; 551–562: the final defeat of the Goths. Following Belisarius' triumph in Sicily, victories on the mainland followed with the siege and fall of Naples (by November 546) and then Rome (winter 536/537). The Goths deposed and murdered the ineffectual King Theodahad, appointing Vitigis in his place. An effective soldier, but not of the royal Amal line, he married Matasuntha despite her aversion to the match. He besieged Rome until the early spring of 538 when the Romans attacked Picenum. Vitigis broke the siege to protect this predominantly Gothic region, but he failed to stop the progress of Belisarius who reinforced Rimini and forced the surrender of Milan and other Ligurian cities. In 539, he recaptured Auximum and Fiesole, and although Vitigis' nephew, Uraias, recovered the Ligurian cities and sacked Milan (amongst the terrible massacre and enslavement, Reparatus, brother of Pope Vigilius, was cut in pieces and thrown to the dogs), support for the Gothic cause waned, leaving Vitigis isolated in Ravenna. He tried to enlist the help of the Lombards but their leader, Wacho, refused, citing the treaty he had agreed with Justinian, and Vitigis even sent an embassy to Persia. Justinian's ambassadors offered favourable terms including the lands north of the Po and an equal division of the Ravenna treasury. But believing that Belisarius would accept the throne, Vitigis opened the gates thus bringing about his own capitulation to Justinian. He and his entourage were taken to Constantinople, along with the treasury when Belisarius returned to his emperor.

Belisarius' recall at this point (December 540) to deal with the Persian war meant that he was unable to complete the imperial reconquest. Lack of military strategy and the rigorous tax demands ruthlessly carried out by the logothete Alexander (the 'snips'), which alienated the resident Italians and Roman soldiers alike, resulted in the pendulum of war swinging back in favour of the Goths. Uraias in Pavia and Hildebad (Ildebadus) in Verona both refused to surrender and thus began the second phase of the war, although a quarrel between the two Gothic leaders quickly resulted in the deaths of both. They were succeeded by Eraric, leader of the Rugi, whose policy of negotiation with Constantinople for a partitioned Italy was unpopular, and his assassination also rapidly followed. Power then passed to Hildebad's nephew, Totila (also known as Baduila), who enjoyed success throughout the 540s. He won a victory at Faenza, south of the Po (spring 542), followed by a victory at Florence, and then moved south, eventually retaking Naples in the spring of 543, and then Auximum. At the end of 545, he began his first siege of Rome; the city surrendered in December 546, although he was impelled to hand over Venetia to the Frankish king, Theudebert, to free up more Goths for active service. Justinian sent Belisarius back in winter 544/545 but with few reinforcements. Having persuaded Totila not to demolish the ancient capital, he went on to retake the city in April 547 but was himself recalled in 549. In his narrative (*Wars* VII.24-6), Procopius celebrates Belisarius' audacious strategy in this, his final accomplishment in Italy. It is clear that the path of Belisarius' generalship in Italy had been anything but smooth; a key characteristic of the war was the quarrelling between the Roman generals, in particular the indecisiveness and rivalry between Belisarius and others, especially John (nephew of Vitalian) and Narses (Fauber 1990). In 538, Justinian had been forced to send a letter stating that Belisarius should lead the whole army, although the qualification 'in the interest of our State' had left his rivals some room for manoeuvre. Returning to the 548 siege of Rome, Procopius proceeded to document the recriminations of the Goths against Totila who, having captured Rome, had allowed it to be retaken. He draws a comparison between the Gothic king and Pericles by evoking the latter's speech (compare Procopius, *Wars* VII.25.4-24 and Thucydides II.60-4); Pericles had also left Athens undefended and vulnerable to Peloponnesian attacks (Pazdernik 2015). Totila later redeemed himself by retaking Rome in January 550 (this time deciding to rebuild and repopulate it) and by recapturing a number of other fortresses including Tarentum and Rimini. He also created a fleet under the command of Indulf (a deserter from the Byzantine army) which ravaged the cost of Dalmatia, took Sicily in 550, and attacked Corfu and Epirus in 551 (Moorhead 2000, Carnevale 2003).

Totila was seen to embody some of the qualities of Theoderic, worshipping at St Peter's, hosting chariot races, and honouring the senate (although at other times he was not averse to doing away with his senatorial hostages). His military victories encouraged Goths to sign up, and his lenient treatment of prisoners likewise encouraged Romans to join his cause, especially those whose pay from Justinian was in arrears. Although he had been relatively successful, he had still been forced to cede territory to the Franks to release manpower, while he knew that although Justinian could command more resources, he was nevertheless stretched by having to fund the Persian war. Totila tried to encourage Justinian to negotiate, sending conciliatory embassies even though he had the upper hand. For example, after his second capture of Rome, he offered to cede Dalmatia and Sicily, pay an annual tribute and provide military assistance to Justinian's campaigns (*Wars* VII.37.1-7 (**II 35**), VIII.24.4, Heather 1996: 267-9).

However, perhaps because the Persian war was winding down, Justinian rejected the advances of Totila, and instead mapped out his next strategy which involved a major land expedition through the Balkans into northern Italy. He began planning in 550 with Germanus (who had married Matasuntha) but following his premature and unexpected death, the expedition finally started in 552 under Narses (Momigliano 1955, Fauber 1990). After a number of victories (including the sea battle of Sena Gallica when the Roman commanders, John and Valerian, triumphed over a Gothic force unused to fighting at sea), Narses met Totila in June/July 552 on a level plain in the northern Apennines called Busta Gallorum. The charge by the Gothic cavalry was unsuccessful: 6,000 died, including Totila. The leadership of the Goths passed to Teias, who gathered as many Goths as possible and sought an alliance with the Franks. Another battle was fought at Mons Lactarius in Campania in which Teias died and remnants of the Goths negotiated an armistice. But in early 553, the help from the Franks arrived and sporadic Gothic resistance continued until c. 555, after which imperial control was re-established above the Po (Agathias II.1-14). In 562, a Gothic count called Widin rebelled in Brescia but his defeat saw the final end of Gothic resistance. It is remarkable that this defeat saw the end of the Ostrogoths who disappeared as a 'nation', leaving no trace of their presence in the archaeological record of Italy.

Lastly, it is worth adding a note on the not inconsequential role of the Franks, masterminded by their ambitious king, Theudebert, who was keen to capitalise on the conflict. He had been pleased to receive territory in Gaul and twenty *centenaria* from Theodahad in return for a military alliance with Theodahad, and later from Totila. In between, he transferred his allegiance to Justinian while accepting

Figure 3.1 Gold solidus of Theudebert © The Trustees of the British Museum.
D N THEODOBERTVS VICTOR ('Our Lord Theudebert the Victorious'); helmeted facing portrait, with spear over shoulder.
VICTORA AVGGGI; facing Angel or Victory holding long cross and globe with cross; below ICONOB; to right, T and star.
The coin copies the designs and inscriptions of imperial Byzantine coins but, very unusually and tendentiously, the emperor's name has been replaced by that of the king: 'it is not right for him [the Persian king] or for any other king among all the barbarians to stamp his own device on a gold stater' (Procopius, *Wars* VII.33.6).

the offer of Raetia from Vitigis. In 539, he led a successful invasion of Italy, attacking both Romans and Goths, but he was ultimately defeated by a bout of dysentery which wiped out a third of his army. In the mid-540s, as he haughtily wrote to Justinian, he enjoyed a kingdom which stretched from the ocean to the borders of Pannonia, including parts of northern Italy (*Epistulae Austrasicae* XX – **II 36**); he minted gold coinage with his own portrait and the word 'victor' (Grierson and Blackburn 1986: 115–16). Perhaps fortunately for Justinian's peace of mind, Theudebert was killed in a hunting accident in 547, although the Franks continued to hold on to their lands until 556; Narses' final victory over the Alamanni-Franks may be followed in Fauber (1990).

Such was the course of the war. Questions remain concerning the complex relationship between the original inhabitants of Italy, the Ostrogothic rulers and the imperial forces; how this relationship both influenced and was influenced by the course of the conflict; and, finally, the impact of the war on the economic and social fabric of Italy. These debates will be considered in turn below.

The Ostrogoths, Italians (Romans) and Romans (Byzantines)

As Justinian had required a trigger to provoke the recovery of North Africa (the usurpation of Gelimer), so the murder of Amalasuntha by Theodahad provided a convenient excuse for war. However, while the traditional view that he had a long-standing plan to reconquer the western empire seems implausible, there is support for the argument that throughout the 520s a programme of propaganda was developed which favoured a single state unified in political rule and religious beliefs: in a word, the Roman Empire restored. This vision required the delegitimisation of the 'barbarian' rule of the west and the repression of other ecclesiastical doctrines (Amory 1997, Mîrşanu 2008, Heydemann 2016: 33–6). Clues that Justinian increasingly had the Goths in Italy in mind in the early 530s have been picked up in his legislation (Barnish and Marazzi 2007: 332). The success of the imperial army in North Africa gave an added boost at a time when Theodahad's regime was troubled and the murder of Amalasuntha provided the final trigger. Heather (2018) in his sweeping 'big picture' view promotes the argument that Justinian was only inspired to consider his western adventures to restore the blow to his prestige following the *Nika* riot, and that a coherent plan was only applied in the mid-530s.

Figure 3.2 Gold medallion of 3-solidi of the Ostrogothic King Theoderic.
REX THEODERICVS PIVS PRINCIS ('King Theoderic the Good Prince'); facing portrait of Theoderic raising right hand and sceptre terminating in a globe surmounted by Victory. Theoderic's gold coinage was made in the name of the Byzantine emperor, but this unique large presentation piece has his portrait and titles. It had been converted into a brooch, was found in northern Italy in 1894, and is today in the Museo Nazionale Romano, Rome. It is the only definite portrait of Theoderic. Photo: author.

But Justinian faced a problem not encountered in recovering Africa. The Ostrogoths had been invited to rule Italy by the Emperor Zeno and on the whole, Theoderic had done so with moderation and success (see Chapter 1). There is a wealth of literature devoted to Theoderic (Moorhead 1992, Arnold 2014), and the *Brill Companion to Ostrogothic Italy* (2016) praises this successful 'barbarian' king for his relatively peaceful rule of a wide geographical area (the Italian peninsula, Sicily, and parts of southern Gaul, Hispania and the Balkans) embracing different religions, and, despite challenging economic and military circumstances, promoting literary and cultural achievements. With some notorious exceptions (Boethius and Symmachus), he also oversaw a relatively successful integration of many of the traditional senators into the new government (Cassiodorus). The prevailing opinion amongst scholars favours a generally peaceful transition (Goffart 1980: 100–2 and 2006: 162–72, Moorhead 1992: chapters 2 and 3, Barnwell 1992: 129–69, Lafferty 2010, 2013), although others argue for a model of greater disruption (Ward-Perkins 2005: 72–3). Besides this, the Gothic elite were highly educated and civilised and many Italians (the popes included) considered the Gothic Church rather more sympathetic than the church of the eastern empire. In dismantling the reality, Procopius' classicising writing was invaluable in ascribing to the Goths all manner of traditional 'barbarian' qualities, highlighting their ferocity, unreliability, adherence to non-Roman laws and Arianism (**II 37**, Amory 1997: 133–47). Procopius was therefore a willing accomplice in conveying Justinian's *renovatio* ideology. A very different interpretation was offered by Jordanes in his *Romana* which he wrote in c. 551 at the request of Vigilius, who had asked for a summary of Roman history. His overall trajectory of the empire sees the Roman world in decline rather than on the rebound, and Justinian's restoration an appearance rather than a reality (Cruse 2015: 240–5).

There is a further dimension to the debate about the identity and ethnicity of the Goths. Barnish and Marazzi's 2007 edited volume includes a valuable introduction by Marazzi and Ausenda which considers current issues and suggests future directions, and an important chapter by Heather. He reprises his view (expressed in his 1996 monograph, and restated in his 2018 book) that resistance to Justinian's aggression came from the highly politicised Gothic freemen elite which numbered thousands rather than hundreds. This elite and privileged group which had been fighting since around 450 to secure a safe homeland for itself would not have lightly given up its assets so hard won. The war eventually ended when casualties and political pressure weakened this elite to such an extent that it could no longer function. Against this view, Amory (1997) believes that resistance came from the descendants of the army Theoderic had brought to Italy in 489 who had intermarried with the Italo-Roman landowning class (and thus forced this class to now take sides). Halsall (2016) also argues against the notion of a defined Gothic identity, and believes that the Italian-born Gothic soldiers formed a well-organised army similar to that of the Romans (*contra* Procopius' traditional ethnic stereotyping), and merely performed badly in the first phase of the war due to political stress and lack of practice.

However, it was undoubtedly with the key figures of the Ostrogothic royal family that the real impetus to direct relations with the eastern empire lay. At the time when Justinian's thoughts were turning towards the west, the Ostrogothic throne was held by Amalasuntha, daughter of Theoderic (see Chapter 1). One of the most divisive figures at the Gothic court, she became the centre of the diplomatic offensive from the Constantinopolitan imperial court. A powerful yet enigmatic female ruler, she has attracted a huge amount of attention, with especial attention now paid to the gender issue (Frankforter 1996, Vitiello 2006, La Rocca 2012, Heydemann 2016, Cooper 2016). The paradoxical nature of her rule stems from the contrasting depictions in our contemporary sources: Procopius (*Wars* V.2) uses the dispute amongst the Goths over her son Athalaric's education (Roman letters versus Gothic military skill) as a means of contrasting the two sides and legitimising Justinian's war. Presented as a victim, she becomes the equivalent of the African king Hilderic whose murder provided the *casus belli* for the African war. Gregory of Tours (3.31), however, presenting a different version of her downfall, portrays her as a monster, guilty of matricide (Joye and Knaepen 2005).

There is no doubt that Amalasuntha was a capable queen. She expanded Ostrogothic territory in the Balkans against the Gepids, taking the Roman city of Gratiana in the process, and she resisted Justinian's attempt to claim the Sicilian port of Lilybaeum. She engaged in talks with Justinian via his envoy, Peter the Patrician, even while she was removing her political opponents from Ravenna, sending them on a military campaign where they were killed (*Wars* V.2.23ff). In 533, she installed Liberius as the new *patricius praesentalis*, while Cassiodorus became praetorian prefect, writing an encomium to Amalasuntha in the form of his acceptance speech (**II 38**). On the other hand, she was doubtful enough to send a ship loaded with treasure to the eastern empire and was ready to follow it should her position in

Italy become untenable. On the death of Athalaric she appointed her cousin Theodahad co-ruler in the hope of strengthening her rule, but he had her murdered on the island of Marta in Lake Bolsena. Procopius (*Wars* V.4.22–3, *Secret History* 16.5, 24.22–3) makes Amalasuntha's assassination the pretext for Justinian's intervention in Italy but, as we saw in Chapter 1, adds a further dimension by making the jealousy of Theodora a reason for the murder through the agency of Peter the Patrician (Cassiodorus, *Variae* X.20 – **II 9**; Vitiello 2014: chapter 4). Letters from Theodahad and his queen Gudeliva to Theodora and Justinian refer to Peter as wise and eloquent, and one letter (*Variae* X.23.1) appears to corroborate the inference that Theodora had masterminded the murder; at the least, the imperial couple would have been pleased with the outcome ('we learn through him that what is established to have happened in this state is agreeable to you'). Known as the philosopher king, yet cowardly and self-interested, Theodahad at first offered to concede sovereignty of Italy in return for securing his own safety and property, but later opted to continue hostilities after the Ostrogothic victory over Mundo in Dalmatia (Barnish 1990, Bjornlie 2013: 311–20, Vitiello 2014: 38–9, 150–1). As we saw in the narrative

Figure 3.3 D N THEODAHATVS REX ('Our Lord King Theodahad'); portrait of King Theodahad, wearing helmet decorated with stars, and royal robe decorated with a pectoral cross.
VICTORIA PRINCIPVM, S C; Victory standing right on prow, holding palm branch and wreath.
This unusual and fine portrait of an Ostrogothic king appears on a large bronze coin. Its reverse was copied from much earlier Roman coins, suggesting that its production was stimulated by the discovery of an earlier hoard. The depiction of the king, however, is entirely original. © The Trustees of the British Museum.

above, he was ousted from the throne and killed on the orders of his successor, the warlike Vitigis.

Another debate relevant to the relationship between the conqueror and the conquered was whether the Italians wished to be rescued from their Ostrogothic rulers and this has been considered at length (Heydemann 2016, Radtki 2016). Belisarius' invasion sparked a division of loyalties: the imperial forces told the Italian citizens of Syracuse and Naples they had come to restore them, while the Goths reminded them how much they had benefited under Theoderic, who had been legally recognised by Constantinople. Clearly there was a wide range of opinion which, filtered through our (biased) sources, makes it difficult to judge. In 535, Cassiodorus represents Pope Agapetus, the senate and Italy's rulers pleading 'if Libya deserved to receive freedom from you, it is cruel for [us] to lose what [we] have already seemed to possess' (*Variae* XI.13.5). On the other hand, it is argued that despite some natural wavering as the war wore on, the loyalty to the imperial cause remained strong (Moorhead 1983). Moorhead argues that even Cassiodorus and Pope Vigilius (who might have their own reasons for being less than supportive of Justinian) were actually both pro-Roman. He refers to the hexameter version of the Acts of the Apostles composed by the subdeacon, Arator, and recited in April–May 544, which stressed the strength of Rome's walls and the promise of freedom. Arator had held office under the Goths but having joined the Roman Church now ranged himself against Totila who, in 544, had written to the senate and displayed notices in Rome (Procopius, *Wars* VII.9.21). The reality is likely to be somewhere in between, with most citizens hoping to avoid being caught up in the conflict, but ultimately siding with whoever could provide the best protection, economic stability and relative peace (Kouroumali 2013). Procopius' concluding remarks (*Wars* VIII.34.3–5) clearly reveal a civilian population treated badly by warring sides and, given the protracted struggle, it is hardly surprising to find both sides committing atrocities, regions continuously switching sides, and frequent mass desertion of troops (Amory 1997). We know most about the high-profile individuals, such as Liberius, who transferred his allegiance to the emperor at the outset, and Cassiodorus, who continued to support the Ostrogothic cause up to 540 when it is likely he left Italy with Belisarius. Theodahad's extreme behaviour, including the murder of Amalasuntha, his mistreatment of members of the senate, his capture of Constantinople's ambassadors, and his coinage which showed a stronger representation of himself as imperator, served to stiffen the competition between those who supported a traditional Gothic versus a traditional Roman way of life. A number of senators left Italy in the early 540s and, ensconced at Justinian's court, were involved in drawing up plans for the future administration of Italy.

Several mentions have been made of the statesman and writer Cassiodorus Senator (c. 485/490–c. 580/585). Fascinating for his own life and the documents he left behind, he is at the heart of the complex relationship between the regime of old Rome, the Ostrogoths and Justinian's eastern empire (MacPherson 1989, Barnish 1992, Gillett 2003: chapter 5, Bjornlie 2013, 2019). The *Variae* (so-called to reflect the varieties of rhetorical style represented) comprise 468 documents arranged in twelve books, including the correspondence and edicts of the Amal rulers. There are many letters drafted by Cassiodorus between 506 and 538 for the Gothic kings, the senate, and himself as praetorian prefect and quaestor. There are also two prefaces which open Books I and XI, and a treatise on the soul (*de anima*). In one of the prefaces, Cassiodorus sets out his motives for assembling this collection, which include satisfying the demands of his friends and supplying models for future administrations. These motives, along with the revelation of Cassiodorus' private views on the masters he was obliged to serve (both Ostrogoths and Romans) and the extent of the authenticity of the documents included in the *Variae* collection, have long been discussed. The intricate relations between Rome, Ravenna and Constantinople are particularly well-illuminated in Bjornlie's studies; while noting that the core content of the letters is probably genuine, he suggests that Cassiodorus deliberately sets out to rehabilitate the Italian elite who had served as the palatine bureaucracy of the Amals by rearranging some of the documents and including a few inventions. Bjornlie notes that there would have been differences of opinion between the Italian exiles at the Constantinopolitan court: the senators from Rome versus the palatine service in Ravenna. And Cassiodorus' own position in a setting where the Anicii held prominent positions would have been complicated and compromised by his connection with the death of Boethius.

The impact of war

The success of Justinian's plan of *renovatio* may be measured in terms of military and economic outcome. The letters of Pope Pelagius (556–561) to Childebert, King of the Franks, and Boethius, the praetorian prefect of Italy, report news of the devastated estates of Italy

(**II 39**; Gasso 1956, Moorhead 2000: 386). The official end of the war was marked by the Pragmatic Sanction in 554 by which act Justinian restored direct imperial control of Italy (*Novels* Appendix 7 (**II 40**), with Miller and Sarris 2018: II.1116–30). It attempted to resolve the economic and social instabilities caused by the conflict, and the stress laid on property and taxation suggests these were key concerns: of the twenty-six sections, fifteen concern property rights and six deal with aspects of taxation. It confirmed all measures passed by legitimate kings on behalf of the Romans or the senate by Theoderic and his successors, but not Totila 'the usurper' (7.1–2). The Sanction was issued at the request of Pope Vigilius, then in Constantinople, and its provisions reflect the concerns of the senatorial and ecclesiastical elites with bishops and local notables being given a role in the election of provincial governors and some control over economic policies (7.12, 18, 19). Justinian reclaimed imperial prerogatives such as coinage, taxes, care of the *annona*, public buildings and law-making. The Justinianic *Code* and *Novels* were to be valid throughout Italy retrospectively. Italy was now part of a single *res publica* again, united by God's will (7.11).

The extent of the damage caused by the twenty-five-year war is still debated; twenty years ago, new research on key sites in northern Italy was considered (Ward-Perkins 1997) but the debate continues today. It is clear that, while there was some continuity, Italy was more susceptible to acute events (Grey 2016, Christie 2006: 34–8, 364–9). In 568, the Lombards overran a northern and central Italy already weakened by warfare and established a Lombard kingdom based in Milan and two Lombard duchies at Spoleto and Benevento. Constantinople installed an exarch to rule from Ravenna over territory which included Rome, Genoa, south Italy, Sicily and the region which would become Venice. Italy would not be a single state again until 1870. As for the social fabric and senatorial rule, these had been badly affected by the long period of fighting and the measures of Totila. As valuable pawns in the military game, both Vitigis and Totila ordered the slaughter of senatorial hostages. Those who survived saw the destruction of the economic and social structures on which their senatorial lifestyle depended, losing the slaves and *coloni* who worked on their estates, and being passed over for administrative positions by emperors who preferred to install eastern senators. There are few mentions of senatorial meetings: the last testimony dates from 578 and 580 when the senate despatched embassies to the Emperor Tiberius (Brown 1984: 21–2). However, the argument that Totila instigated a social and economic revolution by welcoming into the Gothic army large numbers of freed slaves and disposed of the owners of the latifundia, thereby giving peasants control over the lands they worked, has been refuted by Moorhead (2000). He suggests the reason that the Pragmatic Sanction is so hostile to Totila is not because of his 'revolutionary' activities in depriving the senators of their peasant workers, but because in prolonging the war, he caused major devastation of the land hitherto avoided, and thus was responsible for shattering the agrarian economy. The elimination and emigration of the senatorial aristocracy, along with their wealth and experience of governing, necessarily brought about a major change. All taxes were put towards the war effort, rather than any rebuilding, which might only be helped by funds from the sees of Ravenna and Rome and which now played a role in re-establishing imperial rule.

Conflict in the Balkans

While much attention has been directed towards Justinian's policy concerning North Africa and Italy, his strategy regarding the Balkans has not received so much consideration. Suggestions have been made that the area was of low strategic priority, or important only as a gateway to Italy and as a recruiting ground (Pohl 1996, 1997), or that diplomacy and fortification work compensated for a lack of military resources (Pohl 1997). It is the work of Sarantis in recent years (2009, 2013, 2016) which has sought to foreground the Balkans as an important strand to Justinian's western foreign policy. He argues that Justinian devoted considerable political, military and economic resources to the region. However, as most historians have been influenced by Procopius' somewhat cursory treatment of military action in the region, Justinian's attention to the Balkans is often omitted from modern accounts or presented as a minor part of the Italian campaign. Sarantis also suggests that as Procopius had not visited the province himself, he was less interested in recording events there which he had heard about second-hand. On the other hand, the fourth book of the *Buildings* is devoted to the Balkans, and the maps and lists of building works drawn up by provincial authorities provide the basis for a largely accurate account (allowing for the inevitable rhetoric and inclusion of projects already under way by Justinian's predecessors). Sarantis contends that the actual archaeological and epigraphic record supports Procopius' favourable account in the *Buildings* against other views that dispute Procopius' enthusiastic description of towns such as Justiniana Prima (Poulter 2007: 20). Finally, Procopius' critical assessment in the *Secret History* (8.5–6, 11.5–11 – **II 41**) and *Wars* (8.5.16–17, 8.18.19) of the imperial policy of maintaining peace by subsidies brings a third angle to his portrayal of Justinian's Balkans policy.

Justinian's interest in the politics of the Balkans began in the 520s when he strengthened the position of the Heruls with a grant of land in the area of Singidunum, and the baptism of their king, Grepes. However, the successes of the early 530s in recovering Sirmium from the Goths and the achievement of the Slav, Chilbudius, in holding off the Huns, Antae and Sklaveni, were sadly reversed when the Gepids seized Sirmium and Chilbudius was killed in 534. And although the Gepid Mundo, appointed *magister militum per Illyricum*, celebrated an initial victory at the start of the Gothic war, he and his son were later killed. In the autumn of 539, we hear from Procopius about a 'large Hunnic army' which reached as far as the suburbs of Constantinople before retiring with 120,000 captives. Two further raids followed this in c. 544 when one group of Huns again reached the environs of Constantinople, taking prisoners and booty, while a second group breached the defences at Thermopylae and were able to destroy almost all of Greece, except the Peloponnese (*Wars* II.4.1–12 – **II 42**). Successive raids of the Sklaveni in the later 540s and early 550s were directed against Illyricum and Thrace. In 550, Justinian ordered his cousin Germanus to deal with the problem, but he died before he could take action, and after wintering in imperial territory, one force of Sklaveni reached the Long Walls (Sarantis 2016: 278–88).

Justinian responded in three ways to these depredations: administrative reforms, fortifications and diplomacy. In line with his other provincial legislation, he appointed a new official, the *Praetor Justinianus* of Thrace, who combined military and civilian roles. In a law of May 546 (*Novel* 41/50), he also created a new position, the quaestor of the army with responsibility for Moesia Secunda and Scythia, plus Caria, Cyprus and the islands of the Ionian sea (the latter three had previously been part of the remit of the praetorian prefect of the east); the new arrangement was designed to make the defence of the Danube area more efficient and to protect army supplies. *Novel* 11 records Justinian's strengthening of Justiniana Prima as an ecclesiastical and administrative centre (**II 43**). The new archbishopric included a number of places, such as the ancient city of Viminacium which, as Procopius tells us, Justinian had entirely rebuilt. As to fortifications, although Procopius' account cannot be taken completely at face value, certain patterns in the defences have been observed. Defences along the Lower Danube were strengthened, such as at Noviodunum and Dinogetia; fortresses south of the river were built either to defend roads or to supply places of refuge; walls and fortifications were strengthened at sites which had previously been vulnerable such as Thermopylae, Corinth, Gallipoli and the Long Walls of Constantinople. As to Justinian's use of diplomacy, this may most clearly be seen in his dealings with the Gepids and Lombards. Sarantis (2009) argues that the destruction of the Gepids in 567 by the Avars has meant that their threat to the empire in the 540s and 550s has been downplayed. He suggests that Justinian's support of the Lombards' acquisition of Pannonian territories stemmed from his desire to provide a counter-balance to the Gepids, whose capture of Sirmium (along with the threat of the Frankish Theudebert) had vexed the emperor. The series of Gepid-Lombard military and diplomatic disputes played out between the Gepid king, Thorison, and the Lombard king, Audoin, during the years 548–552, allowed Justinian to further favour the Lombards with military support against the Gepids (Sarantis 2016: 266–78). A more devious example of Justinian's diplomacy is found in the year 551 with his dealings with the Kutrigurs and Utrigurs. He encouraged the Utrigurs to desist from raiding imperial lands, and to direct their efforts against the Kutrigurs who, despite receiving subsidies, persisted in attacking the Romans. The Utrigurs duly defeated the Kutrigurs but on learning that 2,000 Kutrigurs had nevertheless been allowed to settle in Thrace sent an embassy to complain at the imperial court (Procopius, *Wars* VIII.19.8–22).

Figure 3.4 Viminacium, early Christian basilica(?) Photo: author.

Figure 3.5 Noviodunum. Photo: author.

Figure 3.6 Dinogetia. Photo: author.

Figure 3.7 Trajan's Bridge across the Danube at Pontes, restored by Justinian (Procopius, *Buildings* IV.6.11-17). Photo: author.

During the 550s, it appears that Justinian's measures were working with evidence of local building initiatives and peaceful conditions; for example, Peter Barsymes was able to requisition grain from Thrace, as well as from Bithynia and Phrygia. However, in March 559, a host of Kutrigurs and Sklaveni crossed the frozen Danube, led by Zabergan. Two divisions were halted by Justinian's new defences at Thermopylae and Gallipoli, but the third, led by Zabergan with 7,000 cavalry, rapidly reached Constantinople, plundering and taking captives; not even a dog barked in resistance as they crossed the Long Walls (Agathias V.13.5–6 – **II 44**). The imperial response is well known and often related: the elderly and overweight Belisarius, struggling into his armour and accompanied by a small force of 300, managed to outwit the enemy and ambush 2,000 of the cavalry (Agathias V.15.7–8 – **II 45**). However, Justinian then recalled him, apparently influenced by the familiar concern that Belisarius might be aspiring to usurp his throne, although his subsequent lengthy stay away from the capital does not suggest that he felt particularly threatened by his general's popularity (Moorhead 1994: 159). Unusually, Justinian visited the scene of combat, remaining in Selymbria for several months supervising the rebuilding of the Long Walls. He promised an annual subsidy to the Kutrigurs in return for their retreat and offered gold as ransom for the prisoners. He enjoyed a triumphal ride back to Constantinople, stopping at the Church of the Holy Apostles and lighting a candle at the tomb of Theodora.

Procopius was scathing of Justinian's policy of too easily offering subsidies to barbarians (*Secret History* 11.5-8 (**II 41**), 19.13-16). In 558 and 561, he sought to appease the Avars, known for their terrifying appearance with their long hair plaited and fastened with ribbons, looking like snakes, and their supremacy as fighters on horseback (Theophanes AM 6050 – **II 46**). Justinian did not agree to offer them land, but instead, with monetary gifts and some diplomacy, he managed to keep them at bay. This policy which so offended Procopius was reversed by Justin II who withdrew the subsidies. The Avars went on to defeat the Gepids, and the Lombards hastily moved into Italy to avoid the same fate. By 626, the Avars and Slavs were besieging the walls of the capital itself.

A last foray: Southern Spain

As a final flourish of western adventurism, in the 550s Justinian also took the opportunity to intervene in the affairs of Spain. This region had been part of Theoderic's vast empire, but his plan that his grandson, Amalaric, should inherit it had gone awry. Spain eventually passed to the Visigothic king, Athanagild, who sought assistance from Justinian. The emperor promptly despatched a fleet under Liberius who, sailing from Sicily, captured many cities and forts, supposedly for Athanagild, but he subsequently refused to hand them over. Liberius established the imperial province of Spania along the coast in Baetica and it remained under rule from Constantinople for the next seventy years. A small mint for gold tremisses also seems to have been established there, perhaps at Cartagena or Malaga. Procopius and Agathias do not record this activity, but evidence is forthcoming from Jordanes (*Getica* 58), from whom we get the date for the expedition of 551, and Isidore (*History of the Goths* 47 – **II 47**, *Chronicon* 399a), and there is a possible mention in the *Greek Anthology* 4.3.82ff.

This chapter has focused primarily on the military and diplomatic aspects of Justinian's foreign policy in the west. We saw that he had to tread carefully when dealing with the African Church; the Nicenes who had been persecuted by the Vandal Arians were now not prepared to compromise. Justinian made the appropriate concessions, but the African Church was soon caught up in the Three Chapters Controversy. As for Justinian's relations with the papacy, we saw in

Chapter 1 that he had worked hard in the early 520s to heal the rift with Rome. However, as he saw for himself the difficulties of keeping the peace within the Church in all parts of the empire, his willingness to defer to successive popes rapidly diminished. The hugely complex problems which engulfed the Church at this time, and the increasing involvement of the emperor, a secular ruler, in this sacred sphere, are the subject of the next chapter.

4

Church and State

Justinian's close attention to the theological matters dominating his reign is not in doubt. His purpose in trying to bring unity to the schismatic factions within the eastern patriarchates and western Church, his interpretation of the role of emperor in directing church affairs, and his success and consequent legacy have been hotly debated. Religious policy at this time was a very complex matter, both theologically and politically. Successive emperors from Constantine onwards had sought to find solutions to the divisions arising over points of doctrine and church organisation between the east and the west, and amongst the eastern patriarchates. No emperor could afford to have serious unrest within his empire, but to Justinian, unity of the Church was all-important as he sought to unite the east and west politically, and to claim his divine right to rule (see Chapter 5). To understand the issues facing Justinian, we must return to the Council of Chalcedon in 451.

The Council of Chalcedon, 451 – the problem

The issues at stake at this council and thereafter have been retold many times, but it is worth repeating them briefly here by way of background. In the early fifth century, following the Antiochene theologians, Diodore of Tarsus and Theodore of Mopsuestia, Nestorius, the patriarch of Constantinople (428–431), attempted to solve the question of how Christ might be both God and a human. He suggested a Christ in whom the divine and human elements were separate: within Christ there was God the Word (the pre-existent creator) and Jesus (the man, who was born, died and rose again). As a consequence, the Virgin Mary who had given birth to a man could no longer be referred to as the 'Theotokos' (mother of God). However, this dualist view was rejected by some who thought that the divine and human aspects of Christ were so close as to form a unity. Cyril, the patriarch of Alexandria (412–444), sought a solution whereby, although God the Word retained its full divinity, the two natures of Christ were united and perfected in one Lord, the Christ and Son, and that God the Word became flesh. He expressed these ideas in his Second Letter to Nestorius written in February 430. Later in the year, Cyril restated his position more powerfully in his Third Letter to Nestorius, referring to the 'One Hypostasis of the Incarnate Word' and 'the Word suffering in the flesh', and he closed with the Twelve Anathemas, statements for Nestorius to anathematise. Unfortunately, these views were seen to be close to those of Apollinarius, a fourth-century heretic. Cyril was therefore criticised by a number of detractors, including Theodoret, Bishop of Cyrrhus. To settle the dispute, the Emperor Theodosius II summoned the Council of Ephesus (431). Nestorius was deposed but argument continued over Cyril's Twelve Anathemas until, in 433, Cyril wrote to John of Antioch accepting the Formula of Reunion, a tactful ambiguous statement of the Antiochene position, and rejoicing in the reconciliation. However, the dispute continued as to whether Cyril's Twelve Anathemas were compatible with the Formula of Reunion. The view that Cyril must have at least tacitly withdrawn his Twelve Anathemas was expressed in a letter to Mari the Persian, attributed to Ibas, Bishop of Edessa.

The question of the nature of Christ was again debated at the Council of Chalcedon in 451 where Christ was acknowledged as one person in two natures 'without confusion, without change, without division, without separation'. The Definition of Faith accepted the Nicene and Constantinopolitan Creeds, the conciliar letters of Cyril (not including his Third Letter to Nestorius) and the Tome of Pope Leo. The omission of the provocative Third Letter made it easier for the council to reinstate Theodoret and Ibas (both condemned at the 499 'Robber' Council of Ephesus) and to pass over Theodore of Mopsuestia.

Following the Council of Chalcedon, a number of different terms are used when discussing the nature of Christ. Those who argued that Christ had one nature became known as the 'monophysites' (from the Greek *monos* (only) plus *physis* (nature)), although this term has been replaced in recent discussions by 'miaphysite' (from the Greek *mia* (one) plus *physis*, the exact opposite of 'dyophysite' – the two-natures formula). The latter term (miaphysite) which still describes the doctrine of the Oriental orthodox churches (including the Copts, Ethiopians, Syrian Orthodox and Armenians) is seen as less pejorative, conveying the meaning that Christ is one nature, possessing divine and human attributes, rather than that he has *only* one nature (Price

2009: 311). Alongside these terms, we refer to those who adhered to the decrees of the Council of Chalcedon as the Chalcedonians, and those who did not as the anti-Chalcedonians or non-Chalcedonians, but as Menze (2008: 2) notes, the latter is the less aggressive, since anti-Chalcedonian implies that they defined themselves and established their church primarily against the council.

In the second half of the fifth century, various attempts were made to bring the two sides together, including Zeno's *Henotikon* in 482. This epistle, masterminded by the patriarch of Constantinople, Acacius, had gone some way to healing the disagreements amongst the eastern sees, but it had provoked a schism with Rome, since the pope could not accept a document which overruled the oecumenical Council of Chalcedon and which had been imposed by imperial edict. Relations had grown worse during the reign of Anastasius, who personally inclined towards miaphysitism, until there was an abrupt change of direction with the accession of Justin (see Chapter 1).

The Theopaschite Formula

The years 519–521 saw the successful healing of the Acacian schism, but the problems arising over how to talk about the divine and human natures of Christ were far from solved. The Scythian monks who were visiting the capital in association with Vitalian argued in favour of the Theopaschite (translated literally as 'God suffered') Formula: 'Christ, one of the Trinity, was incarnate and suffered in the flesh.' Pope Hormisdas rejected the suggestion on the grounds that it was an addition to the Chalcedon Definition rather than because it was heretical. Justinian, at first, supported the pope but quickly changed his mind, adopting the Theopaschite Formula, and attempting to dissuade the pope from insisting on the condemnation of so many key figures in his *libellus* (see Chapter 1; Grillmeier and Hainthaler 1995: II.2, 317–43, Millar 2008: 68–9). The refusal to accept the *libellus* which involved the removal from the diptychs of the key anti-Chalcedonian bishops led to one of the waves of persecution which swept across the east, spearheaded by figures such as the extreme patriarch of Antioch, Paul 'the Jew'. Menze (2008: 67–94) emphasises the importance of the diptychs, the reading out of the names of dead and living persons to be commemorated by the congregation during the liturgy. While churches might normally exclude those who had been excommunicated, significant or well-loved local figures might remain. A requirement to change the names in the diptychs amounted to a public condemnation of individuals and the erasure of the non-Chalcedonian past, which was unacceptable to the miaphysite bishops.

The Conversations of 532

Although Paul's extremism led to his forced resignation, persecutions in the east continued throughout the patriarchate of Euphrasius of Antioch. He burned to death in a vat of boiling wax during the 526 earthquake – a just punishment, according to the miaphysites (Menze 2008: chapter 3). His successor, Ephrem (526–544), carried out an enthusiastic policy of converting or replacing all non-Chalcedonian priests (Hainthaler 2013: II.3, 343–58). John of Tella, with the support of the famous miaphysite patriarch of Antioch, Severus (exiled in 518), began secretly ordaining priests in Syria and such was his success that he came to the notice of the emperor, who invited him to Constantinople in 532 to take part in a three-day event: informal 'conversations' between five Chalcedonian bishops and five or more non-Chalcedonians with a view to affording the latter some 'satisfaction'. Reports survive in a Latin letter by Innocentius, Bishop of Maronia, to the priest Thomas of Thessalonica (Chalcedonian); a short anonymous Syriac document which was a summary of the full (but now incomplete) account; another full (but now incomplete) account, possibly by Severus' biographer, John bar Aphtonia; and the *plerophoria* (doctrinal statement) produced by the Syrian (anti-Chalcedonian) bishops (Pseudo-Zachariah Rhetor IX.15 (**II 48**), with Greatrex 2011: 346, n. 188, Brock 1981). The first day was devoted to Dioscorus, Patriarch of Alexandria (444–451), who had presided over the 'Robber' Council of Ephesus II (449) but been deposed in 451. Although the miaphysites had held him in high honour, they now agreed with the Chalcedonians in admitting that his acceptance of Eutyches (the Constantinopolitan monk who had adopted an extreme miaphysite view) had been in the wrong, while the Chalcedonians admitted that, otherwise, Dioscorus' opinions were 'orthodox'. The second day was devoted to the miaphysites' objections to the Council of Chalcedon, principally Chalcedon's acceptance of Theodoret and Ibas. On the third day, Justinian met with the miaphysites where a relatively amicable exchange took place, the emperor suggesting various concessions 'to achieve the peace of the holy churches'. The miaphysites asked that their opponents 'anathematise those who speak of two natures after the inexplicable union, as well as the Tome of Leo, and what took place at Chalcedon in opposition to the orthodox faith' but did not call for anathemas of particular names 'out of consideration for the accomplishment of universal union' (Brock 1981: 116, anonymous Syriac document, section 5). Justinian suggested that in return for accepting the Tome of Leo and the Council of Chalcedon, but not the dyophysite Definition of Faith, various bishops be anathematised, including Theodore, Theodoret and Ibas. The miaphysite bishops did not accept Justinian's offer, perhaps because the issue of Hormisdas' *libellus* remained, and their leader, Severus, had not been present at the Conversations.

The 530s: The search for a compromise

In 533, in a continued effort to make Chalcedonianism more palatable to its opponents, Justinian published a new 'Edict of Faith' avoiding much of the disputed language and omitting all mention of the Council of Chalcedon (*C.J.* I.1.6, *Chronicon Paschale* 533 (**II 49**) with Whitby and Whitby 1989: 127–30). He sent it to Pope John II for approval, addressing him as the 'head of all the holy churches' but merely asking him to confirm the edict (*Collectio Avellana* 84, 91, *C.J.* I.1.8; see Chapter 3). The pope delayed at first, but in March 534 he agreed the edict and condemned the Chalcedonian Sleepless Monks, who had loyally supported the pope's cause in Constantinople for many years. Justinian incorporated both letters in his *Codex* promulgated in November 534; this synergy between pope and emperor was important timing for both the African and Italian expeditions. At this time (533), he also wrote a similar letter to the patriarch of Constantinople, Epiphanius (*C.J.* I.1.7). He is also credited by some with introducing the 'Only-begotten Son' hymn (a troparion) into the liturgy (although others attribute the composition to Severus; **II 50**).

In 535, Severus, still the effective leader of the miaphysite cause, who had declined Justinian's earlier invitations to the imperial capital, now arrived and took the opportunity to persuade the new patriarch, Anthimus, to support the anti-Chalcedonian cause (Menze 2008: 196–208, Evagrius IV.11, Pseudo-Zachariah Rhetor IX.16, 19–26). At the same time, the newly ordained patriarch of Alexandria, Theodosius, began to ordain miaphysite clergy. Such militant behaviour prompted the resistance of Ephrem of Antioch and the monks of Jerusalem and Syria II who established contact with Pope Agapetus, who, coincidentally, was sent to Constantinople as Theodahad's ambassador. Agapetus had been elected pope in July 535 and, enjoying at least partial support from the senate and good relations with the Goths, he quickly asserted his authority over the western churches and his independence from the emperor. Agapetus supported the African Church's demands against the Arians (*Collectio Avellana* 88) and shortly after Justinian had passed *Novel* 11, which awarded ecclesiastical autonomy to Justiniana Prima, Agapetus reasserted papal authority over the whole province of Illyria. The pope's arrival in Constantinople was marked with an earthquake and the dimming of the sun and moon, and his unexpected death was brought about by a miracle: 'his tongue being eaten away and shredded by his teeth', at least according to the hostile miaphysite source Pseudo-Zachariah Rhetor (IX.19.d–e). He brought about the resignation and condemnation of Anthimus on uncanonical grounds (his illegal transfer from the see of Trapezus) and the appointment of his Chalcedonian successor, Menas (Victor of Tonnena, *Chronicon* 540 – **II 51**). Agapetus also prompted the departure to Egypt of Severus, who died there three years later in 538. In Syria, Ephrem of Antioch, supported by Abraham bar Kaili, the bishop of Amida, unleashed a wave of persecutions which also led to the imprisonment and death of John of Tella. Back in Constantinople, Justinian instructed Anthimus' successor, Menas, to call a synod to investigate the case of Anthimus. The acts of this council were confirmed by Justinian's *Novel* 42 (August 536 – **II 52**).

However, still seeking common ground with the miaphysites, Justinian asked Agapetus to approve the Theopaschite Formula and to condemn the Sleepless Monks. Agapetus reluctantly agreed (*Collectio Avellana* 91) before his sudden death in April 536. A synod held in May–June 536, presided over by Menas and attended by all the western clerics who were present in Constantinople, deposed and condemned Anthimus and repeated the condemnation of Severus and his followers (Grillmeier and Hainthaler 1995: II.2, 351–5, Millar 2008). When the western delegation, leaving behind the deacon Pelagius as an *apocrisarius* to Justinian, returned to bury Agapetus in Rome, they found that the subdeacon Silverius, son of Pope Hormisdas, had already been consecrated. Notwithstanding the Gothic support, Silverius nevertheless welcomed Belisarius and the imperial army to Rome, but he was later arrested by Belisarius on suspicion of treachery with the Goths when the deacon Vigilius arrived from Constantinople with backing from the imperial couple. Vigilius was immediately elected pope. He had let Theodora know that if he were to become pope he would immediately restore Anthimus and, it was rumoured, dismiss the Council of Chalcedon, perhaps encouraged by a bribe (Victor of Tonnena, *Chronicon* 543 – **II 53**). While Rome was under siege there was no communion between emperor and pope but in 540 Vigilius replied to a letter (no longer extant) from Justinian, assuring the emperor he was pleased about his recent military success but urging him to do nothing new in matters of faith or against the see of Rome (*Collectio Avellana* 92). Meanwhile, the fate of the unfortunate Silverius should not be forgotten. Exiled to Patara on the south coast of present-day Turkey, he was supported by the local bishop who argued to Justinian that there were many kings in the world but only one pope. Justinian ordered Silverius to return to Rome but he was swiftly whisked away by Vigilius to Palmaria, a small island in the Tyrrhenian Sea, where he died within the year. Vigilius' rise to power demonstrated that closeness to the imperial power had become important for progressing a career even in the western Church and this was therefore a sign of the expansion of Justinian's power geographically and in church matters.

Meanwhile, while Egypt had escaped the persecutions against the miaphysites so evident in Syria, another issue arose. It stemmed from a disagreement between Severus and Julian of Halicarnassus over whether Christ's human body was subject to corruption (Severus) or not (Julian). From the Greek 'aphthartos' (uncorrupted), the followers of Julian were known as the 'aphthartodocetae' or the 'phantasiasts', as referred to by their opponents. The disagreement escalated into a major schism (Pseudo-Zachariah Rhetor IX.9–13, with Greatrex 2011: 332–43). Theodosius' Julianist successor, Gaianus, was deposed and Theodosius reinstalled, but as he could only hold his position with the help of the imperial army (an army led by Narses was despatched by Theodora), Justinian forced him to resign and summoned him to Constantinople (Grillmeier and Hainthaler 1996: II.4, 53–9). Theodosius was succeeded by Paul the Tabennesiote. He was the first Chalcedonian to be patriarch of Alexandria in half a century and with wise foresight was consecrated in Constantinople before setting out, but even so he lasted only a couple of years before being replaced by the Palestinian monk Zoilus (Hardy 1968, MacCoull 1995, Grillmeier and Hainthaler 1996: II.4, 60–87). From this point, there would be two patriarchs: a Chalcedonian (known as a 'Melchite', a Semitic word meaning 'royal' and thus referring to the clerics who followed Justinian) incumbent in Alexandria, and an anti-Chalcedonian patriarch living in exile in the desert.

The Three Chapters Controversy

Pursuing his policy of making Chalcedon more palatable to its opponents, Justinian sought to rid the council of the taint of Nestorianism implied by the exoneration of Theodore of Mopsuestia, Theodoret and Ibas. Encouraged by his advisor, Theodore Ascidas, Bishop of Caesarea, in late 544/early 545 Justinian issued a decree (of which only fragments remain) condemning the Three Chapters (*In damnationem trium capitulorum*), that is, the person and work of Theodore of Mopsuestia, Theodoret of Cyrrhus' writings against Cyril, and Ibas' letter to Mari the Persian (Grillmeier and Hainthaler 1995: II.2, 421–2). In justification, some ingenious argumentation was used. That Theodore had died in the faith was conveniently undermined by the fact that even in Mopsuestia he had been replaced in the diptychs by Cyril. To condemn Ibas, Justinian claimed that Chalcedon had only exonerated the bishop after he had changed his mind, and that the letter in question was another letter.

This decree followed Justinian's 543 edict in which he condemned Origenism (Grillmeier and Hainthaler 1995: II.2, 385–402). In the *Life of St Sabas* (83–90), Cyril of Scythopolis provides the evidence for the disputes between the Origenists and their opponents in Palestine (Evagrius IV.38 (**II 54**) with Whitby 2000: 243–4, n. 119). So severe was the situation that the patriarchs of Antioch and Jerusalem appealed to Justinian who was pleased to help, seeing an easy way to win favour (Cyril of Scythopolis, *Life of St Sabas* 85 – **II 55**). There has been some attempt to link this earlier edict to Justinian's edict against the Three Chapters but it is unclear that this was the case. In his letter to the Council of 553, Justinian claims that he sought to counter a resurgence in Nestorianism, although again the evidence that there was a resurgence at this time is unclear. It is worth spelling out Justinian's strategy here and explaining why he thought that condemning the Three Chapters would heal the rift between Chalcedonians and non-Chalcedonians. If the former would agree to condemning the Three Chapters then the latter would find it less easy to accuse them of Nestorianism and may be persuaded to join them. However, it would be easy for non-Chalcedonians to argue that the condemnation of the Three Chapters was a tacit admission that the Council of Chalcedon was flawed and was therefore not to be subscribed to. From the unsuccessful outcome of the 532 Conversations, it must have been obvious to Justinian that the miaphysites would be unlikely to accept Chalcedon, and thus a number of scholars (Schwartz 1940, Uthemann 2006, Meier 2003a: 285 and 2004a: 88) have questioned whether winning over the miaphysites could have been the emperor's aim. Price (2009: 16–23) suggests that Justinian's aim was now more modest: rather than accepting Chalcedon, he only hoped that the miaphysites might make their peace with the imperial church, thus preventing the formation of a rival church, made more likely by the successful efforts of ordination by Jacob Baradaeus.

Justinian's policy was resisted in the west, especially in North Africa (see Chapter 2), and he sought secret assurance from Pope Vigilius that he himself would condemn the Three Chapters and would help obtain the agreement of the western churches. In Constantinople, the *apocrisarius*, the deacon Stephen, warned Justinian and Menas that Rome could not accept the condemnation of two bishops who had been exonerated by Chalcedon. Menas reluctantly signed the decree with the caveat that his signature would not be confirmed until he had heard the opinion of the pope. Ephrem of Antioch and Zoilus of Alexandria signed but explained privately that they had done so under duress. Peter of Jerusalem signed but protested publicly. For his part, Vigilius declined to make an official statement and did not break off relations with the east. In November 545, imperial soldiers escorted Vigilius from Rome and, after delaying for a year in Sicily, conveyed him to Constantinople. While the western sources are clear that this was a hostile move on the part of Justinian, who wished to put pressure on Vigilius to agree to the condemnation of the Three Chapters, a more charitable explanation suggests that he was removed to safety before the imminent onset of the Goths. Justinian at least gave the semblance of deference to the pope, coming down to the harbour to greet the arrival of his ship.

Vigilius nevertheless took a firm line in breaking off communion with Menas who naturally reciprocated, resulting in a six-month rift which was only healed in June 547 (Theophanes AM 6039 attributes the reconciliation to the efforts of Theodora). It was probably at this time that the pope signed two secret declarations which he gave to Justinian and Theodora which were later read out in the council. He convened about seventy bishops, mostly westerners, to a synod. In the third session, Facundus of Hermiane embarrassingly produced proof that the letter of Ibas approved by Chalcedon was indeed the very same letter that Justinian had condemned (thus ignoring Justinian's ingenious argument). Backed by imperial agents who were there to coerce and bribe the participants, Vigilius hastily brought the synod to a close, declaring that the vote would be taken at a future date. Later, in 548, he composed the *Iudicatum*, in which he condemned the Three Chapters without implying criticism of Chalcedon. No longer extant, the *Iudicatum* was quoted during the 553 Council.

Unequivocal western opposition was immediately evident in the bishop of Dacia's deposition of Benenatus, the archbishop of Justiniana

Prima, and the actions of the African churchmen Ferrandus and Facundus (see Chapter 3). Justinian responded by not accepting the deposition of Benenatus, and by deposing the bishop of Carthage, Reparatus. He also removed Zoilus of Alexandria and replaced him with the more amenable Apollinaris.

Vigilius, succumbing to pressure, requested Justinian to return his *Iudicatum*, but on 15 August 550, the pope took a secret oath promising that he would do what he could to bring about the condemnation of the Three Chapters, and to inform against anyone who attempted to persuade him to oppose Justinian.

Council of Constantinople 553

In 551, Justinian issued another edict, *On the Orthodox [or True] Faith* (**II 56**). He included the notions of the Word as the subject of his own suffering 'in the flesh'; the one Christ 'composed' of two natures, different in nature, but united by hypostasis (hypostasis unity); and 'one incarnate nature of the Word of God' meaning 'one incarnate hypostasis or person'. All were supported by texts from Cyril and other Fathers. He concentrated on what had become one of the key issues, the propriety of posthumous anathema. For the first time, he added a full and positive exposition of the doctrine on Christ. The edict closed with thirteen anathemas, ten supporting this teaching, and three condemning the Three Chapters (for the text and commentary, Price 2009: 122–59, Grillmeier and Hainthaler 1995: II.2, 425–9). It is striking that while arguing that the duality of Christ's natures must be recognised, the emphasis is on their unity and the new formula, 'one composite hypostasis', is used. This phrase is clearly reminiscent of the 'one incarnate hypostasis' which appeared in Cyril's Third Letter to Nestorius, and it would also appear in the Eighth Session of the 553 Council. This alignment of Cyril's Third Letter and the council was the work of Justinian and a group of theologians, including Ephrem of Antioch, and advocated by the Scythian monks who had arrived in Constantinople at the beginning of Justin's reign. The doctrine was termed 'neo-Chalcedonianism' (Gray 1979: chapter 6, Grillmeier and Hainthaler 1995, Uthemann 1999) and it is clear that Justinian's *Edict on the Orthodox Faith* and the canons of the 553 Council are both neo-Chalcedonian, thus strengthening Price's argument that Justinian's purpose was not to introduce a new Christology but merely to clarify the Definition of Faith agreed at the Council of Chalcedon in 451.

Justinian had promised Vigilius that he would make no further moves until a council had been held, but in the early 550s fresh negotiations took place with the miaphysites. In what would be the last attempt to unite the Christians of the east, the emperor invited the Syrian miaphysites to Constantinople; they remained there for a year before agreeing that they could not agree. There was also some communication with John Philoponus, the Alexandrian miaphysite philosopher and lay theologian, who responded critically to the emperor's edict and refused an invitation to the capital, instead writing a letter to Justinian (Lang 2005).

In response to Justinian's action, Vigilius deposed Theodore Ascidas and excommunicated Menas and all who accepted the new edict, and prudently took refuge in the Church of St Peter. Imperial soldiers were unable to force him from the church but eventually he agreed to return when persuaded by a deputation consisting of Belisarius, Cethegus (leader of the senate in Rome), Peter the Patrician, and Justinian's nephew, Justin. However, in December 551, he sought refuge again, this time – significantly – in the Church of St Euphemia in Chalcedon where the council had taken place exactly 100 years earlier. Here, he published his document of excommunication which he had held off circulating. Those excommunicated requested Justinian's last edict to be withdrawn and condemned the violence against the pope; in June 552, emperor and pope affected a reconciliation.

Between June 552 and January 553, Justinian and Vigilius agreed to call a council to settle the controversy (Grillmeier and Hainthaler 1995: II.2, 438–62). Vigilius was disappointed that his suggestion that the council be held in Sicily, where equal representation of eastern and western bishops may have been more likely, was not agreed. The biographer of Eutychius (Menas' successor who had carefully been selected by Justinian for his reliability) represented the council as a 'new Pentecost'; bishops came from every nation to Constantinople, which was described as the new Jerusalem, although, as predicted by Vigilius, few from the west were able to attend. Of the 170 bishops who gathered in Constantinople, only thirty-one came from the west; 152 actually attended the council, while the remaining eighteen met separately with Vigilius, who declined to attend.

Whilst waiting for Vigilius, Justinian arranged for the bishops to approve a fresh condemnation of Origenism (Evagrius IV.38, with Whitby 2000: 248–9, Grillmeier and Hainthaler 1995: II.2, 402–10, Hainthaler 2013: II.3, 75–82). The emperor did not attend the council himself, giving the illusion that the bishops were free to reach their own decisions, but he did send a letter to be read out at the first session, and all the sessions consequently lack spontaneity. Vigilius still hesitated to attend, and finally wrote the *Constitutum* which was presented to Justinian on 25 May after the council had already met six times. The emperor refused to read it and sent it directly to the council. The quaestor, Constantine, told the council that Justinian had evidence that the pope had already agreed to condemn the Three Chapters, showing as proof the secret declarations of the late 540s, one in the pope's own handwriting and one with his signature. The council duly condemned the pope and the Three Chapters, while affirming the Council of Chalcedon and accepting Cyril's formula: 'one nature incarnate of God the Word'. The first Latin acts of the council naturally included the condemnation of the pope, although Justinian advised that the council must keep union with Rome as Vigilius' 'sulky dithering' must not be allowed to negate the unity of the churches. For Justinian, it must have been a major blow that the very essence of his oecumenical council had been marred by Vigilius' absence. However, he must have been delighted when Vigilius, citing the example of St Augustine's *Book of Retractions*, changed his mind once more, asking for Eutychius to be restored to communion in time to celebrate Christmas mass together. In 554, Vigilius published a new *Iudicatum* condemning the Three Chapters and their defenders including his own deacon Pelagius, now under arrest in a monastery. A second version of the council acts was duly produced recording papal approval, and having wrung affirmation for this doctrine from the pope, Justinian at last allowed Vigilius to return to Italy. He died in Sicily en route to Rome and he is the only pope not to be buried within St Peter's.

In a somewhat surprising move, Justinian promoted the election of Pelagius as pope, responsible for his own pamphlet defending the Three Chapters, perhaps because of his capabilities; it is assumed that they came to an understanding. He duly condemned the Three Chapters and departed for Italy, being consecrated pope in April 556, again with unusual imperial involvement, though the lack of bishops in the vicinity in the aftermath of the war was no doubt significant. However, Pelagius experienced difficulties, caught as he was between the hostile African, Illyrian and Italian bishops and the emperor to whom he owed his appointment. Eventually, he distanced himself from Justinian and his council. In 556, he issued a Profession of Faith in which he accepted only the first four oecumenical councils, and affirmed the orthodoxy of Ibas and Theodoret. With this document, he was able to win over the majority of western clergy, except in northern Italy where the schism with Milan continued until 573 and with Aquileia until the seventh century. Although there was still communication between Rome and Constantinople (Pope John III sent a Profession of Faith to Justinian in 561, and as late as 578 and 580 requests for military help against the Lombards were sent to Constantinople), the popes avoided any discussion of Christology with the emperor in the forty years following Pelagius' election as a way of reassuring hostile western sees (Markus and Sotinel 2007, Straw 2007). However, as Price (2009) argues, Justinian's policy had been successful. The African opposition had collapsed and Vigilius' eventual capitulation had led to the loyalty of the popes from Pelagius to Gregory the Great, leaving aside the local Istrian schism with Aquileia.

After the 553 Council

Justinian continued to seek a solution (in the east) after the 553 Council. In 561, there was a meeting with a number of east Syrian theologians, attended by Paul, the bishop of Nisibis, who was sent to take part by the Persian king, Chosroes. A short extract of the meeting has been preserved, revealing that Justinian was still clearly concerned to negotiate with clerics who held strongly Nestorian views (Guillaumont 1969–70, 1970). In 564/565, he produced an edict on the incorruptibility of Christ's body, influenced by the views of Julian, but still seeking to describe the union of the natures in Christ in a way which would be acceptable to the majority of the non-Chalcedonians. Evagrius observed that Justinian, 'after turning aside from the correct highway of doctrine and walking a path untrodden by the Apostles and Fathers, fell among thorns and prickles' (**II 57**). The Patriarch Eutychius was deposed in January 565, and in Antioch the Patriarch Anastasius, having opposed Justinian, prepared to accept the inevitable sentence of banishment, but was spared by the emperor's death (Evagrius IV.40, Grillmeier and Hainthaler 1995: II.2, 467–73). However, further divisions were caused by the Tritheists (believers in three Gods) who accepted the argument that each person of the Trinity possessed his own individual substance (ousia) and nature (physis). The idea was championed by John Philoponus and led to the schism between Alexandria and Antioch (Grillmeier and Hainthaler 1996: II.4, 107–46, Lang 2005, Hainthaler 2013: II.3, 268–80).

A sincere theologian or pragmatic statesman?

Whether Justinian's drive to eradicate alternative systems and to bring unity to the Church based on a single orthodoxy defined by the oecumenical councils was born out of pragmatism or sincere theological belief, and his competence in these Christological matters, has been much discussed. He is regarded variously as a dilettante (Schwartz 1940), sincere (Anastos 1951), a genuine theologian (Uthemann 1999, Meier 2003a), a politician who merely co-ordinated and endorsed the theological works written by his staff (Gray 1989), and a statesman who was concerned to ensure the co-operation of Constantinople and the pope for his western campaigns (Gray 2005, Markus and Sotinel 2007). It is indisputable that he produced a large corpus of theological writings, the first emperor since Julian to publish works expressing his own convictions, but did this stem from his personal faith or from a concern to unite his subjects in the same faith? Menze (2008: 252) suggests that Justinian had become a 'connoisseur of Christian discourses' over the years but was willing to change his mind (for example, over the Theopaschite Formula) for political expediency. Leppin's 2011 monograph (*Justinian*), which carries the subtitle *Das Christliche Experiment* (*The Christian Experiment*), as might be expected, ascribes to Justinian a commitment to the true faith which was central to his rule. He argues that a concern for religion, fear of God and anxiety to put his realm in order was more understandable in the context of the sixth century than that of the twenty-first, and drove Justinian's policies rather than politics. Leppin (and Meier) argue that Justinian responded to contingent circumstances (for example, the disasters of 540–542) with religious measures, hoping that once again God would favour his military and political enterprises. Moorhead (1994) argues that although Justinian was concerned for correct doctrine as important for the state, he was also a devout and sincere believer who took steps against the pagans and other heretics, insisted that the canons of the oecumenical councils of the Church were to be considered as laws of the empire, and wrote his own works. In Moorhead's view, the difficult constraints of governing the empire, which involved not upsetting intransigent Egypt, which provided Constantinople's grain supply, the west at the time of reconquest, and the important Chalcedonian circles in Constantinople, partly justified his actions in appointing pliable figures, kidnapping and bullying the pope, and calling an oecumenical council.

The question as to whether a solely religious problem (the nature of Christ) could have cultural, ethnic and even political ramifications is an important one. With miaphysitism so firmly established in Syria and Egypt, religious discontent might easily turn to political separation (although there is no real evidence that it did), hence Justinian's care not to alienate his miaphysite provincials (Van Rompay 2005). Browning (1987: 143) also draws attention to the delicate balance of successful governance which required skill and patience which, he argues, wore out as Justinian grew older. Frend (1972) takes the view that any attempt both to gain miaphysite agreement and to please the west was a hopeless policy. He follows Procopius (*Secret History* 18) in judging that Justinian sacrificed the east, allowed the Balkans to be overrun, and became a fanatical opponent to individuals who did not agree with him. And in believing that Justinian (like Justin) prioritised the west he is joined by Meyendorff (1989: chapter 7). Price (2009: 7), however, argues against attaching too much significance to the Illyrian background of uncle and nephew, or indeed to a master plan of Justinian to reconquer the west. He argues instead that the *Henotikon* had failed to unite the eastern churches (as well as aggravating the west) so it was not surprising that Justin and Justinian should try the restoration of Chalcedonianism in an effort to bring unity, and that this policy should not be seen as a sacrifice of the east. Price also argues that Justinian was sincere in his attempt to win over the miaphysites, not because he feared a rebellion but because his sense of duty to God motivated him to work for a reconciliation, even at the risk of upsetting the western Church at a time when the military situation was so dangerous.

That Justinian's goals and methods changed throughout his long reign is hardly surprising, but whether these adjustments were forced upon him as a result of his abrupt change of fortune after 540 (Meier 2003a and 2004a) or were a slower and more continuous process following the ebb and flow of events in his reign is also debated. Leppin (2011) argues that while he was a supporter of Chalcedon, he was willing to make overtures to the miaphysites at certain times, such as in 532, the mid-540s and the early 560s (his devotion to aphthartodocetism was part of the effort to achieve this rapprochement), while the 530s saw a hardening towards the miaphysites culminating in the Council of 536, whose decisions triggered a wave of persecutions. Others (Frend 1972: 255) see the policy changes as less a sensitive reaction to current circumstances and more a 'zigzag policy of Justinian towards the monophysites'. Meyendorff (1989: 246) notes that this 'zig zag' policy had (apart from his support of aphthartodocetism) been only in policy, and not belief. Price (2009: 16), following Meier (2003a, 2004a), stresses the sudden reversals in the 540s which Justinian must have felt were the evidence of divine anger for which he was responsible. Price argues that Justinian, a victim of the plague, might have thought that he had been spared for a reason and that the unification of the Church was that reason. Price also tracks the change in policy from the mid-540s to the 550s. At first, Justinian had worked to restore peace within the divided eastern churches by targeting the already discredited Nestorians with his edict condemning the Three Chapters which bypassed Chalcedon. However, by the time of the council in 553, his priority lay with relations with the Latin west which disapproved of the condemnation of the Three Chapters since it implied the undermining of Chalcedon. Condemnation of the Three Chapters and adherence to Chalcedon were the goals of the council, and an oecumenical council would discourage disagreement from the west.

'Caesaropapism'

It is commonly argued that as time passed and the divisions within the Church continued, Justinian became increasingly autocratic in trying to impose a solution. The extent to which he, as emperor, might legitimately direct affairs of the Church is another important debate and stems from the fact that there was no consensus of an emperor's role in ecclesiastical matters (Sotinel 2005). We are reminded of the close association between Constantine and Christianity, and that therefore the 'particular relationship between the eastern churches and the emperor was not the result of some usurpation of ecclesiastical power by the secular state' (Herrin 1987: 116–19). Justinian could argue that he was responsible for ensuring the correct views of all his subjects, and that his interventions were mere clarifications of some confusing points in the Definition of Faith which had already been agreed. Browning (1987: 142) commends Justinian for not using force, but it is clear that there were some persecutions, and as Gray (2005) argues, Justinian reshaped the imperial role with vigour in desperation to keep the Church united. It is certainly true that Justinian assumed the role of pope-maker and could make or break the powerful eastern patriarchs. He appointed both Vigilius and Pelagius, having deposed Silverius to make way for the latter. He ensured that the patriarchs of Constantinople were loyal to him, deposing Anthimus and appointing Menas and Eutychius. He controlled the seat of Alexandria, recalling Theodosius, and later appointing Paul the Tabennesiote, and then Apollinaris while the previous incumbent Zoilus was still alive. Vigilius protested, conveniently forgetting that he himself had benefited from such high-handed interference by the emperor in church appointments. Other imperial appointments included Primosus of Carthage (installed after the sacking of Reparatus), Vitalis of Milan in 552, and Maximianus, appointed bishop of Ravenna while still in Constantinople.

Price (2009: 36–41) supports Justinian's enhanced role, citing the *Tractatus de Concilio* of Cardinal Jacobatius, prepared for the Council of Trent in 1545 and which argued for a role for the emperor: if the pope himself were to be suspected of heresy, it would be for the emperor to demand from him a statement of faith. With Dagron (2003: 282–312), Price sees the church-state opposition as unhelpful, and in particular the term 'caesaropapism', an eighteenth-century Catholic term which assumes that the Church be run by the pope, not the emperor. Price cautions against mistaking the role of the late Roman emperor in the religious life of the state with the model of early emperors who held the title *pontifex maximus*. Emperors to whom God entrusted earthly affairs must be more significant than mere laymen (Agapetus, *Advice to the Emperor Justinian* 1 - **II 58**).

Justinian could be said to be breaking new ground in three key areas: legislation, church building (discussed in Chapters 5 and 6) and missionary activity. Many (Dvornik 1966, Meyendorff 1968, 1989, Frend 1972) see Justinian as taking the emperor's right to legislate on church matters a step further than previous emperors with his detailed legislation. Anastos notes the significance in Justinian making his various edicts laws (the title of Anastos' 1964 (reprinted 1979) article, 'Justinian's despotic control over the Church', gives a flavour of the author's argument). It is significant that Justinian devoted the first title of the first book of the *Codex Justinianus* (I.1.1–8) to a detailed summary of his theological position: 'Concerning the High Trinity and the Catholic Faith and that no one should dare to contend it publicly' (*de summa trinitate et de fide catholica et ut nemo de ea publice contendere audeat*). Justinian legislated on church matters in a number of his *Novels* (Millar 2008: 168 conveniently provides a complete list). *Novel* 6, addressed to the patriarch, Epiphanius, in Constantinople in 535, rules on the marital status of the clergy, church property and ordination (Meyendorff 1989: 208–10). *Novel* 115 notes that a just cause of disinheritance would be heretical beliefs (including Nestorianism) and *Novel* 131 (**II 59**) concerns ecclesiastical titles and privileges, and its first chapter endorsed four church councils, the condemnation of Nestorianism at Ephesus and anathematisation at Chalcedon. These laws had been drafted by Junillus who served as Justinian's quaestor from 542 to c. 549, following the death of his more famous successor,

Tribonian. Junillus was also responsible for the *Instituta Regularia Divinae Legis* (*Handbook of the Basic Principles of Divine Law*) which was completely in tune with Justinian's Christology and nicely illustrates, as highlighted by Maas (1996, 2003), the increased influence of divine authority on Roman law by Justinian. Several scholars (Gray 2005, Millar 2008) have noted the co-ordination between Justinian's goals with regard to the law codes, the reunification of the Church, and the reconquest of the west which is frequently alluded to in his legislation.

Justinian was the first emperor to make missionary activity a matter of policy. As we have already seen (Chapters 1, 2, 3), the early years of his reign saw a number of politically motivated conversions of client kings: Abasgi (Procopius, *Wars* VIII.3.18–21, Evagrius IV.22); Grepes, king of the Heruls (Procopius, *Wars* VI.14.28–36, Evagrius IV.20, Pseudo-Dionysius of Tel-Mahre 844 – **II 60**; Sarantis 2016: 46–8); Hunnish Grod (Pseudo-Dionysius of Tel-Mahre 845 – **II 61**; Sarantis 2016: 33–4); Tzani (Engelhardt 1974, Moorhead 1994: 141–3); Ḥimyarites (Pseudo-Dionysius 846). Later in his reign, at the request of the Arab phylarch, Harith, Theodora allowed the deposed patriarch of Alexandria to consecrate two bishops for the miaphysites living under Ghassānid rule. The two individuals were Theodore (referred to as the bishop of Bostra), who was to serve in the south, and Jacob Baradaeus, who was to serve in the north. Jacob was consecrated bishop of Edessa but, dressed as a beggar to allude detection, worked enthusiastically throughout Syria, Egypt and Asia Minor as an itinerant bishop; a list of bishops preserved by John of Ephesus (553–566) mentions twenty-seven bishops consecrated by Jacob, in addition to thousands of priests and deacons (Bundy 1978). The results of Jacob's efforts were to have far-reaching consequences for the later history of the miaphysite Church (see below). The imperial couple responded on another occasion to a call for assistance from the bishop of the island of Philae, where Justinian had recently demolished, according to Procopius, the Temple of Isis (see Chapters 2 and 6; Dijkstra 2008: 271–304). We have already referred to the report of John of Ephesus (3.4.6) (**II 22**) that Theodora wrote to the *dux* of the Thebaid with instructions that he should ensure her miaphysite delegation reach the Nobatae before her husband's Chalcedonian envoys. The seriousness of the competition between emperor and empress on this occasion has been debated (Menze 2008: 222 provides a useful summary and recent bibliography) but the general aim in ending the Nubian incursions of Roman Egypt is not in doubt (Grillmeier and Hainthaler 1996: II.4, 267–71). On a rather different scale, Mîrşanu (2008) argues that the Arianism of the barbarians (especially in Africa) was a cogent factor in Justinian's decision to go to war. He can refer to Cyril's account of Sabas' mission to Justinian to ask for various favours which he encourages the emperor to grant by suggesting that God will give him victory over the Goths, Visigoths, Vandals and Gepids, who were all Arians (**II 32**; see Chapter 3).

Finally, it is worth adding a particular note on the efforts of John of Ephesus: miaphysite monk, missionary, church leader, and writer of two works, an *Ecclesiastical History* and the *Lives of the Eastern Saints* (Harvey 1990, Menze 2008: 254–65). Whilst he was in the capital in 542, Justinian enigmatically chose him to lead a campaign of conversion amongst the pagans and heretics still flourishing in Asia Minor; again, the emperor's decision to appoint a miaphysite to this role has caused much puzzlement. John converted tens of thousands of pagans and schismatics and received government aid to found almost 100 churches and twelve monasteries (Trombley 1985, Whitby 1991).

Theodora

The empress' role in the religious policy of the empire has also been the subject of animated debate (see Chapter 1). Theodora's personal miaphysite convictions and open promotion of the miaphysite cause were well known. She housed up to 500 miaphysite bishops in her palace, built a refuge on Chios for banished miaphysite clergy, and gave refuge to a further 300 at a fortress in Thrace. As we have heard, she also engaged in missionary activity which, appearing to run contrary to her husband's support for the Chalcedonian cause, has raised questions about the overall imperial policy. Was Justinian powerless to prevent his wife's support of the miaphysites (Schwartz 1940, Frend 1972), or was it a clever ploy to allow a channel of communication to remain open (Foss 2002, Evans 2002: 72–84)? Even contemporaries seemed uncertain (Procopius, *Secret History* 10.14–15, Evagrius IV.10 – **II 63**, Pseudo-Zachariah Rhetor IX.19a) and John of Ephesus tells us that Justinian continued to show concern for the welfare of the miaphysite community, especially in Constantinople, even after Theodora's death (*Lives* 57); by patronising the miaphysites, Justinian could better understand their position, and give all his subjects the impression he was taking their concerns seriously. More recent assessments have been rather calmer: Leppin (2000) considers that Theodora's actions were not so out of the ordinary for an empress and that she was rather more balanced in her favours than was usually reported, honouring the

Chalcedonian Sabas, and looking after the poor in the city, regardless of their doctrinal persuasion; Menze (2008: 208–29) sees no evidence for a lifelong adherence to miaphysitism, saying she protected (rather than promoted) non-Chalcedonians from the mid-530s. As we saw in Chapter 1, Croke (2006) even diminishes her role in providing for the miaphysites housed in the palace of Hormisdas, attributing the Church of SS Sergius and Bacchus – often ascribed to Theodora – to Justinian, as an early response to Anicia Juliana's St Polyeuktos.

Success and legacy

Many view the Three Chapters Controversy and the 553 Council in a negative light as a long-running and confusing theme of Justinian's rule at times influenced by his military and political goals. In Gray's view (2005), the Three Chapters Controversy led to an oecumenical council, the humiliation and condemnation of a pope, the rewriting of history, the modern west's detestation of Justinian, and caesaropapism. Frend (1972) and Van Rompay (2005) suggest that Justinian's failure to heal the rift with the miaphysites led to the formation in the east of a separate Jacobite and Coptic Church. Markus and Sotinel (2007) point to the negative effect of Justinian's intervention on the political and religious history of early medieval western Europe and North Africa. The attitude of the western bishops (except, for example, the bishop of Ravenna who had been appointed by Justinian) may be summed up by Bishop Nicetius of Trier, who wrote to Justinian informing him that all Italy, Africa, Spain and Gaul grieved over him and anathematised him and asked: 'oh sweet Justinian of ours, who has deceived you?' (*Monumenta Germaniae Historica Epistolae* 3.118f, Moorhead 1994: 139–40).

However, contrary to the negative views of both Justinian's decrees and methods, Price argues that the theology of the 553 Council was positive and that its contribution to Christian unity was relatively successful. He argues that the aim of the Three Chapters Controversy and the 553 Council was not to win over the miaphysites. The condemnation of deceased Church Fathers whom Chalcedon had chosen not to condemn only drew attention to the blunders of the council. The aim was, in fact, to demonstrate that the imperial church was not Nestorian and that therefore the miaphysites had no reason for entering into permanent schism and setting up their own church. As we know, Justinian failed in this endeavour but it was the Muslim conquests of the seventh century which prevented the prospect of a united church (Price 2009: 35).

5

Governing the Empire

Justinian's governance of the empire embraces many aspects: finance and tax; social reform; administration of the provinces; the role of the city and its institutions; building programmes; and religious policy. He also had to deal with specific problems such as the *Nika* riot in 532 (see Chapter 1) and the plague during the 540s (discussed below). All of the actions taken by Justinian, whether long-term policies or short-term fixes, reveal the imperial ideology which underlay his reign, in particular, as we saw most clearly in the last chapter, his belief that he ruled by divine right, as God's representative on earth (Maas 1986, Dvornik 1966, Dagron 2003, Bell 2013).

Codification of the laws

We begin with the cornerstone of Justinian's reforms: the codification of the laws (*Corpus Juris Civilis*), a project which would be instrumental in the development of laws in many European countries and elsewhere, for many centuries. It was a lasting achievement.

Legislative activity lay at the very heart of Justinian's view of what it was to be the emperor, and from his laws emerge so many issues which are key to understanding his character and actions. The laws may have been penned by Tribonian (and others) but they were certainly written to reflect Justinian's personal beliefs and aims, and they are inextricably bound up with his military, religious and other policies, both as vehicles for putting them into effect and for revealing his own personal views. In the preface to *Novel* 1 (535), Justinian represents himself as a busy emperor, looking after the affairs of his people, despite the demands of his foreign policy:

> We are occupied with the concerns of the whole state, and do not choose to consider any small matter, but rather how long the Persians may

remain quiet, how long the Vandals, with the Moors, may be compliant, how long the Carthaginians may retain the ancient liberties which they have regained, how long the Tzani, now recently under the Roman state, may remain among our subjects ... There are also private worries pouring in as continually reported by our subjects, for each of which we give a suitable response.

The codification of the laws was one of Justinian's earliest and most momentous acts. He was not the first Roman emperor to attempt to impose order on the mass of laws, rescripts and commentaries which had been accumulating over the centuries; a hundred years before, in 438, the Theodosian Code had been published by Theodosius II, with the instruction that there should be no further laws promulgated, or further interpolations. Justinian's initiative was more ambitious and he aimed to provide a compilation of all imperial enactments from the Codes of Gregorius, Hermogenes and Theodosius, and those enacted since:

We have therefore taken thought that this *Code*, to last forever, should come to the knowledge of your tribunal, so that all litigants and the most eloquent lawyers may know that they will not be permitted in lawsuits to cite constitutions taken from the three old Codes ... but it is necessary for them in the future to cite only constitutions included in Our *Code*.

With these words in a letter to the praetorian prefect of the east, Menas, on 7/8 April 529, Justinian promulgated the *novus codex* (*Constitutio Summa*) which came into force on 16 April. However, as he continued to pass new laws, another edition of the *Code* (*Codex Repetitae Praelectionis*) was published on 16 November 534, by means of a letter to the senate (*Constitutio Cordi*) which came into effect on 29 December 534. It is this second version which we possess today, although we do have two fragmentary papyri from Egypt dating from 529 to 534 (Corcoran 2008, 2009, 2016). Book one of Justinian's *Code* concerned religious matters, books two to eight concerned civil law, book nine criminal law, and books ten to twelve imperial administration, especially taxation and civic duties.

Related projects included the *Fifty Decisions* (*Quinquaginta Decisiones*), promulgated in batches between summer 530 and spring 531; the *Digest* (or *Pandects* as they are known in Greek) promulgated by Justinian on 16 December 533, a summary of the works of the Roman jurists in fifty books (*Constitutio Deo Auctore* = C.J. I.17.1

and *Constitutio Tanta* = *C.J.* I.17.2); and the *Institutes* (*Institutiones*), an elementary textbook on the model of the work by the classical jurist Gaius. The *Institutes* were published with the *Constitutio Imperatoriam Maiestatem* on 21 November 533, and, although a basic introduction to Roman law, were endowed with the force of law (**II 64**; Birks and McLeod 1987, Metzger 1998). At the same time, the legal studies course at the two major centres of law, Constantinople and Beirut, was lengthened from four to five years and the curriculum laid down by imperial edict, designed around Justinian's *Institutes*, the *Digest* and the *Code*. The freshers taking the course (*dupondii*) were now called 'new Justinians' (*Iustiniani novi*).

The driving force behind all this flourishing legislative activity was Tribonian, whose energy and vision have been highlighted by Honoré in several works (for example, 1978, 2010). Tribonian held the position of *quaestor sacri palatii* from 529 to 542, with a brief break as a sop to his detractors following the *Nika* riot, although Justinian still awarded him an honorary consulship in 533. He is praised for his elegance and erudition in the constitutions (although he himself may well have been the author of these works) by Justinian, as well as by John the Lydian and Procopius, although the latter also accuses him of sycophancy and greed. He died in the early 540s, possibly of the plague.

In the years from 529 to 534, Justinian added new constitutions (*novellae constitutiones*) which were incorporated into the second edition of the *Code*, but from 535 he issued new laws, known as *Novels* (Miller and Sarris 2018). Today, the collection of *Novels* we have is not the result of any formal codification made by Justinian, but it is made up of private collections put together at different times, the core of which is the so-called 'Greek collection of 168 *Novels*' (thirteen of which are in Latin) which include four laws of Justin II and three of Tiberius (Kearley 2010). The fullest and earliest manuscript is the twelfth-century *Codex Marcianus Graecus* 179 which also preserves a further thirteen edicts, including the important Edict 13 dealing with the administration of Egypt. Two significant points follow. First, these laws (unlike those in the *Code*) retain their prefaces which tell us so much about the context of their promulgation. Second, the collecting of *Novels* at different times had different purposes. For instance, the group of 168 *Novels* was compiled to convey a golden age of activity under Justinian, an emperor who restored order and unity, and the compiler was an admirer of the Emperor Tiberius who continued Justinian's policies after the disastrous interruption by Justin II (Miller and Sarris 2018: 14–26). As a result, we do not know what we are missing from the totality of what was originally enacted, an issue which is especially problematic for later laws, and edicts.

Apart from the *Novels* destined for Illyricum, Africa or Italy, or those addressed to officials in Constantinople, which were written in Latin, the *Novels* were mostly composed in Greek in order that they be clearly understood. This shift in use of language may be dated to c. 535 at the instigation of John the Cappadocian, although he may have merely been following the trend as Greek replaced Latin as the language of the state. Even those in Greek usually have an introductory address and were signed off and dated in Latin. On the other hand, Latin translations were also produced to help non-Greek-speaking students, just as Greek translations had been produced of the *Code*.

Below, we will explore further the ideology behind Justinian's legislation, expressed in the titles he awards himself and the prefaces to the *Novels*, and the content of the laws themselves which shed light on the economy and administration of the empire in the sixth century.

The nature and logistics of the laws: Imperial titles, prefaces and audiences

The titles used by Justinian in some of his laws were deliberately employed to create an impression of awe. In his earliest legislation, the first *Code* and the *Constitutio Summa* initiating the *Digest*, he uses the title 'pious, fortunate, illustrious, victorious and triumphant'. However, by 533, his titles already displayed increasing aggrandisement. In his constitution on imperial majesty in which he announced the *Institutes*, the constitution promulgating the *Digest* (*Constitutio Omnen*), and in the second edition of the *Code* (*Constitutio Cordi* of 534), he is described as 'Conqueror of the Alamanni, Goths, Franks, Germans, Antae, Alans, Vandals, Africans – pious, fortunate, illustrious, victorious, triumphant', wording also used in his *Novels* (17, 43, 86, 134 and 137). It has been suggested that after the scare of the *Nika* riot, Justinian needed to show that he could command victory over external enemies and control over troublemakers at home. These images of awe and fear were underlined by the propaganda (Scott 1981, 1985, 1996, Sarris 2006: 1–3).

Each of the *Novels* has a preface, and it is here that Justinian's ideology is most clearly on display, as we have already seen (Maas 1986, Roueché 1998, Pazdernik 2005). In his series of laws aimed at reforming the administration of the provinces, Justinian sought to disguise his innovative measures with a veneer of classicism designed to appeal to the senatorial aristocratic class. Here he highlights legends, ancient titles of magistracies and ties between Rome and the provinces in the Republic. For example, in *Novel* 25 (**II 65**), he justifies creating the position of 'praetor' (combining the civil and military posts) in Lycaonia by linking Lycaonia (conquered by King Lycaon) with Rome (the earliest inhabitants of Italy were a colony founded by King Lycaon's son, Oenotrus, well before the foundation myths of either Romulus or Aeneas). Particularly important is Justinian's mission to bring imperial order to disorder: 'We have always made this one of our aims, to clear away every matter that seemed previously imperfect or confused, and to render it perfect, instead of imperfect' (*Novel* 7 on church property). In *Novel* 31, he explained:

> if those arrangements which have been set out in error or in disorder might come to a proper order and be organised well, some cases would be seen to be different: better instead of worse; elegant instead of indecorous; properly arranged and differentiated, instead of disorganised and confused. This was what we also found had been committed with the province of Armenia, and we have thought it necessary to provide it with one harmonious order, and, as a result of regulation, to grant it the proper strength it needs, and impose good order on it.

In this case, as control of Armenia was crucial to securing the military supply line from the Black Sea to the Persian frontier, military pragmatism was no doubt the driving force, rather than just concern for good order.

The laws were addressed to a variety of individuals, such as civil servants (for example, John the Cappadocian), patriarchs and bishops, or to the people of Constantinople. Some were to be displayed in the capital before being circulated to the provinces, where they might be sent to the governors; to bishops for display in their church porticoes; to teachers and practitioners of law; and to the law schools. A law was deemed to take effect after two months to allow it time to reach the provinces (*Novel* 66.1.3). Sometimes Justinian first tried out a law tentatively; for example, his *Novel* 120, passed as a 'crisis driven reform' (Miller and Sarris 2018: 781) during the plague, was to be advertised first in Constantinople, before being sent to the provinces:

> Therefore, your excellency should be quick to observe undiminished what our Serenity has decreed through the present law, which shall be valid in perpetuity, by posting an edict for ten days, in the established and legal places; nothing is to be sent to the provinces on this occasion, as

we ourselves are making provisions for the manner in which our present general constitution is to become public without any detriment to all subjects.

On other occasions, he was keen that his subjects in the capital should be fully aware of his new law regarding provincial governors. Addressed to his praetorian prefect, John the Cappadocian, Justinian advised in the conclusion:

> Therefore, when your highness learns all this, you should take steps to make it public among all peoples who are subject to you, by means of orders made in the established manner to all governors of provinces, so that they may know our concerns for our subjects, and our intentions for the appointment of judges, and so that they may realise the benefits that are bestowed on them, and that we spare no remedy for their happiness. (*Novel* 8)

But a copy of the edict was addressed to the Constantinopolitans as follows:

> The law recently laid down by us and which we have addressed to our very glorious prefects, shows how much forethought we have taken for our subjects. However, it is also proper for you yourselves to know of our forethought which we have for all men. For this reason, we have also set out the law itself in the fashion of an edict, so that you can rightly render hymns to our Lord God and to our Saviour Jesus Christ, and to our Sovereignty, because we make every effort for your benefit.

In addition, a version in Latin was made available for the praetorian prefect of Illyricum.

Changes to legislation

A survey of Justinian's legislation may seem to give an impression of a strong-minded monarch with a clear sense of his domestic policy, even when responding to petitions. However, a perceptible change takes place in the 540s when the number of *Novels* promulgated drops sharply (the largest number were issued in the 530s and 540s, with thirteen in the 550s and just three in the years 560–565) and some of the early laws were later reversed. The reasons for these changes have been much debated. Does the drop in rate of legislation suggest that the regime had run out of steam? That there were too many external problems? That Justinian had exchanged an interest in civil law for canon law (in keeping with his increased attention to solving the doctrinal schisms)? Can the reversals of the early laws be explained by his sensitivity to his subjects' reactions? Was he responding to the sorts of criticisms which we read in the pages of Procopius' *Secret History*? Or did the practicalities of the disruption brought by the plague force him to review some of his initial measures?

A variety of reasons can explain the changes. Justinian was able to respond when his laws were found to be unwelcome; in 553 (*Novel* 145), he rescinded the provisions he had made for the provinces of Phrygia, Pisidia, Lycaonia and Lydia with a positive spin while noting that 'the burden of the restraints which we have devised cannot be borne'. He could also be flexible towards the landowners over the issue of the illegal employment of imperial troops as private armed retainers (Miller and Sarris 2018: 39–40). He also chose not to enforce certain laws in sensitive places, such as border areas, where the loyalty of the local population was more important than the law. Illicit marriages amongst the population of Osrhoene on the Roman-Persian frontier were allowed (*Novel* 154). Similarly, he could be sensitive to religious sects (when it was pragmatic to do so), such as his treatment of the Samaritans (for example, *Novel* 129). In *Novel* 139, he allowed Jewish communities near Tyre (significantly a major centre for textiles, wool and silk) to contract endogamous marriages in return for a fine (*contra Novel* 12). He also retracted unworkable laws, such as the church ownership of property (*Novel* 46 undoes *Novel* 7).

It is also apparent that Justinian was sensitive to the criticisms which are aired in the *Secret History*. In the preface to *Novel* 60 which refers to various legal officers, including assessors (the position held by Procopius), Justinian justifies the large number of laws he is promulgating, a direct answer to Procopius' criticism that he is forever tampering with the law: 'It is likely that some may find fault with the large number of laws being separately added to by us, without considering that, needs must, we are forced to enact laws that suit their causes, when frequently something unexpected arises and it cannot be remedied by those which have already been enacted.' Again, in the preface to *Novel* 84, Justinian mused: 'Nature is everywhere blessed with many novelties (as has already frequently been said in the preamble to laws, and it will be said again and again, for as long as she bestows the things which are hers), and so forces us to need many laws.' Such statements provide answers to Procopius' remarks: 'And he had no regard for preserving what was established, but he wanted everything new, and, in a word, this man was the greatest destroyer of what has been well established' (*Secret History* 6.21–2; see also 11.2, 28.16).

In his preface to *Novel* 8, Justinian commented that 'it so happens that we pass every day and night in full study and thought as to how something useful and pleasing to God might be granted to our subjects', an observation echoed less charitably by Procopius (*Secret History* 12.20–7). However, it is the third part of the *Secret History* which reads as a point-by-point refutation of Justinian's laws. Using the analogy of a man drinking up the waters in the Bosphorus, Procopius proceeds 'to tell how [Justinian] stole away absolutely all the money' (*Secret History* 19.1–3). Against a background of general complaints, Procopius highlights the specific charges of the harm done by Justinian (and indeed Theodora) to the interests of the landowners, reproaching the imperial couple for not remitting taxes to landowners who lost workers because of the plague, accusing them of devising strategies for seizing estates, and of using trumped-up charges to confiscate lands. John the Lydian, who most likely knew Procopius and had access to the *Secret History* (Cameron 1985: 242–8, Kaldellis 2004a), makes similar criticisms, vilifying John the Cappadocian and praising Phocas, the praetorian prefect of 532.

Neither Procopius nor John the Lydian was taken in by Justinian's attempts to portray change as restoration. One of Justinian's most infamous changes was the downgrading and eventual abolition of the consulship, an office most associated with the great days of the Roman Republic. In *Novel* 47 (**II 66**), he stated that it was the name of the emperor and the year of his reign which were to be used in the dating of documents, rather than the consul's name and indiction. As in other laws, the change was disguised by mention of Aeneas, Romulus, Numa, Caesar and Augustus, but Procopius noted that Justinian was obsessed with 'making everything new and named after him' (*Secret History* 11.2). Indeed, from April 538, copper coins were minted with the dates of Justinian's regnal years (ANNO + a numeral) (**II 67**; Hendy 1985: 539f). In another law (*Novel* 105), Justinian regulated the numbers of celebrations provided by consuls, and decreed that they were to distribute only silver (gold was reserved for the emperor). He presents the latter as a financial advantage, though Procopius naturally disagrees (*Secret History* 26.12–15). In *Novel* 62, Justinian legislated to entrust senators with further judicial responsibilities, on the face of it contradicting Procopius' claim that the emperor sidelined the senate (*Secret History* 14.8), but arguably he was merely making them functionaries of the court system, rather than putting them in charge (Haldon 2005:

39–40). It has, therefore, been suggested that the suppression of the consulship was another indication of Justinian turning away from the senatorial aristocracy and investing power in his own men, until he grew so paranoid and fearful of rivals that he disbanded the office completely in the west after 534, and in the east after 541 (Cameron and Schauer 1982, Meier 2002, Sarris 2011: 153–60, Kruse 2017). On the other hand, he continued to introduce new officers, sometimes disguised with traditional names. In *Novel* 13, Justinian introduced 'praetors of the people', a new judicial and policing post, directly answerable to the emperor, rather than the urban prefect of Constantinople, and he gave the posts the ancient Roman title 'praefecti vigilium'. Similarly, in *Novel* 80, he established a further office, quaestor, also tasked with supervising and policing the people of Constantinople. Procopius criticises both appointments as a means of murdering and robbing the people (*Secret History* 20.9–13, John the Lydian, *de Magistratibus* III.70, Malalas 479, Laniado 2015: 190–254). As for John the Lydian, he was particularly critical of the damage caused by Justinian's tax collectors (*de Magistratibus* III.57). Evagrius also had criticism to offer on the Justinianic regime in his comments on the execution of Aetherius (for treason against Justin II): 'Aetherius ... went through every type of dishonesty and pillaged the property of both the living and the dead in the name of the imperial household, of which he was in charge under Justinian' (V.3).

The accession of Justin II brought an abrupt change of policy, and he reversed a number of his uncle's laws. He quickly sought to rebuild relations between the imperial court and the senatorial and provincial aristocracy with whom Justinian had been in conflict, and imposed his own 'localism' agenda, utterly at odds with Justinian's policy of centralisation. He offered a large-scale tax rebate that favoured the wealthy and he stopped the practice of sending governors from Constantinople to curtail the activities of the local landowners; instead these positions were to be filled with men elected by the provincial landowners and bishops themselves (*Novel* 149).

Legislation and policy

Much of Justinian's legislation was responsive, although he passed a number of laws to strengthen local provincial government and to reduce the numbers of litigants seeking redress from him in Constantinople (*Novels* 10, 20, 23). He often refers to the petitions which prompted him to promulgate a law, thus revealing the issues which were important to ordinary people (Feissel 2010), and several examples can be given. His second *Novel*, concerning remarried women, was formulated in response to the case of a certain Gregoria. He suggests that his *Novel* 64, to regulate market gardeners, was prompted by 'many complaints from everywhere for a very long time [which] have been brought before us, against the market gardeners in this very fortunate city and its suburbs, as everyone is suffering in the face of their wickedness'. In the preface to *Novel* 88, he remarks that, 'recently, while we were hearing a case (something which we do very many times when we are sitting in public at the palace), another dispute arose which we resolved straightaway; indeed learning that there are many instances of this sort of thing, we have judged it right to resolve them with a common and general law'.

However, while Justinian may have often answered his subjects' petitions, he also pursued his own clearly defined programme of social and economic reform, which was both pragmatic and ideological, at least up until the 540s, and many of his views and actions are revealed by the legislation he passed. The subject matter of his legislation had many drivers: a need to improve the efficiency of provincial administration and tax collection (certainly prompted by the pressures on the imperial treasury); a desire to improve the lives of women, widows and children (possibly prompted by Theodora); and a wish to legislate on church matters (prompted by his belief that he ruled by divine right).

Finance

One of the main thrusts of his legislation was directed towards tightening up tax collection to shore up the imperial treasury after the expenses of the early years: the Persian wars, the costly damage of natural disasters (such as the Antioch earthquake), the offensive wars in the west, and the ambitious building policy he pursued, particularly in the capital. Such a rationale was set out uncompromisingly in *Novel* 8.10.2:

> since you, our subjects, knowing that military expenses and the pursuit of enemies require much care, and that these things cannot be carried out without money ... we have restored all of Libya, and reduced the Vandals back to slavery; and we hope to receive from God and to enact still more and greater things, for which fiscal taxes are appropriate without any reduction and that they should be collected dependably and at the defined times.

As well as tax collection, cuts would also be necessary, especially to the staff of government departments, fees to officials, and the imperial post. The category most affected by these reforms was the senatorial and provincial landowning elite, and the emperor's acrimonious relationship is well reflected in Procopius' *Secret History* and John the Lydian's *de Magistratibus*, two figures who instinctively sided with the aristocracy. Justinian's policy was thrown into relief by its sharp contrast with that of the Emperor Anastasius, who had been accused of favouring the rich over the poor. Justinian's humble provincial and military origins naturally brought him into conflict with the social elite, but the revival of warfare with Persia and other financial demands increased pressure on him to deal with the tax evasion of the landed aristocracy, as well as their practice of using imperial troops as private armed retainers on their estates (Sarris 2006: 162–75).

We start with some examples of his measures for provincial administration and tax collection in the *Novels*. Chosroes similarly had made reforms to shore up the Persian treasury during the war (Rubin 1995). Justinian's reforms intensified his conflict with the senatorial and provincial aristocracy, whom he had identified as the 'enemy within' during the *Nika* riot (see Chapter 1; Haldon 2005: 39–41). His anger against the elite is demonstrable; in *Edict* 13, he complains: 'while the taxpayers were all affirming that everything was being exacted in full, the pagarchs, city councillors and tax-collectors, and in particular those in charge at the time, have so arranged the business until now in such a way that nothing can be learnt, and that it benefits only them.' In *Novel* 30 concerning the governance of the province of Cappadocia, the behaviour of the powerful made him 'blush' (with anger or embarrassment) (Sarris 2006: 3, Miller and Sarris 2018: 324).

One of Justinian's main methods of enforcing efficient tax collection was to bolster the position of the provincial governor. In his important *Novel* 8, he improved the stipends of provincial governors so they were not dependent on local patronage networks, stamped out corruption by forbidding payments for office, and issued instructions to governors on maintaining order, collecting tax revenues, and strengthening the provincial courts (see also *Novels* 53, 69, 86, 125, 126). Governors were to check the precise details of the tax collected and what was still owed from the tax collectors, and to cut off their hands if they were not able to provide this information. *Novel* 95 stipulated that governors were to spend fifty days in their province after their period of office had ended in order to answer any charges of wrongdoing. He also strengthened the role of the 'defender of the city' (*defensor civitatis*, *Novels* 15 and 17), and he co-opted bishops and others to check up and report incompetence or venality to the emperor (8.8 with Kelly 2004: 71–81, Sarris 2006: 205–34). The powerful landowners should not steal others' property or *coloni adscripticii* (farmers tied to the land), or their own property would be seized. Private armed retinues should be disbanded and governors should not issue any exemptions in tax collecting (landowners had been collecting taxes and not passing them on to the state (*Novel* 17)).

Justinian also turned his attention to the governance of individual provinces, in 535–539 passing a series of laws on the provincial administration. Again, his aim was to make tax collection more efficient and to strengthen the position of the local governor and provincial courts. One key reform was to amalgamate military and civil power in many provinces (for example, *Novels* 26 (with Sarantis 2016: 139–42), 27 and 28), and he effectively changed the three-tier system of prefectures, dioceses and provinces introduced by Diocletian to a two-tier system consisting of prefectures and provinces (see, for example, *Novels* 8, 20, 23–31, 102, 103).

He also joined a succession of emperors from the fourth century who had sought to prevent the decline of provincial cities, and specifically the decline of the curia (the city council) (*Novels* 38, 45, 70, 89, 101, Laniado 2002, Haarer 2016). Justinian's measures to bolster local governance intersect with the debate about the decline or transformation of the late Roman city. The Romans had traditionally governed through the medium of town councils (*boule* in Greek; *curia* in Latin) made up of the existing landowning elites. These councillors (*curiales*) became responsible for the collection of taxes and the upkeep of the towns. A privilege at first, as a consequence of the empire's financial problems in the third century, these duties became a burden, and the *curiales* sought to find ways to escape their responsibilities. Jones (1964: II, 712–66 and 1998: 192–210) and Liebeschuetz (1972: 2001) favoured the view that the demise of the *curia* inevitably led to the decline of urban prosperity and the weakening of civic life, but more positive views have now been argued. Whittow (1990) led the trend by arguing that the decline of the *curiales* was merely an 'institutional rearrangement', but that the urban elite continued strongly into the seventh century. The twelfth book of the *Theodosian Code* contains 192 constitutions under the title 'de decurionibus' attempting to prevent councillors from leaving their duties, and Justinian adds to this series with a number of *Novels*. In *Novel* 38 (**II 68**), he improved the inheritance rights of children who followed in their fathers' role as a councillor; in *Novel* 45, he legislated that Jews, Samaritans and heretics were to carry out the duties of city councillors (although they could not enjoy the same privileges); in *Novel* 70, councillors were only to be released from their duties if they achieved a genuinely high-ranking position (such as *magister militum* or praetorian prefect); and in *Novel* 89, 'such is our concern for the city councils' that he was willing to legitimise potential heirs to an estate, if they were willing to carry out curial duties. In *Novel* 101, he reiterated the regulations set out in *Novel* 38 after being petitioned: 'A petition from some city councillors has provided us with the occasion for good legislation. . .'.

Justinian's measures, as we have seen, heavily impacted on the landowning elite, themselves the subject of much discussion in recent writing on the sixth-century economy and the functioning of government. Using mainly evidence from Egypt (since the papyri from the village of Aphrodito and the great Apion estate are our most detailed primary sources), we can see the rise of the great estates, and their relationship with local town councils and with the imperial government. One of the key debates today concerns the extent to which the great estates became semi-public institutions, responsible for the collection of taxes from their own tenants and further afield (Gascou 1985, Sarris 2006, Banaji 2007, Nijf and Alston 2011). Justinian's contribution was certainly to ensure that any taxes collected by the powerful landowners were duly passed to the imperial government, for which he was criticised by Procopius (see below).

The public finances were inevitably affected by natural disasters, above all the bubonic plague, which originated in central Africa and first struck in Egypt in the autumn of 541. In 542, it spread to Constantinople, the Near East, the Balkans and Italy. Vivid contemporary descriptions are left by Procopius (*Wars* II.22–3) and Evagrius (IV.29) (**II 69**) who saw for themselves the terrible effects and indeed, in the latter's case, suffered personal losses. The cause, type and spread of the plague have all been thoroughly debated (Stathakopoulos 2004, Horden 2005, Kaldellis 2007b, Little 2007, Meier 2016), and it has been compared with other outbreaks of bubonic plague, and also the plague which struck Athens in the fifth century BC, the description of which by Thucydides is evoked by Evagrius and especially Procopius (Thucydides, *History of the Peloponnesian War* II.47–54). However, here it is the impact of the plague on the functioning of the empire, Justinian's ability to govern, and the nature of his response which are the important issues. There are varying reports on the extent to which the plague affected the countryside, but it is certain that the tax base would have been reduced. Otherwise highly resistant to the alienation of ecclesiastical land, Justinian's priority was now to ensure its continued cultivation, leading him to pass *Novel* 120. In *Novel* 128, he tried to make the rules regarding *adiectio sterilium* (or *epibole* in Greek) fairer; this was the system whereby abandoned or uncultivated land was allocated to neighbouring communities or landowners who became responsible for paying the taxes. The high death rate naturally led to a large amount of land falling vacant all at once, but Justinian was concerned that the remaining taxpayers should not suffer excessively, especially as a result of corrupt officials. He also passed a number of laws on wage control (122) and intestate succession (118) (Sarris 2002, Meier 2016).

There were also abuses at a high level. Procopius criticises Peter Barsymes (*comes sacrarum largitionum* and the praetorian prefect of the east), accusing him of depriving soldiers of their pay, selling offices and reducing pensions, at the same time as embezzling tax revenues himself (*Secret History* 22). He also accuses Peter of issuing the gold coinage 'not at its usual value, but reducing its value materially' – an important matter, since good finances depended on having a good coinage, and vice versa. In 538, Justinian had passed a reform in which he increased the weight standard of the bronze coinage by about twenty per cent, possibly reflecting a change in the value of the gold *solidus* from 210 *folles* (bronze coins marked with their value (40) in Greek (M)) to 180 *folles*. This change turned out not to be successful and the *follis* reverted to something in the region of its former weight in 542/543. In addition to changing the exchange rate between bronze and gold coins, Justinian is also credited with introducing a series of lightweight gold solidi, weighing ten or eleven twelfths of the original solidus. These continued to be minted sporadically but in appreciable numbers until the end of the seventh century. Their purpose has been much debated. Explanations which have been put forward include the facilitation of trade, a reflection of a change to the relative price of gold and bronze, and pressure on the imperial finances, but none has found widespread acceptance. However, Sarris (2006: 218–19) suggests that it is indeed Peter Barsymes in his position as the *comes sacrarum largitionum* (finance minister), which he held from March 542 to July 543 and again between 547 and 550, as Procopius reports, who introduced this change as a response to the shortfall of income to the imperial treasury caused by the plague; according to this view, the government exacted payment in full solidi but disbursed lighter coins. Curiously, although the emperor's portrait on coins is nearly always conventional, it has been suggested that some coins minted in 542 show him with a deformed face as a result of contracting the plague (Pottier 2010).

Figure 5.1 Gold coins of Justinian: the solidus and the lightweight solidus. Solidus: D N IVSTINIANVS P P AVG; facing bust of Justinian, wearing helmet, and holding globe surmounted by cross and shield decorated with cavalryman.
VICTORIA AVGGGΔ; Angel standing facing, holding cross and globe; below, CONOB = CON = Constantinople and OB = obryzum (pure gold). Lightweight solidus: D N IVSTINIANVS P P AVG; facing bust of Justinian, wearing helmet, and holding globe surmounted by cross and shield decorated with cavalryman. VICTORIA AVGGGI; Angel standing facing, holding cross and globe At the bottom of the reverse on the second coin the letters OB XX can be seen, instead of the CONOB. OB again stands for *obryzum*, but XX denotes 20 siliquae, and the coin weighs 3.74 grams, 4 siliquae less than the normal weight of about 4.5 grams (= 24 siliquae). © Classical Numismatic Group LLC MBS 60, lot 1976 and EA 383, lot 574.

Social reform

Another of Justinian's major concerns was social reform. He was sympathetic to the claims of women and children, especially concerning dowries and inheritance. Whether or not we can detect Theodora's influence behind the legislation (see Chapter 1), he did pass a raft of laws to reduce prostitution by forbidding brothels (*Novels* 14 and 51, Harper 2013), a measure presented by Procopius both positively (*Buildings* I.9.2–10 – **II 10**) and negatively (*Secret History* 17.5 – **II 70**); improving the status of concubines; improving inheritance rights, especially for children (18, 22, 68, 74, 78, 118); and on marriage. In *Novel* 12, he increased penalties for illicit or incestuous marriages, but he protected the interests of children born from them. In *Novel* 22, he effectively codified and reformed existing legislation on divorce and remarriage (Feenstra 1983, Fögen 1992). In *Novel* 39, he made further changes to dowry and inheritance law to help widows (*C.J.* V.13.10–11, *Novels* 1, 2, 18 and 22), and defended the interests of married women and widows (*Novels* 61, 91, 97 and 98). Following *C.J.* IX.13.1 in which he overhauled previous legislation, in *Novels* 143 and 150, he strengthened the law on rape, in favour of women.

Homosexuality was now punishable by death, starting with his early constitution when in 528 some homosexual bishops were summoned to Constantinople. Further legislation followed: *Novel* 77 in 535 decreed that male homosexuals should be put to death as they incited God to punish their cities with famine, earthquakes and disease (Malalas 435, *Secret History* 11.34-6), and another *Novel* was published in 559 (141) following the 557 earthquake (Meier 2003a: 587–98). In another bid to win divine approval, he passed various laws reducing the grounds for divorce and forbidding it by mutual consent (*C.J.* V.17.10, *Novel* 117); this unpopular ruling was later reversed by Justin II (*Novel* 140).

Religion

The most significant difference to previous law codes was that legislation on ecclesiastical matters, especially 'orthodox' belief, the powers of bishops, privileges of the clergy and churches, and the non-orthodox, heretics, Jews, Samaritans, Manichaeans and pagans, was now included in the first book of the *Code*, and thereby given emphasis and prominence. Theodosius had added such measures to the end of his *Code*, but, in the intervening century, religious issues had become far more central to daily life, and the importance of regulating them duly increased. Justinian uses the medium of his legislation to set out the relationship between imperial authority and priestly office (*imperium* and *sacerdotium*), saying that each office 'proceeding from one and the same origin enriches life ... if one is blameless in every way and full of faithfulness in the presence of God, the other enriches justly and properly the state which has been entrusted to it' (*Novel* 6, preface, March 535 to the Patriarch Epiphanius).

Justinian also wanted to illustrate his divine right to rule. *Novel* 8 may contain some strongly practical measures for provincial governors to improve tax collection but as he says,

> For we have enacted it for another reason, so that, as a result of the justice which is in the law, we are able to devote ourselves to the Lord God and to

commend our reign to him, and so we may not be seen to think nothing of the oppression of the people whom God has entrusted to us, and so that we may always be merciful towards them and follow his goodness. (8.11)

In *Novel* 86, he asserted,

From the time when God set us up to reign over the Romans, we have been making every effort to do everything to help the subjects of the state entrusted to us by God, and doing whatever may free them from every difficulty, harm and grief, lest for litigation and other reasons they are forced to depart from their homeland and suffer overseas.

Justinian had seen the emergence of alternative law codes produced by 'barbarians' (such as the *Lex Burgundionum*; Fisher Drew 1972) and was keen to remind all that the ability to pass laws was granted to him alone, as emperor, by God. He was the *living law* (*nomos empsychos* or *lex animata*), as he frequently expressed: 'the lot of the emperor ruler is to be exempt from all that has been said [on the consulship]. God has made the very laws subject to him and sent him as the living law unto men' (*Novel* 105.2.4).

Justinian's concern to emphasise his close relationship with God also meant that, although a secular ruler, he nevertheless felt responsible for legislating on sacred matters. He addressed a number of laws to patriarchs and bishops regulating various aspects of ecclesiastical discipline: for example, *Novel* 3 on clergy numbers; 5 on monasteries and monks, with 76; 6 on the ordination and appointment of bishops, priests and deacons; 16 which aimed to curtail high ecclesiastical expenditure resulting from over-manning of the churches; 57 stipulating that communion should not take place in private houses; 67 on further matters of church discipline; 123 which codifies and clarifies a number of regulations on various ecclesiastical matters; 132 edict on faith; 133 regulating monastic life. All these measures underlined his own sense of religious and moral responsibility.

Justinian's support for the Church and desire to assert imperial control over the religious lives of his subjects were both driven by serious pragmatic considerations and had important practical consequences. The Church could become a valuable counter-weight to the landed aristocracy, and he passed a number of *Novels* bolstering the position that ecclesiastical property was inalienable, incurring the wrath of Procopius who noted that Justinian increased ecclesiastical estates at the expense of lay landowners (*Novel* 7, *Secret History* 13.3–7). Pursuit of orthodoxy could also be an excuse for war and the emperor justified his attempt to reclaim North Africa as a war against Arian heretics (*C.J.* I.27.1–9). At the same time, he legislated against educated pagans, heretics and homosexuals, whose activities he believed were displeasing to God who consequently punished the empire with natural disasters (see Chapter 6).

Building programme

Justinian's building and restoration works can be roughly divided into three overlapping categories: defences and fortifications (discussed in Chapters 2 and 3); church building; and utilitarian and public works. We start with churches, and the most famous of Justinian's buildings, Hagia Sophia, still standing in Constantinople today, now deconsecrated as a museum, having been a church until 1453 and a mosque until 1931. Designed by the mathematicians, engineers and architects Anthemius of Tralles and Isidore of Miletus, the project was supervised by the praetorian prefect, Phocas (John the Lydian, *de Magistratibus* III.76). It was first consecrated in 537, and again in 558 after the first dome had to be replaced following an earthquake. Combining the form of an aisled basilica and a centrally planned church, its huge dome rested upon arches which in turn rested on four massive pillars. However, it was not just the architecture which amazed sixth-century witnesses; the decoration, mostly aniconic, which included mirror revetments, intricately carved capitals with monograms of Justinian and Theodora, and entablatures and ornamental mosaics, stunned the contemporary viewers, leading to unstinting praise from Procopius (*Buildings* I.1.20–78). In *Kontakion* 54, Romanos wrote that the church imitated heaven and contrasted its speedy rebuilding with Solomon's Temple in Jerusalem which still lay in ruins (**II 71**). With vivid references to the *Nika* riot, the work has been dated to five years later, to Lent 537, a few months before the official inauguration of Hagia Sophia on 27 December that year. Romanos praised Justinian and Theodora, celebrating them as saviours of Constantinople through their prayers and their rebuilding of the city and Hagia Sophia. The allusion to Solomon's Temple ('decorated with infinite wealth' but remaining 'fallen down and not restored', 54.21) recalls the claims of both Anicia Juliana and Justinian himself to have outdone Solomon (see Chapter 1). We also have another important literary work on Hagia Sophia, Paul the Silentiary's *Ekphrasis (Description) of Hagia Sophia* (**II 72**). This poem was undoubtedly commissioned by Justinian for the re-dedication ceremonies between 24 December 562 and 6 January 563, following the reconstruction of the dome which had collapsed in the 557 earthquake. The poem begins and ends with a double panegyric to the emperor and patriarch, and provides evidence for the ceremony. Mary Whitby (1985: 228) suggests that while Justinian emphasised the ecclesiastical significance of the event (a joint achievement of emperor and patriarch, only made possible by the aid of God), in choosing Paul as the poet, the 'emperor betrayed his earlier ambition to link his city and his reign with the splendours of the classical past'. Paul's friend, the historian Agathias, praised the *ekphrasis*, commenting that 'if anyone who lives far from the capital wishes to get a full and comprehensive picture, as if he were there in person and looking at it, then he could hardly do better than to read the poem in hexameters of Paul' (V.9.5).

Later, in the late tenth or early eleventh century, a new mosaic was installed over an opening into the narthex. This shows the enthroned Virgin holding her Son; to their left, Constantine offers a replica of the city; to their right, Justinian presents a replica of the church (Mathews 1971, Mainstone 1988, Taylor 1996, Ousterhout 2010, Kaldellis 2013, Schibille 2014).

Hagia Sophia was a powerful statement made by Justinian to remind his subjects that, for all emperors from Augustus onwards, building (like passing laws) was an imperial activity. It was the emperor's job to provide amenities and services (such as a reliable water supply) for his

Figure 5.2 Hagia Sophia. Photo: author.

people, places of worship, and protection from enemies by ensuring that defences were in good order. Justinian, conscious of his duties as an emperor and especially keen to underline his relationship with God, was a prolific builder. We can read Procopius' account and indeed the list of constructions repaired or begun under Justinian, bearing in mind, of course, that his *Buildings* is a panegyric, and although Justinian may be credited with completing some buildings, many were started by his predecessor, Anastasius.

As we saw in Chapter 1, Justinian had begun building churches in Constantinople early in his reign, with SS Sergius and Bacchus. However, it was the destruction of the city centre in the *Nika* riot which cleared the way (quite literally) for Justinian to reshape this area of Constantinople. The Church of Hagia Eirene was also destroyed in the riot and rebuilt by Justinian, with a wide nave and two domes. Between Hagia Eirene and Hagia Sophia was the Hospice of Samson. Hagia Sophia was situated north of the Augusteum where an equestrian statue of Justinian stood on a tall column (Procopius, *Buildings* I.2.1–12 – **II 73**; see Chapter 6); there was now access between Hagia Sophia and the imperial palace, thus uniting the religious and civic ceremonies of Constantinople. Later in his reign, Justinian rebuilt the Church of the Holy Apostles in the shape of a cross with a dome over

Figure 5.3 Hagia Eirene. Photo: author.

the middle, during the work conveniently discovering three coffins containing the relics of SS Andrew, Luke and Timothy. The foundation stone had been laid by Theodora, it was said, but the church was dedicated after her death in June 550. Both Theodora and Justinian were buried there. In total (according to Procopius), Justinian built or restored thirty-three churches in Constantinople and the suburbs.

However, Justinian's church-building activity took place across the whole empire, and his churches were characterised by their grandeur and innovative features. Just a few notable examples from the eastern empire will be mentioned here (the remarkable churches of Ravenna will be discussed in Chapter 6). The great Church of St John the Theologian in Ephesus was built to a similar design as the Church of the Holy Apostles in Constantinople. After the sack of Antioch in 540, Justinian constructed a church there dedicated to the Virgin Mary, and another to the Archangel Michael. In Jerusalem, at the request of St Sabas, he completed the *Nea* ('new') church in honour of Mary, Mother of God; it was consecrated in November 543. It was to be the largest church there, over seventy-five metres in length, and was surrounded by a hospital, library, guesthouses and a cistern. At Sinai, he marked the site of Moses and the burning bush with a church. During repair work, an inscription was discovered on one of the roof-beams

Figure 5.4 Basilica Cistern. Photo: author.

of the church commemorating the late Empress Theodora: 'for the memory and repose of our late Empress Theodora' (thus dating the foundation to between 548 and 565). Procopius (*Buildings* V.8.4–9 – **II 74**) also emphasises the dual purpose of the project, in building a fortress to impede the incursions of the Saracens into Palestine (Forsyth 1968). It is also possible that Justinian was responsible for the Church of the Nativity at Bethlehem which had been destroyed in the sixth century, possibly during the Samaritan revolts. The new church managed to escape destruction in the Persian invasion of 614 and although additions were made and redecoration was carried out by the Crusaders, today's church over the cave believed to be the birthplace of Jesus is essentially the structure of the sixth century.

As well as his concern for sacred buildings, Justinian also paid due attention to amenities and public works. In Constantinople he completed the public bath started by Anastasius and he had several cisterns constructed or restored. The most notable is the underground cistern, the Basilica Cistern, now known as the Yerebatan Serai, a popular tourist site today in Istanbul (Procopius, *Buildings* I.11.10–15 – **II 75**), although there were others, including the Cistern of Philoxenos (Binbirdirek Cistern). He also built a huge granary at the nearby island of Tenedos, thus maximising the sailing season for bringing provisions

Figure 5.5 Cistern of Philoxenos. Photo: author.

as grain ships were often unable to reach as far as Constantinople because of the weather. Elsewhere in the empire, Justinian took care to safeguard and improve water supply, restoring or providing from scratch cisterns or aqueducts at Hierapolis, Thermopylae, Heraclea Pontica, Nicaea, Helenopolis and Pythia in Bithynia. He also improved flood defences at Tarsus; he repaired the bridge at Nicaea; and he built a huge bridge, 429 metres long and almost ten metres wide, to span the river Sangarius (see Chapter 6; *Greek Anthology* IX.641 – **II 76**).

All this construction and restoration work helped to enhance the prestige of Justinian. A particular example was the emperor's birthplace, Justiniana Prima (identified with modern-day Caričin Grad in Serbia). We have already seen that Justinian established here a new archiepiscopal see (see Chapter 4). According to Procopius, Justinian provided the city with an aqueduct, numerous churches, lodgings for magistrates, stoas, marketplaces, fountains, streets, baths and shops (*Buildings* IV.1.19–27).

The verdict on Justinian's domestic agenda

In September 560, following a rumour that the emperor had fallen ill, social unrest flared, during which the bakeries were looted and

Figure 5.6 Justiniana Prima, Episcopal Palace. Photo: author.

the *curatores*, George and Aetherius, were accused of plotting to put Theodore, the son of Peter the Patrician, on the throne. In 562, a far more serious incident was discovered (the 'bankers' plot') involving Ablabius, a retired official of the mint, Marcellus, a bullion dealer, and Sergius, nephew of a minor functionary; the bankers were apparently unhappy after Justinian had exacted forced loans (*Novel* 136, Mary Whitby 1985). Worse was the revelation that three members of Belisarius' household were implicated. It seemed that Justinian's long-held suspicions concerning his general's loyalty had been realised, and he summoned a full consistory at which the charges were read out. Belisarius was placed under house arrest and his servants withdrawn, although he was later exonerated. In fact, he died within a few weeks of Justinian in 565. Interestingly, following the excesses of the *Nika* riot, Justinian's reign was largely free from faction rioting, and it did not return until towards the end of his reign when we hear of a number of incidents. Drought triggered fights at the cisterns in 552; a shortage of bread in 556 caused unrest at the games to mark the foundation of Constantinople; riots between the Blues and Greens flared in 561; fires sparked by rioters destroyed the house of the praetorian prefect, Peter Barsymes, in 561; and the city prefect, Andrew, was attacked in 563 (Moorhead 1994: 167–76).

That the major central part of Justinian's reign was free from civil unrest suggests that his domestic rule was, on the whole, peaceful and successful. Clearly, the 560s, when he was elderly, were not filled with the dynamism and determination of his early years on the throne, and the date from which he is perceived to have slowed down, as it were, is much debated. One issue was Justinian's relationship with his officials, especially Belisarius. Parnell (2017) highlights the anxiety felt on both sides, but especially Justinian's not unreasonable concern that a popular general with a loyal army could easily rebel, leading him to prize loyalty over good conduct or military success. As we saw, despite ongoing suspicion, it was only in 562 that Justinian actually took action against him. Another minister who aroused suspicion was John the Cappadocian (*PLRE* IIIA.627–35: Fl. Ioannes 11). Holding the office of praetorian prefect (to which he was reinstated after the *Nika* riot) from 532 to 541, he was accused of avarice and vice by his contemporaries, especially those who were personally affected by some of his measures, such as John the Lydian (*de Magistratibus* II.20, III.58), but they nevertheless admitted his administrative efficiency. However, he incurred the wrath of Theodora who, framing John in a plot to make Belisarius emperor, contrived to have him exiled to Cyzicus – a perfect example of the ease with which Justinian could be persuaded to give in to his suspicions. From Cyzicus John was exiled to Egypt, after Theodora suggested his guilt in the murder of the local bishop. He was finally recalled to Constantinople shortly before his death.

Part of the fascination of Justinian's reign arises from the extreme highs and lows and the seemingly extreme contrast between the glorious first half and the gloomy second half. Of course, it is hard not to be influenced by the writings of Procopius, who emphasises this downward trajectory. The debate centring on this, and how Justinian managed to maintain his grip on power, is more powerfully brought out by Peter Bell (2013). His answer is that through a robust government where political, economic and security issues are all linked, Justinian clearly established the legitimacy of his rule. Strongly driven by an argument based on theoretical models and his own personal experience of working in the civil service and Foreign and Commonwealth Office in areas of conflict, such as the Middle East and Ireland, Bell examines how Justinian managed conflicts not just by creating a culture of fear, but actually by ruling lawfully and justly. He shows how Justinian dealt with criticisms such as vulgarity, oppressiveness and innovation (as explored in the *Secret History*), and setbacks such as military defeats, the collapse of the Hagia Sophia dome, and the plague, which all called into question God's confidence in his earthly vicegerent. We saw above how Justinian counteracted claims of innovation in his provincial reform programme with a veneer of restoration in the prefaces to the laws. Meier (2003a and 2004b) lists the demoralising and delegitimising catastrophes faced by Justinian and contrasts the 'happy' years up to c. 540 with the later years when the emperor was constantly seeking ways to legitimise his rule. Bell argues that apart from Justinian's own religious zeal and appetite for solving administrative problems, there was a necessity for the emperor to build a consensus and conciliate key elements of the elite and wider opinion.

The empire had not seen such active rule since the time of Diocletian (Sarris 2006: 215) in every sphere of life: religious, legal, fiscal, administrative and military. The effects of Justinian's direct interventions were not appreciated by all, hence the tension between Justinian and senatorial and provincial aristocracy. Because we have Procopius' influential *Secret History* this tension is highlighted for us, and it shows that the attempt of Justinian and Tribonian to present reform as restoration did not convince all. However, the constant allusion to what had gone before was at the heart of life in the sixth century, at a time when politics, literature, art and architecture looked back to the classical past, whilst at the same time witnessing many innovations, and it is this tension which forms the subject of Chapter 6.

Culture and Society

The final debate concerns the nature of the transition from a classical, pagan empire to one that was predominantly Christian, in terms of its literary and artistic culture, its festivals, and its way of life. It is especially valid to consider these topics in the context of the age of Justinian since not only was his reign played out against this background of change and transformation, but he himself did more than many other emperors to actively bring about this change. Yet we will find that there are many paradoxes. While Justinian showed an increasing interest in theology and staged several waves of persecutions against the pagans (and heretics), he nevertheless used the past and the ideal of restoration to justify his wars and provincial reform legislation. He desired to be celebrated in art and literature, yet he might have felt uncomfortable about the pagan (or at least Hellenic) traditions from which these panegyrical works stemmed. Further, he knew that propaganda was crucial to portray his ideology and indeed authors writing across all genres sought to offer him praise (or censure), but in fact there is evidence he exercised very little direct patronage. There is no indication that he sought to encourage any literary circles in Constantinople or elsewhere, yet an astonishing number of historians, poets, philosophers, hymnographers and chroniclers all operated during his reign, both in the capital and at various provincial centres. The sheer number will make it hard to offer a succinct summary of the literary output at this time. Certainly, John Zonaras, who wrote in his *Epitome Historiarum* in the twelfth century that 'by making teachers redundant' Justinian was responsible for a new level of 'boorishness' (XIV.6), could not have been more wrong.

Persecution and philosophy

Zonaras' remark about 'making teachers redundant' refers to Justinian's actions against the Academy in Athens. The accusation that he was responsible for the closure of the Academy of Athens in 529, thus bringing to an end a centuries-long tradition of philosophical education, is often levelled against Justinian. However, the case is rather more complex (Alan Cameron 1969, Watts 2004, 2006: chapter 5). Our evidence stems from a law of Justinian in which he targeted heretics, Samaritans and pagans (Hellenes in the Greek) by forbidding them to teach and earn a public salary (*C.J.* I.5.18.4 – **II 77**), and a reference in Malalas (451) suggesting a specific measure against Athens: 'during the consulship of Decius [529], the emperor issued a decree and sent it to Athens ordering that nobody should teach philosophy nor interpret astronomy [law teaching] nor in any city should there be lots cast using dice.' This action has given rise to a number of debates, including the effect of this measure: why did Justinian single out Athens but allow philosophy to continue to be taught in Alexandria? Did the teaching of philosophy suddenly cease in Athens? At this time, the Athens Academy was enjoying a particularly successful phase under the leadership of the energetic Damascius who had travelled to Athens (following the persecution in Alexandria orchestrated by Zeno) and revived the Academy, attracting a number of international students (Athanassiadi 1993). It is possible that a special law was needed for Athens as the Academy was self-supporting and its staff did not receive a public salary. It has also been argued that it was the fact that Athens was so flourishing which caused Justinian anxiety (Alan Cameron 1969). Even then, this measure did not bring about an abrupt end. However, it is likely that another law (*C.J.* I.11.10 (**II 78**)) added to the second edition of Justinian's *Code* (Corcoran 2009) which stipulated (*inter alia*) that pagans (described as those 'infected with Hellenic madness') must be baptised, prohibited from teaching and receiving a public salary, their property confiscated, and they be exiled, finally encouraged Damascius with six followers to leave Athens. They went first to Harran (Carrhae) in the frontier zone with Persia, reputed to be a place of great learning and culture, and then to the Persian court of Chosroes (Agathias II.30.3–4 – **II 79**), who had gained a reputation as an ideal philosopher-king.

It is important to note that those who left were pagans; Christians were at liberty to continue to teach philosophy. Watts (2004, 2006) argues that Justinian's purpose was to stamp out divination (for this linked philosophy, astronomy and dice) and that the Athenian local authorities who had long been engaged in a struggle between the Athenian Platonists and Christians used the measure in particular to eliminate Neoplatonic philosophy as it was taught in Athens. The teaching of philosophy continued in Alexandria with well-known figures such as the Christian John Philoponus (c. 490–570), and even the pagan Olympiodorus (c. 490–after 565). A number of reasons for the continuation of the Alexandrian School have been proposed. First, pragmatic financial expediency: there was much more to be gained from confiscating the property of the rich, privately endowed teachers in Athens, compared with the state-paid teachers in Alexandria. Second, the nature of the teaching: Athens enjoyed a reputation for privileging the teaching of Plato, and 'applied paganism' emphasising cult, magic and pagan ritual, while in Alexandria the focus was on Aristotle and 'theoretical paganism', with an emphasis on shared ancient heritage, a concept familiar from John the Lydian (see below) (Wildburg 2005). As to the fate of the Athens Academy and the group of seven philosophers, there are various theories as to where they ended up. Some have argued that the Academy of Athens continued to flourish late into the sixth century (Alan Cameron 1969); after his dramatic gesture, Justinian did not follow up with any further legislation. Others have linked the archaeological evidence from excavations of the philosophers' houses next to the Areopagus and the departure of their owners. It appears that during the 530s the largest house was renovated: a pagan image in the floor was replaced by a cross, and the statues of the gods were desecrated except

Figure 6.1 Philae. Photo: author.

for seven statues which were found well preserved in a well, as if hidden (Frantz 1988, Watts 2004, 2006).

This incident reveals the complexity of unravelling the effect of Justinian's intentions on the cultural life of the empire. Another such episode concerns his intervention at Philae where the Greek gods Isis, Osiris and Priapus were worshipped by the 'barbarians, even up to my time, but the Emperor Justinian decided to destroy them. Therefore Narses . . . a commander of the troops there, brought down the sanctuaries on the order of the emperor, and put the priests under guard and sent the statues to Byzantium' (Procopius, *Wars* I.19.36; see Chapters 2 and 4). This affair, dated to 535–537, has been studied in detail by Dijkstra (2008), who has taken issue with various assumptions which envisaged a flourishing pagan cult violently brought to an end by Justinian. Today, some of the best-preserved temples in Egypt may be found on Philae, especially the temple of Isis which makes nonsense of the claim that the sanctuaries were torn down. Dijkstra also argues that since a bishop had been in residence at Philae since the fourth century, and the inscriptions associated with the ancient Egyptian cults had come to a sudden end back in 456/457, this does not suggest that Philae saw continuous and solely pagan worship up to 535. He suggests, then, that Narses' actions constituted more of a symbolic closure, and that Procopius was following imperial propaganda.

Figure 6.2 Philae. Christian cross, temple of Isis. Photo: author.

The Philae episode is often linked with another example of Justinian's missionary activity, the conversion of the king of Noubadia, as reported by John of Ephesus (**II 22**). Dijkstra argues that this mission to Noubadia was not a direct consequence of the action on Philae, and the geographical closeness of Philae to Noubadia was the only reason for the possible involvement of the bishop of Philae. Dijkstra also suggests that as portrayed by Procopius, Justinian's 'missionary activities', such as closing temples, building churches, and converting cities and peoples to Christianity, are part of his image as a bringer of civilisation to barbarians, with the emphasis on Byzantine culture, ideology and therefore control, rather than specifically Christianity. Justinian's main aim regarding the Noubades was to encourage their loyalty in maintaining the peace on the southern Egyptian frontier; it is likely that the key function of the first mission was not religious but diplomatic. For John of Ephesus, as a committed miaphysite, on the other hand, the significance lay in the religious (and even doctrinal) conversion, hence his colourful account highlighting the success of Theodora's miaphysite embassy.

Of course, there are other examples of Justinian's missionary activities and his persecution of pagans. Procopius gives us another instance of missionary work, this time in Libya at the city of Augila, where 'from ancient times shrines were dedicated to Ammon and to Alexander the Macedonian' and where 'the natives used to make sacrifices to them even up to the reign of Justinian'. Justinian 'taught them the doctrine of the true faith, making the whole population Christians and bringing about a transformation of their polluted ancestral customs', and 'he built for them a Church of the Mother of God' (Procopius, *Buildings* VI.2.14–20). A far wider programme of conversions was conducted by John of Ephesus from 542, starting in the Maeander Valley in Turkey; John's account (3.3.36) certainly suggests a landscape alive with paganism (Bowersock 1990, Whitby 1991).

Back in Constantinople, we know of three waves of persecutions. As early as 527, a law passed in the name of Justin and Justinian introduced measures against heretics, especially Manichaeans, and pagans (*C.J.* I.5.12 – **II 11**), and later legislation ruled against heretics and pagans holding high office or inheriting an estate, and made apostasy punishable by death. Pagans were given three months to comply. Investigators found several high-profile figures: the former prefect Asclepiodotus, the quaestor Thomas, and the patrician Phocas, possibly a member of the first law commission. Asclepiodotus committed suicide but there were no executions.

In 546, a second investigation was conducted, this time by John of Ephesus, focusing on outing prominent senators, grammarians, lawyers and physicians. This time it was Phocas' turn to commit suicide. John of Ephesus (Pseudo-Dionysius of Tel-Mahre 852 – **II 80**) was pleased to take the credit, although it is likely that Justinian, feeling the pressures of food shortages and earthquake damage, coming so soon after the plague, was encouraged to take steps to reassure himself of God's favour. Similarly, in 562, a year marked by rioting and a conspiracy against the emperor, we hear of a third investigation (Michael the Syrian IX.33). Five priests of the shrines of Athens, Antioch and Heliopolis were arrested and 2,000 cult statues and sacred writings were publicly burnt (Maas 1992: 71–2).

Festivals and lifestyle

It should be clear by now that although Justinian certainly adopted a far more aggressive policy against pagans than his predecessors had done, even his efforts do not quite point to a sustained specific anti-pagan policy. His actions were often triggered by a particular circumstance, a political or civil disturbance, or another agent (John of Ephesus), or were part of a wider policy against heretics, Manichaeans, Samaritans and Jews. When it came to forms of public entertainment, Justinian also found himself in a difficult situation, since the immorality of some forms of entertainment (notably the theatre) and the pagan associations of the festivals did not suit a pattern of life increasingly dominated by religious ceremonies. Strong disapprobation came from the Church as demonstrated by the homilies of the priest Jacob of Serûg, who became the bishop of Batnae in 519. He wrote 760 metrical homilies, including several on Greek theatrical entertainments (Moss 1935). In homily three, Jacob claims that pantomimes in the theatres were so popular that 'Satan wishes to set up paganism by means of the play'. To the Christians who argue that it is innocent entertainment, he replies, 'Who can wallow in mud without being dirty?' Interestingly, we know from the *Life of Severus of Antioch* attributed to John bar Apthonia that Severus, the patriarch of Antioch (512–518), composed his hymns in order to encourage the people of Antioch away from the theatre (60): '[Instead he wrote] chants full of sighs and calling those away from the ruin of the theatre, he made them church-going.'

A somewhat surprising alternative view comes from Choricius, the chair of rhetoric in Gaza, usually considered a Christian operating in a Christian (if highly intellectual) city. Choricius in his *Defence of* the Mimes (*Speech on behalf of those who represent life in the house of Dionysus*) not only defends the mime as morally harmless but even suggests that watching could be morally beneficial. Choricius was the head of the so-called School of Gaza, a group of rhetoricians who together created a flourishing literary and intellectual centre. Choricius succeeded Procopius of Gaza; both were prolific and their output was a mixture of overtly pagan and Christian works (for example, Choricius' wedding song for a Christian couple, complete with references to Eros and Aphrodite, but no biblical allusion). A huge amount of work has recently been produced on this extraordinary provincial town which flourished in this period, with a large-scale building programme of city walls, churches and civic amenities, celebrated by the rhetoricians of the School (for example, Litsas 1982, Glucker 1987, Bitton-Ashkelony and Kofsky 2004, Saliou 2005, Champion 2014, Amato, Corcella and Lauritzen 2017). Most accept the fourth-century Mark the Deacon's *Life of Porphyrius* which relates the conversion of Gaza, and believe that this was a Christian town, but one where festivals, both those in honour of new churches and those with stronger pagan roots, might innocently be enjoyed safely away from the hostile scrutiny of the state and church. Similarly, most believe that the town's celebrated rhetors were Christian in faith, despite the prominence of their classical education in their works (*contra* Barnes 1996).

Justinian's policy concerning forms of public entertainment was guided by political expediency. In 521, he celebrated his consulship with extravagant games, including the exhibition of wild beasts (twenty lions and thirty panthers, amongst others, as we are told by Marcellinus *Comes* 521 – **II 3**); these *venationes* had previously been banned by Anastasius in 498. It is argued that Justinian had been alarmed by the popularity of his rival, Vitalian, who had started his own consulship with magnificent games the previous year, before being murdered (possibly by Justinian) (Lim 1997). Pragmatism also guided his attitude to festivals, and he looked to reinvent such occasions as a means of retaining the structure of the calendar, keeping the *populus* content and, importantly, offering his subjects an opportunity to demonstrate their loyalty. We know that Justin and Justinian were responsible for shutting down the Olympic games in Antioch in 520 and Lim (1997) suggests that it was not that the games had lost relevance or were 'too pagan', but that they provided little opportunity for rebranding as an imperial festival. On the other hand, the *Brumalia* festival offered excellent opportunities as an imperial event. It had originally been connected with various pagan celebrations around the winter solstice, hence the name *bruma* (meaning the 'winter solstice' or 'shortest day' in Latin). From John the Lydian and Malalas we know that this festival evolved to shed its pagan associations but the hospitality associated with it remained. By Justinian's time, it was a long holiday of twenty-four days, starting on 24 November and finishing on 17 December; each day was associated with one letter of the Greek alphabet so that individuals could invite their friends to dinner on the day associated with the first letter of their name. Choricius makes the *Brumalia* the subject of his *Oratio* XIII, incorporating praise of Justinian and Theodora as well as two imperial officials (**II 81**). Thus, Choricius celebrates Justinian's day on 2 December (the ninth day for the ninth letter of the alphabet, iota (the first letter of 'Iustinianos' in Greek)). Theodora celebrated her day the day before (the eighth day for the eighth letter of the Greek alphabet, theta) (Litsas 1980, Mazza 2010). Justinian's take on the *Brumalia* allowed it to continue and thrive as an acceptable festival in Christian times, as well as being a fitting addition to imperial ceremony; we know that by the tenth century, the emperor rewarded his officials with bags of gold in alphabetical order, before receiving the acclamations from the people (*de Caeremoniis* II.18). That the Church still maintained its disapproval of all these age-old forms of entertainment is clear from the Canons of the Council in Trullo (691–692) which include bans for mimes, wild beast hunts and the celebration of various festivals.

The cultural climate: Classicism and Christianity in literary and artistic trends

Similarly, the cultural climate shows not a linear progress from classicising to sacred literature, but an uneven movement, with plenty of seeming contradictions (Cameron 1986, Rapp 2005). Justinian himself made use of archaising language in the prefaces to his *Novels* on provincial reforms, in order to mask or justify his innovations (Maas 1986, Pazdernik 2005). Now it is without doubt that Justinian was a Christian, but what of the writers in his capital and throughout the empire? Procopius, John Lydus, Agathias and the poets who contributed to the *Cycle* produced Hellenistic epigrams (Cameron and Cameron 1966, McCail 1969, Kaldellis 1999) and, along with Choricius of Gaza, have all been the subject of debates as to their beliefs. Given that we hear that the pagan intelligentsia of Constantinople were especially targeted in the periods of persecution, it is not surprising that there are suspicions that some were actually pagans taking pains to cover up. The debate is currently polarised between the views of Kaldellis (most recently 2017), who generally takes the view that these figures were pagan and believes that dissimulation, feared by Justinian in *C.J.* I.5.18.5, was actually taking place, and other scholars, who take the more conventional view that these writers were Christian but that their classical education continued to colour their writings, and that Hellenic culture underlay Christian thought and expression at every level (for example, Cameron 2007, Cameron 2017). The situation may be summarised as follows:

> John the Lydian: Kaldellis 2003a *contra* Maas 1992, Cameron 1996;
> Procopius: Kaldellis 2004b *contra* Cameron 1985, Lung 2017;
> Agathias: Kaldellis 1997, 1999 *contra* Cameron 1970, Lung 2017.

However, it is the case that many sixth-century works simply display a mix of traditions. Malalas, although writing a chronicle rather than a classicising history, gave consideration to the presentation of the past, as he sought to reconcile three streams of the Roman past: Greek mythology, Roman law and Judeo-Christian scripture (Jeffreys 2006, Liebeschuetz 2001: chapter 7). The anonymous *Dialogue on Political Science* wove ideas from the Platonic tradition of the philosopher-ruler and Roman political philosophy as presented in, for example, Cicero's *Republic*. This work was implicitly critical of Justinian, suggesting that political affairs should be run by the emperor's officials, rather than the emperor himself. It has been dated to either the period of the *Nika* riot or the final years of Justinian's reign, both periods when senatorial approval ratings of Justinian were low (O'Meara 2002, Bell 2009). Another unusual composition is the *Christian Topography*, a work by an anonymous Christian author who is known by the name Cosmas Indicopleustes (given in an eleventh-century manuscript). We know that the author was a sixth-century merchant who produced the *Christian Topography* in the mid-540s; it survives in three manuscripts dating from the ninth to the eleventh centuries. He travelled widely and composed the *Christian Topography* in opposition to the cosmological views of John Philoponus and to promote a biblical world view that the cosmos is created in the model of Moses' tabernacle. His work shows that he was familiar with a wide range of classical and Christian writers, although he did not write particularly well himself. Finally, in the mid-sixth century, far away from Constantinople in the Egyptian village of Aphrodito, the lawyer, landowner and village headman Dioscorus wrote a panegyrical poem to John, *dux* of the Thebaid, in flowery classicising language: 'you are a Dionysus giving wine to revelers . . . I beseech you, brave Heracles, put an end to our sufferings at the hands of the tribe of the Blemmyes so that I can find the money which I will take to the emperor as tax' (MacCoull 1988).

Looking back from the ninth century, Photius struggled to understand how the sixth-century authors could, as committed Christians, write so fluently about classical myths and gods. He puzzled over John the Lydian's beliefs ('In matters of religion he seems to have been an unbeliever. He respects and venerates Hellenic beliefs; he also venerates our beliefs, without giving the reader any easy way of deciding whether such veneration is genuine or hypocritical', *Bibliotheca Codex* 180) and was similarly mystified by Choricius ('He is an upholder of the true religion and respects the rites and holy places of the Christians, although for some reason or other, contemptuously and without any excuse, he unjustifiably introduces Greek myths and heathen stories in his writings, sometimes even when discussing sacred things', 160).

Patronage and propaganda

There are only two instances when Justinian directly exercised patronage. In 527, before becoming sole emperor, he granted the post of *cancellarius* (private secretary with senatorial rank) to Marcellinus Comes. Marcellinus came from Illyricum (as did Justinian, of course) and spoke Latin. The reward was probably for the composition of the *Chronicle* which was completed in 518. When Marcellinus updated the work in 534 he showed his gratitude to Justinian by highlighting his subsequent achievements including his accession as emperor, building projects and the victory over the Vandals, which made a convenient endpoint to the narrative (though there is an anonymous edition which deals with the Ostrogothic war up to 548).

The second example is John the Lydian. A native of Philadelphia in Lydia, he came to Constantinople at the age of twenty-one hoping to find employment as a legal secretary. Benefiting from family connections, he received various promotions and eventually he attracted the attention of Justinian and at his invitation delivered an encomium at the court in the presence of celebrities from Rome. He was also commissioned to write a history of the war with Persia. Both works are now lost. Whilst working for the prefecture, he was appointed to an advanced teaching position in Latin in Constantinople and composed two antiquarian works, *de Mensibus* and *de Ostensibus* (concerning the calendar, and divination). Later, after his retirement, he wrote the *de Magistratibus*. When he retired, he was the subject of fulsome praise in a written decree of Justinian which he proudly cites (*de Magistratibus* III.26–30).

As for all the other writers who penned works in praise of Justinian, we can only assume that they did enjoy the patronage of Justinian (but we have no record of the commission), or that they wrote in hope of a reward, or that they wrote in order to avoid suspicion. Procopius of Caesarea is one of the best-known examples. For, after writing the *Wars* (an ostensibly positive account of Justinian's wars against the Persians, Vandals and Goths, although the final book (VIII) came close to revealing an increasingly critical assessment of Justinian's military policy) and the *Secret History* (an invective against Justinian and Theodora, Belisarius and Antonina), he turned to the *Buildings*, a panegyrical work in which he praises Justinian for his territorial gains, religious policy, legal codification and for having 'wedded the state to a life of prosperity' (I.1.10). Justinian's construction of churches, fortifications, bridges and aqueducts is a token of the emperor's paternal care and his lavish generosity to the whole empire. We do not know if Procopius wrote in the hope of receiving a reward, or was motivated by the necessity to clear his name from any association with Belisarius who had been suspected of treason, or wrote in return for a favour already received. The only clue of any direct interaction with the emperor can be found in his remark 'history shows that subjects who have received benefits have proved themselves grateful towards their benefactors, and that they have repaid them with thank-offerings in generous measure' (*Buildings* I.1.4).

Another well-known and well-connected young man operating in the second half of Justinian's reign was Agathias, the continuator of Procopius' history, poet and compiler of the *Cycle*. The *Cycle* includes a hundred of Agathias' own poems, eighty of Paul the Silentiary, and the rest from his friends, all well-educated professionals, including government officials and lawyers. There is debate as to whether the dedicatee of Agathias' *Cycle* was Justin II rather than Justinian, but even if the former, it is still the case that the majority of the poems were the product of the age of Justinian (Cameron and Cameron 1966, McCail 1969, Smith 2019). There are various interpretations as to the extent of the Christian content in the Anthology epigrams (Cameron 1993, Baldwin 1996). McCail detects the influence of the New Testament and the laws of Justinian, and suggests that the absence of homosexual epigrams was a result of Justinian's legislation on the subject (*Novels* 77 and 141). McCail argues further that Agathias' championing of the official line in morality led to him obtaining Justinian's patronage; his building epigram in honour of the emperor was inscribed on the base of the Sangarius Bridge (IX.641 – **II 76**; see Chapter 5). Indeed, inscriptions were a common medium of praise. We have already discussed the dedicatory inscription in SS Sergius and Bacchus, and Justinian was celebrated in an epigram in SS Peter and Paul, another church built early in his reign (*Greek Anthology* I.8 – **II 82**). We have also already come across Paul the Silentiary's *ekphrasis* of Hagia Sophia, written for the re-dedication ceremonies in the 560s (Chapter 5).

A further writer, Romanos the Melode, a Syrian hymn writer who arrived in Constantinople during the reign of Anastasius, had a dream in which he swallowed a scroll from the Virgin Mary, and went on to write more than 800 hymns. He invented a new form known as the *kontakion* which was to become the most popular form of hymn until it was superseded by the *kanon* in the ninth century. Romanos' Greek was the unsophisticated 'koine' Greek, close to the spoken language, with a sprinkling of classical (Attic Greek) forms and poetic and archaic vocabulary, despite his explicit rejection of a classical education and dismissal of pagan philosophers and writers (for example, *Kontakia* 31 and 33; Kaldellis 2007a: 155, 178, 325). His subject matter was naturally mainly ecclesiastical, but his hymns nevertheless contained much political and secular material.

As with the gradual rebranding of pagan festivals discussed above, we can see changes in imperial ceremonies; for example, in 534 Justinian celebrated victory over the Vandals with something very similar to an old Roman triumph, but in 559 he marked the victory over the Kutrigurs with something more like a late antique *adventus* – a formal entry into the city. He stopped off at a church to give thanks to God and pray for the soul of Theodora. Many imperial ceremonies now incorporated religious ritual, and Justinian became increasingly interested in religious liturgy. It is not surprising that he came to realise the power of liturgical hymns for disseminating imperial ideology. Unlike the inscriptions carved in elaborate language high up in churches, hymns could be heard and understood by all, and the refrains, sung by the congregation, would have reinforced the message (Topping 1978, Cameron 1979, Koder 2008).

In addition to the clearly political *Kontakion* 54, *On Earthquakes and Fires*, which refers to Justinian's building of Hagia Sophia after the *Nika* riot (discussed in Chapter 5; **II 71**), Koder (2008) suggests that Justinian encouraged another five hymns (*On the Meeting of Our Lord* (14), *On the Mission of the Apostles* (47), *On the Nativity of the Virgin Mary* (35), *On Lazarus* (27), *On the Resurrection* (43)). We also know of an anonymous hymn, *On the Inauguration of St Sophia*, composed to mark the second dedication of Hagia Sophia in 562 after earthquake damage. Another writer connected with Hagia Sophia was the enigmatic deacon Agapetus, who addressed a work to Justinian.

This composition comprises seventy-two short maxims on how to be a good ruler, and is thought to be the first in the genre of 'Mirror of Princes' works.

Even if Justinian were not a direct patron, nevertheless many writers were attracted to his capital and we can find some trace of the circles of intellectuals who gathered there, many of them exiles from North Africa and Italy, escaping the turmoil which Justinian's foreign policy had brought to their native lands. These included Corippus, who had composed a panegyric for Justinian's general, John Troglyta, back in Carthage in 548, and would go on to compose the panegyric for the accession of Justin II; Victor of Tonnena, who completed his *Chronicle of the World*; Junillus (Tribonian's successor as *quaestor sacri palatii* from 542 to 549), who composed the *Handbook of the Basic Principles of Divine Law* (*Instituta regularia diviniae legis*); Cassiodorus (see Chapter 3), former secretary to the Ostrogothic king Theoderic and future founder of the scholarly monastery of Vivarium, who composed the *Expositio psalmorum* (*Explanation of the Psalms*) whilst in Constantinople, and finished his *Tripartite History* of Greek Church historians (*Historia Tripartita*) and a short biographical pamphlet, the *Ordo generis Cassiodororum*, which he addressed to the Roman aristocrat Cethegus. It is also possible he revised his *Variae* whilst in Constantinople. Jordanes also wrote his *Roman History* (*Romana*, now lost) and his *Gothic History* (*Getica*) in Constantinople c. 551. For this he managed to secure from Cassiodorus' administrator a three-day loan of the latter's *Gothic History*, a text that does not survive. These writers must have been influenced at least to a certain extent by the literary figures they encountered in Constantinople, and efforts have been made to trace the links between, for example, Cassiodorus with Malalas and with John the Lydian (Praet 2019).

Trends in art

The same debates, concerning the mingling of traditions throughout the sixth century and Justinian's role as a patron, are relevant when looking at forms of art. Some have seen the emperor as an 'energetic patron of arts' and have sought to trace the influence from Constantinopolitan workshops in the provinces (Alchermes 2005). As for depictions of Justinian himself, only a few survive, and they combine elements of the Roman imperial tradition with new features designed to highlight Justinian's closeness with Christ. Examples include the massive gold medallion of Justinian, dating to 534/535 and

Culture and Society

weighing half a pound of gold; the original disappeared in 1831 but a cast survived from which some electrotypes were made, such as the one in the British Museum (see cover). Justinian is presented very much as a Roman emperor; on the obverse he wears a breastplate, military cloak, and a diadem topped by a plumed dress helmet. The legend reads 'Our Lord Justinian, perpetual Augustus'. On the reverse he is pictured sitting astride a horse, with a winged Victory carrying a palm frond and captured weapons; the legend describes Justinian as the 'salvation and glory of the Romans'. These elements are also familiar from the 'Barberini Ivory', a diptych of uncertain date, but now most usually thought to depict Justinian, in triumphant pose after his initial victories over the Persians (Cutler 1998). Justinian is depicted both as a victorious emperor and as protected by Christ. In the central panel he is shown as a dominant figure mounted on a horse, and there are signs of various defeated peoples he has conquered (for example, the non-Roman peoples carrying tribute as shown in the lower panel). In the top panel, however, it is clear that victory is granted by God: flying angels hold a roundel which encases a bust of Christ granting his blessing (on the emperor below). The iconography of these angels deriving from classical Victories had earlier appeared on coins struck for Justin and Justinian.

Figure 6.3 Barberini diptych. Photo: public domain.

We also know from extant descriptions of some further depictions of Justinian in Constantinople which no longer survive but clearly sought to portray him as a conquering emperor (despite, of course, the fact that Justinian did not take to the battlefield himself). From Procopius' *Buildings* we learn of the mosaic on the vaulted ceiling of the Chalke (the vestibule of the imperial place), which pictured Justinian and Theodora marking the 'victories over both the king of Vandals and the king of Goths, submissive prisoners of war who approach the imperial couple' (*Buildings* I.10.10–20, Mango 1959). Procopius also includes a description of another lost piece, a colossal equestrian portrait of Justinian that stood near the Chalke, in the Augusteum (*Buildings* I.2.1–12 – **II 73**; see Chapter 5). In this case, we do have a fifteenth-century drawing (now in Budapest). The emperor is presented in a breastplate, boots without greaves, headgear with plumes, but he does not hold any weapons. Instead, he extends his right hand towards the rising sun (which Procopius interprets as ordering the barbarians, presumably the Persians, to remain at home). In the left hand, he holds the *globus cruciger*, a sphere representing the world topped by a cross, a perfect example of a Christianised imperial symbol: Justinian secures his empire with the help of the Christian God.

The other images we know of Justinian may be found in the Church of San Vitale in Ravenna where again we can see a blending of Roman imperial and Christian elements. Justinian, crowned, wearing the

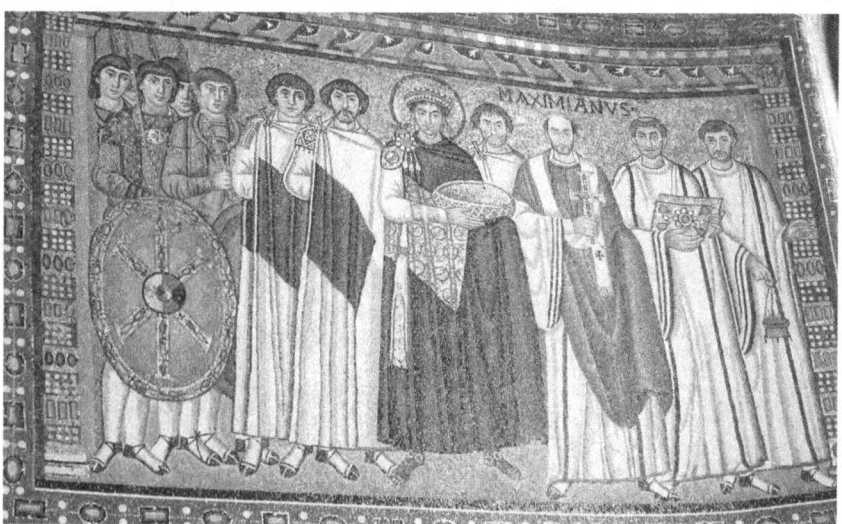

Figure 6.4 Justinian panel, San Vitale, Ravenna. Photo: author.

imperial purple, and holding a liturgical paten or bowl, is shown in a large panel surrounded by his entourage and churchmen, as if taking part in a religious procession. The archbishop of Ravenna, Maximian, is identified by an inscription. Theodora and her retinue are shown in another panel on the opposite wall. She also wears purple, and a tall, jewelled crown and large necklace, and carries a gem-encrusted chalice. The three magi bringing gifts to Christ embroidered on the hem of her cloak have already been noted (see Chapter 2). As for the styling of the figures, it has been pointed out that they share the characteristics (in terms of facial features and dress) with other portraits of this period, for example, the consuls depicted on consul diptychs or sculptures from elsewhere in the empire, such as the well-known statues from Aphrodisias (Smith 1999: 183). If we are surprised that Justinian and Theodora should be depicted with such prominence and magnificence in a church in a place which they had never visited and to which they had never given any donations, we only have to look at the political and religious background. Ravenna was recovered for the east by Belisarius in 540 and the panels portray the allegiance of the Romans in Ravenna to their new rulers. It is likely that the panels were created between 546 (when Justinian appointed Maximian archbishop of Ravenna in the hope he would prove more co-operative than the recalcitrant pope (Vigilius) he was holding in Constantinople) and 548, when

Figure 6.5 Justinian mosaic portrait, San Apollinare Nuovo, Ravenna. Photo: author.

Theodora died. The image then displays the collaboration between Constantinople and Ravenna. Another item which demonstrates this relationship was an ivory throne, today in the Ravenna Museum, with the monogram of the archbishop carved on the front, perhaps a gift from Justinian to Maximian. The throne has suffered various mishaps due to poor restoration and some panels remain missing, but it is generally agreed to date from 547, and although its provenance is not secure, there is a strong argument for Constantinople, given the close resemblance with the various imperial diptychs, including the Barberini diptych. Scenes from the Old and New Testaments depict, notably, the story of Joseph (where it is proposed that the relationship between Joseph and the Pharaoh suggested that between Maximian and Justinian) and the life of Christ.

San Vitale was far from the only church-building activity in Ravenna at this time. San Apollinare Nuovo, an Arian church constructed by Theoderic and known for its three tiers of spectacular mosaic decoration, was converted to an orthodox church following an edict of Justinian. Some of the mosaic figures which had represented Theoderic and his courtiers were replaced by Virgins and Martyrs led by St Martin, to whom the church was now dedicated (it was re-dedicated to

Figure 6.6 Apse mosaic, Church of SS Michael and Gabriel, Ravenna (Bode Museum, Berlin). Photo: author.

San Apollinare in the ninth century). A portrait of Justinian, showing him as rather older and stouter than the San Vitale version, dates from 561; it is possible that this is a reworked image of Theoderic. A third church, San Apollinare in Classe, was consecrated by Maximian in 549. Many of the churches were financed by a local banker, Julianus Argentarius, who also paid for the Church of SS Michael and Gabriel (San Michele in Africisco) which does not survive in Ravenna, but reproductions of the apse and triumphal arch mosaics by the restorer, Giovanni Moro, can be found in the Bode Museum, Berlin.

The workmanship of the Ravenna churches demonstrates a mix of imported materials and local construction, and eastern and western iconography. This process, by which materials might be shipped out (most notably marble from the imperial quarries of Proconnesus) but some or all of the construction and decoration would be carried out by local workmen, is one we see replicated throughout the empire. We have already mentioned this in connection with North Africa (see Chapter 3). Other cases may also be seen at the complex of Bishop Euphrasius at Poreč, and the Church of the Panagia Kanakaria at Lynthrankomi on Cyprus, both dating from the mid-sixth century. At the monastery of St Catherine at Mount Sinai, however, it appears that the capitals and columns are of a lower (local) standard, but the brilliance of the apse mosaic which depicts the Transfiguration suggests that a team of mosaicists was sent out from Constantinople with the materials (Beckworth 1970).

Figure 6.7 Apse mosaic, Church at Poreč. Photo: author.

Evidence that artisans could cater for their wealthy patrons whether they preferred classical or Christian imagery may be found in many art forms: in the marble portrait busts; in the luxurious illustrated purple manuscripts (for example, the Rossano Gospels, the Vienna Genesis and the Codex Sinopensis); and in silverware (for example, the silver plate depicting Hercules and the Nemean lion, now in the Bibliothèque nationale de France). Further evidence for the influence of classical art may be found in the most sacred of items, the icon. Thanks to the iconoclasm of the eighth and ninth centuries, few early icons survive. One example is the icon now preserved in the monastery of St Catherine on Mount Sinai which depicts the image of the Christ blessing. The method used for painting icons was 'encaustic', a technique familiar from the portraits of Roman Egypt attached to mummy cases, and they shared the same sort of imagery and composition, displaying figures in static frontal poses.

Conclusion

The 'long twilight of Byzantine paganism is ... explained as a gradual transmutation of belief in the gods into a reverence for a cultural heritage' (Harl 1990). This is a good way of explaining the long period of transition where both pagans and Christians with a shared educational background could appreciate the same aesthetic values. The spectacular mosaic floors in the Great Palace, with traditional hunting scenes, date from probably c. 580, just after the end of Justinian's reign. However, the enjoyment of classical literature and art forms became a problem if aesthetic appreciation developed into sincere belief and practical application, such as sacrifices to the gods and the use of magic. The line between the two, especially amongst the classically educated elite, was very fine, hence the uneven response from Justinian, and his own use and manipulation of the past. We hear of paganism continuing in pockets in the late sixth century, including at Edessa where sacrifices were still made at the temple there: Anatolius, the *vicarius* of the praetorian prefect, was tried and subsequently lynched and murdered by a mob in Constantinople. There is also evidence that activity at the ancient shrines of Heliopolis (Baalbek) and Carrhae (Harran) continued. However, there were no further major 'pagan scandals' after the mid-sixth century, perhaps suggesting that Justinian's policies had been successful (Whitby 1991).

Finally, it has been said that 'Justinian seems to have been singularly unfortunate in his attempt to find writers to celebrate his regime'

Figure 6.8 Hunting mosaic, Great Palace, Constantinople. Photo: author.

(Cameron 1985: 21). Yet we have found plenty of examples of panegyric within the literary and epigraphic output of Justinian's reign, even if they are not perhaps the conventional imperial encomia we are accustomed to. Whether these writers had been directly commissioned by Justinian, or wrote with some other motivation, it is striking that their presentation of the emperor and his ideology often fitted closely with the emperor's own propaganda to create a coherent picture of his reign.

Conclusion: Longevity and Legacy

Justinian's reign of thirty-eight years was amongst the longest of all Roman emperors. Before him, only Augustus, who ruled for forty-five years (31 BC–AD 14), and Theodosius II, who ruled for forty-eight (402–450), held the throne for longer; after Justinian, we can highlight a few long-reigning emperors such as Heraclius, who enjoyed a thirty-one-year reign (610–641), Basil the Bulgar-Slayer, who ruled for forty-nine years (976–1025), and Alexius I Comnenus, who ruled for thirty-seven years (1081–1118). Justinian was also closely involved in at least the last stages of the reign of his uncle, Justin I, thus extending the period of his influence over the running of the state even further. As for these other emperors, the longevity of Justinian's reign was a key factor in enabling imperial ambitions to be designed and pursued (even if they did not always end in unqualified success), in shaping the era, and in ensuring an enduring legacy.

Justinian shared with Augustus and his successors many of the attributes and ideals of a Roman and Byzantine emperor. Military campaigns, an administrative reform programme and an extensive empire-wide building policy were all aspirations to be prized. Justinian sought to defend the empire against Persia, Rome's ancient enemy, and to recover by military conquest the heart of the Roman Empire. He sought to improve on the codification project attempted by Theodosius II. After the *Nika* riot, he redesigned the centre of Constantinople, including the magnificent Hagia Sophia, an echo of Augustus' claim that he had found Rome a city of bricks and left it a city of marble. The relationship of an emperor to the pagan gods or to the Christian God was also key, whether we think of the deification of Augustus, or the increasing involvement of the later emperors in the affairs of the Church, in which process Justinian played a pivotal role. Finally, a lengthy reign allows us to attribute long-term literary and artistic trends to a particular emperor, and we start to think of the reign as an 'age' or 'era'. Although we have seen that Justinian was not necessarily an active patron, there were certainly a large number of intellectuals and writers working during his reign.

Constant activity and little rest are themes which recur in the sources and Justinian has been characterised as the 'sleepless emperor' (Croke 2011). Despite military setbacks, the complications of the Church, and the challenges caused by the plague, we are left with an impressive legacy of achievements realised over a long reign by an emperor who, as we first discovered in the Introduction from *Novel* 86, made every effort to help the subjects entrusted to him by God.

Part II
Documents

1. *Collectio Avellana* 147

Letter from Justinian to Pope Hormisdas, 7 September 518

Copy of Justinian's letter

Divine Clemency has taken account of the suffering of the human race and consented to grant the desirable time, which we wished for with our best prayers, in which all catholics and those who are perfectly faithful to God may be able to entrust themselves to his majesty. I have, therefore, addressed this letter to your Apostleship, with a free licence now given to me by heavenly good will.

For our lord, the most invincible emperor [Justin I], who has always embraced the orthodox religion with a very passionate faith and desired that the holy churches should be called back to harmony, has now acquired the imperial insignia through the judgment of heaven and has declared to the clergy located here that the churches should be united according to the apostolic regulations. Moreover, a great part of the faith has been established by God's authority; only concerning the name of Acacius is it right for your beatitude to inaugurate your agreement.

For this reason our lord, the most serene prince, has sent the eminent man Gratus, a friend who is of the same mind as me, with a venerable letter to your Holiness, so that by all means it may be thought right for you to come to Constantinople to make the final arrangements for harmony. We expect your arrival without any delay, and if any deferment, which ought not to be the case, perhaps holds it back, then in the meantime make haste to despatch suitable clergy, because the whole world of our provinces does not suffer any delays to unity.

Make haste, therefore, most holy lord, lest the things which must be arranged are arranged in your absence. For we know what the letters of your beatitude and of your predecessors which were sent to the east contained concerning this matter. Moreover, so that nothing may be overlooked, because the matter has been mentioned rather often to the most invincible ruler, any matter of doctrine has also been imparted to your son, the eminent man Gratus, through the favour of our Lord Jesus Christ.

2. Anonymus Valesianus 85–7

(85) After this, the king [Theoderic] began straightaway, when he found an opportunity, to rage against the Romans when a pretext could be found. Cyprianus, who was then a *referendarius*, and afterwards the *comes sacrarum* and a *magister*, was motivated by greed to make an insinuation about the patrician, Albinus, that he had sent the Emperor Justin a letter against Theoderic's rule. Albinus was called for and denied that he had done this, and then the patrician, Boethius, who was the *magister officiorum*, said in the presence of the king: 'The insinuation of Cyprianus is false, but if Albinus did that, so also have I, and the whole senate, done it with a single resolution: it is false, my Lord King.'

(86) Then Cyprianus hesitated but introduced false witnesses, not just against Albinus, but also against his defender, Boethius. Moreover, the king was devising a deception for the Romans and looking for a way to kill them; hence he gave more credence to the false witnesses than the senators.

(87) Then Albinus and Boethius were put in custody in the baptistery of a church. And the king called Eusebius, the prefect of the city, to Ticinum [Pavia], and without listening to Boethius made known his judgment on him. Soon after, at the Ager Calventianus, where Boethius was held in custody, he had him put to an awful death. He was tortured with a cord placed around his forehead for a very long time, so much so that his eyes burst and, while under torture, he was brought to a final death with a club.

3. Marcellinus *Comes* 521

The consul Justinian made this consulship the most well known of all eastern consuls by being truly more generous in his largesse. For two hundred and eighty-eight thousand solidi were distributed amongst the people and expended on spectacles or on their organisation. He displayed in the amphitheatre at the same time twenty lions and thirty panthers amongst other wild beasts. After already donating the chariots, in addition, he provided in the hippodrome numerous horses, richly adorned; only the one last race was denied to the excited people.

4. Diptych announcing the consulship of Justinian, 521

Inscription across the top:

FL[AVIUS] PETRUS SABBAT[IUS] IUSTIN[IANUS] V[IR] I[N]L[USTRIS] / + COM[ES] MAG[ISTER] EQQ[UITUM] ET P[EDITUM] PRAES[ENTALIS] ET C[ONSUL] ORD[INARIUS] +

Flavius Petrus Sabbatius Justinianus, noble man / + Official, Chief of the Cavalry and of the Infantry and Consul normally elected in present times

Central medallions:

+ / MUNERA . PAR / VA . QUIDEM . PRE / TIO . SED HONO / RIBUS ALMA / + / + / PATRIBVS . IS / TA . MEIS . OFFERO / CONS[UL] . EGO / +

I, the consul, offer these gifts, small indeed in value but rich in honours, to my senators.

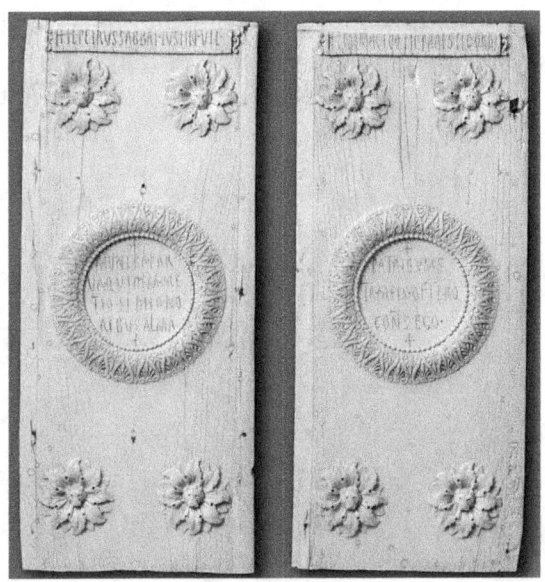

Figure II.4 Diptych announcing the consulship of Justinian, 521. The Met, New York. Photo: public domain.

5. *Greek Anthology* I.10

On the Church of the Holy Martyr Polyeuktos

The dedicatory inscription to the church survives in the *Greek Anthology* and fragments remain in the Istanbul Archaeological Museum. One example, which records part of line 30, is included below; the Greek text and English translation are highlighted in bold.

Lines 14–33
For who has not heard of Juliana, that she, with dutiful devotion, cheered up even her own parents with well-made works? She alone, with righteous toil, built a worthy house to immortal Polyeuktos. For she always knew how to bring blameless gifts to all athletes of the heavenly king. Every country proclaims, and every city, that she made her parents more joyous by more excellent deeds. For where is it not seen that Juliana has raised a glorious temple to the saints? Where are not seen the signs of the pious hands of you alone? What place exists which has not discovered that your purpose is full of piety? The inhabitants of the whole world sing your labours which will be remembered everlastingly. The deeds of piety are not hidden; for oblivion does not extinguish the struggles of benevolent virtue. You yourself do not know how many **houses dedicated to God** your hand **has accomplished**; for you alone, I think, put up innumerable temples all over the world, always fearful of the servants of God in Heaven . . .

Figure II.5 Church of St Polyeuktos inscription. Photo: author.

Line 30 ... πείθεα (θεοπείθεα dedicated to God) δώματα (houses) τεύχει (accomplished)

At the entrance of the same church, outside the narthex, towards the apse:

Lines 42–50
What chorus is sufficient for the works of Juliana who, after Constantine, embellished his Rome, and after the holy all-golden light of Theodosius, and after a royal family of so many ancestors, accomplished in a few years a work worthy of her lineage and even more so? She alone forced time, and she surpassed the wisdom of renowned Solomon, having raised a temple to receive God, whose elaborate and graceful beauty a great age cannot celebrate.

6. Church of SS Sergius and Bacchus inscription

The Greek text of the dedicatory inscription is published in Croke (2006: 47). It is carved into the octagonal nave entablature where it can still be seen today in the Church of SS Sergius and Bacchus, now

... ἀλλὰ (but) Θεοῦ (God) τέτληκεν (he suffered) ὑπὲρ (on behalf of) Χριστοῖο (Christ) δαμῆναι (to be killed)

Figure II.6 Church of SS Sergius and Bacchus inscription. Photo: author.

the Küçük Ayasofya Camii (Little Hagia Sophia Mosque). The Greek text which corresponds to the letters which are legible in the section encircled in black is given in bold beneath the photograph.

Other sovereigns have honoured dead men whose labour was unrecognised; but our sceptred Justinian, cultivating piety, honours with a magnificent abode the Servant of Christ, Begetter of all things, Sergius; whom not the burning fire, nor the sword, nor any other pressure of tortures troubled, but he suffered to be killed for the sake of Christ, the God, gaining by his blood heaven as his home. But in all things may he guard the sovereignty of the sleepless emperor and increase the power of the God-crowned Theodora, whose mind is embellished with piety, whose unceasing labour exists for her unsparing efforts to nourish the poor.

7. Procopius, *Secret History* 9.20–2

(20) Often, even in the theatre, in front of the whole audience, she stripped off and stood naked in their midst, having only a girdle around her private parts and groin, not, however, because she was ashamed to display these parts as well to the people, but because no one is allowed to be there completely naked; that is, not having a girdle around the groin. Thus, wearing this attire, lounging on the floor, she lay on her back. (21) Certain slaves, on whom this task had been inflicted, sprinkled over her private parts grains of barley which geese, which happened to have been trained for this purpose, pecked off with their beaks one by one, and ate them. (22) When she stood up, she did not even blush but she seemed to take pride in this act.

8. John of Ephesus, *Lives of the Eastern Saints* 13

Translated by E. W. Brooks, PO 17 (1923), 187–9

Thomas and Stephen and Zwt' the notaries and *syncelli* of the holy Mare of the metropolitan of Amida

After the decease of the believing king Anastasius who is among the saints, when Justin was set over the kingdom, he was making a beginning of divisions and contentions in the church of God by introducing the impious synod of Chalcedon: and from that time forward by order of the same schismatic king everyone who did not assent to the reception and introduction of the synod lived under persecution and expulsion, and certain members of the church were accordingly banished to various places of exile . . .

These things quickly reached Mesopotamia, and overtook the holy Mare bishop of Amida; . . . [he] therefore, with Sergius and Stephen and Thomas his notaries and *syncelli*, were sent to a hard and distant place of exile at Petra; . . . By reason of this distress therefore the holy Mare was constrained to send the virtuous Stephen his deacon and notary to the royal city, in the hope that he might perhaps by the intercession of anyone whom God might put in his way be able to have that place altered for them. But when he went up, the good God . . . directed the virtuous Stephen to Theodora who came from the brothel, who was at that time a patrician, but eventually became queen also with King Justinian. She therefore, when she learned of that distress, as if by divine instigation, because she saw that saint's distress, made her mercy manifest, and made entreaty to Justinian her husband, who was master of the soldiers and also a patrician and the king's nephew, that he would inform his uncle, and he might order relief to be given to these distressed men, making this entreaty even with tears. And, through the grace which cares for every man's life, it was done . . .

9. Cassiodorus, *Variae* X.20

King Theodahad to Empress Theodora

(1) I have received Your Piety's letters with the thanks which are always due to those things we long for, and I have received with the most reverent rejoicing your verbal message far better than any gift; promising myself everything from such a serene soul, since I have received whatever I could hope for in such a kindly message. (2) For you encourage us to bring to your attention whatever we decide to seek from your husband, the triumphant prince and lord. Who now doubts that whatever so great a power condescends to support will come into effect? Previously we relied on the justice of our cause, but now we rejoice more in your promise. For our wishes cannot be put off when it involves her who deserves to be heard. Now fulfil your promises, in order that you may enable the man to whom you gave a very certain hope to attain his goal. (3) It also adds to my joy that Your Serenity has fixed upon such a man, such as so great a glory ought to send and it is fitting that your service should retain. For there is no doubt that she, who is constantly observed, chose the path of morality, since a mind formed by good precepts is clearly cleansed. Hence it is that, guided by your reverence,

we have thought it right to order that both the most blessed pope and the most distinguished senate should reply without any delay to what you judged should be asked from them, lest your glory will be thought of with less reverence because an eagerness for delay opposed it; and so that the influence they pray for may be increased by their speed of action. (4) For about that person [Amalasuntha] too, about whom some speculative word reached us, know that that has been ordained which we believe will suit your desires. For it is our desire that, since you have extended your favour, you will command no less in my kingdom than in your empire. And so we inform you that the aforementioned reply was made by the venerable pope before your envoy, the carrier of this letter, could leave the city of Rome, lest anything could happen which would obstruct your wishes. (5) Therefore, saluting you with the reverence which ought to be shown to those who are so deserving, we have taken especial care that the office of ambassador to your clemency should be destined for a venerable man distinguished by both his morals and learning, and to be revered for the quality of his piety; for we believe that these persons, whom we judge to have been embraced by the divine mysteries, will be welcomed by you.

10. Procopius, *Buildings* I.9.5–10

(5) The Emperor Justinian and Empress Theodora (who shared between them a common piety in everything they did) made a plan as follows. (6) They cleansed the state of the pollution of the brothels, eradicating the name of the brothel-keepers, and they freed from an intemperance fit for slaves the women who were suffering with great poverty, providing them with an independent living and allowing them to live virtuously. They achieved these things in this way. (7) Near this shore of the strait which is on the right when sailing towards the Euxine Sea, as it is called, they set up a former palace as a grand monastery as a refuge for women repenting of their previous lives; (8) in that place there, through occupying their minds with God and piety, they would be able to cleanse away the sins of their lifestyle in the brothel. (9) Because of this, they name this dwelling place of the women 'Repentance', having the same name as its purpose. (10) And these sovereigns have donated to this monastery a huge income of money, and they have built many buildings which are especially extraordinary in beauty and costliness, as a consolation to these women, so they are never compelled to move away from the practice of virtue in any way whatsoever.

11. *C.J.* I.5.12.4–10

(4) As for the other heretics, whatever their error or name (for we call everyone a heretic who does not adhere to the Catholic Church and our orthodox and holy faith), but also regards the Hellenes (pagans) who are trying to introduce polytheism, and still the Jews and Samaritans, we resolve not only to revive the statutes of existing laws, and to make them more secure in this current law, but also to pronounce more, whereby the security and dignity and honour of those who share in our holy faith will become greater. (5) It will be possible for everyone to perceive, we have said, that those who do not correctly worship God will also be dispossessed of their worldly goods. (6) We therefore prescribe that none of the aforesaid persons may attain any position at all, nor obtain any civilian or military rank, nor reach any order, except that which we call *cohortalini* (for we desire that they are subject to this order from birth, and that they remain subject to it and fulfil all the duties required from it and submit to every burden which is the responsibility of this position; and on the one hand excluded from promotion, and on the other hand from executing sentences against orthodox Christians on account of public and private debts). The descendants of these people will be led into this status if in the meantime they are incapable of escaping notice. And because of their bad reputation we prescribe that they have no defence. (7) We allow the heretics to hold neither the office of defender or of the father of the city, in case by reason of the immunity from this office they harm other Christians and especially bishops most dear to God, and have the ability to judge or condemn them, according to those enactments legislated by our predecessors. (8) We do not allow them to be appointed among the most wise advocates, among whom it is more fitting that they, more so than many, have a correct opinion about divine decrees, as their livelihood is in words. (9) And we also command that those who are heretics and before them Hellenes (pagans) or Jews or Samaritans, and those like them, who already hold any of these offices we have cited and any rank or are on the roster of pleaders, or who acquired a military position, or any other appointment, should be expelled straightaway from holding these positions. (10) We wish that all these aforesaid positions should be purified now both by association of these men, not only in the glorious city but also in every province in every place.

12. Gold coin of Justin and Justinian, 527

Figure II.12 Gold coin of Justin and Justinian, 527. Photo © Classical Numismatic Group LLC Auction 108, lot 717.

DN IVSTIN ET IVSTINIAN PP AVG, CONOB
Our Lords Justin and Justinian emperors for ever. Fine gold, Constantinople

Justin and Justinian nimbate seated on thrones and holding globes with crosses; above, cross

VICTORIA AVGGGZ, CONOB
The Victory of the emperors. Fine gold minted in the seventh workshop at Constantinople

Victory holding a cross and a globe with cross

13. Procopius, *Wars* I.24.33–7

(33) And the Empress Theodora spoke as follows: 'That a woman should not behave boldly among men or speak hot headedly amongst those who shrink in fear, I think that the present time rather allows us to examine this custom in this or some other way. (34) For those whose affairs are in the greatest danger, nothing else seems best other than to resolve these matters in the best possible way. (35) I think that flight indeed now, more than at any time, is not

appropriate even if it brings safety. For although it is not possible for a man who has seen the light of day, not also to die, but for one who has reigned as emperor, it is insufferable to be a fugitive. (36) May I never be parted from this purple, and may I not live to see that day when those who meet me do not address me as mistress. If you wish to save yourself, Emperor, this is no problem. (37) For we have much money, and there is the sea, and here the ships. Nevertheless, consider lest it come about that you, having been saved, would gladly exchange that safety for death. For I favour a certain old saying that royalty is a good burial shroud.'

14. Menander the Guardsman, fragment 6.1

Through the east and Armenia, it seemed that there was a very secure peace between the Romans and Persians and, regarding Lazica, there was a truce between the Romans and Persians. Since, therefore, there was a semi-peace in place, the rulers of the Romans and Persians decided to make a very full peace, and on account of this, Justinian sent Peter, who was the master of the offices, to negotiate a wide-ranging treaty with Chosroes. And so, when Peter arrived at the frontier at Dara, he made it known to the king of the eastern barbarians that he was there to negotiate the laying down of arms everywhere; the ambassador of the Persians, who was called Yazdgushnasp, was also despatched to that place. He held the rank of Zikh, which was the greatest honour among Persians. He was the king's chamberlain . . .

After Peter and Yazdgushnasp had set out their arguments, the account continues:

When the Zikh had said this, the interpreters of both sides gave a report on each part of the speeches and gave an explanation of the proposals. Many other speeches were delivered by both sides, some useful, some for the purpose of boasting and to show they had no less a desire for peace. The Persians thought it right that there should be a permanent truce and, in addition, that a specified amount of gold should be provided by the Romans each year in return for them not taking up arms; and that if forty, or at least thirty, years' worth of the contributions owed, were paid in one payment, they would be willing to lay down their weapons. The Romans, on the contrary, wanted the treaty to be of a short duration, and in addition not to make any contribution for the peace. A long argument over this took place, and no small number of words used up, but finally it was decided that the peace should be established for fifty years; that Lazica be handed over to the Romans; that the treaty be firmly and steadfastly observed on each side; this should be so in the east and in Armenia, but also, of course, in Lazica itself; and that the Persians should receive thirty thousand golden *nomismata* per year for the peace from the Romans. It was also established that the Romans should offer first a down payment of ten years' worth of instalments thus: the amount for seven years would be paid immediately, and after the passing of seven years the contribution for the three remaining years would be paid straightaway. After this, each year the Persians would be provided with the agreed annual payment.

15. C.J. I.29.5

Emperor Justinian Augustus to the illustrious Zetas, Military Commander in Armenia and Pontus Polemoniacus and the nations. Since Roman rule has been conferred on us by divine favour, we have perceived that, having investigated with careful analysis and cautious diligence, it is necessary by this law to appoint a specific Military Commander also for the regions of Armenia and Pontus Polemoniacus and the nations. We are confident that your great qualities, which have been very well commended to us from your deeds, make you suitable for such an appointment, and we have chosen you and entrusted to your care specific provinces, that is, Greater Armenia, which was called Inner (Armenia), and the nations (for example, Anzetana, Ingilena, Asthianena, Sophena, Sophanena, in which Martyropolis is situated, and Balabitena) and First and Second Armenia and Pontus Polemoniacus with their own dukes; the position of the Count of Armenia has completely been abolished, and we have put under your authority certain units, not only new units we have recently formed but also some separated from the *praesentales* [troops serving in the presence of the emperor], those in the east and those other troops, not however lessening the quantity of troops: but because we have added many to them without weighing down the state and increasing expenses, we took away some, in such a way however, that after this reduction more will remain than there were before our happy times.

16. The *Chronicle* of Pseudo-Zachariah Rhetor, IX.8a

Translation from The Chronicle of Pseudo-Zachariah Rhetor: Church and War in Late Antiquity, *edited by Geoffrey Greatrex, translated by Robert R. Phenix and Cornelia B. Horn (Liverpool 2011)*

The eighth chapter of the ninth book is about the Samaritans who rebelled and established for themselves a tyrant in the province of Palestine.

When the Samaritans of the province of Palestine who were near the city of Neapolis and not far from Caesarea learned that the Persians from time to time attacked and invaded Roman territory, and imagining that [the Romans] had shown themselves to be weak [in the face of the Persians], they were emboldened, thinking that they had been deported from Kuth, Babylon, 'Awa, Hamath, and Serafwayim by Shalmaneser [the Fifth] the king of Assyria, and had been settled in the land of Samaria. They made a tyrant as a leader for themselves when they rebelled, and they entered Neapolis and killed Mamona, who was the bishop there. They took up arms and were inflicting harm, causing a disturbance in the province, wanting to help the Persians, because they had been settled from their country in Roman territory. They burned many sanctuaries of saints, and seized the city and collected the spoil. When the emperor heard about this, he sent the *chiliarch* Hadrian; both the *dux* of the province and with him the army of the Romans and Ṭayyayê who were in the 'Arab were assembled, and they engaged the Samaritans, who were slaughtered by the soldiers. The soldiers killed the tyrant, captured the city, and returned it to their control, as by the former arrangement. They also appointed a bishop and an army for his protection and for the [good] order of the [inhabitants] of the province.

17. Procopius, *Wars* I.14.45–54

(45) Therefore, the Persians who held the left wing under the leadership of Baresmanas, with the Immortals, attacked those Romans opposite them at a run. They, not withstanding the attack, started to flee. (46) Then the Romans in the angle, and those who were behind them, went forward with great enthusiasm against the pursuers. (47) As they came against the barbarians from the side, they divided their army into two, and they had the greater part on their right, while some who had been left behind were positioned on their left. And amongst

them, it happened that there was the standard bearer of Baresmanas, whom Sunicas, attacking him, struck with his spear. (48) Already the Persians, who were at the front of the pursuers, realising in what a difficult position they were, turned back and stopped the pursuit. Then they charged against them, and they became exposed to the enemy from both sides. (49) For those fleeing, observing what was happening, turned back again. The other Persians and the unit of the Immortals, seeing the standard falling and lowered to the earth, rushed out against the Romans there with Baresmanas. The Romans came out to meet them. (50) And first Sunicas killed Baresmanas and threw him from his horse to the ground. And because of this, the barbarians, having fallen into great fear, no longer had any thought of defence, but they fled in great disorder. (51) The Romans, having made a circle around them, killed a good five thousand. Thus both armies were in a complete state of motion, the Persians in retreat, and the Romans in pursuit. (52) In this section of the battle, the foot soldiers who were in the Persian army threw down their shields and, being in complete confusion, were killed by the enemy. However, the pursuit of the Romans was short-lived. (53) For Belisarius and Hermogenes absolutely forbade them to go further, fearing that the Persians, driven by necessity, would turn around against their disordered pursuers. It seemed to them sufficient to preserve the victory intact. (54) For on that day, after a long time, the Persians had been defeated in battle by the Romans. Therefore, both armies separated from each other.

18. Malalas, *Chronicle* 477–8

(477) At this time, Hermogenes and Rufinus returned from Persia and brought with them a peace treaty between the two states of Rome and Persia, ... of the two states for the duration of both their lives. The area of Pharangium was restored to the Persians with all the prisoners, while the forts which had been seized by the Persians, along with those who had been captured with them, were returned to the Romans. The two rulers agreed and stated in the treaty that they themselves were brothers according to the ancient custom and that if one of them should need military assistance in either money or men, they should supply it readily.

(478) After these events, both sides withdrew, the Romans and the Persians; the war had occupied thirty-one years from when Kavadh, the king of the Persians, had advanced and made war against the Romans, as was mentioned during the reign of Anastasius, and the

capture of Amida, as was also mentioned before, and the restoration of that city of Amida to the Romans, and the regional wars of the marauding Saracens.

19. Procopius, *Secret History* 24.12–14

(12) I shall add another thing to these since the topic of soldiers leads me to it. The Roman emperors in previous times positioned an absolute mass of soldiers everywhere on the frontiers of the empire for the protection of the borders of the Roman state, especially on the eastern part. In this way, they repulsed the incursions of the Persians and Saracens, and they called these troops the *limitanei*. (13) The Emperor Justinian, from the beginning, treated these troops in such an inferior way and so badly that the paymasters of their units were four or five years behind in their payments to them. Whenever there was peace between the Romans and Persians, these poor men were forced – in as much as that they were also enjoying the benefits of peace – to donate to the treasury what was owing to them for the said time. And later on, he removed from them the very name of soldier. (14) Subsequently, the frontiers of the Roman state remained without guards, and the soldiers straightaway had to look to the hands of those accustomed to offer charity.

20. Evagrius, *Ecclesiastical History* IV.27

The same Procopius also narrates what is recorded by our ancestor about Edessa and Agbar, and how Christ sent to Abgar, and then how Chosroes made another siege assault on the Edessenes, thinking to put an end to the common talk of the faithful: that Edessa would never come under the enemy. This is not in the letter to Agbar by Christ our God, as the diligent can understand from the histories of Eusebius son of Pamphilius, who published the letter itself word for word. This is why it is praised and believed by the faithful, and it received fulfilment, since faith brought about the success of the prediction . . .

Chosroes ordered his forces to gather a large amount of wood from the forest nearby for the siege . . .

Now, those afflicted by the siege saw the mound approaching nearer the city like a moving mountain, and that the enemy were ready to enter the city on foot contrived, as dawn broke, to make by hard work a tunnel under the ground opposite the mound (which was called *agesta* by the Romans), and to introduce a fire there, so that the wood would be destroyed by the flames and bring the mound down to the ground. The work was finished, but in applying the fire their strategy miscarried, as the fire did not have an outlet from which it could obtain air and get a hold on the wood. They were at a complete loss, but they brought the image which had been made by God and not forged by human hands, and which Christ the God had sent to Abgar when he wanted to see Him. Then they brought the all-holy image into the tunnel which they had created and sprinkled it with water, and they spread some of it on to the pyre and the wood. And straightaway the divine power was visited upon the faith of those who had done this, and it completed what had previously been impossible for them. The fire immediately took hold of the timbers, which, quicker than a word, were burnt to a cinder and spread to the parts above, as the fire spread everywhere . . .

So then Chosroes, denied in all his hopes and perceiving that by these actions he had brought great shame on himself, since he had assumed that he would triumph over the God worshipped by us, made his retreat to his own land without any glory.

21. Agathias, *The Histories* IV.30.7–10

(7) Chosroes understood that it was impossible for him to engage with the Romans in Lazica (Colchis), as the sea was under their control, and therefore they could easily send for everything they needed. He, however, was compelled to send only a very few provisions to his army over a long journey through the desert, with the greatest difficulty, by porters and pack animals. Chosroes considered these things, and decided to settle the whole war, since it would not be advantageous for peace to be limited to only certain regions and continue endlessly in a faltering way, but it should be in force everywhere. (8) And so he despatched in an embassy to Byzantion [Constantinople] a very notable Persian man, who was known as 'Zikh'. (9) When this Zikh arrived and met with the Emperor Justinian, he spoke a lot about the present situation, and listened to many in turn. And in the end, it was agreed on these terms, that the Romans and Persians would retain everything which they had already gained in Lazica by right of war up to this point, either towns or forts, and that both sides should maintain peace with each other, and certainly not engage with each other, until there was a greater and more permanent agreement between the two leaders. And therefore Zikh, having accomplished the aims of the embassy, returned to his homeland. (10) When these terms had been announced

to the generals, the powers remained in absolute peace for a long time, and the situation which had previously arisen spontaneously was confirmed by a treaty.

22. John of Ephesus, *Church History* 3.4.6–9

Translated by R. Payne Smith, The Third Part of the Ecclesiastical History of John Bishop of Ephesus *(Oxford 1860) (revised translation)*

Among the clergy in attendance upon pope Theodosius, was a presbyter named Julian, an old man of great worth, who conceived an earnest spiritual desire to christianize the wandering people who dwell on the eastern borders of the Thebais beyond Egypt, and who are not only not subject to the authority of the Roman empire, but even receive a subsidy on condition that they do not enter nor pillage Egypt. The blessed Julian, therefore, being full of anxiety for this people, went and spoke about them to the late queen Theodora, in the hope of awakening in her a smiliar desire for the conversion of these people. And as the queen was fervent in her zeal for God, she received the proposal with joy, and promised to do everything in her power for the conversion of these tribes from the errors of idolatry. In her joy, therefore, she informed the victorious king Justinian of the purposed undertaking, and promised and anxiously desired to send the blessed Julian thither. But when the king heard that the person she intended to send was opposed to the Council of Chalcedon, he was not pleased, and decided to write to the bishops of his own side in the Thebais, with orders for them to proceed thither and instruct them, and plant among them the name of the synod. And as he entered upon the matter with great zeal, he sent thither, without a moment's delay, ambassadors with gold and baptismal robes, and gifts of honour for the king of that people, and letters for the duke of the Thebais, enjoining him to take every care of the embassy, and escort it to the territories of the Nobadae. When, however, the queen learnt these things, she quickly, with much cunning, wrote letters to the duke of the Thebais, and sent an official of her court to carry them to him; and they were as follows: 'Inasmuch as both his majesty and myself have purposed to send an embassy to the people of the Nobadae, I am now despatching a blessed man named Julian; and further, my will is that my ambassador should arrive at the aforesaid people before his majesty's; be warned, that if you permit his ambassador to arrive there before mine, and do not hinder him by various pretexts until mine shall have reached you, and have passed through your province, and arrived at his destination, your life shall answer for it; for I will immediately send and take off your head.'

23. Procopius, *Wars* VIII.17.1–8

(1) Around this time, some monks arrived from India and learned that the Emperor Justinian was keen that the Romans should no longer buy their silk from the Persians. They came into the presence of the emperor thus and agreed to make arrangements regarding silk so that the Romans would no longer make this trade with the Persians, their enemies, or from any other nation. (2) They had spent a long time in the country above the many nations of India, which is called Serinda, and in this place they had learnt precisely the method by which it would be possible for silk to be made in the land of the Romans. (3) The emperor made very persistent and close enquiries if the story was true, and the monks said that certain worms are the makers of silk, nature being their instructor and forcing them to work continually. (4) But while it was not possible to bring the worms there alive, it was straightforward and completely easy for the progeny to travel. They also related that the progeny of these worms were innumerable eggs of each one. (5) And by covering these eggs for a long time in dung, after they had been produced, and keeping them warm for enough time, men made them come to life. (6) After this discussion, the emperor agreed to honour the men with great rewards and persuaded them to make good their account with actions. (7) They went to Serinda again and brought back the eggs to Byzantion [Constantinople], and in the way which has been described they made them grow into worms. They fed them with leaves of the mulberry, and thus they established that from this time silk could be made in Roman territory. (8) Such then were the affairs between the Romans and the Persians regarding the war and silk.

24. Procopius, *Wars* IV.6.30–4

(30) '. . . But farewell, my dear Pharas, and send me, I beg, a lyre, a loaf of bread, and a sponge.'

(31) When Pharas learnt of this letter which had been brought to him, he was at a loss for some time not understanding the very last part of the letter, until the messenger who had brought this missive said that Gelimer needed one loaf of bread, being desirous to see its arrival

and to eat it, since from the time he had gone to Papua, he had not seen a baked loaf. (32) A sponge would also be necessary for him; for one of his eyes, becoming irritated by lack of washing, was very greatly swollen. (33) And being a good harpist, he had written an ode relating to his misfortune which he was eager to sing accompanied by a lyre and to make a loud lament. (34) Hearing this, Pharas, being greatly pained and lamenting the fortune of men, acted according to what was written and he sent all the things which Gelimer asked of him. However, he did not loosen the siege at all, and he guarded him as strictly as before.

25. John the Lydian, *de Magistratibus* III.55

While the state was being tossed about by such great waves and storms of evils, Fortune presented diligence as a counter-balance for the laziness of old, and appointed Justinian, the most vigilant of all emperors for the common good. He thought that damage would occur to his own state, unless they were all wakeful with him and fought on behalf of the state in order that they might capture not only the things which had previously belonged to the Romans which had been lost because of past idleness, but also the things which belonged to the enemy. He gained control of the Persians and undisciplined Chosroes first with gold and then renewing the fight with the sword. Suddenly unleashing war over the Vandals, a Germanic race, who were devouring Libya, he took them in only two months and after taking them by war, he established them in the empire. He handed over to the Romans in slavery Gelimer himself with the most distinguished of his people, whom the barbarians call Hasdings, with his wife and children and great wealth, as if they were good for nothing menials.

26. Corippus, *In laudem Iustini minoris* 1.276–87

And she [Sophia] brought a pall woven with precious purple, where the whole series of Justinian's labours was marked out with gold thread and sparkling gems. There, with great skill, the embroiderer had illustrated, with a fine needle, barbarian phalanxes with bent necks, and slaughtered kings and subject nations in order. And he made the yellow gold stand out from the colours, in order that someone looking at it would think that they were actual bodies: their images were depicted in gold, the blood in purple. He had portrayed Justinian himself as a victor in the middle of his court trampling on the savage neck of the Vandal king: and Libya, applauding, bearing fruit and laurel.

27. Victor of Tonnena, *Chronicon* 534

Justinian was consul for the fourth time. The Emperor Justinian was visited by the bishop Laetus, who later was martyred by Huneric, the king of the Vandals, and he sent an army to Africa against the Vandals, led by his general Belisarius, and this same Belisarius defeated them in battle, and killed Gunthimer and Gebamund, the brothers of the king, Gadinges, and put to flight King Gelimer himself, and captured Africa on the ninety-seventh anniversary of the Vandals' invasion. Also, in that incursion by Belisarius, before he entered Africa, the tyrant, Gelimer, killed King Hilderic along with the latter's family. Belisarius, the general and patrician, captured the tyrant, Gelimer, and brought him to the Emperor Justinian with the riches he had acquired from their looting of Africa.

28. Procopius, *Buildings* I.10.16–18

(16) The themes of these pictures I will show you. On each side is war and battle, and numerous cities are being captured, some in Italy, some in Libya; and the Emperor Justinian enjoys victories won by his general, Belisarius, and the general is returning to the emperor with his whole army unharmed, and he gives him spoils, kings and kingdoms and everything which is exceptional among men. (17) The emperor and the empress, Theodora, stand in the centre, and both seem to rejoice and to celebrate victories over the king of the Vandals and Goths, who come before them as prisoners of war and captives. (18) The Roman Senate, having been specially summoned, stands around them, all in celebration.

29. *C.J.* I.27.1, 12–14

In the name of our Lord Jesus Christ, Emperor Caesar Flavius Justinian Alamannicus, Gothicus, Francicus, Germanicus, Anticus, Alanicus, Vandalicus, Africanus, pious, fortunate, illustrious, victorious and triumphant, Ever Augustus, to Archelaus, praetorian prefect of Africa. pr. What thanks or what praises We should offer to Our Lord Jesus Christ, neither Our mind is able to grasp nor Our tongue profess. (1) Even before this, We have received many prizes from God, and We acknowledge his innumerable benefactions on Our behalf, for which We appreciate that We have done nothing worthy. However, this above all, which Almighty God has now condescended to demonstrate through Us for His praise and His name, exceeds all the wonderful works that have happened in this age: that, through Us, Africa should in such short time regain its freedom, captured one hundred and five years ago by the Vandals, who were enemies of both our souls and bodies . . .

(12) And, with the help of God, with their governors seven provinces shall be formed of which, Zeugi, which was previously called 'Proconsular'; Carthage, Byzacium, and Tripolis will have consular governors; the rest, that is, Numida, the Mauretanias, and Sardinia, will, with the help of God, be governed by *praesides* (ordinary governors). (13) And indeed We decree that three hundred and ninety-six men shall serve in the various bureaus and agencies in the office of your Greatness and also of the interim Prefect of Africa, *vir magnificus*. In the offices of the consular and ordinary governors, We decree that there will be fifty men in each office. (14) A schedule attached below sets out the emoluments which Your Magnificence or the consular or ordinary governors and each of their staffs ought to receive from public funds.

30. Procopius, *Secret History* 18.5–10

(5) For Libya, extending to such a great size, was so utterly destroyed that to make a long journey is difficult and it is worthy of a report to meet another traveller. (6) And yet the Vandals who recently had taken up arms there numbered eighty thousand; and of the women and young children and slaves, who could estimate their number? (7) As for the Libyans who formerly lived in the cities, those who cultivated the land and who worked at sea, which I was fortunate to witness myself – how could anyone estimate the extent of the multitude of all of them? Still, by far more numerous than these, were the Moors there, but it came about that all of these with their wives and offspring were destroyed. (8) The earth has also covered many of the Roman soldiers and those who followed them from Byzantion. So that if someone contends that five million people were destroyed in Libya, he would not be speaking at all accurately about the matter. (9) The reason was that immediately after the Vandals were defeated, Justinian did not concern himself with strengthening his power over the country, and he did not consider beforehand that the protection of its resources should be entrusted to the goodwill of its inhabitants. However, he straightaway summoned Belisarius, with no delay, and with no justification accused him of tyranny, in order that after that, as ruler of Libya, he would grow fat on it and plunder it completely.

(10) Without any consideration, he immediately sent out land surveyors and imposed certain very sharp taxes which had not existed before. And he laid claim to all the best estates.

31. Inscription from Aïn Djelloula (*Cululis*)

A fortunate imperial government accomplished this work, these defences and indeed the orders of the magnanimous Solomon granted them, whom the tribune Nonnus, who built these things, obeys. City, rejoice in your pious emperor and now consider the quantity of misfortunes from which you have been rescued, and with how much grace you have been decorated. Finally, with fear of the Moors removed, you receive power, rank, citizens, justice, duties, fasti, and the empress has conferred her name on you. By the hand of Justinian, the tribe of the Moors has been put to flight, all things have their time, and they grieved for those times.

32. Cyril of Scythopolis, *Life of St Sabas* 74

The emperor, after making all these arrangements and giving his rescripts to the holy old man [Sabas], sent him on his way in peace. God gave the emperor an infinite recompense by fulfilling the prophecy of the old man. For the emperor erected two trophies a short time later by being crowned with two victories such as had never been achieved by any of his predecessors: he recovered Africa and Rome from the rule of usurpers and saw the two kings, Witigis of Rome and Gelimer of Africa, brought to Constantinople. Thus, in a short time, he recovered for the Roman Empire the half part of the land and sea; and liberating all the west from slavery to the said usurpers who were Arians, he issued imperial decrees that the churches of the Arians should everywhere be destroyed, following the orders or at least the prophecy of the godly old man. In addition, nobly exerting himself, he overthrew and anathematised the heresies of Nestorius and Origen, both by the edicts he issued and through the fifth holy oecumenical council lately assembled at Constantinople; but this we shall treat later.

33. *Novel 37, preface, 1, 5*

Preface
We hasten day and night to help the venerable church of our Carthago Justiniana and all the other holy churches of the diocese of Africa, with

imperial benefits, so that, after they had been snatched from the tyrants through the protection of God, and joined with our state, they may also enjoy our generosity.

(1) Therefore, Reparatus, a very holy man, priest of the same city of our Carthago Justiniana, the distinguished head of the venerable council of the most holy churches of the whole of Africa, together with the other most reverend bishops of the same province, beseeched our majesty, in a private letter sent by the religious Theodorus, deacon and *apocrisiarius* of the same venerable church of the city of Carthago Justiniana, that they should securely possess the properties of the churches in the whole of Africa. These were the properties which had been seized from them in the time of the tyrants, and restored to them through the pious disposition of our divinity after the victories against the Vandals that have been given to us through divine protection. Subject to the payment of taxes imposed in each place, we have deliberated that we should with eager and willing spirit grant their petitions, in accordance with the favourable tenor of the law already promulgated on this matter.

(5) It will also be your excellency's concern, that no communion at all in ecclesiastical rites will be granted to the Arians or Donatists or Jews or others who are known not to worship the orthodox religion. But the wicked are to be completely excluded from services and churches, and no licence is conceded to them to ordain bishops or clergy or to baptise anyone at all and to drag them into their own madness. For these sects have been condemned not only by us, but also by previous laws, and they are followed by the most criminal and corrupt men.

34. Facundus of Hermiane, *In Defence of the Three Chapters*, preface

(1) To harm the holy synod of Chalcedon, his Acephali adversaries were stealthily working, through a few individuals, to condemn and anathematise the letter of Ibas, Bishop of Edessa, which had been considered Catholic by the aforementioned synod to which it had been submitted; and also Theodore, Bishop of Mopsuestia and his doctrine, praised in this same letter of Ibas; as well as certain writings of Theodoret, Bishop of Cyrrhus, who defended at the previously mentioned synod of Chalcedon the dogmatic letter of Pope Leo. Urged on by my brothers, I wrote this work to the emperor in Constantinople.

(2) It was not yet finished and worked up when the bishop of Rome was conveyed here. While we were debating this matter under his

examination, taking minutes, he decided, in the middle of the debate, that the proceedings should be interrupted and asked us, all the bishops who were present, to give each in writing our opinion on these chapters.

(3) I was therefore constrained under stern compulsion through the *magister officiorum* to give my answer, but I was barely allowed a pause of seven days, two of which were even feast days. Then, to summarise, I extracted some passages which I judged to be the more important from these books; since I did not have time to develop a completely new argument in this response which now exceeds three thousand lines.

(4) However, as I said, because I had not yet finished these books, certain testimonies, because of faults in the manuscripts from which we had drawn them or the carelessness of the copyists, were reported differently when they were transcribed in that response. This is why I have taken care to add this preface and to give this warning, so that this divergence does not vex anyone who, after having read through my aforementioned response, may have in his hands the present books, but also so that he would pardon my haste then and rather trust now what I write. In fact, some of the things which were presented there in great confusion have been dealt with now in a more moderate and ordered fashion.

35. Procopius, *Wars* VII.37.1–7

(1) Not long before, Totila sent to the court of the ruler of the Franks and he asked him to give his daughter to him in marriage. (2) But he snubbed the request, saying that Totila was not or never would be king of Italy, since although he had taken Rome he had not been able to hold it, but after demolishing part of it, he had surrendered it again to the enemy. (3) On account of this, at the present time, Totila made haste to bring supplies into Rome, and he ordered that everything which he himself had pulled down and destroyed by fire when he captured Rome at a previous time, should be rebuilt as quickly as possible. Then he summoned the members of the Roman Senate and all the others whom he guarded in Campania. (4) After watching the horse-races there, he prepared his whole army to make an expedition against Sicily. (5) At the same time, he also made ready four hundred war-ships in preparation for a sea battle, and a great fleet of many large ships which had been sent there from the east by the emperor, which during this time, he had luckily captured with both their men and their cargoes. (6) He sent a Roman called Stephanus as an envoy to the emperor,

asking him to end this war, and to make a treaty with the Goths, on the understanding that they should fight as his allies when he went against his other enemies. (7) But the Emperor Justinian would not allow the envoy to come into his sight, nor did he pay any attention at all to anything he said.

36. *Epistulae Austrasicae* XX

Theudebert the King to the Illustrious and Most Pre-eminent Lord and Father, Justinian the Emperor.

With the arrival of the *vir expectabilis* Theodore together with Solomon, I received the letters, which the indulgence of your lordship sent, with all the affection and devotion of my nature, because, just as you have a care for me, so I extend the loving friendship of God further through other peoples and provinces. The matter, which you have thought it worthy to ask me, is which provinces I occupy and which of my peoples have, with the help of God, become subject to my dominion. Through the mercy of our God, the Thuringians were defeated and their provinces acquired, and then in time, their kings were done away with. Then the North Swabians were reconciled to our suzerainty and bowed their necks to my commands, as were the Visigoths, and so, by the favour of God, Gaul is now safe. The northern region of Italy and Pannonia, with the Saxons and the Eucii, delivered themselves to us by their own free will. Our rule extends from the Danube and the borders of Pannonia to the shores of the ocean through the protection of God. Since we know, as your letter corroborates, that your August Highness rejoices with a complete joy of the spirit at the progress of the Catholics, in the same way, in accordance with your wish, I send a simple report of what God has granted to me, and I wish with all my heart's desire, that your glory will enjoy success and that you will preserve the old friendship of the rulers who preceded us and we may join together in the friendship which you often promise, for the common benefit.

37. Procopius, *Wars* III.2.1–6

(1) While Honorius was holding imperial power in the west, barbarians seized his land: and I will tell you who they were and in what way they did so. (2) There were many Gothic nations both in previous times and now, but the greatest and most significant of all are the Goths, Vandals, Visigoths and Gepids. In olden times, however, they were called Sauromatae and Melanchlaeni: and some too who called these

nations Getic. (3) All these, differentiated from each other by their names, as has been said, do not differ in any other way at all. (4) For they all have white bodies and fair hair, they are tall and handsome to the eye, and they follow the same laws, and they worship the same God. (5) For they are all of the Arian belief, and they have one language, called Gothic. And it seems to me that they were all from one tribe originally, differentiated later by the names of each of the leaders. (6) From olden times, this people lived above the Ister River. And later the Gepids took hold of the country around Singidunum and Sirmium, both inside and outside the Ister River, where they have settled until my own time.

38. Cassiodorus, *Variae* XI.1

(6) For every kingdom venerates her [Amalasuntha] most fittingly; it is awe-inspiring to see her, and wonderful to hear her speaking. For in what language is she not proven to be very skilled? She is fluent in the clarity of Attic eloquence; she shines in the demonstration of Roman expression; she glories in the riches of her native speech; she surpasses all in their own languages, while she is equally splendid in each . . .

(8) However, while she rejoices in such perfection of languages, in public life she is so quiet that she may be thought to be at leisure. She solves knotty litigation with a few words, she settles irate quarrels with calm, and she governs public life with silence. You do not hear broadcast that which seems to be openly adopted and she achieves with the pretence of incredible moderation that which she recognises must be done at speed . . .

(10) However, under this lady, who had as many kings as she has relatives, with God's blessing, our army terrifies foreign peoples: the army is balanced by a prudent programme, and is neither ground down with continuous wars, nor made soft again by long peace. Also, at the very beginning of her reign, when novelty always tests uncertainties, she made the Danube Roman against the wishes of the Eastern Princeps.

(11) It is well known what the invaders endured: for that reason, I judge these things must be omitted, in case the spirit of an allied Prince should feel shame at his loss. For what he thought about our territory can be understood from the way that after his defeat, he granted a peace which he was unwilling to concede to others when asked. One can add that he honoured us with so many embassies, though only rarely requested, and her singular power has reduced the reverence of eastern majesty so that she could raise the status of the masters of Italy . . .

(14) Rejoice, Goths and similarly Romans: she is a worthy miracle as all may acknowledge. Look how, with the help of God, this blessed woman has achieved what either sex considers remarkable: for she has both given us a glorious king and protected a very large empire with her brave spirit.

(15) These things, mostly, relate to war, as has been mentioned: and if we wish to go into the halls of her piety, 'hardly one hundred tongues and one hundred mouths' would be sufficient for us: for her sense of justice and good will are equal, but her kindness is greater than power.

39. Pope Pelagius, *Letters* 4 and 85

Letter 4
Pelagius to his most beloved brother Sapaudis [in Arles, France] (14 December 556)

… Moreover we urge that you should say to the most magnificent patrician Placidus, our son and your father, that he should agree to give a portion to us of what has been collected from the taxes on the properties of our church, either by his own man or by theirs. The estates of Italy have been so devastated that no one has the means to restore them. And if it is possible, please take steps to procure for us with the money padded cloaks, which could be given out to the poor, and white tunics or hoods or vests, or anything similar which is made in Provence, which could be given to the poor, as we have said. If the opportunity of a ship arises, send them, so that we may express our greatest thanks for your brotherliness, and so that the foresight of your affection may relieve our worries of this sort.

Letter 85
Pelagius to Boethius, Praetorian Prefect of Africa (560/561)

The Church of Rome, over which we preside on the authority of God, has suffered twenty-five years and more from the devastation of the regions of Italy by war, and it has still hardly gone away at all. It receives no money for the clergy and the poor from anywhere else than from remote islands and areas – and that is small and not sufficient.

40. *Novels*, Appendix 7: Pragmatic Sanction, 554

(1) All measures which have been granted by Amalasuntha, Athalaric or Theodahad are to be confirmed.

Pursuant to the petition of Vigilius, venerable bishop of the more ancient Rome, we have decided that matters should be arranged for the benefit of all those who are known to live in the western lands. And so, first, we order that all measures which Athalaric, his royal mother Amalasuntha, or also Theodahad, granted, at the request of the Romans or their senate, should be preserved without violation. But we also wish that those conferred by ourselves or by Theodora Augusta of pious memory, our late consort, to be preserved intact ...

(2) All grants made by Totila are to be invalid.

In no way do we agree that anything done by the usurper Totila, or grant found to have been made by him to any Roman, or to anyone else, should be retained or remain in force. But we order that property, having been taken away from such holders, should be returned to its original owners. We do not permit any act found to have been carried out by him during the period of his usurpation to stigmatise our legitimate times.

(11) Emperors' laws are to circulate throughout their provinces.

In addition, we decree that the ordinances or laws contained in our *Codex*, which we have already previously sent to Italy and proclaimed as an edict, are to continue. But we also order that the constitutions which we have promulgated afterwards are to be published by the proclamation of an edict, and from that time when they are published by the proclamation of an edict, they are to be valid throughout the regions of Italy, and now that the republic has been united by the will of God, the authority of our laws should also be circulated everywhere.

41. Procopius, *Secret History* 11.5–8

(5) So then, as there was peace amongst the Romans towards all men, he did not know what to do, but, due to his lust for blood, he brought into conflict all the barbarians with one another, and summoning the leaders of the Huns for no reason, he delivered to them large donatives with great generosity, doing this, in truth, as a pledge of friendship; it was said that he himself had done this also during the time of the Emperor Justin. (6) They, even after having received this money, sent some of their fellow rulers with some of their followers, ordering them to attack and raid the lands of the emperor, with the intention that they themselves would be able to sell the peace to the very person who wished in no way to purchase it. (7) And straightaway, they began to

enslave the Roman Empire and they were no less in receipt of pay from the emperor; after them, others immediately set about looting the suffering Romans, and after plundering, they received the munificence of the emperor as a reward for the attack. (8) Thus they all collectively, it is said, harassed and plundered all at once, not letting up for any season in rotation.

42. Procopius, *Wars* II.4.4–11

(4) Immediately a huge Hunnic army crossed the Ister (Danube) River and fell upon all of Europe, which had already happened frequently, but which had never before brought such a host or such a magnitude of evils to the men here. For from the Ionian Gulf, these barbarians pillaged everything, one after another, up to the suburbs of Byzantion. (5) They captured thirty-two fortresses in Illyricum, and they seized by force the city of Cassandria (which the ancients called Potidaea, as far as we know), never having fought against walls before. (6) They took the money and carried off one hundred and twenty thousand prisoners. Then they all withdrew home, not meeting any opposition. (7) They often came on later occasions, and they brought ruinous disasters upon the Romans. (8) They also attacked the wall of the Chersonese, overwhelming those defending from the wall, and through the surf of the sea they scaled the fortification which is on the so-called Black Gulf; so arriving within the Long Walls and falling upon the Romans in the Chersonese unexpectedly, they killed many and enslaved almost all of them. (9) A few of them also crossed the strait between Sestus and Abydus, and, after plundering the country of Asia, they went back to the Chersonese, together with the rest of the army, and they carried all the plunder home. (10) In another invasion, they plundered Illyricum and Thessaly, and attempted to storm the wall at Thermopylae. The guards on the walls defended them very strongly, so, tracking down the paths around, they surprisingly found the path which leads to the mountain which arises there. (11) Thus having destroyed almost all the Greeks except the Peloponnesians, they withdrew.

43. *Novel* 11, preface, 4

Archbishop of Justiniana Prima: archbishop's privileges

The same Augustus to Catellianus, most blessed archbishop of Justiniana Prima

Desiring to increase in many and various ways our native land in which God granted to us to first come into this world which he himself created, we also wish to amplify with maximum increments its priestly office: thus the current most holy primate of Justiniana Prima, our birthplace, is to be not only a metropolitan, but also an archbishop, and certain provinces are to be under his authority: that is, Mediterranea and Ripensis Dacia, also the First Moesia, Dardania, the province of Praevalitana, the Second Macedonia, and the part of the Second Pannonia which is under the city of Bacis.

(4) And so your beatitude and all most holy primate archbishops of the aforesaid Justiniana Prima are to have the prerogative and complete licence to bestow their own authority on others and to appoint them; and in all the above-mentioned provinces they are to hold primacy of honour, primacy of rank, the highest priesthood and the highest sacred position: they are to be appointed by your seat and they are to have you as their only archbishop, with no contribution maintained by the archbishop of Thessalonica. But you yourself and all the primates of Justiniana Prima are to be their judges and arbitrators: whatever difference arises between them, they themselves should reconcile this and impose an end to it and to manage them, and nor should this be brought to anyone else, but all the aforesaid provinces should recognise their own archbishop and recognise his appointment, and either through himself or through his own authority or through those sent by clerics, he is to have all power and priestly office and licence to appoint.

44. Agathias, *The Histories* V.13.5–6

(5) For the affairs of the Romans had been driven to such misfortune that in the suburbs themselves of the imperial city such terrible violence was brutally perpetrated by a few barbarians. However, the boldness of these men did not end here, but going along the road, they easily passed inside the Long Walls as they are called, and approached the fortifications inside. For everywhere the building of the great defence had fallen and collapsed through time and neglect. One part the barbarians themselves demolished without fear and so easily, as if destroying houses. (6) There was no impediment to this nor military guard posted here, nor defence engines, nor those who knew how to operate these things; but not even the bark of a dog could be heard, unless – to make an absurd comparison – as if in a pigsty or a farmyard.

45. Agathias, *The Histories* V.15.7–8

(7) When the capital had been greatly in chaos and the barbarians had not let up ravaging whatever came to hand, then Belisarius, already worn down by old age, was nevertheless sent against them by the emperor. (8) And now, the old man put on his breastplate and helmet again after such a long time, and threw on the uniform that was so familiar from his youth. He was refreshed by the memory of his previous actions and his energy was restored. He completed this very last contest of his own life, and won no less glory than when he had raised the victory monuments over the Vandals and Goths.

46. Theophanes AM 6050

At the same time, the extraordinary race of the so-called Avars reached Byzantium and the whole city ran out at the sight of them, as they had never seen such a people. They wore their hair very long at the back, tied up with ribbons and braided. The rest of their clothing was like that of the other Huns. They had fled from their own country and had come to Scythia and Mysia and sent envoys to Justinian asking to be admitted.

47. Isidore, *History of the Goths* 47

In the year 592, in the 29th year of the Emperor Justinian, after the death of Agilans, Athanagildus held the kingdom which he had invaded for fourteen years. He had taken up his tyranny long before, and in the attempt to deprive Agilans of his kingdom, he had asked the Emperor Justinian for the help of soldiers whom afterwards, when he tried, he was unable to remove from the boundaries of his kingdom. Conflict broke out with them at this point. They had fallen previously in many battles, and now they were broken and finished by many misfortunes. Then Athanagildus died at Toledo by a natural death, and the kingdom had no ruler for five months.

48. The *Chronicle* of Pseudo-Zachariah Rhetor, IX.15j

Translation from The Chronicle of Pseudo-Zachariah Rhetor: Church and War in Late Antiquity, *edited by Geoffrey Greatrex, translated by Robert R. Phenix and Cornelia B. Horn (Liverpool 2011)*

When the letter of the defence of the faith [written out above] had been given to the emperor and was read and many [things] were discussed for the not insignificant [length of] time of one year by the faithful bishops who were assembled there in the royal city at the command of the emperor . . . while joined with them was the learned archimandrite John bar Aphthonia, who recorded these [proceedings], the emperor did not ban the Council of Chalcedon from the church. When he summoned by letter the holy Severus, the head of the priests, who was hiding in various places, [Severus] declined to come to him, sending [a letter] to the emperor. Each one of these faithful bishops then went away from Constantinople, to any place [where] he chose to hide himself, as he deemed suitable for him.

49. C.J. I.1.6 and *Chronicon Paschale* 533

Theopaschite Edict

The same emperor to the Constantinopolitans

Serving the Saviour and Lord of all, Jesus Christ, our true God, we strive in every way to imitate his humility, as far as it is possible for a human mind to comprehend.

(1) And having found some overpowered by the sickness and madness of the impious Nestorius and Eutyches, the enemies of God and the Holy Catholic and Apostolic Church, who refuse to name the holy glorious ever-Virgin Mary properly and truly as the Mother of God, we have strived for them to be taught the correct faith of the Christians.

(2) However, they, being incurable, have hidden their error and go around, as we have learnt, upsetting and offending the souls of ordinary people and speaking against the Holy Catholic and Apostolic Church.

(3) Therefore, we have thought it necessary to dismiss the lies of the heretics, and to make clear to all what the Holy Catholic and Apostolic Church of God believes, and what its most holy priests proclaim. We, who follow them, make clear what are the hopes within us, and we do not make any innovation to the faith – not at all – but we refute the madness of those who share the beliefs of the impious heretics. We did this at the beginning of our reign and made it clear to everyone.

(4) For we believe in one God, Father Almighty and in one Lord Jesus Christ, the Son of God, and in the Holy Spirit, worshipping one being in three substances, one deity, one power, a consubstantial Trinity.

(5) At the end of days, we acknowledge that Our Lord Jesus Christ, the only begotten Son of God, true God of true God, begotten of the Father before the ages and without time, co-eternal with the Father,

from whom and through whom are all things, descended from the heavens, was made flesh through the Holy Spirit and the holy, glorious ever-Virgin Mother of God, Mary, and was made man, suffered on a cross for us under Pontius Pilate, was buried and rose on the third day, and we recognise the miracles and sufferings of the one and same, which he willingly suffered in the flesh.

(6) For we do not know one as God the Word and the other as Christ, but as one and the same, consubstantial with the Father according to his divine nature, and consubstantial with us according to his human nature. For he is perfect in his divine nature just as he is also perfect in his human nature. We accept and acknowledge the unity in substance. For the Trinity remained a Trinity even when one of the Trinity, God the Word, became flesh. For the Holy Trinity does not accept an addition of a fourth person.

(7) Therefore, since these things are thus, we anathematise every heresy, and especially Nestorius the worshipper of man and those who have shared or do share his beliefs, those who distinguish between the one Lord of us, Jesus Christ the Son of God, and Our God; and those who do not accept the holy glorious ever-Virgin Mary properly and truly as the *Theotokos*, the Mother of God, but say there are two sons, one who is God the Word begotten from the Father, and the other from the holy ever-Virgin Mother of God Mary, through the grace, nature and kinship to God the Word and is God himself; and they deny and do not acknowledge that our Lord Jesus Christ, the Son of God and our God, who was made flesh and became man and was crucified, is one of the holy and consubstantial Trinity. For he alone is the one who is worshipped and glorified with the Father and the Holy Spirit.

(8) And we anathematise Eutyches the madman and those who have followed and follow his beliefs, those who introduce an apparition and deny the true incarnation from Mary the holy, ever-Virgin Mother of God of Our Lord and Saviour Jesus Christ, that is our salvation; and who do not acknowledge that he is consubstantial with the Father according to his divine nature and consubstantial with us according to his human nature.

(9) In the same way, we also anathematise Apollinarius the destroyer of souls and those who have shared or share his beliefs, saying that Our Lord Jesus Christ the Son of God and Our God was without mind and introducing confusion or indeed chaos to the incarnation of the only-begotten Son of God, and we anathematise all those who have shared or share their beliefs.

15 March 533

50. 'Only-begotten Son' troparion

Only-begotten Son and Word of God,
Being Immortal in existence,
And who accepted, for our salvation,
To become flesh from the holy Mother of God
And ever-Virgin Mary,
Being immutable, he became a man, and was crucified, Christ the God,
Crushing death with death,
Being one of the holy Trinity,
Glorified with the father and the Holy Spirit,
Save Us.

51. Victor of Tonnena, *Chronicon* 540

In the consulship of the most illustrious Justin, Agapetus, the archbishop of Rome, comes to Constantinople, and deposes Anthimus, the bishop of Constantinople, who had corrupted the Church of Constantinople and was hostile towards the Council of Chalcedon. He deprives his patron, the Empress Theodora, of communion, and, in addition, he immediately makes Menas bishop of the Church of Constantinople.

52. *Novel* 42, preface

Concerning the deposition of Anthimus, Severus, Peter, Zoaras and others.

The same Sovereign to the most holy and most blessed Menas, archbishop and universal patriarch.

Preface
We have come to the present law, after we also have carried out a practice not unusual for an emperor. For as often as a decree of the priests deposes anyone unworthy of their priesthood from their priestly seat, as were Nestorius, Eutyches, Arius, Macedonius and Eunomius, and also some others who were no less wicked than they, so often the emperor has been of the same opinion as the authority of the priesthood, so that the more sacred and the secular may run together and create harmony with their just decisions. We know something like this happened recently with Anthimus, who was expelled from his seat in this royal city by Agapetus of holy and celebrated memory, the bishop of the most holy Church of the elder Rome, since he usurped, contrary

to all lawful canons, a seat in no way fitting for him. Indeed, by a universal decision, first from that man of holy memory, and from the celebrated holy council which took place here, he was condemned and deposed, because he had departed from the correct doctrines and had later strayed away from various beliefs which he had at first seemed to embrace on many different occasions. Pretending to follow the four holy synods (those of the three hundred and eighteen fathers in Nicaea, the hundred and fifty in this fortunate city, the two hundred gathering earlier at Ephesus and the six hundred and thirty God-beloved fathers at Chalcedon), however, he did not in fact follow the decrees of these councils; nor did he wish to accept the condescension and clemency to which we had consented for the sake of his safety; nor himself to repudiate the leaders of impious doctrines who were expelled by the earlier holy councils. However, he thought in himself that both those who had been condemned and those who condemned them ought to be considered as equal. For, once he had become enslaved by thoughts which were foreign to the most holy church and alienated from orthodox doctrines, he accordingly did not think it right to return to their orthodoxy, even though he was invited and guided by us to do so, and though we made every effort for his salvation.

53. Victor of Tonnena, *Chronicon* 543

In the second year after the consulship of the most illustrious Basilius, at the making of the Empress Theodora, who has never ceased to be secretly hostile to the Council of Chalcedon from the time when she had begun to reign, secret preparations are made for proscriptions. The bishop of Rome, Silverius, is sent into exile, and Vigilius is ordained in his place. And before he becomes pope, the aforementioned Empress Theodora lured him with a secret agreement that when he had been made pope he would condemn and ban the Three Chapters of the Council of Chalcedon, that is, the letter of Ibas of Edessa to the Persian Mari, that was approved of by the judgement of the Council of Chalcedon and judged to be orthodox, and related to the councils which had been held. Then Theodore, Bishop of Mopsuestia, was praised in the acts of the council which was similarly held in Antioch under John, the bishop of the same Church, and in Chalcedon. And the sayings of Theodoret, Bishop of Cyrrhus, were praised by the declarations of the Council of Chalcedon with the same Theodoret.

And so this Vigilius is made pope, and is forced by Antonina, the patrician wife of the patrician Belisarius, to write to Theodosius at

Alexandria, Anthimus at Constantinople and Severus at Antioch, long since condemned by the apostolic see, as if he was writing to true Catholics and felt about their faith just as they did.

The essence of his letter is shown to consist of this:

'Bishop Vigilius to Bishops Theodosius, Anthimus and Severus, my lords and brothers joined in the love of Christ our God and Saviour.

I know, indeed, that a plausible report of my faith reached Your Holinesses before, with God's help. But my glorious mistress and my most Christian and patrician daughter, Antonina, has now made me be filled with the desire to send the present letter to Your Fraternities. I greet you with the grace with which we are joined together in Christ our Lord and Saviour, and I notify you that I have held and am holding that faith which you hold, with God's help, in the knowledge that we preach and read it in common between us, because we have one soul and one heart in God. I have made haste to announce to you the joy of my advancement, which is yours, with the help of God, as I know well in my mind that Your Fraternities will gladly welcome what you wish for.

And so it is necessary that nobody should know what I am writing to you, but rather, let Your Wisdoms affect that you regard me as if more suspect than others, so that what God has begun to do may be more easily brought.'

Below was written: 'Pray for me, my lords and brothers, bound together by the love of Christ, our Lord and Saviour.'

54. Evagrius, *Ecclesiastical History* IV.38

When Vigilius was responsible for the older Rome, and, for the new Rome, first Menas and then Eutychius, Apollinarius for Alexandria, Domninus for Antioch, and Eustochius for Jerusalem, Justinian summoned the Fifth Council for the following reason: Eustochius made every effort to drive out those who worshipped the dogmas of Origen who were gaining in power, especially in the so-called New Lavra [in Judaea]. And after arriving at the New Lavra itself, he expelled everyone, driving them far off, as being common evils; and they were scattered and united many to their side.

Vigilius agreed in writing, but he did not choose to attend [the Fifth Council]. Justinian, having learnt from the assembled council what was said about Theodore and what Theodoret had said against Cyril and his Twelve Chapters, and the so-called letter of Ibas to Mari the Persian; and after the many writings of Theodore and Theodoret had been read, and it had been demonstrated that long ago even Theodore had been condemned and erased from the sacred diptychs, and that heretics ought to be condemned even after their death, they all anathematised Theodore, as has been reported, and the sayings of Theodore against the Twelve Chapters of Cyril and the correct faith, and the letter of Ibas to Mari the Persian, saying in the following words: 'Our great God and saviour Jesus Christ, according to the parable in the Gospels . . .'

And afterwards:
'We condemn and anathematise, as well as all other heretics who have been condemned and anathematised by the aforesaid four holy synods and from the Holy Catholic and Apostolic Church, both Theodore, who is said to be the bishop of Mopsuestia, and his impious writings, and what was impiously written by Theodoret against the correct faith and the Twelve Chapters of Cyril, who is among the saints, and the first holy synod at Ephesus, and all that he composed in defence of Theodore and Nestorius. And in addition to these, we also anathematise the impious letter said to have been written by Ibas to Mari the Persian.'

55. Cyril of Scythopolis, *Life of St Sabas* 85

The fathers prepared this dossier [against the Origenists] and presented it. The archbishop, on receiving it, sent it to the emperor and wrote to him of the innovations of the Origenists. When our most devout emperor received this dossier, he made an edict against the doctrines of Origenists. Menas, the patriarch of Constantinople, subscribed his name, together with the synod under him.

56. Justinian, *On the Orthodox Faith*

In the name of God the Father and his only-begotten Son Jesus Christ our Lord and the Holy Spirit. The Christ-loving Emperor Caesar Flavius Justinian Alamannicus, Gothicus, Francicus, Germanicus, Anticus, Alanicus, Vandalicus, Africanus, pious, fortunate, illustrious, victorious, triumphant, ever-venerable Augustus, to the whole complement of the Catholic and Apostolic Church.

Knowing that nothing so honours the mankind-loving God as all Christians holding one and the same belief about the correct and faultless faith and there being no schisms in the holy church of God, we have thought it necessary, taking away every excuse from those who are offended or cause offence, to make clear through the current edict the confession of the orthodox faith which is proclaimed in the holy church of God, so that those who confess the correct faith may guard it securely, and that those who are contentious, learning the truth, should hasten to be at one with the holy church of God.

Therefore, we confess that we believe in the Father and Son and Holy Spirit, the consubstantial Trinity, glorifying the one Godhead or verily the nature and essence and power and authority in three hypostases or persons, in whom we were baptised, in whom we have believed, and under whom we have been placed. We distinguish their properties but unite their divinity. For we worship unity in trinity and trinity in unity, retaining the paradox in respect of both their division and union; they are a unity according to their essence or certainly their Godhead, and a trinity according to their properties or certainly their hypostases or persons (for they are separated inseparably, as we should say, and are joined separably, for the Godhead is one in three, and the three in which is the Godhead are one, or to speak more accurately, which are the Godhead); each is God, if he is seen alone with the mind dividing those things which are indivisible, and God is three when they are contemplated with each other in their identity of movement and nature, since it is necessary both to confess the one God and to proclaim the three hypostates or indeed three persons, each with its own properties. We do not make the union a confusion like Sabellius, who said that the Trinity is one person with three names, and the Father and the Son and the Holy Spirit are the same. We do not separate them and alienate the Son of the Holy Spirit from the essence of God the Father according to the madness of Arius who divided the Godhead into three different essences. There is, therefore, one God the Father, from whom are all things, and one only-begotten Son, through whom are all things, and one Holy Spirit, in whom are all things.

57. Evagrius, *Ecclesiastical History* IV.39

At that time, Justinian, after turning aside from the correct highway of doctrine and walking a path untrodden by the Apostles and Fathers, fell among thorns and prickles ... he wrote what is called by the Romans an edict, in which he called the body of the Lord incorruptible and not subject to the natural and innocent passions, thus stating that the Lord ate before the Passion just as He ate after the resurrection, and that his all-holy body did not undergo any change or alteration from the time of its formation in the womb neither in the voluntary nor natural passions, not even after the resurrection; he forced priests everywhere to agree to this.

58. Agapetus, *Advice to the Emperor Justinian*

(1) Having a worthiness beyond all other honour, Emperor, honour God, who made you worthy, beyond all; since even according to the likeness of the kingdom of heaven, he gave you the sceptre of earthly rule in order that you might teach men the protection of justice and repulse the bark of those who rave against it, since you are ruled by the laws of justice, and you rule lawfully those subject to you.

59. *Novel* 131, preface, 1–4

Concerning Church canons and titles

Preface
We are issuing the current law regarding ecclesiastical canons and privileges, and with other chapters regarding the most holy churches and other venerable houses.

(1) Therefore, we decree that the holy ecclesiastical canons are to have the standing of laws – those which were issued or confirmed by the four holy councils, that is, that of the three hundred and eighteen at Nicaea, that of the one hundred and fifty holy fathers at Constantinople, the first at Ephesus, at which Nestorius was condemned, and that at Chalcedon, at which Eutyches was anathematised together with Nestorius. For we accept the decrees of the aforesaid four councils, just as we accept the holy scriptures, and we preserve their canons as laws.

(2) And therefore, we decree according to their definitions, that the most holy pope of the older Rome holds the first place of all priests, and that the most blessed archbishop of Constantinople, the new Rome, holds the second place after the holy apostolic see of the elder Rome, but takes precedence over all other sees.

(3) Also (we decree that) the most blessed archbishop at the time of Justiniana Prima, our native city, is always to have under his jurisdiction the bishops of Dacia Mediterranea and Dacia Ripensis, Praevalitana, Dardania, Upper Moesia and Pannonia; and they are to be appointed by him, and he himself should be appointed by his own synod; and in the provinces under him he is to take the place of the apostolic seat of Rome, according to that which was agreed by the most holy Pope Vigilius.

(4) In a similar way, we also order that the status of the high priesthood, which we gave to the bishop of the city of Carthago Justiniana in Africa, from the time when God restored it to us, should be maintained. The other cities and their bishops, in various places, which enjoy the right of metropolitan status, are to enjoy such a privilege in perpetuity. All privileges and exemptions which have been conferred on holy churches or other venerable places by imperial munificence or in any other way whatsoever are to be securely maintained for them for ever.

60. Pseudo-Dionysius of Tel-Mahre, *Chronicle* 844

Translation from Pseudo-Dionysius of Tel-Mahre, Chronicle Part III, *translated by Witold Witakowski (Liverpool 1996)*

The year 844 (AD 532/533): Grepes, the king of the Heruli, with all his army, all his nobles and twelve members of his family, came to Justinian. He greeted (the emperor) and declared himself willing to become a Christian. The Emperor Justinian rejoiced on hearing it, since he devoted much care and much zeal to converting erring peoples to the faith. He gave instructions and (Grepes) was baptised on the holy feast of the Epiphany, along with his family, his nobles and his army; the victorious emperor was his godfather. (Then) he gave (Grepes) many gifts and sent him back.

61. Pseudo-Dionysius of Tel-Mahre, *Chronicle* 845

Translation from Pseudo-Dionysius of Tel-Mahre, Chronicle Part III, *translated by Witold Witakowski (Liverpool 1996)*

The year 845 (AD 533/534): Grod, the king of the Huns, together with a numerous army, arrived in the capital and asked to become a Christian. He was instructed (in the faith) and baptised, Justinian being his godfather. He honoured (Grod), gave him many gifts and dismissed him to his country. When he came to his country he found his brother, whom he had appointed chief over his troops, and he told him about his (conversion to) Christianity. Also, he showed him the riches and gifts from the Roman emperor, and (the brother) was astonished. Then (Grod) removed the idols of silver and gold which they used to worship, since he believed that only One was the true God, and those idols were deaf and were not gods. He broke them up and sent them to the city of Bosporos to exchange them for *miliaresia*. When his brother and all his troops saw it they became full of anger against him, and having devised a plot against him, together with the priests of the idols they killed him. Since they were afraid of the Roman emperor, they fled to another region.

62. Cyril of Scythopolis, *Life of St Sabas* 72

... the emperor sent for the sanctified Sabas and said to him: 'It has been said to me, father, that you have established very many monasteries in the wilderness, and wherever you may wish, ask for an income for the needs of those who live there and we will provide it, so that they may pray for the state which has been entrusted to our care.' However, he said, 'Those praying for Your Reverence have no need of such an income. For their allowance and income is the Lord, who in the wilderness showered the bread of heaven on a disobedient and quarrelsome people and made quails stream forth for them. But we, all-devout king, ask for a remission in taxes for the care of the holy churches in Palestine, the reconstruction of the sacred buildings burnt by the Samaritans, and succour for the Christians of Palestine, who have been lessened in number and plundered. We also call on you to establish a hospital in the holy city for the care of sick foreigners, and to build and ornament the new church of the Mother of God whose foundations were previously laid down by our archbishop Elias. This is especially appropriate for Your Reverence. And on account of the incursions of the Saracens we call on Your Tranquillity to order the most glorious Summus to build at public expense a fort in the desert below the monasteries which were established through my guidance. I believe that God, for these five acts of yours which will gratify him, will add to your empire Africa, Rome and all the rest of the empire of Honorius, which the royal predecessors of Your all-devout Tranquillity lost, in order that you may cast out the Arian heresy, together with those of Nestorius and Origen, and free the city and the Church of God from the outrage of the heresies.'

63. Evagrius, *Ecclesiastical History* IV.10

Therefore, Justinian very rigorously supported those who gathered at Chalcedon and the decisions which had been resolved by them, as did his wife Theodora, as they spoke of one nature. Either they truly held these views – for whenever a debate about faith is proposed, fathers are against children, children in turn are against those who bore them, a wife is against her own husband, and a husband is against his own wife – or they had contrived some arrangement, in order that he would oppose those who spoke of two natures in Christ our God instead of one, while she would oppose those who urged one nature. Equally, they did not give in to each other; but he very enthusiastically upheld what had been set down at Chalcedon, while she went with those on the opposite side and provided complete support for those speaking for one nature; and she looked after the locals, and welcomed the foreigners with lots of money. She also persuaded Justinian to have Severus summoned.

64. *Institutes*, preface

In the name of our Lord Jesus Christ

The Emperor Caesar Flavius Justinian Alamannicus, Gothicus, Francicus, Germanicus, Anticus, Alanicus, Vandalicus, Africanus, pious, fortunate, illustrious, victorious and triumphant ever-Augustus

To eager young lawyers

Imperial majesty should not only be enhanced with arms, but also armed with laws, so that it may be ruled justly in times of both war and peace; and the Prince of the Roman state may be victorious not only over enemies in war, but may also expel the iniquities of evil-doers by legitimate methods, and may be as very respectful of the law as he is triumphant over his conquered enemies.

(1) We have achieved the path to both of these, with the help of God, through great vigilance and great care. Barbarian nations, brought under our yoke, recognise our efforts in war. Africa as well as other numerous provinces have again been added to Roman rule and our empire, and bear witness to our victories, granted after such a long space of time through the power of heaven. Indeed, all our peoples are ruled by laws which have already been promulgated or gathered by us.

(2) We have brought into transparent harmony the sacred constitutions which were previously confused, and we then extended our care also to the immense volumes of old law, and we completed, with the favour of heaven, a task which appeared hopeless, as if going through the middle of the deep.

(3) And when this had been done, with the help of God, we called Tribonian, a man of distinguished rank and former quaestor of the sacred palace, and also Theophilus and Dorotheus, law professors

of illustrious rank, whose general skill, legal knowledge and loyalty concerning our orders we already knew from many examples; and we ordered them to compose the *Institutes* with our authority and with our encouragement. In this way, you might learn about the first foundations of the law not from old fables but you might get them from the splendour of the emperor; and your ears and your minds may receive nothing useless and nothing misplaced, but only what comes from the actual reality of the cases. Because in previous times, it was the case that after four years the former students could hardly read the imperial pronouncements, but you have been found worthy of such great honour and so great a happiness to do so from the beginning and to have a legal education which, from start to finish, proceeds from the voice of the emperor.

(4) Therefore, after fifty books of the Digest or Pandects, into which all classical law has been collated (which we achieved through the same excellent Tribonian and other illustrious and very learned men), we ordered that the *Institutes* be divided up into these four books, in order to form the first principles of all learning in law.

(5) In them, it is explained briefly both how things used to be and how afterwards, having been obscured by disuse, they were illuminated by imperial remedies.

(6) Having composed the work from all the *Institutes* of the ancients and especially from the commentaries of our Gaius – his *Institutes* and his everyday laws – and from many other treatises, the three above-named learned commissioners presented it to us, and we have read and examined and bestowed on them the full strength of our own constitutions.

(7) And so receive our laws with great energy and keen enthusiasm and show that you yourselves are so learned that our very fine hope favours you to complete the whole law course and also to be able to govern whatever part of our state is entrusted to you.

Given at Constantinople on 21 November 533, the year of the third consulate of our lord Justinian, forever Augustus.

65. *Novel* 25, preface

Concerning the Praetor of Lycaonia

Emperor Justinian Augustus to John, for the second time Most Illustrious prefect of the sacred praetoria of the east, ex-consul, patrician

We have thought it was just to adorn the people of Lycaonia with a higher rank than at present, looking back at earlier administrations in the sources where those who have written about and narrated the past have handed down to us, since they are very closely related to the Romans and arose from almost the same events. For Lycaon, once ruler in Arcadia in Greece, also happened to live in the land of the Romans and when he acquired their ancestors, the Oenotri, he provided a prelude to the empire of the Romans (we are speaking, however, of things that are really ancient, and much older than the times of Aeneas and Romulus); he sent out a colony to these parts, and took away a part of Pisidia and gave it his own name, Lycaonia, and called the province after himself. It will, therefore, be right to adorn its office and label it with the ancient name of a Roman post, and at the same time also to combine its magistracies together (we mean the holder of the civil governor and military commander) into one and to adorn it with the title of praetor. For this name is traditional for a rank of the Romans and was used in the great city of the Romans even before there were consuls. For the Romans once called their leaders praetors and they ordered them to be in charge of the armies and they obeyed the laws written by them: and it was an office regulated in each aspect – it included and demonstrated both bravery in battles and rigour in legislation.

66. *Novel* 47, preface

About the placing of the name of the emperor in contracts and records, and that dates should be written more clearly in Latin letters

The same Sovereign to John, for the second time prefect of praetoria, ex-consul, patrician

Preface
    Any contract and record, and whatever else has been devised by man for the remembrance of an era, is regarded as the most honourable of all when it is also enhanced by a mention of the emperor. For the consuls and indictions, and whatever indication of time is in use with us, do indeed indicate what is intended, and we will certainly not abolish any of them, but we will make a further addition to them, so that the course of time will be designated more fully and more completely. For if someone were to look back to the oldest of all and ancient time of the Republic, Aeneas the Trojan king was for us the first ruler of the republic and we are called 'the sons of Aeneas' after him; but if someone were to look back to that second start, from

when the name of the Romans really shone with lustre among men, the kings Romulus and Numa established it: one built the city, and the other ordered it and enhanced it with laws; or again someone could take, as the third start of the empire, the very great [Julius] Caesar and the pious Augustus and so one would find that this our present state is now powerful – and may it remain immortal as proceeding from them. Therefore, it will be absurd if, in contracts and those matters which take place in the courts and in fact in absolutely everything on which there is a mention of the date, the reign is not placed at their head.

67. Justinian, the first dated copper coin, AD 538

Figure II.67 Justinian, first dated copper coin, AD 538. Photo © The Trustees of the British Museum.

D(ominus) N(oster) IVSTINIANVS P(er)P(etuus) AVG(ustus), facing bust of Justinian, wearing helmet, and holding globe surmounted by cross and shield decorated with cavalryman; to right, cross

M (= 40 nummi), CON (mint of Constantinople) B (workshop 2) ANNO XII (= in the year 12)

68. *Novel* 38, preface

Concerning the City Councillors and their Sons

The same Sovereign to John, for the second time Most Illustrious prefect of the sacred praetoria of the east, ex-consul, patrician

Preface

Those who originally established our republic thought that, following the model of the imperial city, in every city the nobles should be brought together, and that each one should be given a local council, through which all public business should be transacted and everything should be done in the proper order. For this flourished so much and appeared so splendid that the houses of the councillors were large and populous, and there was a mass of those willing and what had seemed to be the burden of public service was by no means unbearable for anyone: for dividing the burden between a mass made it pretty well unnoticeable for those who endured. When, however, bit by bit, some began to remove themselves from the lists of the councillors and to find excuses with which they could somehow make themselves free of it, thus gradually the councils dwindled away and an infinite number of excuses were thought up, through which private fortunes could do well, but common and public affairs would be diminished through all of them. For this reason, liturgies fell on only a few men and their resources were eaten up, so that they fell under these ruinous contractors who are called 'vindices'. As a result it happened that city governance became full of defects, and full of every kind of injustice.

69. Evagrius, *Ecclesiastical History* IV.29

I will come to the business of the plague which struck, now in its fifty-second year, and has not been described before, and which increased in strength and spread over the whole world. For two years after the capture of Antioch by the Persians, a pestilential suffering settled down, in some ways similar to that in the writing of Thucydides but in some ways very different. It was, and is now, said to have begun from Ethiopia. It ran through the whole inhabited world in turn, leaving, I think, no one among mankind who was not affected by the plague. And some cities were affected to such an extent that they became completely empty of inhabitants. However, there were places where it fell more lightly before moving on. It did not strike at any fixed time, and when it struck it did not go away in the same way: but it took hold of some places at the beginning of winter, others while spring was ending, others in the summer, and some places when late autumn was coming on. And there were places where parts of cities were touched but other parts escaped: and often you could see in a city, which did not have the disease, that certain households had been completely destroyed. There were places where one or two houses were destroyed, but the rest of the city has remained untouched: but as we have discovered by close investigation, the households that remained untouched were the only ones to suffer in the following year. But, most amazing of all, if the inhabitants of affected cities happened to be living somewhere else where the disease had not struck, they alone were struck with the disease, that is, those who were from those cities which had been overcome but who were living in the unaffected cities.

And these things often happened in the cities and other places at the times of the periods called indictions. Most of all, an almost complete destruction struck in the first or second year of the fifteen-year cycle. And this also happened to me, who has written these things – for I resolved to weave into my history matters concerning myself, fitting in what is relevant in the relevant place. At the beginning of this plague, I was afflicted by what are called buboes, while I was still studying with the elementary teacher: in the various onslaughts of these sufferings I lost many of my offspring, my wife and other relations, and very many servants and neighbours, as if it was the indictional cycles which were assigning the misfortunes on me. So, at the time of writing, during the fifty-eighth year of my age, no more than two years ago, when the plague struck Antioch for the fourth time when the fourth cycle had passed its beginning, I lost a daughter and the son she had borne, in addition to the previous losses.

The suffering was made up of various illnesses. For in some it began from the head, making the eyes bloodshed and face swollen, it went down to the throat, and having taken hold of someone, it dispatched him from mankind. In others, a flowing out of the stomach occurred. In some, the buboes swelled up and from there terrible fevers arose: and on the second or third day they died, equally in possession of their mental and physical powers as those who had suffered nothing. Others became deranged and laid down their life. And carbuncles broke out and did away with men. There were places where some were affected once or twice and escaped, but, being affected again, they perished.

And there were different ways, beyond telling, of passing it on. Some were killed just by being and living together, some only by touching, some remaining inside their houses, and others in the open space. Some fled from diseased cities and remained untouched, but passed on the disease to those who were not sick. Some have not caught it at all, although living with many who are sick, and who have touched not only many who were sick, but also those who had died. Others who were eager to perish because they had suffered the complete loss of their children or relatives, and because of this they were especially involved with the sick, but nevertheless they were not overcome, as if the disease was struggling against their wish. And so, as I have said, this suffering has been dealt out now for fifty-two years, exceeding all before. For Philostratus was amazed that the pestilence continued for fifteen years in his time. And the future is unclear, as it moves from here to where God will decide; he understands the causes and where they lead. And I will return to where I set out and speak of the remainder of Justinian's affairs.

70. Procopius, *Secret History* 17.5

But Theodora was also concerned to plan punishments for sins against the body. For instance, after she had gathered more than five hundred prostitutes, who earned at the rate of three obols in the middle of the marketplace, just enough to live on, she sent them to the mainland opposite, and shut them up in the convent called Repentance, as it is called, compelling them to change their way of life.

71. Romanos, *Kontakion* 54, 14–25

On Earthquakes and Fires

(14) The Creator, inflicting a first, and then a second blow, but finding men had not become better, but were worse still than they were before, then inflicts despondency at the very table of grace itself, by allowing the sanctuaries of the Church to be burned, just as in the past he had granted the divine ark to foreigners. And the lamentations of the crowd were spreading in the squares as in the churches; for the fire would have destroyed everything, if they had not had the God who provides for all eternal life.

(15) Everyone apparently knows what happened then, and its memory rightly holds your mind and your thought captive, and also makes our language more timid to tell its tale. Because the fire was fed by the wood, and was eager to spread, and, pushed by terrifying winds, to burn it all completely. And we, suffering before this misfortune, transform our anger into wickedness. For we do not know how to repent in a way to have eternal life.

(16) Like a cloud, the fire rumbled through the whole air, dazzling and consuming everything, noisy, frightening, without yielding to the many headwinds, and having no fear of the water. In addition, the water in the sea rose up. The men's hands were ineffective to help. The fire

resisted them and overwhelmed them, and the sea itself beat them, for it obstructed those who hastened to flee: so they called for eternal life.

(17) But to speak concisely: everything in the city, with the churches and at the same time the palace, was without all hope, at least in man; but God as usual observed everything. Because of those who live in mercy, the Lord makes supplicants wise and grants mercy to all; but because of the wicked who do not want to be made wise by the very threat, he arouses anger at the point of the sword, so that they may know eternal life.

(18) The city was gripped by these terrible things, and it held a great lamentation. Those who feared God stretched out their hands to him, begging for mercy and an end from their misfortunes. With them, as is right, the emperor also prayed, looking up to the Creator, and with him his consort: 'Grant me, Saviour,' he cried, 'as also to your David, to overcome Goliath. For I have hope in you. Save your faithful people and have mercy on those to whom you will also give eternal life.'

(19) When God heard the voices of those who cried out and of the royals, he granted to the city compassion from his love of man, for a bitter lament had arisen for those who had been exterminated with the sword: the wives lamented being widowed, the children being orphaned, the fathers being childless, and the relatives being deprived of their families. Others mourned the loss of their situations, and grief was common in all the city. On the ground lay the throne of the Church, which provides eternal life.

(20) The sons of baptism once honoured with psalms, Sophia and Irene, the glorious powers of the world above; now, they saw the sacred churches lying on the ground. The glorious beauty that came from them was full of decay; the place which had shone with radiance now held out fear. Once the light of beauty shone out, now the fire drove the spectators away. The only salvation we could hope for is that which provides eternal life.

(21) Always, all the faithful who trust in God rightly hope to deserve greater things, because this is the way of God. Indeed, if one were to contemplate Jerusalem and the very great temple that Solomon, that wisest man of all, who had taken a very long time to raise and adorn it, decorated with infinite wealth; how it was cast down and delivered to destruction, and how it remains fallen down and not restored, one will be able to see the grace granted to this church, which provides eternal life.

(22) The people of Israel are deprived of their temple; but we, in its place, now have the Holy Resurrection and Zion which Constantine and the faithful Helena donated to the world, two hundred and fifty

years after it was thrown down. But here, one day after the collapse, they began the work of resurrecting the church. And it is splendidly adorned, and finished. The royals present the cost, and the Lord, eternal life.

(23) Those who presently govern with piety the affairs of the Romans have brought forth great and dazzling things, worthy of marvel and surpassing all the kings of the past. For, in a short time, they have restored the whole city, so that they enable those who have suffered all the misfortunes to forget. The building itself of the church is constructed with such quality that it imitates heaven, a divine throne which provides eternal life.

(24) All of us who love Christ and hasten to send him in glory, we ask the Lord and Creator of Heaven to strengthen the enterprise and establishment of his church, so that we may rightly see it completely filled [with the glory of our God] and brimming with grace for those who see it during liturgies, canticles and hymns, so that the royals, the citizens and the priests rejoice in it, that everyone is given eternal life.

(25) Saviour, Immortal Son of a Father who was before time, save the whole city, save the churches, also save the royals. Deliver the city from all upheavals, earthquake, famine and plague. Preserve the whole state, Lord of all wisdom. And grant to me in my misery forgiveness for my sins. Take me away from the terrible things that surround me and heal my unhappiness. Grant me to travel through this life free from harm, and there, eternal life.

72. Paul the Silentiary, *Ekphrasis of Hagia Sophia*, lines 1–80

Is it possible to find a day greater than today, on which both God and emperor are revered? It is not possible to name one. We know that Christ is Lord, we know it totally; for you make this known by your words, Almighty One, even to barbarians. For this reason, you have Him as a partner in your actions: in passing laws, in founding cities, in erecting churches, in calling to arms (if needed), in arranging treaties and in ending fighting. For this reason, victory is an intrinsic part of your work, as if it were a badge. Is it not the Ocean to the west for us the limit of your empire after we have raced across the world? And to the east, have you not already overturned all men, some in battle, and taking hold of others before it came to that? Have you not long since held all Libya [Africa] as your slave? For this reason, you escape lightly from diseases, against everyone's expectations. For this reason, truly you always learn of hidden dangers, Almightiest, and avoid them: guarded not by spears or shields, but by the very hand of God.

I admire you, Almighty One, for your good courage, I admire you for your knowledge and for your faith. The ambush was set, the sword was prepared and ready, the appointed time was now. The conspirators had already passed inside the palace and were grabbing the inner door, through which they were intending to strike against your throne. But since you knew this and had learnt of it long since, you remained resolute, trusting in your only defender – I mean God – through whom you triumph in all things: and you were not frustrated in your aim.

For what came after this? The leader of the ambush fell by your own hand: for Justice did not wish to save him. She knew clearly from the tyrants who had often fallen that if you held him while he was still alive, you would surely turn straight to pity and to mercy – in these, too, you surpass all mankind. With your sympathy for the faults of life, you have often sighed at our false steps, Best of Men; you often moisten your gentle eyes with tears, in royal fashion, distressed on our behalf; and particularly when you observe that lack of self-control, which is life's fellow inmate, you release everyone from their evil debts, like God, and rush to forgive. You ask yourself, when the scale of accusations does not permit the others to begin their entreaties. Indeed, you never allow the pity of another to be realised, when it is yours absolutely. And through the acts of impious audacity which we commit you have occasion for speaking freely from above.

Does he not arm himself completely against God himself, the man who is not willing for this emperor to rule, an emperor who is gentle and kind-hearted, and who does good in measure both to those who are friends and to those who are not friends? This is your salvation. This, Almighty One, makes the soul of the empress, she who is fortunate, the best of all, beautiful and most wise, to speak freely to God on your behalf. While alive she was your devout partner, but when she departed, she provided for your subjects a supportive oath, an unbreakable oath, which you have not transgressed and which you would not willingly neglect.

Such are these things. But grant courage to those who already wish to go to the church. And let this also be among your marvels, that bold words should appear to describe a work which surpasses everything by the superiority of its marvels. Proof of the magnitude of your marvels is that great love which the whole city nurtures for you, Mightiest King, and for your church. For when you were celebrating the festival, as was right, straightaway all the people, the senate and those who affect safety of a moderate life, asked you to extend the days of the festival. You approved. The days ran on. They asked again. Again you approved. By doing this repeatedly, you richly extended the festival.

73. Procopius, *Buildings* I.2.1–12

(1) There happened to be a marketplace in front of the Senate House; the Byzantines call the marketplace the Augusteum. There, a structure of stones has been made up no less than seven in a rectangle, all lying next to each other at their ends, but each is smaller than the one below and falls short of it, so that each of the stones, by the way it is placed, becomes a projecting step and the people who gather there sit on them as if on steps. (2) At the top of the stones, a column rose up to a really extraordinary height, but it is not one piece, but made up of large stones in a circular course forming an angle inside where they are cut, and fitted to each other by the skill of the stone masons. (3) The best brass, cast in panels and garlands, encircles the stones on all sides, binding them firmly, and covering them in decorations, and in almost every aspect they resemble a column, especially at the top and the bottom. (4) The colour of this brass is paler than pure gold, and in value it is not much less than the same would be in silver. (5) A huge bronze horse stood on the top, turned towards the east, a sight worth talking about. He seems to be walking and to be clearly moving forward. (6) He is actually raising up his left fore foot, as if about to advance on the ground before him, and the other presses down on the stone which is underneath him, as if awaiting the step. He holds his back feet together in such a way as if he were in readiness to go forwards whenever he is ready not to stand still. (7) Mounted on this horse is a bronze image of the emperor, like a colossus. The image calls Achilles to mind; (8) for this is how they call the costume which he wears. He has put on boots and his legs are without greaves. (9) He also wears a breastplate in the manner of a hero and the helmet which covers his head gives the impression that it is nodding up and down, and a kind of brilliance radiates from it. (10) One might say poetically that it is the star of Autumn. He looks towards where the sun is rising and making his direction towards the Persians, I suppose. (11) And he carries in his left hand a globe, with which the sculptor has shown that the whole earth and sea are subject to him, but he holds neither sword or spear nor any other weapon, but a cross surmounts his globe, from which alone he has gained his empire and his victory in war. (12) Stretching forward his right hand to the rising sun and spreading out his fingers, he orders the barbarians there to stay at home and not to advance. So much for these things.

Figure II.73 Fifteenth-century drawing of the statue of Justinan. Photo: copy of the drawing in Budapest University Library MS 35, taken from P. A. Dethier, 'Augusteon', Magyar Tudományos Akadémia XI (1869).

74. Procopius, *Buildings* V.8.4–9

(4) On this Mt Sinai live monks, whose life is an exact practice for death, and they enjoy without fear the solitude which is dear to them. (5) For these monks (since there is nothing they desire, as they are above all human needs, and nor do they desire to own anything, or to care for their bodies, nor do they have any enthusiasm to benefit by anything else), the Emperor Justinian built a church, which he dedicated to the Mother of God, in order that they may spend their time there praying and worshipping. (6) He built this church not on the top of the mountain but much further down below. (7) For it was impossible for a man to spend the night on the summit, since continuous crashes and other signs of divinity are heard at night, terrifying the body and soul of man. (8) It was there, they say, that Moses received the laws from God and brought them forth. (9) And at the foot of the mountain this emperor also built a very strong fortress and established a very important garrison of soldiers, in order that the barbarian Saracens would not be able to attack in great secrecy the lands of Palestine from that place which, as has been related by me, is deserted.

75. Procopius, *Buildings* I.11.10–15

(10) I will now set out what works were carried out here by this emperor for a plentiful water supply. In the summer, the imperial city had a scarcity of water for the most part, although there was plenty in other seasons. (11) For at that time, droughts occur, since the springs flow with less water than at other times and make the water conduits to the city underprovided. (12) On account of this, the emperor planned the following. At the imperial stoa, where the lawyers, prosecutors and any others who are involved in this sort of work prepare their cases, there is a very large court, very long and sufficiently wide, with a peristyle around its four sides. It was not made on an earth base by those who built it, but on rock. (13) Four stoas, one standing on each side, surround the court. Deeply excavating under this and the stoa which faces towards the south wind, the Emperor Justinian made a storage area, fit for purpose in the summer, for the water which was lost through its excess in the other seasons. (14) This reservoir receives the run-off from the overflowing aqueduct and so freely provides a space for the overfull water, and furnishes a supply to those who want it when it becomes needed in the season. (15) Thus the Emperor Justinian provided that there should be no lack of drinking water for the people of Byzantium.

76. Greek Anthology IX.641

On a Bridge over the Sangarius

And you too, Sangarius, after haughty Italy and after the peoples of the Medes and all the barbarian host, your streams were fettered by strong vaults, and so as you have been enslaved by the royal hand; you who previously was impassable by boats, previously unyielding, lie tightly held with bonds of stone.

77. C.J. I.5.18.4

Concerning all other heresies (by heresies we call those which think and worship contrary to the Catholic and Apostolic Church and orthodox faith), we desire that the law already set down by us and our father of divine memory should pertain, in which suitable measures were established not only against them but also against both the Samaritans and Hellenes (pagans): so that those who are ill with this sickness may neither serve in the army or enjoy any office, nor indeed in the guise of a teacher of any discipline draw the minds of the more simple into their own error and in this way make them more lazy towards the true and the pure faith of the orthodox. We permit, however, only those who are of orthodox faith to teach and to receive a public salary.

78. *C.J.* I.11.10

Since some are found, who are imbued with the error of the impious and sinful and do what moves a merciful god to a just anger: so that we should not allow what relates to them to remain uncontrolled, but knowing that they have abandoned the worship of true and only God, that they have made sacrifices to images in their foolish sin and that they have celebrated rituals full of every sort of impiety; those indeed who now, after they have had the blessing of holy baptism, have committed them, and when the wickedness of which they have been convicted has been duly observed, we compassionately lay down this: for the future we order through the present law to all those who have been made Christians and have enjoyed at any time the blessing of a holy and saving baptism, if it still shall be seen that they have remained in pagan sin, they shall suffer the ultimate penalty.

79. Agathias, *The Histories* II.30.3–4

(3) . . . Damascius of Syria, Simplicius of Cilicia, Eulamius of Phrygia, Priscian of Lydia, Hermias and Diogenes of Phoenicia and Isidore of Gaza, all of them, as the poem has it [Pindar, *Isthmian Ode* 7], the very zenith of the philosophers of our age, thought that, since the religion which was for the most part dominant among the Romans was not to their liking, the Persian state was much better. Moreover, they were convinced by those widespread rumours that it would be the state that was most just for them, and that it was just what the argument of Plato wanted, a place where philosophy and monarchy came together as the same thing; the state of the subjects was particularly just and orderly; no thefts or robberies took place, and they truly did not share in any other sort of injustice. Even if one of their valuable possessions were left in some indescribably remote place, nobody who came across it would take it away, and so it would remain, even

if it were unguarded, and it would be kept safe for whoever left it until he came back.

(4) Taking this as all true, and in addition because they were forbidden by law here to take part in politics without penalty (since they did not follow the established religion), they left immediately and set off for a foreign and inhospitable land, so that they might spend the rest of their lives there.

80. Pseudo-Dionysius of Tel-Mahre, *Chronicle* 852

Translation from Pseudo-Dionysius of Tel-Mahre, Chronicle Part III, *translated by Witold Witakowski (Liverpool 1996)*

In the 19th year of the Emperor Justinian (AD 545/6) by encouragement of our humble self the affair of the pagans was investigated. There were found in the capital famous persons, notables and others – *grammatici*, sophists, *scholastici* and physicians, and when they were exposed, on being tortured they denounced each other. They were arrested, scourged and imprisoned. (Then) these patricians and nobles were sent into churches to learn the faith of the Christians, as benefited pagans.

One noble and rich pagan among them, whose name was Phocas, and who was a patrician, seeing the intensity of the investigation and also (knowing) that those (pagans) who had been arrested informed (the authorities) that he was a pagan (as well), and that a heavy sentence was prepared against him because of the emperor's severe zealousness, took poison in the night and ended (his) life here. When the emperor was informed of it he made a very just decision giving instructions that (Phocas) should be buried (with) the burial of an ass, that is without people attending or any prayer for him. So members of his household carried him on a bier at night, went out (of the city), opened a tomb and threw him in like a dead beast. Thus for some time fear seized all the pagans.

81. Choricius, *Oratio* XIII, preface, 10–16

For the Brumalia [winter festival] of the Emperor Justinian. Impromptu [after 532, before 539].

The address acknowledges that the virtue of the emperor shines through even without any words, but it is moved by pleasure to speak the words that the occasion grants.

(10) So they held a festival for each letter. And in my judgement the one for the present day seems to be imperial. For it is a figure and a symbol that is straight, simple and free from embellishment, just as, for us, the emperor sits in judgement 'with straight verdicts', as the Askraian says [the early Greek poet Hesiod], if the tragic discourse wants the myth to be as the simple truth.

(11) And indeed the letter is straightforward for everyone, and old men, children and young persons write it just the same. For the emperor hands out goods not according to the measures of age, but he grants to everyone to draw water from the same spring.

(12) And if it has ever come into your head to you to count the syllables, you have seen, I suppose, that appropriately it comes first in the number of its letters; for the emperor indeed is the greatest of all the dignities.

(13) It was indeed proper, I think, that he was also not divided from his spouse in the letters; even in them, it seems that there is a single and mutual harmony between both of them. In no way does anything come in the middle and divide their letters.

(14) Therefore everything which the emperor may decide, is of benefit to human life. I myself also simply wonder at them and praise them, and not even Momus, so to speak [Momus was the personification of mockery; his name and 'find fault with' are puns in Greek], would find fault with them. And when I was reflecting on which of them is the finest, suddenly Summus [the governor of Palestine, where Gaza was situated] appeared as leader of the chorus, he who was impervious to the strokes of gold and he who at last brought Peace into the light for us, when it was a long cause of anxiety and was no less needed than when Comedy brought her to Dionysus [Aristophanes' comic play *Peace* was performed in 430 BC at the Theatre of Dionysus in Athens, at the end of the ten-year war between Athens and Sparta].

(15) But as the saying goes, 'brother may stand by brother'. Knowing this proverb very well, you do not depend completely on your own nature, and although you are capable of quick understanding and of fulfilling in action whatever comes to your mind, nevertheless you make your brother [Julian, Summus' brother and one of Justinian's ambassadors] a partner in your deliberations, whom Aristides would say came to men as a model of Hermes the Orator.

(16) Having prepared such a feast, I have come to you, my friends; but time, being short, did not grant me to gather the usual 'chefs of words'.

82. Greek Anthology I.8

On the Church of the Holy Apostles Peter and Paul near St Sergius in the property of Hormisdas

Honouring Christ, the Absolute King, with his devoted labours, Justinian built this very glorious church to Peter and Paul; for by granting the prayers of his servants, a man brings great honour to the King himself. Here is ready gain for the soul and for the eyes; let each one gain what he has need of by his prayers, and take joy seeing the beauty and glory of the house.

Chronology

482/3	Birth of Justinian
491	Anastasius becomes emperor
500?	Birth of Procopius
c. 503	Birth of Theodora
518	Justin becomes emperor
519	The Acacian schism ends
521	First consulship of Justinian
524/5	Justinian and Theodora marry
525	Justinian becomes Caesar
526	Earthquake destroys Antioch
527	Justinian becomes co-emperor; death of Justin
528	Second consulship of Justinian
529	Academy of Athens closed; Samaritan revolt; promulgation of the first edition of the *Codex Iustinianus*; Saracens plunder Syria
530	Belisarius defeats the Persians at Dara
531	Persians defeat Belisarius at Callinicum
532	'Endless Peace' signed with Persians; *Nika* riot; work begins on Hagia Sophia
533	Belisarius sent to overthrow Vandals; *Digest* and *Institutes* promulgated
534	Belisarius returns in triumph from North Africa; the Berbers in Africa revolt; second edition of the *Codex Iustinianus*; death of Athalaric in Italy
535	Theodahad murders Amalasuntha in Italy and becomes king; Belisarius conquers Sicily; Justinian begins his programme of provincial reform
536	Mutiny of Stotzas in Carthage; Belisarius takes Naples and Rome; Vitigis becomes king after Theodahad murdered
537–8	Siege of Rome; Hagia Sophia is dedicated (27 December 537)

539	Hunnic raid
540	Chosroes breaks the 'Endless Peace' and sacks Antioch; Vitigis surrenders Ravenna and Belisarius is recalled
541	Consulship is abolished; bubonic plague reaches Egypt from Africa; Chosroes recaptures Lazica; exile of John the Cappadocian; Totila becomes king in Italy
542	Plague arrives in Constantinople
543	Berber revolt in North Africa
544	Belisarius is sent back to Italy; Solomon is killed in North Africa; Chosroes invades Roman provinces
545	Five-year truce agreed with Persia (excluding Lazica)
546	Totila recaptures Rome
547	Belisarius recaptures Rome
548	Death of Theodora; victory of John Troglita against the Berbers
549	Belisarius recalled from Italy; plot by Artabanes and Arsaces against Justinian
550	silkworms brought to the Roman Empire Totila recaptures Rome
551	Justinian's *Edict on the True Faith*; Justinian sends an expedition under Liberius to Spain
552	Battle of Busta Gallorum; death of Totila
553	Fifth Council of Constantinople
554	Legislation ('Pragmatic Sanction') was passed for the rule of Italy after the defeat of the Ostrogoths; silkworms brought to Roman Empire
558	Conquest of Visigothic Spain; collapse of Hagia Sophia dome; Avar embassy to Constantinople
559	Belisarius wards off an invasion by the Kutrigur Huns which threatens Constantinople
562	Peace treaty with Persia to last for fifty years; bankers' plot against Justinian; re-dedication of Hagia Sophia
564	Justinian imposes aphthartodocetism
565	Death of Justinian

Popes and Patriarchs

Rome

Hormisdas	514–523
John I	523–526
Felix IV	526–530
Boniface II	530–532
John II	533–535
Agapitus	535–536
Silverius	536–537
Vigilius	537–555
Pelagius	556–561

Constantinople

John II the Cappadocian	518–520
Epiphanius	520–535
Anthimus	535–536
Menas	536–552
Eutychius	552–565
John Scholasticus	565–574

Alexandria

Timothy IV	517–535
Theodosius	535–536
Gaianus	535
Paul the Tabennesiote	538–540
Zoilus	540–551
Apollinaris	551–570

Antioch

Paul II	518–520
Euphrasius	520–526
Ephraem	526–545
Domnus III	545–559
Anastasius I	559–570

Jerusalem

John III	516–524
Peter	524–552
Macarius	552
Eustochius	552–563
Macarius	563/4–574

Glossary

Words marked with an asterisk (*) can also be found elsewhere in the Glossary.

Abasgi A people from Abasgia (modern Abkhazia, in modern Georgia).

Acacian schism A doctrinal division which arose in the late fifth century between the western and eastern churches. Named after Acacius, the *patriarch of Constantinople from 471 to 489, who had prepared the *Henoticon* for the Emperor Zeno which was not accepted by the pope in Rome.

Academy of Athens A school of philosophy in Athens. The original academy founded by Plato was destroyed in the first century BC. A revived academy was established in AD 410 by the leading Neoplatonists.

Acculturation The assimilation of one culture to another.

Acephali The extreme miaphysites. They broke off communion from all the *patriarchs and were therefore known as the 'headless ones' (*acephali* in Greek).

Alamanni A confederation of German peoples, from the Upper Rhine. After their defeat, Justinian styled himself Alamannicus.

Alans Originally a nomadic people living north of the Black Sea. In the fifth century, one group settled in southern Spain, and migrated with the *Vandals to North Africa. After their defeat, Justinian styled himself Alanicus. Another group remained in the Caucasus and allied themselves with the Persians against the Romans.

Alexandrian Christology Doctrine developed especially by Cyril of Alexandria (d. 444) which emphasised the divine nature of Christ and the unity of the person of Christ.

Anathema Meaning 'curse' or 'excommunication', it refers to the banning of a religious doctrine which was regarded as heretical.

Annona Meaning 'grain'; it refers to both the distribution of food and a land tax.

Antae Tribes who occupied territory to the north-east of the Black Sea. After their defeat, Justinian styled himself Anticus.

Anti-Chalcedonian see *Chalcedon.

Antiochene Christology Doctrine associated with the see of Antioch, developed especially by Diodore of Tarsus, Theodore of Mopsuestia, Theodoret of Cyrrhus and Nestorius. They emphasised the humanity of Christ and saw a looser union of the divine and human in Christ than envisaged by the Alexandrians.

Aphthartodocetism The theory that Christ's body was incorruptible argued for by Julian of Halicarnassus and adopted by Justinian in 564/565. The Greek word *aphthartodocetai* means 'those who believe in incorruptibility'. Exponents were also known as the phantasiasts.

Apocrisarius The representative of a bishop.

Apsilii A people from Apsilia (modern Abkhazia, in modern Georgia).

Archimandrite A senior monk.

Arians Followers of Arius, priest in Egypt during the late third and early fourth centuries. He denied the full divinity of Christ, arguing that he had been created by God and was therefore inferior to him. Arius' views were condemned as heresy by the *Council of Nicaea in 325.

Armenia Sometimes a Roman province, on the frontier between Rome and Persia, and roughly the same area as modern Armenia.

Assessor A legal advisor to, for example, a provincial governor.

Augustus The title of the most senior member of the imperial family (compare *Caesar*).

Avars A confederation of peoples who lived to the north of the Black Sea; they made an alliance with Justinian in the late 550s.

Axumites The kingdom of Axum was located in modern Eritrea, in Ethiopia. It played an important role in the Red Sea trade.

Berbers see *Moors.

Blemmyes A people inhabiting Nubia (Noubadia), in southern Egypt and Sudan. See *Nobades.

Blues One of the *circus factions.

Boule The Greek word for *Curia*.

Brumalia A winter festival, held in November and December of each year.

Burgundians Originally a Germanic tribe, they established a kingdom in modern Burgundy and Savoy which was annexed by the *Franks in 534, although it later emerged as one of the sub-kingdoms of Merovingian France.

Caesar The title of a junior emperor.

Caesaropapism The authority of the secular head of state (e.g. an emperor) over the Church.

Candidatus An elite unit of guards, originally named after their white tunics.

Chalcedon A city near Constantinople, where the fourth oecumenical council was convened by the Emperor Marcian in 451. It produced the formula that Christ was one person in two natures (*dyophysite), the divine *consubstantial with the Father, the human consubstantial with us. It failed to unite the eastern patriarchates and was not adopted by the pope in Rome.

Chiliarch An army officer.

Circus factions Groups of supporters of different teams at the games, particularly for the chariot races held at the hippodrome, and divided between the Blues, Greens, Reds and Whites. They could also have a political role (for example, during the *Nika* riot) and help to defend cities from foreign invaders.

Codex 'Codex' means 'book' and is the origin of our word 'code'. Here it refers to the bodies of laws drawn up by Theodosius II (*Codex Theodosianus*) and Justinian (*Codex Justinianus*).

Codex Justinianus (**Code of Justinian**) The body of laws drawn up under the Emperor Justinian in 534 (a first edition was published in 529, but it does not survive).

Codex Sinopensis Part of an illuminated copy of the New Testament, made in the sixth century, bought in 1799 by a Frenchman in Sinope (Sinop, Turkey) and today in the Bibliothèque nationale de France.

Codex Theodosianus (*Theodosian Code*) The body of laws drawn up under the Emperor Theodosius II in 438.

Comes domesticorum The 'count of the domestics', a senior military commander in charge of the *domestici* (imperial bodyguards).

Comes excubitorum The 'count of those out of bed', the commander of a unit of elite palace guards called *Excubitors.

Comes Orientis The 'count of the east' was the governor of the Oriens, one of the principal administrative areas or dioceses, consisting mostly of modern Syria, Lebanon, Cyrpus, Israel and Jordan, with its capital at Antioch.

Comes sacrarum (*largitionum*) Chief finance minister.

Constantinoplitan Creed A modification of the Nicene Creed (see *Council of Nicaea), made by the council held at Constantinople in 381.

Consubstantial A translation of the Greek word *homoousion* (also translated as 'of the same essence').

Consul Originally one of the two principal Roman magistrates, the office survived into the late empire, when it became largely honorary, but involved the holder in the colossal expense of holding games. The consulship was held from time to time by the emperor. Justinian abolished it in the west after 534, and in the east after 542.

Council of Chalcedon see *Chalcedon.

Council of Constantinople Held in 553, in which Justinian aimed to reconcile the *miaphysites and *dyophysites.

Council of Ephesus see *Ephesus.

Council of Nicaea First oecumenical council held in 325 by Constantine in Nicaea (in north-west modern Turkey). Produced the Nicene Creed which emphasised the equality of God the Father and God the Son through the *homoousion* formula.

Council in Trullo Held in 691–692, in the domed hall ('troulos') in the emperor's palace in Constantinople.

Creed A statement of religious belief. See *Constantinopolitan Creed and *Nicene Creed.

Curator Superintendent. The 'superintendents of the divine house' (*curatores divinae domus*) administered the personal property of the imperial family.

Curia City council. *Boule* in Greek.

Curiales City councillors; see *Curia*.

Cycle An anthology of epigrams produced in the sixth century by Agathias.

Definition of Faith The agreement made at the *Council of Chalcedon in 451.

Delphax A grand courtyard in the emperor's palace in Constantinople.

Digest (called *Pandects* in Greek). A summary of the works of earlier jurists, published by Justinian in 533.

Diocese A geographical administrative unit, made up of several provinces and commanded by a vicar (*vicarius*). Mostly abolished by Justinian.

Diptychs 'Two-leaves', a diptych was an ancient writing tablet made of two joined parts. In ecclesiastical terms, it comes to refer to the names of dead and living persons listed on the diptychs who were commemorated in church services (removal of a name signified their excommunication). Secular diptychs were used to enclose letters, but in particular carved ivory diptychs were used by consuls to mark the holding of the consular games.

Dux A military commander.

Dux Numidiae The military commander of Numidia, in North Africa.

Dyophysite 'Two natures' (in contrast to *miaphysite), whereby the divine and human natures of Christ are separate.

Ekphrasis A literary description of a work of art or fine building.

Encaustic 'Burnt-in': a technique of painting, in which colours are mixed with hot wax.

Ephesus One of the principal cities of ancient Asia Minor (on the western coast of modern Turkey), where the Emperor Theodosius II summoned the third oecumenical council in 431 to settle doctrinal differences about the nature of Christ. It brought about a schism between the patriarchates of Antioch and Alexandria (see *patriarch), which was ended in 433 by the *Formula of Reunion. A second council, known as the 'Robber' Council, was held at Ephesus in 449.

Excubitors Elite palace guards.

Formula of Reunion John, the *patriarch of Antioch, put forward this compromise between the different religious views debated at the *Council of Ephesus.

Franks The Franks established a kingdom in France and Germany, based between the Loire and the Rhine. Their king, Theudebert, lent his support to the Ostrogoths against Justinian. After their defeat, Justinian styled himself Francicus.

Gepids A Germanic people who lived to the west of the Black Sea.

Ghassānids An Arab family dynasty (see *Jafnids) located to the east and south of Jordan.

Goths A generic name for a number of Germanic peoples, particularly used of the *Ostrogoths. After their defeat, Justinian styled himself Gothicus.

Greens One of the *circus factions.

Hellenes Those who followed 'hellene' or Greek views of paganism.

Henoticon The name of the document of doctrinal unity (*henosis*) prepared by Acacius for the Emperor Zeno in 482 as a compromise between the Chalcedonians and non-Chalcedonians. It led to the *Acacian schism.

Heruls A Germanic people who lived in the middle Danube; often unreliable allies of the Romans; they were eventually defeated by the *Lombards.

Ḥ**imyarites** A people living in southern Arabia.

Homoousion The *Nicene Creed states that the Son is 'of the same essence' ('homoousion' in Greek; 'consubstantial' in Latin), i.e. Christ possesses the same divine attributes as the Father.

Ḥ**ujrids** An Arab dynasty living in the Arabian peninsula.

Huns There were various groups of Huns (see *Sabir Huns, *Kutrigurs, *Utrigurs), but the term was used more specifically to mean the people living to the north-east of the Black Sea.

Hypostasis Meaning 'substance', it referred to the individual 'reality' of the Father, the Son and the Holy Spirit (i.e. each member of the Trinity).

Indiction The tax and administrative cycle of fifteen years.

Institutes A textbook for legal students, based on the model of the classical jurist Gaius. The work was published in 533, and given the force of law.

Isaurians People who lived in southern Turkey.

Jafnids An Arab family dynasty (see *Ghassānids) located to the east and south of Jordan.

Kathisma 'Seat', meaning the emperor's box at the hippodrome.

Kutrigurs A people living to the north of the Black Sea.

Lakhmids An Arab dynasty (see *Naṣrids) living in the Arabian peninsula.

Latifundia Large estates.

Lazi People living in Lazica (Colchis in classical times), to the north-east of the Black Sea.

Libellus A 'little book'; for example, the dossier made by Pope Hormisdas, incorporating statements of faith.

Limes Frontier.

Logothete The logothete (literally translated as the 'calculator') was in charge of tax gathering.

Lombards A people originally from northern Europe who defeated the *Gepids and moved to northern Italy, where they established a kingdom.

Magister militum A 'master of the soldiers' was a senior military regional commander.

Magister militum per Orientem The 'master of the soldiers throughout the east' was the military commander of the *Oriens*.

Magister militum praesentalis The 'master of the soldiers of the imperial presence' was the general stationed in Constantinople.

Magister officiorum The 'master of the offices' was the senior civil servant.

Manichaean Manichees were the followers of the third-century Persian gnostic Mani who believed in a dualist (good versus evil) view of the world. Manichaeism was viewed as heretical and outlawed in imperial legislation throughout the fourth and fifth centuries.

Miaphysite Meaning 'one nature', it refers to the view that Christ had a single nature, with a human and divine aspect, the exact opposite of *dyophysite. In recent literature, 'miaphysite' has replaced the term 'monophysite' (meaning Christ had *only* one nature). Miaphysites were found in the eastern provinces, especially Egypt.

Milaresia Silver coins.

Misimiani A people who lived to the east of the Black Sea.

Monophysite see *miaphysite.

Montanist A person who believed in the teaching of Montanus, named after a prophet of the second century from Turkey. Montanism was regarded as a heresy.

Moors Native tribes of North Africa, both within the territory conquered by Rome (who might become allies) and outside of it. The Moors were later referred to as the Berbers.

Nakhveragan The title of a Persian military commander.

Narthex The porch of a church.

Naṣrids An Arab dynasty (see *Lakhmids) living in the Arabian peninsula.

Nestorian An adherent of the religious views of Nestorius, the *patriarch of Constantinople from 428 to 431, who denied that the Virgin Mary was the *theotokos (Mother of God) and accepted the duality of natures of Christ (human and divine). Nestorius was deposed at the *Council of Ephesus in 431.

Nicene Creed/Church Used of the church or creed which followed the *Council of Nicaea.

***Nika* riot** The riot in Constantinople of 532, which destroyed large parts of the city.

Nimbate Wearing a nimbus or halo.

Nobades A people (Nobades or Noubades) inhabiting Nubia, in southern Egypt and northern Sudan.

Nomisma Gold coin.

Non-Chalcedonians Those who rejected the Council of Chalcedon's Definition of Faith which defined that Christ has two natures.

Noubades see *Nobades.

Novels or *novella* The Latin word means 'new' and is applied to any law (*novella constitutio*) passed after the *Codex Theodosianus* in 438 and after the publication of the *Codex Justinianus* in 534. Justinian's new laws or novels (*novellae constitutiones*) were collected together on several occasions during the centuries after his death.

Obol The name of a small Greek coin or sum of money. It played no part in the Byzantine monetary system but the word *triobelos* (three obols) was still used to denote a derisory sum.

Origenism Named after Origen, a third-century theologian, whose views were condemned by a local council in Constantinople in 543.

Ostrogoths Often referred to more simply as 'Goths', they were a Germanic people who eventually captured and settled in Italy (under the direction of the Emperor Zeno) under various kings such as Theoderic and Totila. Justinian waged a long war against them to recover Italy.

Pandects The Greek name for the *Digest.

Patriarch The name given to the archbishop of the patriarchal sees of Constantinople, Antioch, Jerusalem and Alexandria (the fifth see was Rome whose leader is, of course, referred to as the pope).

Patrician The term originally referred to the descendants of the Roman kings, and later became an honorary title.

Phantasiast see *aphthartodocetism.

Phylarch A title bestowed on Arab chieftains.

Praesentales Troops serving in the presence of the emperor.

Praetor Originally a Roman magistrate, the title was revived by Justinian. The *praetores Justiniani* combined military and civil command in the provinces, while the *praetor plebis* (praetor of the people) was the chief police and law officer in Constantinople. Not to be confused with the *praetorian prefect.

Praetorian prefect The governor of one of the largest administrative units of the empire (*prefecture). The name was derived from that of the original commander of the praetorian guard, the emperor's corps of bodyguards.

Pragmatic Sanction The law with which Justinian re-established direct imperial control in Italy in 554.

Prefecture A very large military and administrative unit, governed by a *praetorian prefect. They were originally subdivided into dioceses and then provinces, but Justinian effectively abolished the dioceses.

Presbyter A religious official.

Quaestor Originally a Roman administrative or financial magistrate, the title was used for several roles in the late empire. The senior legal official was the *quaestor sacri palatii*, and in 536 Justinian used the title for the commander of a large area to the west of the Black Sea (*quaestor exercitus*). Another post of quaestor was created by Justinian to work with the *praetor plebis* in Constantinople.

Reds A *circus faction.

Referendarii Judicial clerks and messengers at the imperial court.

Rossano Gospels An illustrated copy of the Gospels, made in the sixth century and today in the Cathedral of Rossano, Italy. It is one of the earliest illustrated versions of the New Testament.

Rugi A people living in the Danube area, in modern Austria.

Sabir Huns A people who lived to the north of the Caspian Sea.
Samaritan A religious minority in the Levant, who rebelled in 529 and were regarded as heretics.
Saracens A term used for Arabs.
Scholae palatinae The 'palatine schools' were an elite unit of the imperial guard.
Scymni A people living to the east of the Black Sea.
Scythian monks A community of monks, originally from Scythia, the original name of the area to the west of the Black Sea. See also *Theopaschite.
Silentiary Palace official of high rank.
Sklaveni A people living on the Danube frontier.
Sleepless Monks Monks who held services throughout the day and night, without any break, and played a role in the religious controversies of the time.
Solidus/i Gold coin(s).
Suani A people who lived to the east of the Black Sea.
Syncellus A senior church official.
Theopaschite 'God suffered': if only applied to Christ, this avoided attributing suffering to God (which would be heretical).
Theotokos Meaning 'Mother of God', the Virgin Mary.
Three Chapters A decree issued by Justinian in 544/545, condemning Theodore of Mopsuestia, Theodoret of Cyrrhus' writings against Cyril of Alexandria, and Ibas' letter to Mari the Persian.
Triclinium Dining room.
Tzani A people living in the Caucasus.
Utrigurs A people living to the north-east of the Black Sea.
Vandals The Germanic people who invaded North Africa and established a kingdom there in the fifth century. It lasted for almost a century until it was conquered by Justinian in 534. After their defeat, Justinian styled himself Vandalicus.
Venatio An animal hunt, conducted in the games.
Vicarius A term used for various positions including the governor of a *diocese.
Vienna Genesis An illustrated manuscript of the Book of Genesis, probably produced in Syria in the sixth century, and today in the Österreichische Nationalbibliothek.
Visigoths The Gothic people who settled in Spain.
Whites A *circus faction.
Zikh A Persian nobleman.
Zoroastrianism The religion of the Persian Empire, in which Ahura Mazda was the supreme god.

Further Reading

There are many monographs devoted to the reign of Justinian, such as Barker 1966, Browning 1971 (reprinted 1987), Moorhead 1994, Evans 1996a, Sarris 2006 and Rosen 2007. In 2013, Bell published a monograph on social conflict with a distinctive take on the political and cultural history using social theory and personal experience. The most recent addition is the monograph by Heather (2018) who explores the extent to which Justinian was responsible for the problems which beset the empire in the seventh century. There are also monographs focusing on particular aspects such as the Persian wars (Börm 2007), religious studies (Menze 2008) and the Balkans (Sarantis 2016). There have been a number of studies in other languages such as French (Maraval 1999) and especially German, with the works of Mazal (2001), Meier (2003a and 2004a), Brodka (2004) and Leppin (2011). *The Cambridge Companion to the Age of Justinian* (Maas 2005) offers a clear and reliable introduction to all the individual themes of the period.

An overview of Justinian's reign can be found in the relevant chapters of the *Cambridge Ancient History XIV: Late Antiquity: Empire and Successors* A.D. *425–600* (Cameron, Ward-Perkins and Whitby 2000). The reign of Justinian is also covered in the traditional accounts of the later Roman Empire (Bury 1923, reprinted 1958, Stein 1949, Jones 1964, reprinted 1986). We have already discussed in the Introduction the expanding offering of English translations and commentaries on our primary sources. Key among these are the flourishing Procopian studies, and the invaluable Translated Texts for Historians series published by Liverpool University Press.

Chapter 1: Rise to power

There have been recent attempts to re-evaluate Justinian's role during the period 518–527 when Justin was on the throne (Croke 2007 and

Greatrex 2007). Chapter 1 also focused on the rise to power of Theodora as much as Justinian and there have been several studies on the empress, her early life and the influence she had over Justinian (Evans 2002 and 2011, Cesaretti 2004, Potter 2015). The *Nika* riot is a defining moment in the early years and the key study here is Greatrex 1997.

Chapter 2: Conflict and diplomacy on the eastern frontier

Narratives of Justinian's Persian wars may be found in most of the general monographs devoted to Justinian, as well as the helpful sourcebook by Greatrex and Lieu (2002). There has been a huge amount of interest in the Persians and recent studies (Canepa 2009 and Sauer et al. 2013) help to throw light on their relations with the Roman Empire and motivation for their hostility. New research has also been carried out on the Arab tribes (Fisher 2011, Dijkstra and Fisher 2014 and Fisher 2015) which builds on the research carried out by Shahîd (1995). Not so much research has been published on Lazica: Adontz (1970) and Braund (1994) remain the basic accounts, but Colvin (2013) is also very helpful.

Chapter 3: The wars of reconquest

There is a growing body of works on North Africa, including the large number of studies by Modéran (as listed in the Bibliography), the important edited volumes by Merrills and Miles (2010) and Stevens and Conant (2016), and recent individual studies by Wilhite (2017) and Whelan (2018). An understanding of the economy and towns of North Africa can be found in the works of Leone (2003 and 2007). The Ostrogothic king Theoderic was always a popular topic for research (Moorhead 1992 and Arnold 2014), but research has also been carried out on the Ostrogoths themselves (Barnish and Marazzi 2007 and Arnold, Bjornlie and Sessa 2016). As mentioned above, the main study on the Balkans is now Sarantis (2016).

Chapter 4: Church and state

Justinian's religious policy is covered in many general books on Christianity in the late antique world, such as Frend (1972), Gray (1979), Grillmeier and Hainthaler (1995 and 1996) and Hainthaler (2013). Studies which focus on elements of Justinian's policy include Millar (2008), and the edited volume by Chazelle and Cubitt (2007) contains a very helpful selection of papers. The Translated Texts for Historians edition of the Acts of the Council of Constantinople of 553 by Price (2009) contains an invaluable introduction which offers a clear summary of the issues which form the background to Justinian's reign as well as his own efforts to solve the divisions within the Church.

Chapter 5: Governing the empire

The new editions of the *Codex* (Frier 2016) and the *Novels* (Miller and Sarris 2018) with their very useful introductions are critical in opening up the study of the codification of the laws and Justinian's reform programme. For discussion and analysis, see the monographs by Sarris (2006) and Bell (2013). For a general overview of the developments in the governance of provincial cities and the economy see, for example, Laniado (2002), Banaji (2007) and Nijf and Alston (2011).

Chapter 6: Culture and society

Watts (2004, 2005, 2010) has done much to elucidate Justinian and the philosophers, including the closure of the Academy of Athens, and Dijkstra (2008) has explored the situation at Philae and Justinian's actions there. There have been many studies on Gaza and its culture (Litsas 1982, Glucker 1987, Bitton-Ashkelony and Kofsky 2004, Saliou 2005, Champion 2014, Amato, Corcella and Lauritzen 2017). We have already noted the rise in Procopian studies (Cameron 1985, Kaldellis 2004b, Lillington-Martin and Turquois 2017, Greatrex and Janniard 2018). A glance at the Bibliography will indicate the immense contribution of Kaldellis to this area of study, although his argument that many of the standard writers of Justinian's day are pagans is not the conventional view today. For a good introduction to the art and architecture of the sixth century, see Beckworth (1993), Cormack (2018) and Krautheimer (1986), and on Ravenna, see Deliyannis (2010) and Herrin (2020).

Essay Questions and Exercise Topics

The early years

Questions

1. How influential was Justinian during the reign of Justin (518–527)?
2. Identify and discuss the main elements of foreign policy during the period 518–527.
3. Why was it important to heal the Acacian schism?

Topics

4. Analyse the role of Theodora, including her religious beliefs. In what ways did she influence Justinian's governance of the empire and his policy towards the Church?
5. Discuss the episode of the *Nika* riot. What was the background to the riot and what long-term effects did it have?

Foreign policy in the east

Questions

6. What was the motivation of the Persians kings (Kavadh and Chosroes) in pursuing military action against the Romans?
7. Was Justinian's policy against the Persians active or passive?
8. What was the importance of Lazica in the Persian war?

Topics

9. Discuss the role of diplomacy in the Persian war. How did Justinian use acculturation and conversion to Christianity to secure the loyalty of his allies?

10. Consider the importance of the role of the Arabs to both the Romans and the Persians during the conflict.

The wars of reconquest

Questions

11. Did Justinian's reconquest of North Africa bring prosperity to the region?
12. Why was the reconquest of Italy so problematic?
13. How important was the defence of the Balkans to Justinian?

Topics

14. Consider why Justinian sought to recover the western provinces for the Eastern Roman Empire? Was it a long-held objective or more opportunistic?
15. Was Justinian motivated by religious fervour or military glory?

Religious policy

Questions

16. Identify the main issues in the religious controversies of the sixth century.
17. Discuss the major steps taken by Justinian to resolve the issues leading up to the 553 Council of Constantinople.
18. To what extent did the 553 Council of Constantinople resolve the issues?

Topics

19. Discuss the extent to which Justinian's actions arose from sincere belief or political pragmatism.
20. Do the personal beliefs of our sources mean that we will never attain objectivity in understanding the religious problems of the day?

Governance

Questions

21. What were the main changes Justinian made to provincial administration?

22. What was the impact of the plague on the empire?
23. What was Justinian's social policy?

Topics

24. Discuss the significance of Justinian's codification of the laws.
25. Consider the extent and range of Justinian's building programme. Why was church building, in particular, so important?

Culture and society

Questions

26. Why did Justinian close the Academy of Athens?
27. Discuss the role of festivals and games in the sixth century.
28. Was Justinian a patron of the arts?

Topics

29. How do you account for the regular appearance of classical mythology in a Christian context?
30. To what extent can the literary works of the time be regarded as imperial propaganda?

General questions

31. How useful are coins and inscriptions for understanding Justinian's reign?
32. Consider the works of Procopius and discuss the different viewpoints he presents in his three works.
33. Discuss the importance of other key figures in the reign of Justinian.
34. Was the influence of Theodora as a woman untypical in the late antique world?
35. Is Justinian relevant to the modern world?

Primary Sources

English translations are given where available. Otherwise, translations in other modern languages are given; if none are readily available then the edition in the original language is cited. Multiple editions are cited if they are referred to in the text.

Acts of the Council of Constantinople of 553 with Related Texts on the Three Chapters Controversy, translated into English with an introduction and notes by R. Price, Translated Texts for Historians 51, Liverpool: Liverpool University Press, 2009.

Agapetus, *Advice to the Emperor*, translated into English by P. N. Bell, *Three Political Voices from the Age of Justinian*, Translated Texts for Historians 52, Liverpool: Liverpool University Press, 2009, 99–122.

Agathias, *The Histories*, translated into English by J. D. Frendo, Corpus Fontium Historiae Byzantinae IIA: Series Berolinensis, Berlin and New York: De Gruyter, 1975.

Anonymus, *Kontakion on the Rededication of Hagia Sophia*, translated into English by A. Palmer with L. Rodley, 'The inauguration anthem of Hagia Sophia in Edessa: A new edition and translation with historical and architectural notes and a comparison with a contemporary Constantinopolitan kontakion', BMGS 12 (1988), 117–68.

Anonymus, *Dialogue on Political Science*, translated into English by P. N. Bell, *Three Political Voices from the Age of Justinian*, Translated Texts for Historians 52, Liverpool: Liverpool University Press, 2009, 123–88.

Anonymus, *Narratio de Sancta Sophia*, translated into English by C. Mango, *The Art of the Byzantine Empire 312–1453: Sources and Documents*, Toronto: University of Toronto Press, 1986, 96–102.

Anonymus, *The Book of the Himyarites: Fragments of a Hitherto Unknown Syriac Work*, edited with introduction and translation into English by A. Moberg, Lund: C. W. K. Gleerup, 1924.

Anonymus Valesianus, translated into English by J. C. Rolfe, *Ammianus Marcellinus*, vol. III, Loeb Classical Library, Cambridge, MA, and London: Harvard University Press, 1986, 509–69.

The Burgundian Code: Book of Constitutions or Law of Gundobad, translated into English by K. Fisher Drew, Philadelphia: University of Pennsylvania Press, 1972.

Cassiodorus, *The Variae of Magnus Aurelius Cassiodorus Senator*, translated into English by S. J. B. Barnish, Translated Texts for Historians 12, Liverpool: Liverpool University Press, 1992; *The Variae: The Complete Translation*, translated into English by M. S. Bjornlie, Oakland, CA: University of California Press, 2019.

Chalcedon in Context: Church Councils 400–700, translated into English by R. Price and Mary Whitby, Translated Texts for Historians Contexts 1, Liverpool: Liverpool University Press, 2009.

Choricius of Gaza. 'Choricius of Gaza: An approach to his work. Introduction, translation, commentary', by F. K. Litsas, unpublished PhD thesis, University of Chicago, 1980. Can be found online at the ProQuest website; *Rhetorical Exercises from Late Antiquity: A Translation of Choricius of Gaza's Preliminary Talks and Declamations*, translated into English by R. J. Penella, Cambridge: Cambridge University Press, 2009.

Chronicon Paschale 284–628 AD, translated into English with notes and introduction by Michael Whitby and Mary Whitby, Translated Texts for Historians 7, Liverpool: Liverpool University Press, 1989.

Collectio Avellana. Epistulae Imperatorum Pontificum aliorum inde ac a. XVII usque ad a. DLIII datae Avellana quae dicitur collectio, edited with a critical commentary by O. Günther in the series *Corpus Scriptorum Ecclesiasticorum Latinorum* 35, Prague, Vienna and Leipzig: F. Tempsky, 1895–8; partial translation into English by P. R. Coleman-Norton, *Roman State and Christian Church: A Collection of Legal Documents to AD 535*, London: SPCK, 1966.

Constantine VII Porphyrogenitus, *The Book of Ceremonies*. A. Moffatt and M. Tall, *Constantine Porphyrogenitus, The Book of Ceremonies*, 2 vols, Byzantina Australiensia 18, Canberra: Australian Association for Byzantine Studies, 2012.

Corippus, *In laudem Iustini Minoris Libri IV*, edited with translation into English and commentary by Averil Cameron, London: Athlone Press, 1976; *The Iohannis, or, De Bellis Libycis of Flavius Cresconius Corippus*, with introduction and translation into English by G. W. Shea, Lewiston, NY, and Lampeter: Edwin Mellen Press, 1998; *Flavii Cresconii Corippi Iohannidos Liber III*, translated into Italian by C. O. Tommasi Moreschini, Florence: Le Monnier, 2001; *Flavii Cresconii Corippi Iohannidos Liber primus. Introduzione, testo critico, traduzione e commento*, translated into Italian by M. A. Vinchesi, Koinonia 9, Napoli: D'Auria, 1983.

Cosmas Indicopleustes. *The Christian Topography of Cosmas, an Egyptian Monk*, translated and edited by W. McCrindle, London: Hakluyt Society, 1897.

Cyril of Scythopolis. *Lives of the Monks of Palestine by Cyril of Scythopolis*, translated into English by R. M. Price with an introduction and notes by J. Binns, Cistercian Studies 114, Kalamazoo, MI: Cistercian Publications, 1991.

Epistulae Austrasicae, edited by W. Gundlach, in *MGH, Epistolarum Tomus II, Merowingici et Karolini Aevi I*, Berlin: Weidmann, 1892, 110–53; edited and translated into Italian by E. Malaspina, *Il 'Liber Epistolarum' della Cancellaria Austrasica (Sec. V–VI)*, Rome: Herder, 2001.

Evagrius. *The Ecclesiastical History of Evagrius Scholasticus*, edited and translated into English by Michael Whitby, Translated Texts for Historians 33, Liverpool: Liverpool University Press, 2000.

Facundus of Hermiane, *In Defence of the Three Chapters. Facundi episcopi Ecclesiae Hermianensis, Opera omnia*, edited by J.-M. Clément and R. Vander Plaetse, in the series *Corpus Christianorum Series Latina* 90A, Turnhout: Brepols, 1974; *Facundus d'Hermiane, Défense des Trois Chapitres (à Justinien)*, text edited by J.-M. Clément and R. Vander Plaetse, translation into French by A. Fraïsse-Bétoulières in the series *Sources Chrétiennes* 471, 478–9, 484, 499, Paris: Cerf, 2002–6.

Fulgentius Ferrandus, *Letters*. Original text in *Dionysii Exigui, Viventioli, Trojani, Pontiani, S. Caesarii ... Fulgentii Ferrandi et Rustici ... Justi, Facundi Opera Omnia*, edited by J. P. Migne in the series *Patrologia Latina* 67, Paris, 1848, cols. 887–78.

The Greek Anthology, with an English translation by W. R. Paton, 5 vols, Loeb Classical Library, London: Heinemann and New York: G. P. Putnam's Sons, 1916–1918.

Gregory of Tours, *The History of the Franks*, introduction and translation into English by L. Thorpe, Harmondsworth and Baltimore: Penguin, 1974.

Isidore of Seville, *Chronicon*, edited by J. C. Martín, *Isidori Hispalensis Chronica*, in the series *Corpus Christianorum Series Latina* 112, Turnhout: Brepols, 2003; *Isidore of Seville's History of the Kings of the Goths, Vandals and Suevi*, translated into English by G. Donini and G. B. Ford, Leiden: Brill, 1966.

Jacob of Edessa, *Chronicon Iacobi Edesseni*, text and English translation by E. W. Brooks, 'The chronological canon of James of Edessa', *Zeitschrift der Deutschen Morgenländischen Gesellschaft* 52 (1898), 261–327.

Jacob of Serugh. C. Moss, 'Jacob of Serugh's homilies on the spectacles of the theatre', *Le Muséon. Revue d'Études Orientales* 48 (1935), 87–112 (English translation and edition); reprinted as C. Moss, *Jacob of Serugh's Homilies on the Spectacles of the Theatre*, Analecta Gorgiana 496, Piscataway, NJ: Gorgias Press, 2010.

John of Antioch, *Ioannis Antiocheni Fragmenta quae Supersunt*, text and English translation by S. Mariev, Corpus Fontium Historiae Byzantinae 47, Berlin and New York: De Gruyter, 2008; *Ioannis Antiocheni Fragmenta ex Historia Chronica. Introduzione, Edizione Critica e Traduzione*, text and Italian translation by U. Roberto, Texte und Untersuchungen zur Geschichte der altchristlichen Literatur 154, Berlin: De Gruyter, 2005.

John of Ephesus, *Ecclesiastical History*. The First Part is lost. The Second Part is preserved in various sources especially in: *Pseudo-Dionysius of Tel-Mahre: Chronicle (known also as the Chronicle of Zuqnin) Part III*, translated with notes and introduction by W. Witakowski, Translated Texts for Historians 22, Liverpool: Liverpool University Press, 1996; *The Chronicle of Zuqnīn, Parts III and IV, AD 488–775*, translated from Syriac with notes and introduction by A. Harrak, Medieval Sources in Translation 36, Toronto: Pontifical Institute of Mediaeval Studies, 1999. The Third Part survives intact: *The Third Part of the Ecclesiastical History of John Bishop of Ephesus*, translated by R. Payne Smith, Oxford: University Press, 1860.

John of Ephesus, *Lives of the Eastern Saints*. *John of Ephesus: Lives of the Eastern Saints*, translated by E. W. Brooks, *Patrologia Orientalis*, Paris: Firmin-Didot, 17 (1923): 1–307; 18 (1924): 513–698; 19 (1926): 153–285.

John the Lydian (John Lydus). *Ioannes Lydus: On Powers or the Magistracies of the Roman State*, with English translation, introduction and commentary by A. C. Bandy, Memoirs of the American Philosophical Society 149, Philadelphia: American Philosophical Society, 1983; T. F. Carney, *Bureaucracy in Traditional Society: Romano-Byzantine Bureaucracies Viewed from Within*, Book III (English translation), Lawrence, KA: Coronado Press, 1971.

John of Nikiu, *The Chronicle of John, Bishop of Nikiu*, translated by R. H. Charles, London: Norgate, 1916.

Jordanes, *Iordanis Romana et Getica*, edited by T. Mommsen, *MGH Auctorum Antiquissorum*, vol. 1, Berlin: Weidmann, 1882; Jordanes, *The Gothic History of Jordanes in English Version*, with an introduction and commentary by C. C. Mierow, Cambridge: Speculum Historiale, New York: Barnes and Noble, 1966.

Justinian, *Code*. P. Krüger (ed.), *Codex Iustinianus*, in *Corpus Iuris Civilis*, 16th edn, vol. 2, Berlin: Weidmann, 1928; B. W. Frier (ed.), *The Codex of Justinian: A New Annotated Translation*, 3 vols, Cambridge: Cambridge University Press, 2016.

Justinian, *Digest*. T. Mommsen and P. Krüger (eds), *Digesta*, in *Corpus Iuris Civilis*, 16th edn, vol. 1, Berlin: Weidmann, 1928; A. Watson, *The Digest of Justinian*, 4 vols, Philadelphia: University of Pennsylvania Press, 1998.

Justinian, *Dogmatic Writings*. E. Schwartz, *Drei dogmatische Schriften Justinians*, Abhandlungen der Bayerischen Akademie der Wissenschaften Philosophisch-historische Abteilung 18, Munich: Bayerischen Akademie der Wissenschaften, 1939; K. P. Wesche, *On the Person of Christ: The Christology of Emperor Justinian*, English translation and introduction, Crestwood, NY: St. Vladimir's Seminary Press, 1991.

Justinian, *Institutes*. T. Mommsen and P. Krüger (eds), *Institutiones*, in *Corpus Iuris Civilis*, 16th edn, vol. 1, Berlin: Weidmann, 1928; P. Birks and G. McLeod, *Justinian's Institutes*, Latin text and English translation with introduction, London: Duckworth, 1987, with E. Metzger (ed.), *A Companion to Justinian's Institutes*, London: Duckworth, 1998.

Justinian, *Novels* and *Edicts*. R. Schöll and G. Kroll (eds), *Novellae*, in *Corpus Iuris Civilis*, 16th edn, vol. 3, Berlin: Weidmann, 1928; D. J. D. Miller and

P. Sarris, *The Novels of Justinian: A Complete Annotated English Translation*, 2 vols, Cambridge: Cambridge University Press, 2018.

Liber Pontificalis. R. Davis, *The Book of Pontiffs (Liber Pontificalis): The Ancient Biographies of the First Ninety Roman Bishops to* AD *715*, English translation with introduction, Translated Texts for Historians 6, Liverpool: Liverpool University Press, 2000.

Malalas, John, *Chronicle*. E. Jeffreys, M. Jeffreys and R. Scott, *The Chronicle of John Malalas: A Translation*, Byzantina Australiensia 4, Melbourne: Australian Association for Byzantine Studies, 1986.

Marcellinus, Comes. B. Croke, *The Chronicle of Marcellinus: A Translation and Commentary*, Byzantina Australiensia 7, Sydney: Australian Association for Byzantine Studies, 1995.

Martyrs of Najrân. I. Shahîd, *The Martyrs of Najrân: New Documents*, Subsidia Hagiographica 49, Brussels: Société des Bollandistes, 1971.

The Martyr St. Arethas. M. Detoraki (ed.), *Le martyre de Saint Aréthas et de ses compagnons (BHG 166). Édition critique, étude et annotation*, trans. J. Beaucamp, Centre de recherche d'histoire et civilisation de Byzance, Monographies no. 27, Paris: Association des amis du Centre d'histoire et civilisation de Byzance, 2007.

Menander Protector (the Guardsman). R. C. Blockley, *The History of Menander the Guardsman*, Liverpool: Francis Cairns, 1985.

Michael the Syrian. J.-B. Chabot, *Chronique de Michel le Syrien Patriarche Jacobite d'Antioche (1166–1199), Éditée pour la Première Fois et Traduite en Français*, Paris: Leroux, 1899–1924, 4 vols; M. Moosa, *The Syriac Chronicle of Michael Rabo (the Great): A Universal History from the Creation: Translation and Introduction*, Teaneck, NJ: Beth Antioch Press, 2014.

Nonnosus. K. Müller (ed.), *Fragmenta Historicorum Graecorum*, vol. 4, Paris: Firmin Didot, 1851, 178–80.

Paul the Deacon. W. D. Foulke (trans.) and E. Peters (ed.), *Paul the Deacon: History of the Lombards*, Philadelphia: University of Pennsylvania Press, 1907.

Paul the Silentiary, *Description of Hagia Sophia*. P. N. Bell, *Three Political Voices from the Age of Justinian*, Translated Texts for Historians 52, Liverpool: Liverpool University Press, 2009 (partial translation and notes), 189–212; C. Mango, *The Art of the Byzantine Empire 312–1453: Sources and Documents*, Toronto: University of Toronto Press, 1986, 91–6 (partial translation); C. De Stefani (ed.), *Paulus Silentiarius: Descriptio Sanctae Sophiae; Descriptio Ambonis*, Berlin and New York: De Gruyter, 2011; M. L. Fobelli, *Un Tempio per Giustiniano, Santa Sofia di Constantinopoli e la Descrizione di Paolo Silenziario*, Rome: Viella, 2005 (edition with Italian translation); P. Friedländer, *Johannes von Gaza und Paulus Silentiarius, Kunstbeschreibungen Justinianischer Zeit*, Leipzig: Teubner, 1912, repr. Hildesheim and New York: Olms, 1969.

Pelagius. P. M. Gasso (ed.), *Pelagii I Papae Epistulae quae Supersunt (556–561)*, Scripta et Documenta 8, Montserrat: Abbey, 1956.

Peter the Patrician. T. Banchich (trans.), *The Lost History of Peter the Patrician: An Account of Rome's Imperial Past from the Age of Justinian*, Abingdon: Routledge, 2015.

Photius, *Bibliotheca*. R. Henry, *Photius. Bibliothèque. Texte Établi et Traduit*, 8 vols, Paris: Belles Lettres, 1959–1977.

Procopius, *Buildings*. Greek text and English translation by H. B. Dewing and G. Downey, Loeb Classical Library Procopius 7, New York and London: Harvard University Press, 1949.

Procopius, *History of the Wars*. Greek text and English translation by H. B. Dewing, Loeb Classical Library Procopius 1–5, New York and London: Harvard University Press, 1914–1928; *The Wars of Justinian, Prokopios*, translated by H. B. Dewing, revised and modernised, with introduction and notes, by Anthony Kaldellis, Indianapolis: Hackett, 2014.

Procopius, *The Persian Wars*. *Procopius of Caesarea*, translation by G. Greatrex with acknowledgements to Averil Cameron, Cambridge: Cambridge University Press, forthcoming 2021; G. Greatrex, *Procopius' Persian Wars: A Historical Commentary*, Cambridge: Cambridge University Press, forthcoming 2021.

Procopius, *Secret History*. *The Anecdota or Secret History*, Greek text and English translation by H. B. Dewing, Loeb Classical Library Procopius 6, New York and London: Harvard University Press, 1935; G. A. Williamson and P. Sarris, *Procopius: The Secret History*, English translation, with introduction, London: Penguin, 2007; A. Kaldellis, *Prokopios: The Secret History with Related Texts*, edited and translated, with an introduction, Indianapolis: Hackett, 2010.

Pseudo-Dionysius of Tel-Mahre: Chronicle (known also as the Chronicle of Zuqnin) Part III, translated with notes and introduction by W. Witakowski, Translated Texts for Historians 22, Liverpool: Liverpool University Press, 1996.

Pseudo-Zachariah. G. Greatrex (ed.), *The Chronicle of Pseudo-Zachariah Rhetor: Church and War in Late Antiquity*, translated from Syriac and Arabic sources by Robert R. Phenix and Cornelia B. Horn, with introductory material by Sebastian P. Brock and W. Witakowski, Translated Texts for Historians 55, Liverpool: Liverpool University Press, 2011.

Romanos, *Kontakia*. M. Carpenter (trans. and ed.), *Kontakia of Romanos: Byzantine Melodist*, 2 vols, Columbia: University of Missouri Press, 1970–1972; *Kontakia: On the Life of Christ. St. Romanos the Melodist*, translated with an introduction by Ephrem Lash, San Francisco: HarperCollins, 1995; A. Mellas, *Hymns of Repentance: Saint Romanos the Melodist*, English translation and introduction, Crestwood, NY: St. Vladimir's Seminary Press, 2020; R. J. Schork, *Sacred Song from the Byzantine Pulpit: Romanos the Melodist*, Gainesville: University Press of Florida, 1995.

Severus of Antioch. E. W. Brooks (ed. and trans.), *The Sixth Book of the Select Letters of Severus, Patriarch of Antioch in the Syriac Version of Athanasius of Nisibis*, 2 vols, London: Williams and Norgate, 1902–4; S. Brock and B. Fitzgerald, *Two Early Lives of Severos, Patriarch of Antioch*, translated with an introduction and notes, Translated Texts for Historians 59, Liverpool: Liverpool University Press, 2013.

S. Symeon Stylites the Younger. P. van den Ven (ed. and trans.), *La Vie Ancienne de Syméon Stylite le Jeune*, 2 vols, Subsidia Hagiographica 32, Brussels: Société des Bollandistes, 1962–1970.

Al-Tabari. C. E. Bosworth, *The History of al-Tabari, Vol. 5: The Sāsānids, the Byzantines, the Lakmids, and Yemen*, New York: State University of New York Press, 1999.

Theophanes, *Chronicle*. C. Mango and R. Scott, with the assistance of G. Greatrex, *The Chronicle of Theophanes Confessor: Byzantine and Near Eastern History, AD 284-813*, translated with introduction and commentary, Oxford: Clarendon Press, 1997.

Thucydides: The Peloponnesian War, edited by M. Hammond and P. J. Rhodes, Oxford World's Classics, Oxford: Oxford University Press, 2009.

Victor Tunnensis. J. R. C. Martyn, *Arians and Vandals of the 4th-6th Centuries*, Newcastle: Cambridge Scholars Publishing, 2009, 130–66 (English translation).

Vigilius, *Letters (Epistles)*. E. Schwartz (ed.), *Vigiliusbriefe: Zur Kirchenpolitik Iustinians*, Sitzungsberichte der Bayerischen Akademie der Wissenschaften zu München, Philosophisch-Historische Abteilung 2, Munich: Verlag der Bayerischen Akademie der Wissenschaften, 1940.

Zonaras, *Chronicle*. L. Dindorf (ed.), *Ioannis Zonarae Epitome Historiarum*, 6 vols, Leipzig: Teubner, 1868–1875; M. Pinder and T. Büttner-Wobst (eds), *Ioannis Zonarae Annales*, 3 vols, in the series *Corpus Scriptorum Historiae Byzantinae*, Bonn: Weber, 1841–1897.

Bibliography

Abramowski, L. (2001), 'Die Mosaiken von S. Vitale und S. Apollinare in Classe und die Kirchenpolitik Kaiser Justinians', *ZAC* 5, 289–341.

Adontz, N. (1970), *Armenia in the Period of Justinian: The Political Conditions Based on the Naxarar System*, trans. and rev. N. G. Garsoïan, Lisbon: Gulbenkian Foundation.

Adshead, K. (1993), 'The Secret History of Procopius and its genesis', *Byzantion* 64, 5–28.

Adshead, K. (2000), 'Justinian and aphthartodocetism', in S. Mitchell and G. Greatrex (eds), *Ethnicity and Culture in Late Antiquity*, London: Duckworth and Classical Press of Wales, 331–6.

Agusta-Boularot, S., J. Beaucamp, A.-M. Bernardi and E. Caire (eds) (2006), *Recherches sur la Chronique de Jean Malalas*, vol. 2, Paris: Association des amis du Centre d'histoire et civilisation de Byzance.

Alchermes, J. D. (2005), 'Art and architecture in the age of Justinian', in M. Maas (ed.), *The Cambridge Companion to the Age of Justinian*, Cambridge: Cambridge University Press, 343–75.

Allen, P. (1979), 'The "Justinianic" plague', *Byzantion* 49, 5–20.

Allen, P. (1981), *Evagrius Scholasticus, the Church Historian*, Leuven: Spicilegium Sacrum Lovaniense.

Allen, P. (1992), 'Contemporary portrayals of the Byzantine Empress Theodora (A.D. 527–548)', in B. Garlick, S. Dixon and P. Allen (eds), *Stereotypes of Women in Power*, Westport, CT: Greenwood Press, 93–103.

Allen, P., and C. T. R. Hayward (2004), *Severus of Antioch*, Abingdon: Routledge.

Allen, P., and E. Jeffreys (eds) (1996), *The Sixth Century: End or Beginning?*, Byzantina Australiensia 10, Brisbane: Australian Association for Byzantine Studies.

Amato, E., A. Corcella and D. Lauritzen (eds) (2017), *L'École de Gaza: Espace Littéraire et Identité dans l'Antiquité Tardive. Actes du Colloque International de Paris, Collège de France, 23–25 mai 2013*, Leuven: Peeters.

Amory, P. (1997), *People and Identity in Ostrogothic Italy, 489–554*, Cambridge: Cambridge University Press.

Anastasiou, I. E. (1968), 'Relation of Popes and Patriarchs of Constantinople in the frame of imperial policy from the time of the Acacian Schism to the death of Justinian', in *I Patriarcati Orientali nel Primo Millennio: Relazioni del Congresso tenutosi al Pontificio Istituto Orientale nei Giorni 27-30 Dicembre 1967*, Rome, 55-69.

Anastos, M. V. (1951), 'The Immutability of Christ and Justinian's condemnation of Theodore of Mopsuestia', *DOP* 6, 125-60.

Anastos, M. V. (1964, repr. 1979), 'Justinian's despotic control over the Church as illustrated by his Edicts on the Theopaschite Formula and his Letter to Pope John II in 533', *Zbornik Radova Vizantoloskog Instituta* 8.2, 1-11.

Andreescu, I., and W. Treadgold (1997), 'Procopius and the imperial panels of S. Vitale', *Art Bulletin* 79, 708-23.

Angold, M. (1996), 'Procopius' portrait of Justinian', in C. N. Constantinides, N. M. Panagiotakes, E. Jeffreys and A. D. Angelou (eds), *ΦΙΛΕΛΛΗΝ, Studies in Honour of Robert Browning*, Venice: Istituto Ellenico di Studi Bizantini e Postbizantini, 21-54.

Arentzen, T. (2017), *The Virgin in Song: Mary and the Poetry of Romanos the Melodist*, Philadelphia: University of Pennsylvania Press.

Arnold, J. J. (2014), *Theoderic and the Roman Imperial Restoration*, Cambridge: Cambridge University Press.

Arnold, J. J., M. S. Bjornlie and K. Sessa (eds) (2016), *A Companion to Ostrogothic Italy*, Leiden and Boston: Brill.

Athanassiadi, P. (1993), 'Persecution and response: The evidence of Damascius', *JHS* 113, 1-29.

Athanassiadi, P., and M. Frede (eds) (1999), *Pagan Monotheism in Late Antiquity*, Oxford: Clarendon Press.

Bagnall, R. (1993), *Egypt in Late Antiquity*, Princeton: Princeton University Press.

Bagnall, R. (ed.) (2007), *Egypt in the Byzantine World*, Cambridge: Cambridge University Press.

Baldwin, B. (1978), 'The career of Corippus', *CQ* 72, 372-6.

Baldwin, B. (1996), 'Notes of Christian epigrams in Book One of the Greek Anthology', in P. Allen and E. Jeffreys (eds), *The Sixth Century: End or Beginning?*, Byzantina Australiensia 10, Brisbane: Australian Association for Byzantine Studies, 92-104.

Banaji, J. (2007), *Agrarian Change in Late Antiquity: Gold, Labour and Aristocratic Dominance*, 2nd edn, Oxford: Oxford University Press.

Bardill, J. (1999), 'The Great Palace of the Byzantine emperors and the Walker Trust excavations', *Journal of Roman Archaeology* 12, 216-30.

Bardill, J. (2000), 'The Church of Sts. Sergius and Bacchus in Constantinople and the monophysite refugees', *DOP* 54, 1-11.

Bardill, J. (2006), 'Visualising the Great Palace of the Byzantine emperors at Constantinople: Archaeology, text and topography', in F. A. Bauer (ed.),

Visualisierung von Herrschaft: Frühmittelalterlicher Residenzen: Gestalt und Zeremoniell, Istanbul: Ege Yayınları, 5–45.

Barker, J. W. (1966), *Justinian and the Later Roman Empire*, Madison: University of Wisconsin Press.

Barkhuizen, J. H. (1990), 'Romanos and the Nika riots: A religious perspective', *Ekklesiastikos Pharos*, n.s.1, 30–9.

Barnes, T. D. (1996), 'Christians and the theater', in W. J. Slater (ed.), *Roman Theater and Society: E. Togo Salmon, Papers I*, Ann Arbor: University of Michigan Press, 161–80.

Barnish, S. J. (1985), 'The wealth of Iulianus Argentarius: Late antique banking and the Mediterranean economy', *Byzantion* 55, 5–38.

Barnish, S. J. (1990), 'Maximian, Cassiodorus, Boethius, Theodahad: Literature, philosophy and politics in Ostrogothic Italy', *Nottingham Medieval Studies* 34, 16–32.

Barnish, S. J., and F. Marazzi (eds) (2007), *The Ostrogoths from the Migration Period to the Sixth Century: An Ethnographic Perspective*, Woodbridge and Rochester: Boydell Press.

Barnwell, P. S. (1992), *Emperor, Prefects and Kings: The Roman West 395–565*, London: Duckworth.

Beaucamp, J., F. Briquel-Chatonnet and C. Robin (1999–2000), 'La persécution des chrétiens de Nagrān et la chronologie himyarite', *ARAM* 11, 15–83.

Beck, H. G. (1986), *Kaiserin Theodora und Prokop: Der Historiker und sein Opfer*, Munich: Piper Verlag.

Beckworth J. (1970, repr. 1993), *Early Christian and Byzantine Art*, London: Penguin Books; repr. New Haven and London: Yale University Press.

Bell, P. N. (2013), *Social Conflict in the Age of Justinian: Its Nature, Management and Mediation*, Oxford: Oxford University Press.

Bellinger, A. R. (1966), *Catalogue of the Byzantine Coins in the Dumbarton Oaks Collection and in the Whittemore Collection, Vol. 1: Anastasius I to Maurice 491–602*, Washington, DC: Dumbarton Oaks Research Library and Collection.

Belting, H. (1994), *Likeness and Presence: A History of the Image before the Era of Art*, trans. E. Jephcott, Chicago: University of Chicago Press.

Bernardi, A.-M. (2006), 'Regards croisés sur les origins de Rome: La fête des Brumalia chez Jean Malalas et Jean Lydos', in S. Agusta-Boularot, J. Beaucamp, A.-M. Bernardi and E. Caire (eds), *Recherches sur la Chronique de Jean Malalas*, vol. 2, Paris: Association des amis du Centre d'histoire et civilisation de Byzance, 53–68.

Bitton-Ashkelony, B., and A. Kofsky (2004), *Christian Gaza in Late Antiquity*, Leiden: Brill.

Bjornlie, M. S. (2013), *Politics and Tradition between Rome, Ravenna and Constantinople: A Study of Cassiodorus and the Variae*, Cambridge: Cambridge University Press.

Blockley, R. C. (1985), 'Subsidies and diplomacy: Rome and Persia in Late Antiquity', *Phoenix* 39, 62–74.
Boojamra, J. L. (1975), 'Christian *Philanthropia*: A study of Justinian's welfare policy and the Church', *Byzantina* 7, 345–73.
Börm, H. (2006), 'Der Perserkönig im Imperium Romanum: Chosroes I. und der sasanidische Einfall in das Oströmische Reich 540 n. Chr.', *Chiron* 36, 299–328.
Börm, H. (2007), *Prokop und die Perser: Untersuchungen zu den römisch-sasanidischen Kontakten in der Ausgehenden Spätantike*, Stuttgart: Steiner Verlag.
Börm, H. (2010), 'Herrscher und Eliten in der Spätintike', in H. Börm and J. Wiesehöfer (eds), *Commutatio et Contentio: Studies in the Late Roman, Sasanian and Early Islamic Near East in Memory of Zeev Rubin*, Düsseldorf: Wellem Verlag, 159–98.
Börm, H. (2015), 'Procopius, his predecessors, and the genesis of the *Anecdota*: Anti-monarchic discourse in late antique historiography', in H. Börm (ed.) *Antimonarchic Discourse in Antiquity*, Stuttgart: Steiner Verlag, 1–32.
Bowersock, G. W. (1990), *Hellenism in Late Antiquity*, Ann Arbor: University of Michigan Press.
Bowersock, G. W. (2006), *Mosaics as History: The Near East from Late Antiquity to Islam*, Cambridge, MA: Harvard University Press.
Bowersock, G. W., P. Brown and O. Grabar (eds) (1999), *Late Antiquity: A Guide to the Postclassical World*, Cambridge, MA: Belknap Press.
Brandes, W. (2002), *Finanzverwaltung in Krisenzeiten: Untersuchungen zur Byzantinischen Administration im 6.–9. Jahrhundert*, Forschungen zur Byzantinischen Rechtsgeschichte 25, Frankfurt am Main: Löwenklau-Gesellschaft E.V.
Brands, G. (2002), *Die Bauornamentik von Resafa-Sergiupolis: Studien zur Spätantiken Architektur und Bauausstattung in Syrien und Nordmesopotamien*, Mainz: Zabern Verlag.
Braund, D. (1994), *Georgia in Antiquity: A History of Colchis and Transcaucasian Iberia 550 BC–AD 562*, Oxford: Clarendon Press.
Breck, J. (1982), 'The Troparion Monogenes: An Orthodox Symbol of Faith', *St Vladimir's Theological Quarterly* 26, 203–28.
Brock, S. (1980), 'The Orthodox–Oriental Orthodox Conversations of 532', *Apostolos Barnabas* 41, 19–227.
Brock, S. (1981, repr. 1992), 'The conversations with the Syriac Orthodox under Justinian (532)', *Orientalia Christiana Periodica* 47, 87–121; repr. in S. Brock, *Studies in Syriac Christianity: History, Literature and Theology*, Aldershot: Variorum.
Brodka, D. (2004), *Die Geschichtsphilosophie in der Spätaniken Historiographie: Studien zu Prokopios von Kaisareia, Agathias von Myrina und Theophylaktos Simokattes*, Frankfurt am Main: Lang Verlag.
Brodka, D. (2018), *Narses – Politik, Krieg und Historiographie im 6. Jahrhundert n. Chr.*, Berlin: Peter Lang.

Brown, P. R. L. (1971), *The World of Late Antiquity*, London: Thames and Hudson.
Brown, P. R. L. (1992), *Power and Persuasion in Late Antiquity*, Madison: University of Wisconsin Press.
Brown, P. R. L. (1995), *Authority and the Sacred: Aspects of the Christianisation of the Roman World*, Cambridge: Cambridge University Press.
Brown, P. R. L. (2003), *The Rise of Western Christendom*, 2nd edn, Oxford: Blackwell.
Brown, T. S. (1984), *Gentlemen and Officers: Imperial Administration and Aristocratic Power in Byzantine Italy A.D. 554–800*, London: British School at Rome.
Browning, R. (1971, repr. 1987), *Justinian and Theodora*, London: Weidenfeld and Nicolson and New York: Thames and Hudson.
Brubaker, L. (2004), 'Sex, lies and intertextuality: The Secret History of Prokopios and the rhetoric of gender in sixth-century Byzantium', in L. Brubaker and J. M. H. Smith (eds), *Gender in the Early Medieval World: East and West 300–900*, Cambridge: Cambridge University Press, 83–101.
Brubaker, L., and H. Tobler (2000), 'The gender of money: Byzantine empresses on coins (324–802)', *Gender and History* 12, 572–94.
Bundy, D. D. (1978), 'Jacob Baradaeus: The state of research, a review of sources, and a new approach', *Le Muséon* 91, 45–86.
Bury, J. B. (1897), 'The Nika riot', *JHS* 17, 92–119.
Bury, J. B. (1923, repr. 1958), *History of the Later Roman Empire from the Death of Theodosius I to the Death of Justinian II*, New York: St. Martin's Press; repr. New York: Dover.
Cambridge Ancient History XIV: Late Antiquity: Empire and Successors A.D. 425–600, (2000), ed. A. Cameron, B. Ward-Perkins and M. Whitby, Cambridge: Cambridge University Press.
Cambridge History of the Byzantine Empire, c. 500–1492 (2008), ed. J. Shephard, Cambridge: Cambridge University Press.
Cambridge History of Greek and Roman Warfare, Vol. 2: Rome from the Late Republic to the Late Empire (2007), ed. P. Sabin, H. van Wees and M. Whitby, Cambridge: Cambridge University Press.
Cameron, Alan (1969), 'The last days of the Academy at Athens', *Papers of the Cambridge Philological Society* 195, 14–30.
Cameron, Alan (1973), *Porphyrius the Charioteer*, Oxford: Clarendon Press.
Cameron, Alan (1976), *Circus Factions: Blues and Greens at Rome and Byzantium*, Oxford: Clarendon Press.
Cameron, Alan (1977), 'Some prefects called Julian', *Byzantion* 47, 42–64.
Cameron, Alan (1978), 'The house of Anastasius', *GRBS* 19, 259–76.
Cameron, Alan (1982), 'The death of Vitalian (520 A.D.)', *ZPE* 48, 93–4.
Cameron, Alan (1993), *The Greek Anthology: From Meleager to Planudes*, Oxford and New York: Clarendon Press.

Cameron, Alan (2007), 'Poets and pagans in Byzantine Egypt', in R. Bagnall (ed.), *Egypt in the Byzantine World, 300–700*, Cambridge: Cambridge University Press, 21–45.
Cameron, Alan (2011), *The Last Pagans of Rome*, Oxford and New York: Oxford University Press.
Cameron, Alan, and D. Schauer (1982), 'The last consul: Basilius and his diptych', *JRS* 72, 126–45.
Cameron, Alan, and Averil Cameron (1966), 'The Cycle of Agathias', *JHS* 86, 6–25.
Cameron, Averil (1969), 'Agathias on the Sassanians', *DOP* 23–4, 67–183.
Cameron, Averil (1970), *Agathias*, Oxford: Clarendon Press.
Cameron, Averil (1979), 'A nativity poem from the sixth century AD', *Classical Philology* 79, 222–32.
Cameron, Averil (1981a), *Continuity and Change in Sixth-Century Byzantium*, London: Variorum.
Cameron, Averil (1981b), 'Images of authority: Elites and icons in late sixth-century Byzantium', in M. Mullett and R. Scott (eds), *Byzantium and the Classical Tradition*, Birmingham: Centre for Byzantine Studies, 204–34.
Cameron, Averil (1982), 'Byzantine Africa: The literary evidence', in J. H. Humphrey (ed.), *Excavations at Carthage (1977–78), Conducted by the University of Michigan*, Ann Arbor: University of Michigan Press, 29–62.
Cameron, Averil (1984), 'Corippus' Iohannis: Epic of Byzantine Africa', *Papers of the Liverpool Latin Seminar 4* (1983), ARCA 11, Liverpool: F. Cairns, 167–80.
Cameron, Averil (1985), *Procopius and the Sixth Century*, London: Duckworth.
Cameron, Averil (1986), 'History as text: Coping with Procopius', in C. Holdsworth and T. P. Wiseman (eds), *The Inheritance of Historiography 350–900*, Exeter: University of Exeter Press, 53–66.
Cameron, Averil (1989), 'Gelimer's laughter: The case of Byzantine Africa', in F. M. Cliver and R. S. Humphreys (eds), *Tradition and Innovation in Late Antiquity*, Madison: University of Wisconsin Press, 171–90.
Cameron, Averil (1991), *Christianity and the Rhetoric of Empire*, Berkeley: University of California Press.
Cameron, Averil (1993), *The Mediterranean World in Late Antiquity AD 395–600*, London: Routledge.
Cameron, Averil (1996), *Changing Cultures in Byzantium*, Aldershot: Variorum.
Cameron, Averil (1997), 'Gibbon and Justinian', in R. McKitterick and R. Quinault (eds), *Edward Gibbon and Empire*, Cambridge: Cambridge University Press, 34–52.
Cameron, Averil (2017), 'Writing about Procopius then and now', in C. Lillington-Martin and E. Turquois (eds), *Procopius of Caesarea: Literary and Historical Interpretations*, London and New York: Routledge, 13–25.
Canepa, M. (2009), *The Two Eyes of the World: Art and Ritual Kingship between Rome and Sassanian Iran*, Berkeley: University of California Press.

Carnevale, L. (2003), 'Totila comes *perfidus rex* tra stroria e agiografia', *Vetera Christianorum* 40, 43–69.
Carney, T. F. (1971), *Bureaucracy in Traditional Society: Romano-Byzantine Bureaucracy Viewed from Within*, Kansas: Coronado Press.
Cavallo, G. (1992), *Codex Purpureus Rossanensis*, Rome: Salerno Editrice.
Cesa, M. (1981), 'La politica di Giustiniano verso l'Occidente nel giudizio di Procopio', *Athenaeum* 59, 389–409.
Cesaretti, P. (2004), *Theodora: Empress of Byzantium*, trans. R. M. Giammanco Frongia, New York: Vendome Press.
Chadwick, H. (1981), *Boethius: The Consolation of Music, Logic, Theology and Philosophy*, Oxford: Clarendon Press.
Champion, M. (2014), *Explaining the Cosmos: Creation and Cultural Interaction in Late-Antique Gaza*, Oxford: Oxford University Press.
Charanis, P. (1939, repr. 1974), *Church and State in the Later Roman Empire: The Religious Policy of Anastasius I, 418–518*, Thessalonica: Centre for Byzantine Research.
Chazelle, C. M., and C. Cubitt (eds) (2007), *The Crisis of the Oikoumene: The Three Chapters and the Failed Quest for Unity in the Sixth-Century Mediterranean*, Turnhout: Brepols.
Christensen, A. S. (2002), *Cassiodorus, Jordanes and the History of the Goths: Studies in a Migration Myth*, Copenhagen: Museum Tusculanum Press.
Christie, N. (2006), *From Constantine to Charlemange: An Archaeology of Italy AD 300–800*, Aldershot: Ashgate.
Chuvin, P. (1990), *A Chronicle of the Last Pagans*, trans. B. A. Archer, Cambridge, MA: Harvard University Press.
Colvin, I. (2013), 'Reporting battle and understanding campaigns in Procopius and Agathias: Classicising historians' uses of archived documents as sources', in A. Sarantis and N. Christie (eds), *War and Warfare in Late Antiquity: Current Perspectives*, Late Antique Archaeology 8, Leiden and Boston: Brill, 571–95.
Conant, J. P. (2012), *Staying Roman: Conquest and Identity in Africa and the Mediterranean, 439–700*, Cambridge: Cambridge University Press.
Conant, J. P. (2016a), 'Donatism in the fifth and sixth centuries AD', in R. Miles (ed.), *The Donatist Schism: Controversy and Contexts*, Liverpool: Liverpool University Press, 345–61.
Conant, J. P. (2016b), 'Sanctity and the networks of empire in Byzantine North Africa', in S. T. Stevens and J. P. Conant (eds), *North Africa under Byzantium and Early Islam*, Washington, DC: Dumbarton Oaks Research Library and Collection, 201–14.
Constantelos, D. J. (1964), 'Paganism and the state in the age of Justinian', *The Catholic Historical Review* 50.3, 372–80.
Cooper, K. (2016), 'The heroine and the historian: Procopius of Caesarea on the troubled reign of Queen Amalasuntha', in J. J. Arnold, M. S. Bjornlie and K. Sessa (eds), *A Companion to Ostrogothic Italy*, Leiden and Boston: Brill, 296–315.

Corcoran, S. (2008), 'Justinian and his two Codes: Revisiting P. Oxy. 1814', *Journal of Juristic Papyrology* 38, 73–112.

Corcoran, S. (2009), 'Anastasius, Justinian, and the Pagans: A tale of the two Law Codes and a papyrus', *Journal of Late Antiquity* 2, 183–208.

Corcoran, S. (2016), 'The Codex of Justinian: The life of a text through 1,500 years', in B. W. Frier (ed.), *The Codex of Justinian*, vol. 1, Cambridge: Cambridge University Press, xcvii–clxiv.

Cormack, R. (1997), *Painting the Soul: Icons, Death Masks, and Shrouds*, London: Reaktion Books.

Cormack, R. (2000, repr. 2018), *Byzantine Art*, Oxford: Oxford University Press.

Croke, B. (1982), 'Mundo the Gepid: From freebooter to Roman general', *Chiron* 12, 125–35.

Croke, B. (1983), 'A.D. 476: The manufacture of a turning point', *Chiron* 13, 81–119.

Croke, B. (2001), *Count Marcellinus and his Chronicle*, Oxford: Oxford University Press.

Croke, B. (2005a), 'Jordanes and the immediate past', *Historia* 54, 473–94.

Croke, B. (2005b), 'Procopius' *Secret History*: Rethinking the date', *GRBS* 45, 405–31.

Croke, B. (2006), 'Justinian, Theodora, and the Church of Saints Sergius and Bacchus', *DOP* 60, 25–63.

Croke, B. (2007), 'Justinian under Justin: Reconfiguring a reign', *Byzantinische Zeitschrift* 100, 13–56.

Croke, B. (2011), 'Justinian, the "Sleepless Emperor"', in G. Nathan and L. Garland (eds), *Basileia: Essays on Imperium and Culture in Honour of E. M. and M. J. Jeffreys*, Brisbane: Byzantina Australiensia 17, 103–8.

Crown, A. D. (1986), 'The Samaritans in the Byzantine Orbit', *Bulletin of the John Rylands Library* 69, 96–138.

Cruse, M. (2015), 'A Justinianic debate across genres on the state of the Roman Republic', in G. Greatrex and H. Elton (eds), *Shifting Genres in Late Antiquity*, Farnham: Ashgate, 233–45.

Cutler, A. (1984), 'The making of the Justinian diptychs', *Byzantion* 54, 75–115.

Cutler, A. (1998), 'Barberiniana: Notes on the making, content, and provenance of Louvre, OA. 9063', in *Late Antique and Byzantine Ivory Carving*, IV, Aldershot: Variorum, 329–39.

Dagron, G. (2003), *Emperor and Priest: The Imperial Office in Byzantium*, trans. J. Birrell, Cambridge: Cambridge University Press.

Dagron, G., D. Feissel, A. Hermary, J. Richard and J.-P. Sodini (1987), *Inscriptions de Cilicie*, Travaux et mémoires du Centre de recherche d'histoire et civilisation de Byzance, Monographies 4, Paris: De Boccard.

Daryaee, T. (2009), *Sasanian Persia: The Rise and Fall of an Empire*, London and New York: I. B. Tauris.

Daube, D. (1966–7), 'The marriage of Justinian and Theodora: Legal and theological reflections', *Catholic University Law Review* 16, 380–99.

Deichmann, F. W. (1958–89), *Ravenna: Hauptstadt des spätantiken Abendlandes*, 2 parts in 6 vols, Wiesbaden: F. Steiner.
Deliyannis, D. (2010), *Ravenna in Late Antiquity*, Cambridge: Cambridge University Press.
Delmaire, R. (1989), *Largesses Sacrées et Res Privata: L'Aerarium et son Administration du IVe au VIe siècle*, Rome: École française de Rome.
Delmaire, R. (1995), *Les Institutions du Bas-Empire Romain, de Constantin à Justinien, Vol. 1: Les Institutions Civiles Palatines*, Paris: Cerf.
Diehl, C. (1893), *Excursions in Greece to Recently Explored Sites of Classical Interest*, London and New York: Grevel.
Diehl, C. (1901, repr. 1969), *Justinien et la Civilization Byzantine au VIe siècle*, Paris: Leroux; repr. New York: Franklin.
Diehl, C. (1972), *Theodora: Empress of Byzantium*, trans. S. R. Rosenbaum, New York: Frederick Ungar.
Dignas, B., and E. Winter (2007), *Rome and Persia in Late Antiquity: Neighbours and Rivals*, Cambridge: Cambridge University Press (originally published in German in 2001).
Dijkstra, J. H. F. (2008), *Philae and the End of Ancient Egyptian Religion: A Regional Study of Religious Transformation (298–642 CE)*, Leuven: Peeters.
Dijkstra, J. H. F., and G. Fisher (eds) (2014), *Inside and Out: Interaction between Rome and the Peoples on the Arabian and Egyptian Frontiers in Late Antiquity*, Leuven: Peeters.
Dmitriev, S. (2010), 'John Lydus and his contemporaries on identities and cultures of sixth-century Byzantium', *DOP* 64, 27–42.
Dossey, L. (2016), 'Exegesis and dissent in Byzantine North Africa', in S. T. Stevens and J. P. Conant (eds), *North Africa under Byzantium and Early Islam*, Washington, DC: Dumbarton Oaks Research Library and Collection, 251–68.
Downey, G. (1958), 'The Christian schools of Palestine: A chapter in literary history', *Harvard Library Bulletin* 12.3, 297–319.
Downey, G. (1959), 'The tombs of the Byzantine emperors at the Church of the Holy Apostles in Constantinople', *JHS* 79, 27–51.
Downey, G. (1960), *Constantinople in the Age of Justinian*, Norman: University of Oklahoma Press.
Downey, G. (1961), *A History of Antioch in Syria from Seleucus to the Arab Conquest*, Princeton: Princeton University Press.
Downey, G. (1963), *Gaza in the Early Sixth Century*, Princeton: Princeton University Press.
Durand, J. (1992), *Byzance: L'Art Byzantine dans les Collections Publiques Françaises*, Paris: Princeton University Press.
Durliat, J. (1981), *Les Dédicaces d'Ouvrages de Défense dans l'Afrique Byzantine*, Rome: École française de Rome.
Dvornik, F. (1966), *Early Christian and Byzantine Political Philosophy*, vol. 2, Washington, DC: Dumbarton Oaks Center for Byzantine Studies.

Elsner, J. (2007), 'The rhetoric of buildings in the *de Aedificiis* of Procopius', in L. James (ed.), *Art and Text in Byzantine Culture*, Cambridge: Cambridge University Press, 33–57.

Engelhardt, I. (1974), *Mission und Politik in Byzanz: Ein Beitrag zur Strukturanalyse Byzantinischer Mission zur Zeit Justins und Justinians*, Munich: Institut für Byzantinistik und neugriechische Philologie.

Evans, J. A. S. (1971), 'Christianity and paganism in Procopius of Caesarea', *GRBS* 12, 81–100.

Evans, J. A. S. (1996a), *The Age of Justinian: The Circumstances of Imperial Power*, London and New York: Routledge.

Evans, J. A. S. (1996b), 'The dates of Procopius' works: A recapitulation of the evidence', *GRBS* 37, 301–13.

Evans, J. A. S. (2002), *The Empress Theodora: Partner of Justinian*, Austin: University of Texas Press.

Evans, J. A. S. (2005), *The Emperor Justinian and the Byzantine Empire*, Westport, CT, and London: Greenwood Press.

Evans, J. A. S. (2011), *The Power Game in Byzantium: Antonina and the Empress Theodora*, London: Continuum.

Farrokh, K. (2007), *Shadows in the Desert: Ancient Persia at War*, Oxford: Osprey.

Fauber, L. (1990), *Narses, Hammer of the Goths: The Life and Times of Narses the Eunuch*, New York: St. Martin's Press.

Fayant, M.-Ch. (2001), 'Le poète, l'empereur: L'éloge de Justinien dans la Description de Paul de Silentaire', in L. Mary and M. Sot (eds), *Le Discours d'Éloge entre Antiquité et Moyen Age*, Paris: Picard, 69–78.

Feenstra, R. (1983), 'The "poor widower" in Justinian's legislation', in P. Stein and A. D. Lewis (eds), *Studies in Justinian's Institutes in Memory of J. A. C. Thomas*, London: Sweet and Maxwell, 39–44.

Feissel, D. (1992), 'Trois inscriptions de Justinian Ier du IVe au VIe siècle', *Bulletin de Correspondance Hellenique* 116, 383–96.

Feissel, D. (2000), 'Les édifices de Justinien au témoignage de Procope et de l'épigraphie', *Antiquité Tardive* 8, 81–104.

Feissel, D. (2004), 'Un rescript de Justinien découvert à Didymes (Ier avril 533)', *Chiron* 34, 285–365.

Feissel, D. (2010), *Documents, Droit, Diplomatique de l'Empire Romain Tardif*, Paris: Association des amis du Centre d'histoire et civilisation de Byzance.

Feissel, D., and I. Kaygusuz (1985), 'Un mandement impérial du VIe siècle dans une inscription d'Hadrianoupolis d'Honoriade', *Travaux et Mémoires* 9, 397–419.

Fentress, E., and A. I. Wilson (2016), 'The Saharan Berber diaspora and the southern frontiers of Byzantine North Africa', in S. T. Stevens and J. P. Conant (eds), *North Africa under Byzantium and Early Islam*, Washington, DC: Dumbarton Oaks Research Library and Collection, 41–63.

Fisher, E. A. (1978), 'Theodora and Antonina in the Historia arcana: History and/or fiction?', *Arethusa* 11, 253–79.
Fisher, G. (2011), *Between Empire: Arabs, Romans and Sasanians in Late Antiquity*, Oxford: Oxford University Press.
Fisher, G. (2014), 'State and tribe in late antique Arabia: A comparative view', in J. H. F. Dijkstra and G. Fisher (eds), *Inside and Out: Interaction between Rome and the Peoples on the Arabian and Egyptian Frontiers in Late Antiquity*, Leuven: Peeters, 281–97.
Fisher, G. (ed.) (2015), *Arabs and Empire before Islam*, Oxford: Oxford University Press.
Fobelli, M. L. (2005), *Un Tempio per Giustiniano: Santa Sofia di Costantinopoli e la Descrizione di Paolo Silenziario*, Rome: Viella.
Fögen, M. Th. (1992), 'Muttergut und Kindesvermögen bei Konstantin d. Gr., Justinian und Eustathios Rhomaios', in D. Simon (ed.), *Eherecht und Familiengut in Antike und Mittelalter*, Munich: De Gruyter, 15–27.
Forsyth, G. H. (1968), 'The Monastery of St. Catherine at Mount Sinai: The church and fortress of Justinian', *DOP* 22, 1–19.
Forsyth, G. H., and K. Weitzmann (1973), *The Monastery of Saint Catherine at Mount Sinai*, Ann Arbor: University of Michigan Press.
Foss, C. (2002), 'The Empress Theodora', *Byzantion* 72, 141–76.
Frankforter, A. D. (1996), 'Amalasuntha, Procopius, and a woman's place', *Journal of Women's History* 8.2, 41–57.
Frantz, A. (1988), *The Athenian Agora XXIV: Late Antiquity, A.D. 267–700*, Princeton: American School of Classical Studies at Athens.
Frend, W. H. C. (1972), *The Rise of the Monophysite Movement*, Cambridge: Cambridge University Press.
Gador-Whyte, S. (2017), *Theology and Poetry in Early Byzantium: The Kontakia of Romanos the Melodist*, Cambridge: Cambridge University Press.
Garland, L. (1999), *Byzantine Empresses: Women and Power in Byzantium, AD 527–1204*, London: Routledge.
Gärtner, T. (2008), *Untersuchungen zur Gestaltung und zum Historischen Stoff der Johannis Coripps*, Berlin: De Gruyter.
Gascou, J. (1985), 'Les grands domaines, la cité et l'état en Égypte byzantine: Recherches d'histoire agraire, fiscal et administrative', *Travaux et Mémoires* 9, 1–90.
Gauthier, G. (1998), *Justinien: Le Rêve Imperial*, Paris: Éditions France-Empire.
Gillett, A. (2003), *Envoys and Political Communication in the Late Antique West, 411–533*, Cambridge: Cambridge University Press.
Glucker, C. A. M. (1987), *The City of Gaza in the Roman and Byzantine Periods*, Oxford: BAR International Series 325.
Goffart, W. (1980), *Barbarians and Romans A.D. 418–585: The Techniques of Accommodation*, Princeton: Princeton University Press.
Goffart, W. (2006), *Barbarian Tides: The Migration Age and the Late Roman Empire*, Philadelphia: University of Pennsylvania Press.

Graves, R. (1938, rev. 1954), *Count Belisarius*, London: Penguin Books.
Gray, P. T. R. (1979), *The Defense of Chalcedon in the East (451–553)*, Leiden: Brill.
Gray, P. T. R. (1989), '"The Select Fathers": Canonizing the patristic past', *Studia Patristica* 23, 21–36.
Gray, P. T. R. (1997), 'Covering the nakedness of Noah: Reconstruction and denial in the age of Justinian', in L. Harland (ed.) *Conformity and Non-Conformity in Byzantium*, Amsterdam: Byzantinische Forschungen 24, 193–206.
Gray, P. T. R. (2005), 'The legacy of Chalcedon: Christological problems and their significance', in M. Maas (ed.), *The Cambridge Companion to the Age of Justinian*, Cambridge: Cambridge University Press, 215–38.
Greatrex, G. (1996a), 'Flavius Hypatius: *Quem vidit validum Parthus sensitque timendum*: An investigation into his career', *Byzantion* 66, 120–42.
Greatrex, G. (1996b), 'Stephanus, the father of Procopius of Caesarea?', *Medieval Prosopography* 17.1, 125–45.
Greatrex, G. (1997), 'The Nika riot: A reappraisal', *JHS* 117, 60–86.
Greatrex, G. (1998), *Rome and Persia at War, 502–532*, Leeds: F. Cairns.
Greatrex, G. (2003), 'Recent work on Procopius and the composition of Wars VIII', *BMGS* 27, 45–67.
Greatrex, G. (2007), 'The early years of Justin I's reign in the sources', *Electrum* 12, 99–113.
Greatrex, G. (2014), 'Perceptions of Procopius in recent scholarship', *Histos* 8, 76–121.
Greatrex, G. (2017), 'The emperor, the people and urban violence in the fifth and sixth centuries', in J. H. F. Dijkstra and C. R. Raschle (eds), *Religious Violence in the Ancient World*, Cambridge: Cambridge University Press, 389–405.
Greatrex, G. (ed.) (2019), 'Work on Procopius outside the English-speaking world: A survey (2019)', *Histos* Supplement 9, <https://histos.org/SV09Procopius.html> (last accessed 6 May 2021).
Greatrex, G., and S. Janniard (2018), *Le Monde de Procope/The World of Procopius*, Paris: De Boccard.
Greatrex, G., and S. N. C. Lieu (eds) (2002), *The Roman Eastern Frontier and the Persian Wars, Part II: 363-630*, London and New York: Routledge.
Greatrex, G., and J. Watt (1999), 'One, two or three feasts? The Brytae, the Maiuma and the May festival at Edessa', *Oriens Christianus* 83, 1–21.
Grey, C. (2016), 'Landowning and labour in the rural economy', in J. J. Arnold, M. S. Bjornlie and K. Sessa (eds), *A Companion to Ostrogothic Italy*, Leiden and Boston: Brill, 263–95.
Grierson, P. (1982), *Byzantine Coins*, London: Methuen.
Grierson, P., and M. Blackburn (1986, repr. 2007), *Medieval European Coinage: With a Catalogue of Coins in the Fitzwilliam Museum, Cambridge 1: The Early Middle Ages (5th–10th Centuries)*, Cambridge and New York: Cambridge University Press.

Grierson, P., C. Mango and I. Sevcenko (1962), 'The tombs and obits of the Byzantine emperors (337–1042) with an additional note', *DOP* 16, 3–63.

Grillmeier, A., and T. Hainthaler (1995), *Christ in Christian Tradition II: From the Council of Chalcedon (451) to Gregory the Great (590–604), Part 2: The Church in Constantinople in the Sixth Century*, London: Mowbray.

Grillmeier, A., and T. Hainthaler (1996), *Christ in Christian Tradition II: From the Council of Chalcedon (451) to Gregory the Great (590–604), Part 4: The Church of Alexandria with Nubia and Ethiopia after 451*, London: Mowbray.

Guillaumont, A. (1969–70), 'Justinien et l'église de Perse', *DOP* 23–4, 39–66.

Guillaumont, A. (1970), 'Un colloque entre orthodoxes et théologiens nestoriens de Perse sous Justinien', *Académie des Inscriptions et Belles Lettres: Comptes rendus*, 201–7.

Gunn, J. D. (2000), *The Years without Summer: Tracing A.D. 536 and its Aftermath*, Oxford: Archaeopress.

Haarer, F. K. (2006), *Anastasius I: Politics and empire in the late Roman world*, Cambridge: F. Cairns.

Haarer, F. K. (2016), 'Developments in the governance of late antique cities', in U. Roberto and L. Mecella (eds), *Governare e riformare l'impero al momento della sua divisione*, Rome: École française de Rome, 125–62.

Hahn, W. (2005), *Zur Münzprägung des Frühbyzantinischen Reiches: Anastasius I. bis Phocas und Heraclius-Revolte, 491–610*, Vienna: Money Trend Verlag.

Hahn, W., with M. A. Metlich (2013), *Money of the Incipient Byzantine Empire: Anastasius I–Justinian I*, 2nd edn, Vienna: Veröffentlichen des Instituts für Numismatik und Geldgeschichte 15.

Hainthaler, T. (2007), *Christliche Araber vor dem Islam*, Leuven: Peeters.

Hainthaler, T. (2013), *Christ in Christian Tradition II: From the Council of Chalcedon (451) to Gregory the Great (590–604), Part 3: The Churches of Jerusalem and Antioch from 451 to 600*, Oxford: Oxford University Press.

Haldon, J. (2001), *The Byzantine Wars*, Stroud: History.

Haldon, J. (2005), 'Economy and administration: How did the empire work?', in M. Maas (ed.), *The Cambridge Companion to the Age of Justinian*, Cambridge: Cambridge University Press, 28–59.

Halsall, G. (2016), 'The Ostrogothic Military', in J. J. Arnold, M. S. Bjornlie and K. Sessa (eds), *A Companion to Ostrogothic Italy*, Leiden and Boston: Brill, 173–99.

Hardy, E. R. (1968), 'The Egyptian policy of Justinian', *DOP* 22, 21–41.

Harl, K. W. (1990), 'Sacrifice and pagan belief in fifth- and sixth-century Byzantium', *Past and Present* 128, 7–27.

Harper, K. (2013), *From Shame to Sin: The Christian Transformation of Sexual Morality in Late Antiquity*, Cambridge, MA: Harvard University Press.

Harries, J. (1999), *Law and Empire in Late Antiquity*, Cambridge: Cambridge University Press.

Harrison, M. (1989), *A Temple for Byzantium: The Discovery and Excavation of Anicia Juliana's Palace-Church in Istanbul*, Austin: Harvey Miller and Texas University Press.

Harvey, S. A. (1990), *Asceticism and Society in Crisis: John of Ephesus and the Lives of the Eastern Saints*, Berkeley: University of California Press.

Harvey, S. A. (2001), 'Theodora the "believing queen": A study in Syriac historiographical tradition', *Hugoye* 4, 1–32.

Hatlie, P. (2007), *The Monks and Monasteries of Constantinople ca. 350–850*, Cambridge: Cambridge University Press.

Hays, G. (2016), 'Sources from a silent land: The Latin poetry of Byzantine North Africa', in S. T. Stevens and J. P. Conant (eds), *North Africa under Byzantium and Early Islam*, Washington, DC: Dumbarton Oaks Research Library and Collection, 269–94.

Heather, P. (1994), 'New men for new Constantines? Creating an imperial elite in the eastern Mediterranean', in P. Magdalino (ed.), *New Constantines: The Rhythm of Imperial Renewal in Byzantium, Fourth–Thirteenth Centuries*, Aldershot: Variorum, 11–33.

Heather, P. (1996), *The Goths*, Oxford: Blackwell.

Heather, P. (2005), *The Fall of the Roman Empire: A New History*, London: Macmillan.

Heather, P. (2018), *Rome Resurgent: War and Empire in the Age of Justinian*, Oxford: Oxford University Press.

Hendy, M. (1985), *Studies in the Byzantine Monetary Economy, c. 300–1450*, Cambridge: Cambridge University Press.

Henry, P. (1967), 'A mirror for Justinian: The *Ethesis* of Agapetus Diaconus', *GRBS* 8, 281–308.

Herrin, J. (1987), *The Formation of Christendom*, Oxford: Oxford University Press.

Herrin, J. (2020), *Ravenna. Capital of Empire, Crucible of Europe*, London: Allen Lane.

Heydemann, G. (2016), 'The Ostrogothic kingdom: Ideologies and transitions', in J. J. Arnold, M. S. Bjornlie and K. Sessa (eds), *A Companion to Ostrogothic Italy*, Leiden and Boston: Brill, 17–46.

Hickey, T. (2012), *Wine, Wealth and the State in Late Antique Egypt: The House of Apion at Oxyrhynchus*, Ann Arbor: University of Michigan Press.

Hodges, R., and W. Bowden (eds) (1998), *The Sixth Century: Production, Distribution and Demand*, Leiden: Brill.

Honoré, T. (1975), 'Some Constitutions composed by Justinian', *JRS* 65, 107–23.

Honoré, T. (1978), *Tribonian*, London: Duckworth.

Honoré, T. (2010), *Justinian's Digest: Character and Compilation*, Oxford: Oxford University Press.

Horden, P. (2005), 'Mediterranean plague in the age of Justinian', in M. Maas (ed.), *The Cambridge Companion to the Age of Justinian*, Cambridge: Cambridge University Press, 134–60.

Howard-Johnston, J. (1995), 'The two great powers in late antiquity: A comparison', in A. Cameron (ed.), *The Byzantine and Early Islamic Near East, III: States, Resources and Armies*, Princeton: Darwin Press, 157–226.

Howard-Johnston, J. (2006), *East Rome, Sasanian Persia and the End of Antiquity*, Aldershot: Variorum.

Howard-Johnston, J. (2013), 'Military infrastructure in the Roman provinces north and south of the Armenian Taurus in late antiquity', in A. Sarantis and N. Christie (eds), *War and Warfare in Late Antiquity: Current Perspectives*, Late Antique Archaeology 8, Leiden and Boston: Brill, 853–91.

Hoyland, R. (2001), *Arabia and the Arabs: From the Bronze Age to the Coming of Islam*, London: Routledge.

Hoyland, R. (2014), *In God's Path: The Arab Conquests and the Creation of an Islamic Empire*, Oxford: Oxford University Press.

Humfress, C. (2007), *Orthodoxy and the Courts in Late Antiquity*, Oxford: Oxford University Press.

Hurst, H. R. (ed.) (1994), *Excavations at Carthage: The British Mission, Volume II.1: The Circular Harbour, North Side – The Site and Finds Other Than Pottery*, British Academy Monographs in Archaeology 4, Oxford: Oxford University Press.

James, L. (2001), *Empresses and Power in Early Byzantium*, Leicester: Leicester University Press.

Jeffery, A. (1945), 'Three documents on the history of Christianity in south Arabia', *Anglican Theological Review* 27, 185–205.

Jeffreys, E. (2006), 'Writers and audiences in the early sixth century', in S. F. Johnson (ed.), *Greek Literature in Late Antiquity: Dynamism, Didacticism, Classicism*, Aldershot and Burlington, VT: Ashgate, 127–40.

Jeffreys, E., with B. Croke and R. Scott (1990), *Studies in John Malalas*, Byzantina Australiensia 6, Sydney: Australian Association for Byzantine Studies.

Johnson S. F. (ed.) (2006), *Greek Literature in Late Antiquity: Dynamism, Didacticism, Classicism*, Aldershot and Burlington, VT: Ashgate.

Jones, A. H. M. (1940, repr. 1998), *The Greek City from Alexander to Justinian*, Oxford: Clarendon Press.

Jones, A. H. M. (1964, repr. 1986), *The Later Roman Empire 284–602: A Social, Economic and Administrative Survey*, 2 vols, Oxford: Blackwell; repr. Baltimore: Johns Hopkins University Press.

Joye, S., and A. Knaepen (2005), 'L'image d'Amalasonthe chez Procope de Césarée et Grégoire de Tours: Portraits contrastés entre Orient et Occident', *Le Moyen Âge* 11, 229–58.

Kaegi, W. E. (1965), 'Arianism and the Byzantine army in Africa 533–546', *Traditio* 21, 23–53.

Kaegi, W. E. (1968), 'The fifth-century twilight of Byzantine paganism', *Classica et Mediaevalia* 27, 243–75.

Kaldellis, A. (1997), 'Agathias on history and poetry', *GRBS* 38.3, 295–305.

Kaldellis, A. (1999), 'The historical and religious views of Agathias: A reinterpretation', *Byzantion* 69, 206–52.
Kaldellis, A. (2003a), 'The religion of Ioannes Lydos', *Phoenix* 57.3–4, 300–6.
Kaldellis, A. (2003b), 'Things are not what they are: Agathias *Mythistoricus* and the last laugh of classical culture', *CQ* 53, 295–300.
Kaldellis, A. (2004a), 'Identifying dissident circles in sixth-century Byzantium: The friendship of Prokopius and Ioannes Lydos', *Florilegium* 21, 1–17.
Kaldellis, A. (2004b), *Procopius of Caesarea: Tyranny, History and Philosophy at the End of Antiquity*, Philadelphia: University of Pennsylvania Press.
Kaldellis, A. (2005), 'Republican theory and political dissidence in Ioannes Lydos', *BMGS* 29.1, 1–16.
Kaldellis, A. (2007a), *Hellenism in Byzantium: The Transformations of Greek Identity and the Reception of the Classical Tradition*, Cambridge: Cambridge University Press.
Kaldellis, A. (2007b), 'The literature of the plague and the anxieties of piety in sixth-century Byzantium', in F. Mormando and T. Worcester (eds), *Piety and Plague: From Byzantium to the Baroque*, Kirksville, MO: Truman State University Press, 1–22.
Kaldellis, A. (2009), 'The date and structure of Procopius' *Secret History* and his projected work on Church history', *GRBS* 49, 585–616.
Kaldellis, A. (2013), 'The making of Hagia Sophia and the last pagans of New Rome', *Journal of Late Antiquity* 6.2, 347–66.
Kaldellis, A. (2016), 'Prokopios' Vandal War: Thematic trajectories and hidden transcripts', in S. T. Stevens and J. Conant (eds), *North Africa under Byzantium and Early Islam*, Washington, DC: Dumbarton Oaks Research Library and Collection, 13–21.
Kaldellis, A. (2017), 'Epilogue', in C. Lillington-Martin and E. Turquois (eds), *Procopius of Caesarea: Literary and Historical Interpretations*, London and New York: Routledge, 261–70.
Kaplan, M. (1992), *Les Hommes et la Terre à Byzance du VIe au XIe siècle: Propriété et exploitation du sol*, Byzantina Sorbonensia 10, Paris: Éditions de la Sorbonne.
Kaster, R. A. (1988), *Guardians of Language: The Grammarian and Society in Late Antiquity*, Berkeley: University of California Press.
Kearley, T. (2010), 'The creation and transmission of Justinian's Novels', *Law Library Journal* 102, 377–97.
Kelly, C. M. (2004), *Ruling the Later Roman Empire*, Cambridge, MA: Harvard University Press.
Kelly, C. M. (2006), 'John Lydus and the eastern praetorian prefecture in the sixth century AD', *Byzantinische Zeitschrift* 98.2, 431–58.
Kennedy, H. (1985a), 'From *Polis* to Madina: Urban changes to late antique and early Islamic Syria', *Past and Present* 106, 3–27.
Kennedy, H. (1985b), 'The last century of Byzantine Syria: A reinterpretation', *Byzantinische Forschungen* 10, 141–83.

Key Fowden, E. (1999), *The Barbarian Plain: Saint Sergius between Rome and Iran*, Berkeley: University of California Press.
Key Fowden, E. (2000), 'An Arab building at al-Rusafa-Sergiopolis', *Damaszener Mitteilungen* 12, 303–24.
Kislinger, E., and D. Stathakopoulos (1999), 'Pest und Perserkriege bei Prokop: Chronologische Überlegungen zum Geschehen, 540–545', *Byzantion* 69, 76–98.
Kitzinger, E. (1977), *Byzantine Art in the Making: Main Lines of Stylistic Development in Mediterranean Art, 3rd–7th Century*, Cambridge, MA: Harvard University Press, and London: Faber & Faber.
Koder, J. (2008), 'Imperial propaganda in the Kontakia of Romanos the Melode', *DOP* 62, 275–91.
Koehn, C. (2018), *Justinian und die Armee des Frühen Byzanz*, Berlin: De Gruyter.
Kominko, M. (2013), *The World of Kosmas: Illustrated Byzantine Codices of the Christian Topography*, Cambridge: Cambridge University Press.
Kouroumali, M. (2013), 'The Justinianic reconquest of Italy: Imperial campaigns and local responses', in A. Sarantis and N. Christie (eds), *War and Warfare in Late Antiquity: Current Perspectives*, Late Antique Archaeology 8, Leiden and Boston: Brill, 969–99.
Kovalchuk, K. (2007), 'The founder as a saint: The image of Justinian I in the Great Church of St Sophia', *Byzantion* 77, 205–37.
Krautheimer, R. (1965, repr. 1986), *Early Christian and Byzantine Architecture*, Harmondsworth: Penguin Books Ltd.
Krautheimer, R. (1983), *Three Christian Capitals: Topography and Politics*, Berkeley: University of California Press.
Kruse, M. (2017), 'Justinian's *Laws* and Procopius' *Wars*', in C. Lillington-Martin and E. Turquois (eds), *Procopius of Caesarea: Literary and Historical Interpretations*, London and New York: Routledge, 186–200.
La Rocca, C. (2012), '*Consors regni*: A problem of gender? The *consortium* between Amalasuntha and Theodahad in 534', in J. Nelson, S. Reynolds and S. M. Johns (eds), *Gender and Historiography*, London: Institute of Historical Research, 127–43.
Lafferty, S. (2010), 'Law and society in Ostrogothic Italy: Evidence from the *Edictum Theoderici*', *Journal of Late Antiquity* 3.2, 337–64.
Lafferty, S. (2013), *Law and Society in the Age of Theoderic the Great: A Study of the Edictum Theoderici*, Cambridge: Cambridge University Press.
Lang, U. M. (2005), 'John Philoponus and the Fifth Ecumenical Council: A study and translation of the letter to Justinian', *Annuarium Historiae Concilium* 37, 411–36.
Laniado, A. (2002), *Recherches sur les Notables Municipaux dans l'Empire Protobyzantin*, Travaux et Mémoires Monographies 13, Paris: Association des amis du Centre d'histoire et civilisation de Byzance.
Laniado, A. (2015), *Ethnos et Droit dans le Monde Protobyzantin, V–VIe siècle*, Geneva: Droz.

Laporte, J.-P. (2003), 'Zabi, Friki: Notes sur la Maurétanie et la Numidie de Justinien', *Antiquité Tardive* 10, 151–67.
Lassère, J.-M. (2015), *Africa, quasi Roma, 256 av. J.C. – 711 apr. J.C.*, Paris: CNRS Éditions.
Lee, A. D. (1993a), 'Evagrius, Paul of Nisibis and the problem of loyalties in the mid-sixth century', *Journal of Ecclesiastical History* 44, 569–85.
Lee, A. D. (1993b), *Information and Frontiers: Roman Foreign Relations in Late Antiquity*, Cambridge: Cambridge University Press.
Lee, A. D. (2007), *War in Late Antiquity: A Social History*, Oxford: Blackwell.
Lee, A. D. (2008), 'Treaty-making in late antiquity', in P. de Souza and J. France (eds), *War and Peace in Ancient and Medieval History*, Cambridge: Cambridge University Press, 107–9.
Lee, A. D. (2013), *From Rome to Byzantium AD 363–565: The Transformation of Ancient Rome*, Edinburgh: Edinburgh University Press.
Leone, A. (1999), 'Change or no change? Revised perceptions of urban transformation in late antiquity', in P. Baker, C. Forcey, S. Jundi and R. Wircher (eds), *TRAC 98: Proceedings of the Eighth Annual Theoretical Roman Archaeology Conference, Leicester 1998*, Oxford: Oxbow Books, 121–30.
Leone, A. (2003), 'Topographies of production in the cities of late antique North Africa', in L. Lavan and W. Bowden (eds), *Theory and Practice in Late Antique Archaeology*, Leiden: Brill, 257–87.
Leone, A. (2007), *Changing Townscapes in North Africa from Late Antiquity to the Arab Conquest*, Bari: Edipuglia.
Leppin, H. (2000), 'Kaiserliche Koohabitation: Von der Normalität Theodoras', in C. Kunst and U. Riemer (eds), *Grenzen der Macht: Zur Rolle der römischen Kaiserfrauen*, Potsdamer Altertumswissenschaftliche Beiträge 3, Stuttgart: Steiner, 75–85.
Leppin, H. (2002), 'Theodora und Iustinian', in H. Temporini-Gräfin Vitzthum (ed.), *Die Kaiserinnen Roms: Von Livia bis Theodora*, Munich: C. H. Beck, 437–81.
Leppin, H. (2006), 'Zu den Anfängen der Kirchenpolitki Justinianins', in H.-U. Wiemer (ed.), *Staatlichkeit und Politisches Handeln in der Römischen Kaiserzeit*, Berlin and New York: De Gruyter, 187–208.
Leppin, H. (2007), '(K)ein Zeitalter Justinians: Bemerkungen aus althistorischer Sicht zu Justininian in der jüngeren Forschung', *Historische Zeitschrift* 284, 659–86.
Leppin, H. (2009), 'Power from humility: Justinian and the religious authority of monks', in A. Cain and N. Lenski (eds), *The Power of Religion in Late Antiquity*, Farnham: Ashgate, 155–64.
Leppin, H. (2011), *Justinian: Das Christliche Experiment*, Stuttgart: Klett-Cotta.
Leven, K.-H. (1987), 'Die "Justiniansche" Pest', *Jahrbuch der Instituts für Geschichte der Medizin der Robert-Bosch-Stiftung* 6, 137–61.
Liebeschuetz, J. H. W. G. (1972), *Antioch: City and Imperial Administration in the Later Roman Empire*, Oxford: Clarendon Press.

Liebeschuetz, J. H. W. G. (1996a), 'Administration and politics in the cities of the 5th and 6th centuries with special reference to the circus factions', in C. Lepelley (ed.), *La Fin de la Cité Antique et le Début de la Cité Médiévale de la Fin du III*^{e} *siècle à l'Avènement de Charlemagne: Actes du colloque tenu à l'Université de Paris X-Nanterre les 1,2, et 3 avril 1993*, Bari: Edipuglia, 161–82.

Liebeschuetz, J. H. W. G. (1996b), 'Civic finance in the Byzantine period: The laws and Egypt', *Byzantinische Zeitschrift* 89, 389–408.

Liebeschuetz, J. H. W. G. (2001), *The Decline and Fall of the Roman City*, Oxford: Oxford University Press.

Lillington-Martin, C. (2007), 'Archaeological and ancient literary evidence for a battle near Dara Gap, Turkey, AD 530: Topography, texts and trenches', in A. Lewin and P. Pellegrini (eds), *The Late Roman Army in the Near East from Diocletian to the Arab Conquest*, BAR International Series 1717, Oxford: Archaeopress, 299–311.

Lillington-Martin, C. (2013), 'Procopius on the struggle for Dara in 530 and Rome in 537–538: Reconciling texts and landscapes', *Late Antique Archaeology* 8.2, 599–630.

Lillington-Martin, C., and E. Turquois (eds) (2017), *Procopius of Caesarea: Literary and Historical Interpretations*, London and New York: Routledge.

Lim, R. (1997), 'Consensus and dissensus on public spectacles in early Byzantium', *Byzantinische Forschungen* 24, 159–79.

Litsas, F. K. (1982), 'Choricius of Gaza and his descriptions of festivals at Gaza', *Jahrbuch der Österreichischen Byzantinistik*, 32.3, 427–36.

Little, L. K. (2007), *Plague and the End of Antiquity: The Pandemic of 541–750*, Cambridge: Cambridge University Press.

Lizzi Testa, R., and G. Marconi (2019), *The Collectio Avellana and its Revivals*, Newcastle upon Tyne: Cambridge Scholars Publishing.

Lung, E. (2017), 'Religious identity as seen by sixth-century historians and chroniclers', in M. Sághy and E. M. Schoolman (eds), *Pagans and Christians in the Late Roman Empire: New Evidence, New Approaches (4th–8th Centuries)*, Budapest: Central European University Press, 119–30.

Maas, M. (1986), 'Roman history and Christian ideology in Justinianic reform legislation', *DOP* 40, 17–31.

Maas, M. (1992), *John Lydus and the Roman Past: Antiquarianism and Politics in the Age of Justinian*, London: Routledge.

Maas, M. (1996), 'Junillus Africanus' *Instituta Regularia Divinae Legis* in its Justinianic context', in P. Allen and E. Jeffreys (eds), *The Sixth Century: End or Beginning?*, Byzantina Australiensia 10, Brisbane: Australian Association for Byzantine Studies, 131–44.

Maas, M. (2003), *Exegesis and Empire in the Early Byzantine Mediterranean: Junillus Africanus and the 'Instituta Regularia Divinae Legis'*, Tübingen: Mohr Siebeck.

Maas, M. (ed.) (2005), *The Cambridge Companion to the Age of Justinian*, Cambridge: Cambridge University Press.

McCail, R. C. (1969), 'The Cycle of Agathias: New identifications scrutinised', *JHS* 89, 87–96.

McCail, R. C. (1970), 'The early career of Agathias Scholasticus', *Revue des Études Byzantines* 28, 141–51.

McCail, R. C. (1971), 'The erotic and ascetic poetry of Agathias', *Byzantion* 41, 205–67.

MacCormack, S. G. (1981), *Art and Ceremony in Late Antiquity*, Berkeley: University of California Press.

McCormick, M. (1986), *Eternal Victory: Triumphal Rulership in Late Antiquity, Byzantium and the Early Medieval West*, Cambridge: Cambridge University Press.

MacCoull, L. S. B. (1988), *Dioscorus of Aphrodito: His Work and his World*, Berkeley: University of California Press.

MacCoull, L. S. B. (1995), '"When Justinian was upsetting the world": A note on soldiers and religious coercion in sixth-century Egypt', in T. S. Miller and J. Nesbitt (eds), *Peace and War in Byzantium: Essays in Honor of George T. Dennis, S. J.*, Washington, DC: Catholic University of America Press, 106–13.

McDonough, S. (2013), 'Military and society in Sasanian Iran', in B. Campbell and L. A. Tritle (eds), *The Oxford Handbook of Warfare in the Classical World*, Oxford: Oxford University Press, 601–20.

MacPherson, R. (1989), *Rome in Involution: Cassiodorus' Variae in their Literary and Historical Setting*, Seria Filologia Klasyczna 14, Poznań: Wydawnictwo Naukowe Uniwersytetu im. Adama Mickiewicza w Poznaniu.

Macrides, R., and P. Magdalino (1988), 'The architecture of *ekphrasis*: Construction and context of Paul the Silentiary's *ekphrasis* of Hagia Sophia', *BMGS* 12, 47–82.

Mainstone, R. J. (1988), *Hagia Sophia: Architecture, Structure and Liturgy of Justinian's Great Church*, London: Thames and Hudson.

Mango, C. (1959), *The Brazen House: A Study of the Vestibule of the Imperial Palace of Constantinople*, Arkaeologisk-kunsthistoriske meddelelser IV.4, Copenhagen: Kommission hos Munksgaard.

Mango, C. (1993), 'The columns of Justinian and his successors', in C. Mango (ed.), *Studies on Constantinople*, Aldershot: Variorum, 1–20.

Mango, C. (2004), *Le développement urbain de Constantinople* (IVe–VIIe siècles), Paris: De Boccard.

Maraval, P. (1999), *L'empereur Justinien*, Paris: Presses universitaires de France.

Markus, R. A. (1979), 'Carthage – Prima Justiniana – Ravenna: An aspect of Justinian's *Kirchenpolitik*', *Byzantion* 49, 277–302.

Markus, R. A., and C. Sotinel (2007), 'Introduction', in C. M. Chazelle and C. Cubitt (eds), *The Crisis of the Oikoumene: The Three Chapters and the Failed Quest for Unity in the Sixth-Century Mediterranean*, Turnhout: Brepols, 1–14.

Mathews, T. F. (1971), *The Early Churches of Constantinople: Architecture and Liturgy*, University Park and London: Pennsylvania State University Press.

Matthews, J. (1981), 'Anicius Manlius Severinus Boethius', in M. Gibson (ed.), *Boethius: His Life, Thought and Influence*, Oxford: Blackwell, 15–43.

Mattingly, D. J., and R. B. Hitchner (1995), 'Roman Africa: An archaeological review', *JRS* 85, 165–213.

Mayerson, P. (1978), 'Procopius or Eutychius on the construction of the monastery at Mount Sinai: Which is the more reliable source?', *Bulletin of the American Schools of Oriental Research* 230, 33–8.

Mazal, O. (2001), *Justinian I. und seine Zeit: Geschichte und Kultur des Byzantinischen Reiches im 6. Jahrhundert*, Cologne: Böhlau.

Mazza, R. (2010), 'Choricius of Gaza, *Oration XIII*: Religion and state in the age of Justinian', in R. M. Frakes (ed.), *The Rhetoric of Power in Late Antiquity*, London and New York: Tauris Academic Studies, 172–93.

Meier, M. (1999), 'Beobachtungen zu den sogenannten Pestschilderungen bei Thukydides II.47–54 und bei Prokop, Bell. Pers. II 22–23', *Tyche* 14, 177–210.

Meier, M. (2000), 'Die Erdbeben der Jahre 542 und 554 in der byzantinischen Überlieferung: Quellenkritische Überlegungen zur Geschichte des 6. Jahrhunderts n. Chr.', *ZPE* 130, 287–95.

Meier, M. (2002), 'Das Ende des Konsulats im Jahr 541/42 und seine Gründe: Kritische Anmerkungen zur Vorstellung eines "Zeitalters Justinians"', *ZPE* 138, 277–99.

Meier, M. (2003a), *Das andere Zeitalter Justinians, Kontingenzerfahrung und Kontingenzbewältigung im 6. Jahrhundert n. Chr.*, Göttingen: Vandenhoeck & Ruprecht.

Meier, M. (2003b), 'Die Inszenierung einer Katastrophe Justinian und der Nika-Aufstand', *ZPE* 143, 273–300.

Meier, M. (2004a), *Justinian: Herrschaft, Reich und Religion*, Munich: C. H. Beck.

Meier, M. (2004b), 'Prokop, Agathias, die Pest und das Ende der antiken Historiographie: Naturkatastrophen und Geschichtsschreibung in der ausgehenden Spätantike', *Historische Zeitschrift* 278, 281–310.

Meier, M. (2004c), 'Zur Funktion der Theodora-Rede im Geschichtswerk Prokops (BP 1, 24, 33–37)', *Rheinisches Museum für Philologie* 147, 88–104.

Meier, M. (2007), 'Σταυρωθεὶς δι' ἡμᾶς – Der Aufstand gegen Anastasios im Jahr 512', *Millennium* 4, 157–237.

Meier, M. (ed.) (2011), *Justinian: Neue Wege der Forschung*, Darmstadt: WBG, Wissenschaftliche Buchgesellschaft.

Meier, M. (2016), 'The "Justinianic Plague": The economic consequences of the pandemic in the Eastern Roman Empire and its cultural and religious effects', *Early Medieval Europe* 24.3, 267–92.

Menze, V.-L. (2008), *Justinian and the Making of the Syrian Orthodox Church*, Oxford: Oxford University Press.

Merrills, A. H. (ed.) (2004), *Vandals, Romans and Berbers: New Perspectives on Late Antique North Africa*, Aldershot: Ashgate.

Merrills, A. H. (2010), 'Justinian and the end of the Vandal kingdom', in A. H. Merrills and R. Miles, *The Vandals*, Oxford: Wiley-Blackwell, 228–55.

Merrills, A. H. (2016), 'Gelimer's slaughter: The case for late Vandal Africa', in S. T. Stevens and J. P. Conant (eds), *North Africa under Byzantium and Early Islam*, Washington, DC: Dumbarton Oaks Research Library and Collection, 23–40.

Merrills, A. H., and R. Miles (2010), *The Vandals*, Oxford: Wiley-Blackwell.

Metcalf, W. E. (1988), 'Joint reign of Justin I and Justinian I', in W. Hahn and W. E. Metcalf (eds), *Studies in Early Byzantine Gold Coinage*, Numismatic Studies 17, New York: American Numismatic Society, 19–27.

Meyendorff, J. (1968), 'Justinian, the empire and the Church', *DOP* 22, 43–60.

Meyendorff, J. (1989), *Imperial Unity and Christian Division: The Church 450–680 A.D.*, Crestwood, NY: St Vladimir's Seminary Press.

Miguélez Cavero, L. (2008), *Poems in Context: Greek Poetry in the Egyptian Thebaid, 200–600 AD*, Berlin: De Gruyter.

Miles, R. (2015), 'Byzantine Carthage and its Vandal legacy', in É. Wolff (ed.), *Littérature, Politique et Religion en Afrique Vandale*, Paris: Institut d'Études augustiniennes, 73–92.

Millar, F. (2008), 'Rome, Constantinople and the Near Eastern Church under Justinian: Two synods of CE 536', *JRS* 98, 62–82.

Millar, F. (2010), 'Rome's Arab allies in late antiquity: Conceptions and representations from within the frontiers of the empire', in H. Börm and J. Wiesehöfer (eds), *Commutatio et Contentio: Studies in the Late Roman, Sasanian, and Early Islamic Near East in Memory of Zeev Rubin*, Düsseldorf: Wellem Verlag, 199–226.

Mîrşanu, D. (2008), 'The imperial policy of otherness: Justinian and the Arianism of barbarians as a motive for the recovery of the west', *Ephemerides Theologicae Lovanienses: Louvain Journal of Theology and Canon Law* 84, 477–98.

Modéran, Y. (1986), 'Corippe et l'occupation byzantine de l'Afrique: Pour une nouvelle lecture de la Johannide', *Antiquités Africaines* 22, 195–212.

Modéran, Y. (1996), 'La renaissance des cités dans l'Afrique du VIe siècle d'après une inscription récemment publiée', in C. Lepelley (ed.), *La fin de la cité antique et le début de la cité médiévale*, Bari: Edipuglia, 85–114.

Modéran, Y. (2003a), 'Une guerre de religion: Les deux églises d'Afrique à l'époque vandale', *Antiquité Tardive* 10, 21–44.

Modéran, Y. (2003b), *Les Maures et l'Afrique Romaine (IVe–VIe siècle)*, Rome: École française de Rome.

Modéran, Y. (2007), 'L'Afrique reconquise et les Trois Chapitres', in C. M. Chazelle and C. Cubitt (eds), *The Crisis of the Oikoumene: The Three Chapters and the Failed Quest for Unity in the Sixth-Century Mediterranean*, Turnhout: Brepols, 39–82.

Momigliano, A. (1955), 'Cassiodorus and Italian culture of his time', *Proceedings of the British Academy* 40, 207–25.
Moorhead, J. (1983), 'Italian loyalties during Justinian's Gothic War', *Byzantion* 53, 575–96.
Moorhead, J. (1992), *Theoderic in Italy*, Oxford: Clarendon Press.
Moorhead, J. (1994), *Justinian*, Harlow: Longman.
Moorhead, J. (2000), 'Totila the revolutionary', *Historia* 49.3, 382–6.
Moorhead, J. (2009), 'Boethius' life and the world of late antique philosophy', in J. Marenbon (ed.), *The Cambridge Companion to Boethius*, Cambridge: Cambridge University Press, 13–33.
Morrisson, C. (2004), 'L'atelier de Carthage et la diffusion de la monnaie frappée dans l'Afrique vandale et byzantine (439–695)', *Antiquité Tardive* 11, 65–84.
Morrisson, C. (2016), 'Regio dives in omnibus bonis ornata: The African economy from the Vandals to the Arab Conquest in the light of coin evidence', in S. T. Stevens and J. P. Conant (eds), *North Africa under Byzantium and Early Islam*, Washington, DC: Dumbarton Oaks Research Library and Collection, 173–200.
Morrisson, C., and J.-P. Sodini (2002), 'The sixth-century economy', in A. E. Laiou (ed.), *The Economic History of Byzantium from the Seventh through the Fifteenth Century*, vol. 1, Washington, DC: Dumbarton Oaks Research Library and Collection, 165–220.
Nijf, O. M. van, and R. Alston (2011), *Political Culture in the Greek City after the Classical Age*, Leuven: Peeters.
Noethlichs, K. L. (2000), '*Quid possit antiquitas nostris legibus abrogare?* Politische Propaganda und praktische Politik bei Justinian I. im Lichte der kaiserlichen Gestzgebung und der antiken Histoiriographie', in *ZAC* 4, 116–32.
Noethlichs, K. L. (2007), 'Jews, heretics or useful farm workers? Samaritans in late antique imperial legislation', in J. Drinkwater and B. Salway (eds), *Wolf Liebeschuetz Reflected*, London: Institute of Classical Studies, 57–65.
Nöldeke, T. (1897), *Geschichte der Perser und Araber zur Zeit der Sassaniden*, Leiden: Brill.
O'Daly, G. J. P. (1991), *The Poetry of Boethius*, London: Duckworth.
O'Donnell, J. J. (1979), *Cassiodorus*, Berkeley: University of California Press.
O'Meara, D. (2002), 'The Justinianic dialogue *On Political Science* and its Neoplatonic sources', in K. Ierodiakonou (ed.), *Byzantine Philosophy and its Ancient Sources*, Oxford: Clarendon Press, 49–62.
O'Meara, D. (2003), *Platonopolis: Platonic Political Philosophy in Late Antiquity*, Oxford: Oxford University Press.
Obolensky, D. (1971), *The Byzantine Commonwealth, 500–1453*, London: Weidenfeld and Nicolson.
Oikonomidès, N. (1986), 'Silk trade and production in Byzantium from the sixth to the ninth century: The seals of kommerkiarioi', *DOP* 40, 33–53.

Osler, D. J. (1985), 'The compilation of Justinian's Digest', *Zeitschrift der Savigny-Stiftung für Rechtsgeschichte: Romische Abteilung* 102, 129–84.

Ousterhout, R. (2010), 'New temples and new Solomons: The rhetoric of Byzantine architecture', in P. Magdalino and R. Nelson (eds), *The Old Testament in Byzantium*, Washington, DC: Dumbarton Oaks Research Library and Collection, 223–54.

Oxford Dictionary of Byzantium (1991), (ed.) A. P. Kazhdan, 3 vols, New York and Oxford: Oxford University Press.

Palmer, A. (1990), *Monk and Mason on the Tigris Frontier: The Early History of Tur 'Abdin*, Cambridge: Cambridge University Press.

Parker, S. T. (1986), *Romans and Saracens: A History of the Arabian Frontier*, Boston: American Schools of Oriental Research.

Parnell, D. A. (2017), *Justinian's Men: Careers and Relationships of Byzantine Army Officers, 518-610*, London: Palgrave Macmillan.

Patout Burns, J., and R. M. Jensen (2014), *Christianity in Roman Africa: The Development of its Practices and Beliefs*, Grand Rapids: William B. Eerdmans.

Pazdernik, C. (1994), '"Our most pious consort given us by God": Dissident reactions to the partnership of Justinian and Theodora, AD 525–548', *Classical Antiquity* 13, 256–81.

Pazdernik, C. (2000), 'Procopius and Thucydides on the labors of war: Belisarius and Brasidas in the field', *Transactions of the American Philological Association* 130, 149–87.

Pazdernik, C. (2005), 'Justinianic ideology and the power of the past', in M. Maas (ed.), *The Cambridge Companion to the Age of Justinian*, Cambridge: Cambridge University Press, 185–212.

Pazdernik, C. (2006), 'Xenophon's *Hellenica* in Procopius' *Wars*: Pharnabazus and Belisarius', *GRBS* 46, 175–206.

Pazdernik, C. (2015), 'Belisarius' second occupation of Rome and Pericles' last speech', in G. Greatrex and H. Elton (eds), *Shifting Genres in Late Antiquity*, Farnham: Ashgate, 207–18.

Pfeilschifter, R. (2013), *Der Kaiser und Konstantinopel: Kommunikation und Konfliktaustrag in einer spätantiken Metropole*, Millennium-Studien 44, Berlin and Boston: De Gruyter.

Piccirillo, M. (2001), 'The Church of Saint Sergius at Nitl: A centre of the Christian Arabs in the steppe at the gates of Madaba', *Liber Annuus* 51, 267–84.

Pilara, G. (2006), *La città di Roma fra Chiesa e impero durante il conflitto gotico-bizantino*, Rome: Aracne.

PLRE = J. R. Martindale (ed.) (1980), *The Prosopography of the Later Roman Empire, Vol. 2: A.D. 395-527*, and (1992), *The Prosopography of the Later Roman Empire, Vol. 3: A.D. 527-641*, Cambridge: Cambridge University Press.

Pohl, W. (1996), 'Die Langobarden in Pannonien und Justinians Gotenkrieg', in D. Bialeková and J. Zabojnik (eds), *Ethnische und Kulturelle Verhältnisse an der Mittleren Donau im 6.–11. Jahrhundert*, Bratislava: Veda, Verlag der Slowakischen Akademie der Wissenschaften, 27–35.

Pohl, W. (ed.) (1997), *Kingdoms of the Empire: The Integration of Barbarians in Late Antiquity*, Leiden: Brill.

Potter, D. (2015), *Theodora: Actress, Empress, Saint*, Oxford: Oxford University Press.

Pottier, H. (2010), 'L'empereur Justinien survivant à la peste bubonique (542)', in *Mélanges Cécile Morrisson*, Travaux et Mémoires 16, Paris: Association des amis du Centre d'histoire et civilisation de Byzance, 685–91.

Poulter, A. (ed.) (2007), *The Transition to Late Antiquity on the Danube and Beyond*, Oxford: Oxford University Press.

Praet, R. (2019), 'Malalas and erudite memory in sixth-century Constantinople', in J. Borsch, O. Gengler and M. Meier (eds), *Die Weltchronik des Johannes Malalas im Kontext spätantiker Memorialkultur*, Stuttgart: Steiner Verlag, 219–39.

Price, R. (2009), *The Acts of the Council of Constantinople of 553, translated with an introduction and notes*, Translated Texts for Historians, Liverpool: Liverpool University Press.

Pringle, D. (1981), *The Defence of Byzantine Africa from Justinian to the Arab Conquest*, Oxford: BAR International Series 99.

Pringle, D. (2002), 'Two fortified sites in Byzantine Africa: Ain Djelloula and Henchir Sguidan', *Antiquité Tardive* 10, 269–90.

Prinzing, G. (1986), 'Das Bild Iustinians I. in der Überlieferung der Byzantiner vom 7. bis 15. Jahrhundert', *Fontes Minores* 7, 1–99.

Pummer, R. (2002), *Early Christian Authors on Samaritans and Samaritanism*, Tübingen: Mohr Siebeck.

Rabello, A. M. (1987–8), *Giustiniano, Ebrei e Samaritani alla Luce delle Fonti Storico-Letterarie, Ecclesiastiche e Giuridiche*, 2 vols, Milan: Giuffrè.

Radtki, C. (2016), 'The Senate at Rome in Ostrogothic Italy', in J. J. Arnold, M. S. Bjornlie and K. Sessa (eds), *A Companion to Ostrogothic Italy*, Leiden and Boston: Brill, 140–4.

Rance, P. (2005), 'Narses and the Battle of Taginae (Busta Gallorum) 552: Procopius and sixth-century warfare', *Historia* 54.4, 424–72.

Rapp, C. (2005), 'Literary culture under Justinian', in M. Maas (ed.), *The Cambridge Companion to the Age of Justinian*, Cambridge: Cambridge University Press, 376–97.

Reynolds, J. (2000), 'Byzantine Buildings, Justinian and Procopius in *Libya Inferior* and *Libya Superior*', *Antiquité Tardive* 8, 169–76.

Reynolds, P. (2016), 'From Vandal *Africa* to Arab Ifrīqīiya: Tracing ceramics and economic trends through the fifth to the eleventh centuries', in S. T. Stevens and J. P. Conant (eds), *North Africa under Byzantium and Early Islam*, Washington, DC: Dumbarton Oaks Research Library and Collection, 129–72.

Riedlberger, P. (2010), *Philologischer, historischer und liturgischer Kommentar zum 8. Buch der Johannis des Goripp nebst kritischer Edition und Übersetzung*, Groningen: Egbert Forsten.

Robin, C. J. (2008), 'Les Arabes de Himyar, des "Romains" et des Perses (IIIe–VIe siècles de l'ère chrétienne)', *Semitica et Classica* 1, 167–202.

Robin, C. J. (2012), 'Ethiopia and Arabia', in S. F. Johnson (ed.), *The Oxford Handbook of Late Antiquity*, Oxford: Oxford University Press, 297–306.

Robin, C. J. (2014), 'The people beyond the Arabian frontier in late antiquity: Recent epigraphic discoveries and latest advances', in J. H. F. Dijkstra and G. Fisher (eds), *Inside and Out: Interaction between Rome and the Peoples on the Arabian and Egyptian Frontiers in Late Antiquity*, Leuven: Peeters, 33–82.

Rompay, L. Van (2005), 'Society and community in the Christian East', in M. Maas (ed.), *The Cambridge Companion to the Age of Justinian*, Cambridge: Cambridge University Press, 239–66.

Rosen, W. (2007), *Justinian's Flea: Plague, Empire and the Birth of Europe*, New York: Viking.

Rothstein, G. (1899), *Die Dynastie der Lahmiden in al-Hîra: Ein Versuch zur Arabisch-Persischen Geschichte zur Zeit der Sasaniden*, Berlin.

Roueché, C. M. (1998), 'Provincial governors and their titulature in the sixth century', *Antiquité Tardive* 6, 83–9.

Roueché, C. M. (ed.) (2000), 'Le *de Aedificiis* de Procope: Le texte et les réalités documentaires', *Antiquité Tardive* 8, 7–180.

Rousseau, Ph. (1998), 'Procopius' Buildings and Justinian's pride', *Byzantion* 68, 121–30.

Roussel, P. (1939), 'Un monument d'Hiérapolis-Bambykè relative à paix <<perpétuelle>> de 532 ap. J.-C.', in *Mélanges syriens offerts a M. René Dussaud*, Paris: P. Geuthner, vol. 1, 367–72.

Rubin, B. (1960, 1995), *Das Zeitalter Iustinians*, 2 vols, Berlin: De Gruyter.

Rubin, Z. (1989), 'Byzantium and South Arabia: The policy of Anastasius', in D. H. French and C. S. Lightfoot (eds), *The Eastern Frontier of the Roman Empire*, Oxford: BAR, 383–420.

Rubin, Z. (1995), 'The reforms of Khusro Anushirwan', in A. Cameron (ed.), *The Byzantine and Early Islamic Near East, Vol. 3: States, Resources and Armies*, Princeton: Darwin Press, 227–97.

Ruffini, G. R. (2008), *Social Networks in Byzantine Egypt*, Cambridge: Cambridge University Press.

Rummel, P. von (2016), 'The transformation of ancient land- and cityscapes in early medieval North Africa', in S. T. Stevens and J. P. Conant (eds), *North Africa under Byzantium and Early Islam*, Washington, DC: Dumbarton Oaks Research Library and Collection, 105–17.

Ruscu, D. (2008), 'The revolt of Vitalianus and the "Scythian Controversy"', *Byzantinische Zeitschrift* 101, 773–85.

Russo, E. (2004), 'La scultura di S. Polieucto e la presenza della Persia nella cultura aristica di Constantinopoli nel VI secolo', in *La Persia e Bisanzio: Atti del Convegno internazionale (Roma, 14–18 ottobre 2002)*, Rome: Accademia nazionale dei Lincei, 737–826.

Sabin, P., H. van Wees and M. Whitby (2007), *The Cambridge History of Greek and Roman Warfare, Vol. 2: Rome from the Late Republic to the Late Empire*, Cambridge: Cambridge University Press.

Saliou, C. (ed.) (2005), *Gaza dans l'Antiquité Tardive: Archéologie, Rhétorique, et Histoire: Actes du Colloque International de Poitiers, 6–7 mai 2004*, Salerno: Helios.

Saradi, H. (2006), *The Byzantine City in the Sixth Century: Literary Images and Historical Reality*, Athens: Society of Messenian Archaeological Studies.

Sarantis, A. (2009), 'War and diplomacy in Pannonia and the north-west Balkans during the reign of Justinian: The Gepid threat and imperial responses', *DOP* 64, 15–40.

Sarantis, A. (2013), 'Fortifications in Africa: A bibliographic essay', in A. Sarantis and N. Christie (eds), *War and Warfare in Late Antiquity: Current Perspectives*, Late Antique Archaeology 8, Leiden and Boston: Brill, 297–315.

Sarantis, A. (2016), *Justinian's Balkan Wars: Campaigning, Diplomacy and Development in Illyricum, Thrace and the Northern World A.D. 527–65*, Prenton: Francis Cairns Publications.

Sarantis, A., and N. Christie (eds) (2013), *War and Warfare in Late Antiquity: Current Perspectives*, 2 vols, Late Antique Archaeology 8, Leiden and Boston: Brill.

Sarris, P. (2002), 'The Justinianic Plague: Origins and effects', *Continuity and Change* 17, 169–82.

Sarris, P. (2006), *Economy and Society in the Age of Justinian*, Cambridge: Cambridge University Press.

Sarris, P. (2011), *Empires of Faith: The Fall of Rome to the Rise of Islam*, Oxford: Oxford University Press.

Sartre, M. (1982), *Trois Études sur l'Arabie Romaine et Byzantine*, Brussels: Revue d'études latines.

Sauer, E. (2017), *Sasanian Persia: Between Rome and the Steppes of Eurasia*, Edinburgh: Edinburgh University Press.

Sauer, E., T. J. Wilkinson, H. O. Rekavandi and J. Nokandeh (2013), *Persia's Imperial Power in Late Antiquity: The Great Wall of Gorgān and Frontier Landscapes of Sasanian Iran*, British Institute of Persian Studies Archaeological Monographs Series II, Oxford: Oxbow Books.

Scarborough, J. (2013), 'Theodora, Aëtius of Amida and Procopius: Some possible connections', *GRBS* 53, 742–62.

Schibille, N. (2014), *Hagia Sophia and the Byzantine Aesthetic Experience*, Farnham: Ashgate.

Schindler, C. (2009), *Per Carmina Laudes: Untersuchungen zur spätantike Verspanegyrik von Claudian bis Coripp*, Berlin: De Gruyter.

Schwartz, E. (1940), 'Zur Kirchenpolitik Justinians', *Sitzungsberichte der Bayerischen Akademie der Wissenschaften* 2, 32–81.

Scott, R. (1981), 'Malalas and Justinian's codification', in E. and M. Jeffreys and A. Moffatt (eds), *Byzantine Papers: Proceedings of the First Australian Byzantine Studies Conference, Canberra, 17–19 May 1978*, Byzantina Australiensia V.1, Canberra: Australian Association for Byzantine Studies, 21–31.

Scott, R. (1985), 'Malalas, the *Secret History*, and Justinian's propaganda', *DOP* 39, 99–109.

Scott, R. (1992), 'Diplomacy in the sixth century: The evidence of John Malalas', in J. Shepard and S. Franklin (eds), *Byzantine Diplomacy: Papers from the Twenty-Fourth Spring Symposium of Byzantine Studies*, Aldershot: Variorum, 159–65.

Scott, R. (1996), 'Writing the reign of Justinian: Malalas *versus* Theophanes', in P. Allen and E. Jeffreys (eds), *The Sixth Century: End or Beginning?*, Byzantina Australiensia 10, Brisbane: Australian Association for Byzantine Studies, 20–34.

Sessa, K. (2016), 'The Roman Church and its bishops', in J. J. Arnold, M. S. Bjornlie and K. Sessa (eds), *A Companion to Ostrogothic Italy*, Leiden and Boston: Brill, 425–50.

Shahîd, I. (1964), 'Byzantino-Arabica: The Conference of Ramla AD 524', *Journal of Near Eastern Studies* 23, 115–31.

Shahîd, I. (1984), *Byzantium and the Arabs in the Fourth Century*, Washington, DC: Dumbarton Oaks Research Library and Collection.

Shahîd, I. (1989), *Byzantium and the Arabs in the Fifth Century*, Washington, DC: Dumbarton Oaks Research Library and Collection.

Shahîd, I. (1995), *Byzantium and the Arabs in the Sixth Century*, Washington, DC: Dumbarton Oaks Research Library and Collection.

Shahîd, I. (2002), *Byzantium and the Arabs in the Sixth Century, Vol. 2, Part 1: Toponymy, Monuments, Historical Geography, and Frontier Studies*, Washington, DC: Dumbarton Oaks Research Library and Collection.

Shahîd, I. (2010), *Byzantium and the Arabs in the Sixth Century, Vol. 2, Part 2: Economic, Social and Cultural History*, Washington, DC: Dumbarton Oaks Research Library and Collection.

Shayegan, M. R. (2011), *Arsacids and Sasanians: Political Ideology in Post-Hellenistic and Late Antique Persia*, Cambridge: Cambridge University Press.

Signes Codoñer, J. (2003), 'Prokops *Anecdota* und Justinians Nachfolge', *Jahrbuch der Österreichischen Byzantinistik* 53, 47–82.

Sirks, A. J. B. (2008), 'The colonate in Justinian's reign', *JRS* 98, 120–43.

Sivan, H. (2008), *Palestine in Late Antiquity*, Oxford: Oxford University Press.

Smith, R. R. R. (1999), 'Late antique portraits in a public context: Honorific statuary at Aphrodisias in Caria, A.D. 300–600', *JRS* 89, 155–89.

Smith, S. D. (2019), *Greek Epigram and Byzantine Culture: Gender, Desire, and Denial in the Age of Justinian*, Cambridge: Cambridge University Press.

Snively, C. S. (2001), 'Justiniana Prima (Caričin Grad)', *Reallexikon für Antike und Christentum* 19, 638–68.
Sotinel, C. (1992), 'Autorité pontificale et pouvoir imperial sous le règne de Justinien: Le pape Vigile', *Mélanges de l'École française de Rome: Antiquité* 104.1, 439–63.
Sotinel, C. (2000), 'Le concile, l'empereur, l'évêque', in S. Elm, É. Rebillard and A. Romano (eds), *Orthodoxie, Christianisme, Histoire/Orthodoxy, Christianity, History*, Rome: École française de Rome, 275–99.
Sotinel, C. (2005), 'Emperors and popes in the sixth century', in M. Maas (ed.), *The Cambridge Companion to the Age of Justinian*, Cambridge: Cambridge University Press, 267–90.
Sotinel, C. (2010), *Church and Society in Late Antique Italy and Beyond*, Aldershot: Variorum.
Speigl, J. (1984), 'Das Religionsgespräch mit den severianischen Bischöfen in Konstantinopel im Jahr 532', *Annuarium Historiae Conciliorum* 16, 264–85.
Speigl, J. (1994), 'Die Synode von 536 in Konstantinopel', *OS* 43, 105–53.
Speigl, J. (1995), 'Formula Iustiniani: Kircheneinigung mit kaiserlichen Glaubensbekenntnissen (Codex Iustinianus I.1.5–8)', *Ostkirchliche Studien* 44, 105–34.
Stathakopoulos, D. (2000), 'The Justinianic plague revisited', *BMGS* 24, 256–76.
Stathakopoulos, D. (2004), *Famine and Pestilence in the Late Roman and Early Byzantine Empire: A Systemic Survey of Subsistence Crises and Epidemics*, Birmingham: Ashgate.
Stein, E. (1949), *Histoire du Bas-Empire, Tome II: De la Disparition de l'Empire d'Occident à la Mort de Justinien (476–565)*, Paris: Desclée de Brouwer.
Stevens, S. T., and J. P. Conant (eds) (2016), *North Africa under Byzantium and Early Islam*, Washington, DC: Dumbarton Oaks Research Library and Collection.
Straw, C. (2007), 'Much ado about nothing: Gregory the Great's apology to the Istrians', in C. M. Chazelle and C. Cubitt (eds), *The Crisis of the Oikoumene: The Three Chapters and the Failed Quest for Unity in the Sixth-Century Mediterranean*, Turnhout: Brepols, 121–60.
Tate, G. (1999), 'La route de la soie au VIe siècle', *Les Annales archéologiques de Syrie* 43, 195–201.
Tate, G. (2004), *Justinien: L'Épopée de l'Empire d'Orient*, Paris: Fayard.
Taylor, R. (1996), 'A literary and structural analysis of the first dome of Justinian's Hagia Sophia, Constantinople', *Journal of the Society of Architectural Historians* 55, 66–78.
Thiel, R. (1999), *Simplikios und das Ende der neuplatonischen Schule in Athen*, Mainz: Akademie der Wissenschaften und der Literatur.
Toivanen, H. R. (2003–4), 'The Church of St. Polyeuktos: Archaeology and texts', *Acta Byzantina Fennica* 2, 127–59.
Topping, E. C. (1976), 'The Apostle Peter, Justinian, and Romanos the Melodos', *BMGS* 2, 1–15.

Topping, E. C. (1977), 'Romanos, "On the entry into Jerusalem": A *Basilikos Logos*', *Byzantion* 47, 65–91.

Topping, E. C. (1978), 'On Earthquakes and Fires: Romanos' encomium to Justinian', *Byzantinische Zeitschrift* 71, 22–35.

Töth, A. J. (2017), 'John Lydus – Pagan and Christian', in M. Sághy and E. M. Schoolman, *Pagans and Christians in the Late Roman Empire: New Evidence, New Approaches (4th–8th Centuries)*, Budapest: Central European University Press, 59–68.

Treadgold, W. (2007), *The Early Byzantine Historians*, New York: Palgrave.

Trombley, F. R. (1985), 'Paganism in the Greek world at the end of antiquity: The case of rural Anatolia and Greece', *Harvard Theological Review* 78, 327–52.

Trombley, F. R. (1994a), *Hellenic Religion and Christianisation c. 370–529*, Leiden: Brill.

Trombley, F. R. (1994b), 'Religious transition in sixth-century Syria', *Byzantinische Forschungen* 20, 153–95.

Trombley, F. R. (1997), 'War and society in rural Syria c. 502–613 A.D.: Observations on the epigraphy', *BMGS* 21, 154–209.

Trousset, P. (2003), 'Les limites sud de la reoccupation byzantine', *Antiquité Tardive* 10, 143–50.

Ure, P. N. (1951), *Justinian and his Age*, Harmondsworth: Penguin.

Uthemann, K.-H. (1999), 'Kaiser Justinian als Kirchenpolitiker und Theologe', *Augustinianum* 39, 5–83.

Uthemann, K.-H. (2006), 'The Emperor Justinian', in A. De Berardino (ed.), *Patrology: The Eastern Fathers from the Council of Chalcedon (451) to John of Damascus (d. 750)*, Cambridge: James Clarke, 53–92.

Vasiliev, A. A. (1950), *Justin the First: An Introduction to the Epoch of Justinian the Great*, Cambridge, MA: Harvard University Press.

Vitiello, M. (2006), '"Nourished at the breast of Rome": The queens of Ostrogothic Italy and the education of the Roman elite', *Rheinische Museum für Philologie* 149, 398–412.

Vitiello, M. (2014), *Theodahad: A Platonic King at the Collapse of Ostrogothic Italy*, Toronto and London: University of Toronto Press.

Vitiello, M. (2017), *Amalasuintha: The Transformation of Queenship in the Post-Roman World*, Philadelphia: University of Pennsylvania Press.

Vössing, K. (2010), 'Africa zwischen Vandalen, Mauren und Byzantinern (533–548 n. Chr.)', *ZAC* 14, 196–225.

Ward-Perkins, B. (1997), 'Catastrophists, and the towns of post-Roman northern Italy', *Papers of the British School at Rome* 65, 157–76.

Ward-Perkins, B. (2005), *The Fall of Rome and the End of Civilisation*, Oxford: Oxford University Press.

Watts, E. J. (2004), 'Justinian, Malalas, and the end of Athenian philosophical teaching in AD 529', *JRS* 94, 168–83.

Watts, E. J. (2005), 'Where to live the philosophical life in the sixth century? Damascius, Simplicius and the return from Persia', *GRBS* 45, 285–315.

Watts, E. J. (2006), *City and School in Late Antique Athens and Alexandria*, Berkeley and London: University of California Press.

Watts, E. J. (2010), *Riot in Alexandria: Tradition and Group Dynamics in Late Antique Pagan and Christian Communities*, Berkeley: University of California Press.

Webb, R. (2008), *Demons and Dancers: Performance in Late Antiquity*, Cambridge, MA: Harvard University Press.

Weitzmann, K. (1976), *The Monastery of Saint Catherine on Mount Sinai: The Icons, Vol. 1: From the Sixth to the Tenth Century*, Princeton: Princeton University Press.

Weitzmann, K. (ed.) (1979), *Age of Spirituality: Late Antique and Early Christian Art, Third to Seventh Century*, New York: Metropolitan Museum of Art.

Welsby, D. A. (2002), *The Medieval Kingdoms of Nubia: Pagans, Christians and Muslims along the Middle Nile*, London: British Museum Press.

Whelan, R. (2018), *Being Christian in Vandal Africa: The Politics of Orthodoxy in the Post-Imperial West*, Oakland: University of California Press.

Whitby, Mary (1985), 'The occasion of Paul the Silentiary's *Ekphrasis* of S. Sophia', *CQ* 35, 215–28.

Whitby, Mary (1987), 'On the omission of a ceremony in mid-sixth-century Constantinople: Candidati, Curopalatus, Silentiarii, Excubitores and Others', *Historia* 36, 462–88.

Whitby, Mary (2003), 'The vocabulary of praise in verse celebration of 6th-century building achievements: *AP* 2.398–406, *AP* 9.656, *AP* 1.10 and Paul the Silentiary's description of St Sophia', in D. Accorinti and P. Chuvin (eds), *Des géants à Dionysos: Mélanges de mythologie et de poésie grecques offerts à Francis Vian*, Alessandria: Edizioni dell'Orso, 593–606.

Whitby, Mary (2006), 'The St. Polyeuktos epigram (AP 10): A literary perspective', in S. F. Fitzgerald (ed.), *Greek Literature in Late Antiquity: Dynamism, Didacticism, Classicism*, Aldershot: Ashgate, 159–88.

Whitby, Michael (1985), 'Justinian's bridge over the Sangarius and the date of Procopius' *De Aedificiis*', *JHS* 105, 129–54.

Whitby, Michael (1989), 'Procopius and Antioch', in D. H. French and C. S. Lightfoot, *The Eastern Frontier of the Roman Empire: Proceedings of a Colloquium Held at Antioch in September 1988*, BAR International Series 553, British Institute of Archaeology at Ankara Monograph 11, Oxford: BAR, 537–53.

Whitby, Michael (1991), 'John of Ephesus and the Pagans: Pagan survivals in the sixth century', in M. Salamon (ed.), *Paganism in the Later Roman Empire and in Byzantium*, Cracow: Universitas.

Whitby, Michael (2001), 'Pride and prejudice in Procopius' *Buildings*: Imperial images in Constantinople', *Antiquité Tardive* 8, 59–66.

White, D. (1982), 'Property rights of women: The changes in the Justinianic legislation regarding the dowry and the parapherna', *Jahrbuch der Österreichischen Byzantinistik* 32, 539–48.

Whittow, M. (1990), 'Ruling the late Roman and early Byzantine city: A continuous history', *Past and Present* 129, 3–29.

Whittow, M. (1999), 'Rome and the Jafnids: Writing the history of a sixth-century tribal dynasty', in J. H. Humphrey (ed.), *The Roman and Byzantine Near East, Vol. 2: Some Recent Archaeological Research*, JRA Supplement 31, Portsmouth, RI: JRA, 207–24.

Wickham, C. (2005), *Framing the Early Middle Ages: Europe and the Mediterranean 400–800*, Oxford: Oxford University Press.

Wiemer, H.-U. (2013), 'Die Goten in Italien: Wandlungen und Zerfall einer Gewaltgemeinschaft', *Historische Zeitschrift* 296.3, 593–628.

Wildburg, C. (2005), 'Philosophy in the age of Justinian', in M. Maas (ed.), *The Cambridge Companion to the Age of Justinian*, Cambridge: Cambridge University Press, 316–40.

Wilhite, D. E. (2017), *Ancient African Christianity: An Introduction to a Unique Context and Tradition*, London: Routledge.

Winkler, S. (1965), 'Die Samariter in den Jahren 529/30', *Klio* 43–5, 435–57.

Wolfram, H. (1988), *History of the Goths*, trans. T. J. Dunlap, Berkeley: University of California Press.

Wolfram, H. (1997), *The Roman Empire and its Germanic Peoples*, trans. T. J. Dunlap, Berkeley: University of California Press.

Wood, P. (2011), 'Being Roman in Procopius' Vandal "Wars"', *Byzantion* 81, 424–47.

Wood, P. (2014), 'Christianity and the Arabs in the sixth century', in J. H. F. Dijkstra and G. Fisher (eds), *Inside and Out: Interaction between Rome and the Peoples on the Arabian and Egyptian Frontiers in Late Antiquity*, Leuven: Peeters, 353–68.

Wroth, W. W. (1908), *Catalogue of the Imperial Byzantine Coins in the British Museum*, 2 vols, London: British Museum.

Yardley, J. C. (1980), 'Paulus Silentiarius, Ovid, and Propertius', *CQ* 30.1, 239–43.

Zarini, V. (2003), *Rhétorique, poétique, spiritualité: La technique épique de Corippe dans la Johannide*, Turnhout: Brepols.

Zuckerman, C. (2002), 'The dedication of a statue of Justinian at Antioch', in T. Drew-Bear, M. Taslialan and Ch. M. Thomas (eds), *Actes du Ier Congrès International sur Antioche de Pisidie*, Lyon: Université Lumière-Lyon 2, and Paris: De Boccard, 243–55.

Zuckerman, C. (2003), 'La haute hiérarchie militaire en Afrique byzantine', *Antiquité Tardive* 10, 169–75.

Zuckerman, C. (2004), 'Les deux Dioscore d'Aphroditè ou les limites de la pétition', in D. Feissel and J. Gascou (eds), *La petition à Byzance*, Centre de recherche d'histoire et civilisation de Byzance Monographies 14, Paris: Association des amis du Centre d'histoire et civilisation de Byzance, 75–94.

Zuckerman, C. (2013), 'Silk "Made in Byzantium": A study of economic policies of emperor Justinian', *Travaux et Mémoires* 17, 323–50.

Index

Page numbers in *italics* denote figures and maps

Abasgi, 36, 42, 44, 92
Ablabius, 118
Abraham (Ḥimyarite king), 45
Abraham (Justin's envoy), 17
Abraham bar Kaili, 80
Abramus, 46–7
Abundantius, 16
Abyssinia *see* Ethiopia
Acacius (Theodora's father), 23
Acacius, Patriarch of
  Constantinople, 14–15,
  77, 145
Academy of Athens, 5, 120–3
Aetherius, 103, 118
Africa *see* North Africa
Agapetus, Pope, 65, 79–80, 178
Agapetus, Deacon, *Advice to the
  Emperor Justinian*, 10, 91,
  131–2, 183
Agathias, 7, 10, 43, 59, 72–3, 113,
  121, 160, 174, 175, 199
  beliefs, 10, 127–8
  Cycle, 7, 127, 130
  The Histories, 7, 174, 175, 199
Agbar, 159–60
Ain Djelloula (*Cululis*),
  inscription, 53–4, 166
Alans, 42, 98

Albinus, 16, 146
Alexander (the 'snips'), 57
Alexandria, 23, 81, 87, 90, 92
Alexandrian School, 121–2
Amalafrida, 15
Amalaric, 73
Amalasuntha, 15–16, 24–6, 61,
  63–5, 152, 170–2
Amantius, 13, 18
Amida, 159
'Amr, 44
Anastasius, Emperor, 12–15, 18,
  20–1, 25, 30–1, 105, 126, 131,
  150, 158
  building works, 114, 116
  Ghassanids, 18, 35
  Persian War, 39, 158
  religious policy (miaphysitism)
  14, 77
Anastasius, grandson of
  Theodora, 18
Anastasius, Patriarch of
  Antioch, 87
Anatolius, 138
Andrew, city prefect, 118
Anicia Juliana, 14–15, 19–20, 94,
  112, 148–9
Anonymus Valesianus 16, 146

Anthemius of Tralles, 112
Anthimus, Patriarch of
    Constantinople, 79, 80, 90,
    178, 180
anti-Chalcedonianism, 4, 75–94
    Anastasius, 14
    Ghassanids, 18
    John of Ephesus, 9
    Theoderic, 15
    see also miaphysites
Antioch, 37
    church building, 25
    defence of, 47
    earthquake, 18, 27, 37, 104
    Olympic games, 19, 126
    plague, 190–2
    sack of, 4, 33, 40–1, 48, 115
    paganism, 125
Antiochene christology, 75–6,
    82, 97, 179
Antonina, 25, 26, 28, 41, 179–80
    Procopius, 6–7, 130
aphthartodocetism, 81, 89
Apollinarius, 76, 177, 180
Apsilii, 36, 42
Arabia, 33, 45–6
    map, xviii
Arabs, 34–7, 39, 44–7, 51
Arator, 65
Areobindus, 30
Ariadne, Empress, 25
Arianism (Arian, Arians) 93,
    136
    Goths and Theoderic, 15–16, 62
    persecution of, 166, 167, 185
    Vandals and war in Africa, 50,
    55–6, 73, 80, 111
Aristotle, 122
Armenia, 36, 155–6
    administrative reorganisation
    of, 40, 45, 48, 99, 156

conflict with Persia, 18, 33,
    37–40, 42, 44, 51, 99
Asclepiodotus, 124
Asia Minor, 92, 93
Athalaric, 15, 16, 63, 64, 171–2
Athanagild, 73, 175
Athanasius, 25, 43
Athens, 58, 107, 125, 201;
    see also Academy of Athens
Audoin, 70
Augila, 124
Auximum, 57, 58
Avars, 70, 73, 175

Baduila see Totila
Balkans, 5, 89
    building programme, 6
    conflict in the, 6, 59, 68–73
    map, xix
    plague, 107
    Ostrogoths, 62, 63
bankers' plot, 118
Baresmanas, 157–8
Basilica Cistern, 115, 116
Basilides, 30
Batzas, 39
Belisarius, 28
    conflict with Italy, 57–8, 65
    conflict with Persia, 18, 36–7,
    41, 158
    Dara, 38–9
    Joannina, 25
    Kutrigurs, 72, 175
    Nika riot, 28, 30, 31
    North Africa, 49–53, 164
    Procopius and, 6, 130
    Ravenna, 10, 135
    Silverius, 80
    suspect competence, loyalty,
    47, 72, 118, 130, 165
    Vigilius, 85, 179

Barberini Ivory, 133, *133*, 136
Berbers *see* Moors
Bessas, 42, 43
Bibliotheca Codex, 129
Blemmyes, 46, 128
Boethius, 15–16, 62, 66, 146
  Consolation of Philosophy, 16
  Boethius, praetorian prefect of Africa, 171
Bolum border fort, 38, 39
Book of the Himyarites, 17
brothels, 23–5, 109, 151, 152
Brumalia festival, 11, 126–7, 200–1
Buildings, x, 6, 7, 51, 114, 130, 134, 164
  Augila, Libya, 124
  Balkans, 68–9, 72, *72*
  brothels, 24, 109, 152
  Eastern Frontier, 47–8
  equestrian statue, Augusteum, 114, 134, 196
  Hagia Sophia, 112
  Justiniana Prima, 117
  Mount Sinai, 116, 197
  North Africa, 53, 55
  Python, 25
  water supply, 116, 198
Busta Gallorum, 59

C. J.
  Africa, 52, 53, 111, 164–5
  Armenia, 37, 156
  Constitutio Deo Auctore, 96
  Constitutio Tanta, 97
  Edict of Faith, 79
  Justinian and Justin I, 27
  marriage legislation, 22
  orthodoxy of soldiers (Justin), 15
  pagans and heretics, 27, 121, 124, 128, 153, 198–9
  Theopaschite Edict, 176–7
  women and children, 109–10
Caesarea, Palestine, 37–8, 157
Caesaropapism, 5, 90–3, 94
Callinicum, 39, 41
Cappadocia, 105
Carthage, 49, 50–6, 83–4, 132, 165
Carthago Justiniana, 166–7, 184
Caspian Gates, 34, 39, 41
Cassandria, 173
Cassiodorus, 10, 62, 63, 65–6, 132
  Expositio psalmorum, 132
  Ordo generis Cassiodorum, 132
  Tripartite History, 132
  Variae, 10, 16, 24, 64, 66, 132, 151, 170
Celer, 14–15
Cethegus, 85, 132
Chalcedonianism, 4, 6, 75–94
  al-Ḥārith, 46
  Anicia Juliana, 20
  Cyril, Patriarch of Alexandria, 9
  Euphemia, 22
  Justin, 17
  neo-Chalcedonianism, 84
  Nobadia, 46
  Theoderic, 15
  Theodora, 23, 25
  Vitalian, 13
Childebert, 66–7
Chios, 93
Choricius, 126, 127, 129
  Defence of the Mimes, 125–6
  Oratio XIII, 10–11, 127, 200–1
Chosroes
  Edessa, 159–60
  Eternal Peace, 39, 155
  military action, 34, 40–3, 163
  peace treaty, 160

philosophers, 121
religious policy, 87
succession, 17, 19, 39
tax collection, 105
Theodora, 24
Chronicon Paschale, 8, 28, 30–1, 79, 176–7
church building, 5, 91, 112–16
  Anicia Juliana, 20–1
  North Africa, 55
  Ravenna, 136–7
  Theodora, 25
Church of St Euphemia, Chalcedon, 85
Church of St John, Pamphylia, 27
Church of St John the Theologian, Ephesus, 115
Church of SS Michael and Gabriel, 136–7, *136*
Church of SS Peter and Paul, 131, 202
Church of St Polyeuktos, Constantinople, *20*, 20–1, 34, 94, 147–8
Church of SS Sergius and Bacchus, 20–1, *21*, 94, 114, 130–1, 149–50, 202
Church of the Holy Apostles Peter and Paul, 114–15, 202
Church of the Nativity, Bethlehem, 116
Church of the Panagia Kanakaria at Lynthrankomi, Cyprus, 137
circus factions, 18, 19, 23–4, 29–30, *29*, 118
Cistern of Philoxenos, 116, *116*
Codex Marcianus Graecus, 97
Codex of Justinian (also *Codex Iustinianus*; Code), 11, 54, 67, 79, 91, 97, 98, 110, 121, 172
Codex Repetitae Praelectionis, 96

Codex Sinopensis, 138
Codex Theodosianus see Theodosian Code
coinage,
  Africa, 53
  Justin I and Justinian, 27, 154
  Justin II, 15
  Justinian, 67, 102, 108–9, *109*, 133, 189
  Theodahad, 64, *64*, 65
  Theoderic, 61, *61*
  Theodora, 25
  Theudebert, 60, *60*
Collectio Avellana, 9, 14, 56, 79–81, 145
Constantine, Emperor, 3, 31, 75, 90, 113, 149, 193
Constantine (quaestor), 86
Constantine Porphyrogenitus, *de Caeremoniis*, 44
Constantiniolus, 30
Constantinople
  buildings, 5–6, 9, 20, 114, 116–17, 134, 140, 139, *139*
  coins, 27
  Huns, 69
  and Italy, 15, 58, 65, 67, 135–6
  Kutrigurs, 72–3
  map, *xvi*
  and Persia, 36, 42
  plague, 107
  riots, 118
  writers in, 6, 8–10, 129, 131–2
Constantinopolitan Creed, 76, 210
Constitutio Cordi, 96, 98
Constitutio Deo Auctore, 96–7
Constitutio Imperatoriam Maiestatem, 97
Constitutio Omnen, 98
Constitutio Summa, 96, 98
Constitutio Tanta, 97

Corippus, 50, 132
  Iohannis or *de Bellis Libycis*, 51
  In laudem Iustini minoris, 49, 163
Corpus Juris Civilis, 95–8
Cosmas Indicopleustes, *Christian Topography*, 128
Council of Antioch, 179
Council of Chalcedon, 75–94, 176, 179, 183, 185–6
  Anthimus, Patriarch of Constantinople, 178–9
  Conversations of 532, 78–9
  Council of 553, 84, 86
  Edict of Faith, 79
  Facundus, 167
  Henoticon, 14
  Justin I, 150–1
  nature of Christ, 4
  Theodora, 161, 179, 185–6
  Theopaschite formula, 77
  Three Chapters Controversy, 56, 167–8
  Vigilius, 80
Council of Constantinople 553, 4, 9, 82–7, 90, 94, 166, 180, 183
Council of Ephesus 431, 4, 76, 91, 179, 181, 183
Council of Ephesus ('Robber') 499, 76, 78
Council of Nicaea, 4, 179, 183
Council of Trento 154–5, 91
Cyprianus, 146
Cyril, Patriarch of Alexandria
  dualism, 75–6
  Third Letter to Nestorius, 76, 84
  Three Chapters Controversy, 82, 86
  Twelve Anathemas, 76, 180–1

Cyril of Scythopolis
  Life of St Sabas, 9, 38, 55, 82, 93, 166, 181, 185

Dagisthaeus, 42
Dalmatia, 57–9, 64
Damascius, 121, 199–200
Dara, 33, 38–9, 41, 43–4, 155
Dariel Pass *see* Caspian Gates
Definition of Faith, 76, 79, 84, 90
Dhu Nuwas, 16
Dialogue on Political Science, 10, 128
Digest, 96–8, 187; *see also Pandects*
Dinogetia, *71*
Diodore of Tarsus, 75
Dioscorus, Patriarch of Alexandria, 78
Dioscorus of Aphrodito, 128
diptychs
  consular, 19, 135–6, 146–7
  sacred, 14, 77–8, 82, 181
  see also Barberini
Dorotheus
  lawyer, 186–7
  Magister militum per Armeniam, 38
dyophysites, 76–7, 79

earthquakes
  Antioch, 18, 25, 27, 37, 78, 104
  Constantinople, 80
  Hagia Sophia, 112, 125, 131
  Kontakion, 192–4
  legislation, 110
Eastern Frontier, 33–48
  map, *xvii*
Edessa, 18, 41, 138, 159
Edict 13, 3, 97, 105
Edict of Faith, 79
Edict of Toleration, 50

Egypt
  Aphthartodocetism, 81
  buildings, 6
  Dioscorus of Aphrodito, 128
  foreign policy, 33, 35–6, 46, 92
  great estates, 107
  Jacob Baradaeus, 92
  John the Cappadocian, 119
  law codes, 96
  map, *xviii*
  miaphysitism, 88–9, 161
  Philae temples, 123
  plague, 107
  Severus, Patriach of
    Antioch, 80
Ephrem of Antioch, 78, 79, 80,
  83, 84
Epiphanius, Patriarch of
  Constantinople, 79, 91, 110
Epistulae Austrasicae XX, 169
Eraric, 58
Ethiopia, 16–17, 46–7, 190
Eudaemon, 30
Euphemia, 14–15, 21–2, 26
Euphrasius, Bishop of Poreč, 137
Euphrasius, Patriarch of
  Antioch, 78
Eusebius, city prefect, 146
Eusebius (of Caesarea), 159
Eutharic, 15
Eutyches, 78, 176–7, 178, 183
Eutychius, 10, 85, 86, 87, 90, 180
Evagrius Scholasticus
  Aetherius, 103
  aphthartodocetism 87, 182–3
  client kings, 92
  Council of 553, 180–2
  Ecclesiastical History, 9
  Edessa, 41, 159–60
  Origenism, 82, 85
  plague, 107, 190–2
  Severus, 79
  Theodora, 93, 185–6

factions, 18–19, 21, 23, 27–32,
  29, 40, 47, 118
Facundus of Hermiane, 83–4
  *In Defence of the Three
  Chapters*, 56, 167
Felix III, Pope, 14
Ferrandus, 56, 84
festivals, 5, 11, 120, 125–7, 131
Fiesole, 57
*Fifty Decisions (Quinquaginta
  Decisiones)*, 96
Formula of Reunion, 76
Franks, 7, 59–60, 66–7, 70, 168–9

Gaius, 97, 187
games, 19, 30, 118, 126
Gaza, 10, 125–6, 201
Geiseric, 50
Gelimer, 49–51, 61, 162–4, 166
George, 118
Gepids, 63, 69, 70, 73, 93, 169–70
Germanus, 12, 40, 51, 59, 69
Ghassānids, 18, 35, 45–6, 92
Golden Horn, 14
Goths, 98, 169–70
  Agapetus, 79
  Amalasuntha, 171
  Chalke mosaic, 134, 164
  Procopius, 130
  recovering Italy, 57–60, 175
  Sabas, 93
  Silverius, 80
  Sirmium, 69
  Vigilius, 83
  see also Ostrogoths; Visigoths
Gourgenes, 37, 44
granaries, 116–17
Gratiana, 63

Gratus, 14, 145
Great Palace, 6, 138–9
Greek Anthology, 147–8, 198, 202
  Sangarius Bridge, 117, 198
  Spain, 73
  SS Peter and Paul, 131, 202
  St Polyeuktos, 20, 147–8
Gregory of Tours, 63
Grepes, 69, 92, 184
Grod, 92, 184–5
Gubazes, 42–4
Gudeliva, 24, 64
Guntarith, 51

Hadrian, 157
Hagia Eirene, 114, *114*
Hagia Sophia, 3, 20, 30, 32, 112–14, *113*, 119, 140
  Agapetus, 131
  On the Inauguration of St Sophia, 131
  Paul the Silentiary, 112, 131, 194
  Procopius, 6
  Romanos, 11, 131
al-Ḥārith, 35, 37, 41, 43–6
Harran (Carrhae), 121, 138
Hecebolus of Tyre, 23–4
Heliopolis, 125, 138
Hellenes *see* paganism
heretics, 27, 88, 93, 107, 110–12, 120–1, 124–5, 153, 176, 181, 198–9
Hermogenes, 38, 96, 158
Heruls, 69, 92, 184
Hildebad (Ildebadus), 58
Hilderic, 15, 50, 63, 164
Ḥimyarites, 16–17, 45, 47, 92
hippodrome, 14, 19, 23, 26, 28, 30–1, 146
homosexuality, 110–12, 130

Honorius, 169–70, 185
Hormisdas, Palace of, 15, 79
Hormisdas, Pope, 2, 14–16, 77, 80, 145
  libellus, 15, 79
Ḥujrids (Kindites), 35, 47
Huns, 42, 69, 172–3, 175, 184–5
  Sabir, 17, 34, 42–3
Hypatius, 15, 18, 28, 31, 36

Ibas, Bishop of Edessa, 56, 76, 78–9, 82–3, 86, 167, 179, 180–1
Iberia, 17, 36–7, 42–4
Illyria, 80, 86, 89
Illyricum, 69, 98, 129, 173
Indulf, 58
Innocentius, Bishop of Maronia, 78
inscriptions
  from Ain Djelloula (*Cululis*), 53–4, 166
  Hierapolis column, 39
  Justinian and Theodora, 24
  Justinian diptych, 19, 146
  Philae temples, 123
  San Vitale, Ravenna, 135
  Sangarius Bridge, 130
  Sinai, 115–16
  St Polyeuktos, Constantinople, 20, 147–9
  SS Sergius and Bacchus, 130, 149–50
Institutes (Institutiones), 97, 186
Isidore of Miletus, 112
Isidore of Seville
  History of the Goths 73, 175
Italy
  map, *xxi*
  relations with the Church, 15–16, 56, 86–7

war with, 4, 6, 40, 50, 57–60, 66–8, 164, 169
writers in, 132

Jacob Baradaeus, 45–6, 83, 92
Jacob of Edessa, *Chronicon*, 15
Jacob of Serûg, 125
Jacobatius, Cardinal, 91
Jafnids, 35, 37, 40, 45–8
Jerusalem, 5, 9, 19, 25, 41, 79, 82, 112, 115, 180, 193
Jews, 16–17, 27, 37, 101, 107, 110, 125, 153, 167
Joannina, 25
John (nephew of Vitalian), 58–9
John (Theodora's grandson), 25
John, *dux* of the Thebaid, 128
John, Pope, 16, 205
John bar Aphtonia,
  Life of Severus of Antioch, 78, 125, 176
John II, Pope, 56, 79
John III, Pope, 87
John, Patriarch of Antioch, 76, 179
John of Ephesus
  conversions, 93, 124–5
  Ecclesiastical History, 9, 23, 93
  Jacob Baradaeus, 92
  Lives of the Eastern Saints, 9, 23, 93
  Nubia mission, 46, 92, 124, 161
  Theodora, 23–4, 150
John of Tella, 78, 80
John Philoponus, 85, 87, 122, 128
John the Cappadocian
  criticism of, 10, 102, 118
  Greek language, 98
  laws, 99, 100, 187–90
  Nika riot, 27–30
  North Africa, 50
  Theodora, 25, 118–19

John the Lydian (John Lydus)
  beliefs, 10, 122, 127–9
  Brumalia festival, 127
  criticisms by, 102, 103, 105, 118
  de Magistratibus (On the Magistracies), 10, 129, 163
  de Mensibus, 129
  de Ostensibus, 129
  Hagia Sophia, 112
  links with other writers, 132
  patronage, 129
  Theodora, 24
  Tribonian, 97
  writers, 10
John Troglita, 51, 132
Jordanes
  Gothic History (Getica), 73, 132
  Roman History (Romana), 62, 132
Julian (Samaritan leader), 37–8
Julian of Halicarnassus, 81, 87
Julianus Argentarius, 137
Junillus,
  Handbook of the Basic Principles of Divine Law, (*Instituta Regularia Divinae Legis*) 91–2, 132
Justin I, 12–18
  Agapetus, 178
  Albinus, 146
  Huns, 172
  Justinian and, 12–13, 18–21, 26–7, 89, 124, 126, 133, 140, 145, 154
  Lazica, 44
  Najran massacre, 46
  persecutions, 45
  religious policy, 77, 150–1
  Scythian monks, 84

Justin II
  accession, 103
  Aetherius, 103
  Agathias, 130
  coins, 15
  Corippus, 132
  legislation, 97, 110
  Sophia, 25
  subsidies, 73
  Vigilius, 85
Justinian
  amenities and public works, 116–17
  building programme, *72*, 112–17
  Church and state, 75–94
  codification of the laws, 95–100
  coins, *109*
  Conversations of 532, 78–9
  Council of 553, 84–7
  culture and society, 120–39
  eastern frontier, 20–48
  festivals, 125–7
  governing the empire, 95–119
  images of, 132–7, *134*, *135*
  Justin, 26–7
  longevity and legacy, 140–1
  Nika riot, 27–32
  Novels, 100–12; finance, 104–9; social reform, 109–10; religious legislation 110–12
  On the Orthodox Faith, 181
  paganism, 120–5
  panegyrical works, 10–11
  patronage and propaganda 129–32
  renovatio, 62, 66–8
  rise to power, 18–32
  'sleepless emperor', 141
  sources and scholarship, 3–11
  Theodora, 21–6, 93–4
  Theopaschite Formula, 8, 77–8, 80, 88, 124, 176–7
  Three Chapters Controversy, 81–4
  wars of reconquest, 49–74; North Africa, 49–56; Italy 57–68; Balkans, 68–73; Spain, 73–4
Justiniana Prima, 40, 68–9, 80, 83–4, 117, *117*, 173–4, 183

Kavadh, 17–9, 34–9, 158–9
kontakion, 131; *see also* Romanos
Kutrigurs, 70, 72, 131

Laetus, 164
Lakhmids, 17–18, 35, 45
landowners, 52, 101–3, 106–8, 111
Lazica, 6, 17, 33–48, 155–6, 160
legislation, 95–112
  adiectio sterilium, 108
  city councils, 106–7
  codification of the laws, 27, 95–8
  finance, 104–9
  imperial titles, 98–100
  prefaces, 98–100
  religion, 110–12
  social reforms, 109–10
  women, 22, 24, 40, 104, 109–10
  see also Novels
Leo, Emperor, 12
Leo I, Pope,
  Tome, 76, 78–9, 167
Libelarius, 18
Liberius, 63, 65, 73
Libya, 65, 104, 124, 163–5, 194
Lilybaeum, 63
Lombards, 57, 67, 70, 73, 87,

Long Walls, 69–70, 72, 173–4
Lycaonia, 99, 101, 187–8
Lydia, 101, 129, 199

Malalas, John, 8, 10, 103, 128, 132
  Academy of Athens, 121
  Brumalia festival, 127
  Consulship, 28
  Dara, 39
  factional violence, 27
  Justin I, 18, 27
  legislation, 110
  Nika riot, 30–1
  Persians, 17, 38, 39, 158
  Samaritans, 38
  Theodora, 24–5
Marcellinus *Comes*, 9, 19, 126, 129, 146
Marcellus (banker), 118
Mare, Bishop of Amida, 150–1
Mark the Deacon, 126
Martin, 43
Martyrdom of Arethas, 17
Matasuntha, 15, 57, 59
Maximian, Archbishop of Ravenna, 135–7
Menander the Guardsman, 7–8, 33, 155
Menas, Patriarch of Constantinople, 80, 83, 85, 90, 178, 180, 181
Menas, Praetorian Prefect, 98
Mesopotamia, 33, 36–40, 44, 45, 151
Miaphysites (miaphysitism), 76–83, 89
  Anicia Juliana, 20
  Ethiopia, 16–17
  Ghassānids, 18, 35
  Jafnids, 45–6, 48
  Theodora, 23–5, 92–4, 124
  Three Chapters Controversy, 56
Mihr-Mihroe (Mermeroes), 38, 42–3
Milan, 4, 57, 67, 87, 91
missionary activity, 91–3, 123–4
'monophysites' *see* miaphysites
Mons Lactarius, Campania, 59
Moors, 6, 49–53, 56, 96, 165–6
al-Mundhir, 18, 36–7, 43–8
Mundo, 57, 64, 69
Mundus, 30, 31

Najran, 16–17, 46
Naples, 57, 58, 65
Narses, 7, 28, 31, 38, 58–60, 81, 123
Naṣrids, 35, 37, 40, 44, 45, 47, 48
Nea Church, Jerusalem, 115
Neapolis, 37–8, 157
Nestorianism, 56, 81–2, 87, 90, 91, 94
Nestorius, Patriarch of Constantinople, 75–6, 84, 166, 176–9, 181, 183, 185
Nicene Church, 15, 50, 55–6
Nicene Creed, 76
Nicetius, Bishop of Trier, 94
Nika riot, 4, 19, 27–32, 39, 50, 61, 95, 97–8, 105, 118
  building programme, 114, 140
  Chronicon Paschale, 8
  Dialogue on Political Science, 128
  Kontakion (54), 11, 112, 131
  Pseudo-Zachariah Rhetor, 8–9
Nobadae, 46, 48, 161–2
Nonnus, 54, 166

North Africa, 4, 6, 40, 46, 49–56, 94
  Belisarius, 28
  building programme, 53–5, 166
  Church, 55–6, 80, 83, 86–7, 111, 137, 166–7, 184
  governance and the economy, 52–3
  map, xx
  military action, 50–2, 164–5
  writers from, 132
Noubadia, 124
Novels, 4–5, 11, 95–112, 127, 130
Noviodunum, *71*
Nubia, 46, 92

Olybrius, Emperor, 19
Olybrius, son of Anicia Juliana, 21
Olympic Games, Antioch, 19, 126
On the Inauguration of St Sophia, 131
On the Orthodox [or True] Faith, 84, 181
Origenism, 82, 85–6, 166, 180, 181, 185
Osrhoene, 17, 37, 101
Ostrogoths, 4–5, 16, 61–6
  Cassiodorus, 10, 132
  Italy, military conflict, 58–60
  Marcellinus *Comes*, 129
  Persia, 40
  rule in Italy, 61–6
  Theoderic, 15
  Theodora, 24

paganism, 5–6, 120–8, 138, 140
  conversion, 9, 44, 46, 92–3, 124, 161, 184
  festivals, 11, 19, 131
  legislation and persecution, 27, 88, 110–12, 153, 199, 200
  writers, 7, 10

Palestine, 6, 10, 185
  Chosroes, 41
  Origenism, 82
  Samaritans, 37, 157
  Saracens, 116, 198
Paul, Bishop of Nisibis, 87
Paul, Patriarch of Antioch, 77–8
Paul the Silentiary
  Cycle, 130
  Ekphrasis (Description) of Hagia Sophia, 10, 112–13, 131, 194–5
Paul the Tabennesiote, 81, 90
Pavia, 16, 57–8
Pelagius, Pope, 66–7, 80, 86–7, 90, 171
  Letters, 171
Persia
  Eternal Peace, 27, 34, 36–7, 39–40
  Justin I, 17–18
  peace treaty of 561, 155–6
  philosophers, 121
Persian wars, 33–48, 140
  Agathias, 7
  Dara, 157–8
  John the Lydian, 129
  Menander the Guardsman, 7
  Procopius, 6
  Pseudo-Zachariah Rhetor, 8–9
Peter Barsymes, 72, 108, 118
Peter Mongus, Patriarch of Alexandria, 14
Peter of Jerusalem, 83
Peter the Patrician, 33, 44, 63–4, 85, 118, 155–6
Petra, 40, 42, 151
phantasiasts, 81
Pharangium border fort, 38, 39, 158
Pharas, 162–3
Philae, 46, 92, 122–4, *122, 123*

philosophy
  Academy of Athens, 120–2, 128, 199–200
  Dialogue on Political Science, 128
Phocas, 10, 102, 112, 124–5, 200
Photius, 129
Phrygia, 72, 101
Picenum, 57
Placidus, 171
Plague, 4, 90, 95, 107–9, 119, 141
  Chosroes, 41
  Evagrius Scholasticus, 9, 190–2
  legislation, 99–102
  persecution, 125
  Procopius, 4
  public finances, 107–9
  Tribonian, 97
plerophoria, 78
Pompey, 31
Pontianus, Bishop of Thaenae, 56
Pragmatic Sanction, 67–8, 171
Probus, 30
Procopius, 6–8
  Agbar, 159
  Amalasuntha, 64
  Balkans, 68–70
  'barbarians', 73
  beliefs, 127–8
  brothels, 109
  conflict on the Eastern Frontier, 38
  downward trajectory of Justinian, 119
  Edessa, 159
  Egypt, 46
  factional violence, 29
  Goths, 62
  Justin I and Justinian, 12
  missionary activity, 124
  Nika riot, 30–1
  North Africa, 50–1, 52

Peter Barsymes, 108–9
plague, 4
Theodora, 22, 23, 24, 26
Tribonian, 97
see also Buildings; Secret History; Wars
prostitutes, 21, 24, 109, 151, 152, 192
Pseudo-Dionysius of Tel-Mahre, 9, 17, 92, 125, 184, 200
Pseudo-Zachariah Rhetor, 8–9, 17, 37–8, 78–81, 93, 157, 175
public baths, 116

Ramla conference, 17
Ravenna
  Belisarius, 10
  churches, 115, 134–7
  conflict with Constantinople, 10, 15, 66
  exarch, 67
  Maximian, Archbishop of Ravenna, 91, 94, 135
  Vitigis, 57
  see also San Vitale
Reparatus, 56, 57, 84, 91, 167
Rimini, 57, 58
Romanos the Melode, 11, 131
  On Earthquakes and Fires, 11, 20, 112, 131, 192
Rufinus, 38, 39, 158
Rusticus, 43

Sabas, 9, 93–4, 115, 166, 185; *see also* Cyril of Scythopolis
Sabir Huns, 17, 34, 42–3, *see also* Huns
Samaritans, 37–8, 101, 107, 116, 121, 153, 157, 185, 199
St Catherine monastery, Mount Sinai, 137–8
San Apollinare in Classe, 137

San Apollinare Nuovo, 135–7, *135*
San Vitale, Ravenna, *22*, 22–3, 34, *134*, 135–6
Sangarius Bridge, 117, 130, 198
Sapaudis, 171
Saracens, 44, 116, 159, 185, 198
Sarapanis border fort, 39, 42
Sardou, Victorien, 22
Satala, battle of, 38–9
Scanda border fort, 39, 42
School of Gaza, 10–11, 125–6
Scythian monks, 14, 77, 84
Secret History, 6–7, 12, 28
   Amalasuntha, 64
   criticisms of Justinian, 47, 55, 101–3, 105, 108–11, 119, 130, 172
   foreign policy, 41, 47, 68–9, 73, 89, 172–3
   Libya, 165–6
   prostitutes, 192
   soldiers, 40, 159
   Theodora, 22–4, 26, 41, 47, 93, 149–50, 192
Sena Gallica sea battle, 59
Sergius (banker), 118
Sergius (nephew of Solomon), 51
Sergius, Bishop of Cyrrhus, 15
Serinda (Sogdiana), 47, 162
Severus, Patriarch of Antioch, 23, 78–81, 125, 176, 178–80, 186
Sicily, 50, 57–9, 62, 67, 73, 83, 85–6, 168
Silverius, 80–1, 90, 179
Simeon of Bet Arsham, 17
Sinai, 115–16, 137–8, 197
Singidunum, 69, 170
Sirmium, 69–70, 170
Sittas, 18, 24, 37, 38
Sklaveni, 69, 72

Sleepless Monks, 79, 80, 141
Solomon, 51–4, 166
Sophia, 25, 49, 163
Soterichus, 43
Spain, 15, 73, 94
Stephanus, 168–9
Stephen, Deacon, 83, 151
Suania, 34, 42–3
Summus, 185, 201
Sumyaf 'a Ashw' a, 46
Sunicas, 158
Symeon the Younger, 44
Syria, 35
   Arabs, 45–6
   religious policy, 78–81, 85, 87, 89, 92
   war, 40

tax collection, 27, 29, 52, 57, 67–8, 96, 102–10, 166, 171
Teias, 59
Thebais, 92, 128, 161–2
Theodahad, 57, 61, 64–6
   Agapetus, 79–80
   Pragmatic Sanction, 171–2
   and Theodora, 24, 151–2
   Theudebert, 59
Theoderic, 58, 62–3, 65, 67
   Boethius, 146
   Cassiodorus, 132
   coinage, 61, *61*
   San Apollinare Nuovo, 136–7
   Spain, 73
   Totila, 58–9
Theodora, 21–6, 151, 172, 178
   Amalasuntha, 64, 151–2
   conversions, 45–6, 92, 124, 161
   Brumalia festival, 127
   Chalke Gate mosaic, 134, 164
   Church of SS Sergius and Bacchus, 149

Church of the Holy Apostles,
     73, 115, 131
  death of, 4
  Hagia Sophia, 112
  John the Cappadocian, 118–19
  Nika riot, 28, 31, 154–5
  Pragmatic Sanction, 172
  Procopius, 6–7, 102, 130, 154–5
  religious policy, 93–4, 185
  St Catherine's, 115–16
  San Vitale, Ravenna, *22*, 34, 135
  social reform, 104, 109–10,
     152, 192
  Vigilius, 80, 83, 179
Theodore (son of Peter the
  Patrician), 118
Theodore, Bishop of Bostra, 92
Theodore Ascidas, Bishop of
  Caesarea, 82, 85
Theodore of Mopsuestia, 56,
  75–6, 82, 167, 169, 179, 180–1
Theodore Simus, 37–8
Theodoret, Bishop of Cyrrhus,
  15, 76, 78, 82, 86–7, 167,
  180–1
Theodosian Code, 96, 106, 110,
  209
Theodosius, Patriarch of
  Alexandria, 79, 81, 90, 179–80
Theodosius II, 17, 19, 76, 96, 140
Theodotus, 19
Theopaschite Edict / Formula, 8,
  77–8, 80, 88, 176–7
Theophanes, 18, 28, 31, 73,
  83, 175
Theophilus, 186–7
Thermopylae, 69–70, 72, 117, 173
Theudebert, 58–60, *60*, 70, 169
Thomas of Thessalonica, 78
Thomas, quaestor, 124
Thorison, 70

Thrace, 12, 30, 69, 70, 72, 93
Thrasamund, 15
Three Chapters Controversy, 9,
  56, 73, 81–4, 86, 90, 94, 179
Thucydides, 6, 8, 58, 107, 190
Totila, 57–9, 65, 67–8, 168–9, 172
Tribonian, 28–30, 92, 95, 97,
  119, 132, 186–7
Tribunus, 42
Troparion, 'Only begotten Son',
  79, 178
Tzani, 37, 43, 44, 92, 96
Tzath, 17, 43, 44

Uraias, 57–8
Uthimereos fort, 42
Utrigurs, 70

Valerian, 59
Vandals, 16, 49–56, 96, 98, 104,
  163–5, 167, 169–70, 175
  Chalke Gate, 134, 164
  Hilderic, 15
  imperial ceremonies, 131
  Marcellinus *Comes*, 129
  Procopius, 6, 130
  Sabas, 93
Venetia, 58
Verona, 58
Victor of Tonnena, 51, 56, 132,
  164, 178–9
Vienna Dioscorides, 20
Vienna Genesis, 138, 214
Vigilius, Pope, 65, 80–7, 90–1,
  179–83
  Iudicatum, 83–4, 86
  Jordanes, 62
  Pragmatic Sanction, 67, 172
  Ravenna, 136
  Reparatus, 57
Viminacium, *70*

Visigoths, 73, 93, 169–70
Vitalian, 12–14, 18–19, 58, 77, 126
Vitigis, 40, 57, 60, 65, 67

Wacho, 57
water supply, 113, *115*, *116*, 117, 198
women, 22, 24–5, 26, 40, 104, 109–10

Yazdgushnasp, 33, 43–4, 155–6

Zabergan, 72
Zaberganes, 24
Zeno, 14–15, 62, 77, 121
Zilgibis, 17
Zoilus, 81, 83–4, 90
Zonaras, 26–7, 120
Zoroastrianism, 17, 42

EU representative:
Easy Access System Europe
Mustamäe tee 50, 10621 Tallinn, Estonia
Gpsr.requests@easproject.com